PRAISE FOR *BLUE POWER*

"*Blue Power* is a tour de force. Beautifully researched and written, this book shows how police officers transformed whining about respect into wielding political clout. Schrader tells a big, lively, harrowing story. And as the best big stories always do, the book doesn't exhaust what can and should be known. Rather, it offers readers and strategists tools to make sense of the forces of organized violence on the make. Read it now."

—Ruth Wilson Gilmore, author of *Abolition Geography*

"Stuart Schrader's sweeping history of the political mobilization of the police makes clear just how historically distinctive the role of the police in our society is today. *Blue Power* chronicles the rise of the police as a political force, and the lobbying strategies, rhetorical campaigns, and legal gambits police unions and associations have deployed to protect the power and autonomy of their members. This has indelibly shaped not only American cities and criminal justice policies, but our society and politics as a whole. The book is a remarkable achievement."

—Kim Phillips-Fein, author of *Fear City*

"In *Blue Power*, Stuart Schrader tells the story of how local, state, and federal governance in the United States was diverted to the purpose of protecting and serving the police rather than the people. This is an urgent book—deeply researched and boldly argued."

—Walter Johnson, author of *The Broken Heart of America*

"Every thin blue line flag should come with a copy of this book. For half a century police have worked the beat that matters most to them—not the anti-crime beat but the pro-police beat, where they have lobbied and campaigned, rioted and lied, to secure their funding, build their ranks, and insulate themselves from every tedious intrusion of oversight and democratic process. By exploiting the bipartisan law-and-order consensus, police have put themselves beyond the reach of even the most powerful elites. Politicians flog and ridicule chants to 'defund the police,' but this book helps us to hear those chants anew as an essential first stand—no fascism, no fascism, no fascism."

—Naomi Murakawa, author of *The First Civil Right*

Also by Stuart Schrader

Badges Without Borders: How Global Counterinsurgency Transformed American Policing

BLUE POWER

HOW POLICE ORGANIZED TO PROTECT AND SERVE THEMSELVES

STUART SCHRADER

BASIC BOOKS

New York

Basic Books
Hachette Book Group
1290 Avenue of the Americas, New York, NY 10104
www.basicbooks.com

Printed in the United States of America

First Edition: April 2026

Published by Basic Books, an imprint of Hachette Book Group, Inc. The Basic Books name and logo is a registered trademark of the Hachette Book Group.

The Hachette Speakers Bureau provides a wide range of authors for speaking events. To find out more, go to hachettespeakersbureau.com or email HachetteSpeakers@hbgusa.com.

Basic books may be purchased in bulk for business, educational, or promotional use. For more information, please contact your local bookseller or the Hachette Book Group Special Markets Department at special.markets@hbgusa.com.

The publisher is not responsible for websites (or their content) that are not owned by the publisher.

Library of Congress Control Number: 2025036667

ISBNs: 9781541608030 (hardcover), 9781541608047 (ebook)

LSC-C

Printing 1, 2026

CONTENTS

ABBREVIATIONS

AFL	American Federation of Labor
AFSCME	American Federation of State, County and Municipal Employees
CIO	Congress of Industrial Organizations
CLEAT	Combined Law Enforcement Associations of Texas
COPS	California Organization of Police and Sheriffs
CORE	Congress of Racial Equality
DARE	Drug Abuse Resistance Education
DOJ	Department of Justice
FBI	Federal Bureau of Investigation
FOP	Fraternal Order of Police
IACP	International Association of Chiefs of Police
LEAA	Law Enforcement Assistance Administration
MOU	memorandum of understanding
NAACP	National Association for the Advancement of Colored People
PBA	Patrolmen's/Police Benevolent Association
PCLEAJ	President's Commission on Law Enforcement and Administration of Justice
PERB	Public Employment Relations Board
POPAC	Peace Officers Political Action Council
PORAC	Peace Officers Research Association of California

INTRODUCTION

Cops were pissed off. They felt disrespected by protesters, underpaid by mayors, and abused by commanding officers. Forced to accept worsening working conditions without complaint, cops were dejected, fragmented, and disorganized. At the national level, they lacked an obvious way to mount a cohesive response, vocalize their political positions, and assert their indispensability. If Americans wanted to take power away from the police, many cops felt, maybe they did not deserve police protection at all.

One officer crystallized these frustrations while testifying before Congress. Jerome Dudzik was a leader of a nascent police union in Milwaukee, and he had come to Washington to demand that Congress protect police from unfair labor practices, particularly where overtime pay was concerned. He was direct, if a bit contorted. "Gentlemen, we are getting stronger and more unified," he declared. "The probability of a nationwide police walkout could be a possibility." Police certainly had leverage, but whether they were as able to use it as Dudzik suggested was another question.[1]

The year was 1970. The last time police had mounted a real strike was 1919. Then, Boston's police commissioner refused to allow officers to join the American Federation of Labor, spurring over 1,000 cops to decline to report for work. Nine people died in the street violence, fires, and looting that ensued. Police had been wary of even threatening unlawful strikes and slowdowns ever since. Labor unions steered clear of cops, seeing them largely as protectors of business interests and the status quo, while cops mistrusted organized labor, believing it was nothing but a den of pinkos.[2]

Without organized bottom-up power, top-down power filled the void. The police organization most actively involved in lobbying legislators in

Washington did not speak for rank-and-file officers—the International Association of Chiefs of Police represented their bosses. Its greatest accomplishment, the 1968 Omnibus Crime Control and Safe Streets Act, signed by President Lyndon Johnson, enabled the federal government to offer fiscal assistance to police agencies through the Law Enforcement Assistance Administration. But this new outfit's focus on research and reform had little to offer cops on the beat.

A new generation was realizing that if regular cops wanted change, they would have to accomplish it themselves. In 1967, the president of the Detroit Police Officers Association, Carl Parsell, broke the taboo on police strikes when he organized officers to call out sick en masse. John Cassese, leader of New York City's Patrolmen's Benevolent Association, had organized an effective campaign to convince voters to strike down civilian review of police misconduct. His successors would follow in his footsteps to become national figures, shaping the profession far beyond the Big Apple. In Baltimore, the local Fraternal Order of Police was contending with a chapter of the American Federation of State, County and Municipal Employees to represent cops at the bargaining table, and each was trying to outdo the other through political appeals beyond the workplace. A few San Francisco cops calling themselves the Bluecoats remade their officers' association into one of California's most fearsome political outfits, able to get what it wanted from the state legislature if local officials refused to cave. And when Parsell could not get a flight to Washington, the Milwaukee Professional Policemen's Protective Association took the case to Congress, putting Dudzik and his colleague Robert Kliesmet briefly into the spotlight. A few months after their appearance, John Harrington, national president of the Fraternal Order of Police, brought as many as 3,500 cops from forty-four states to Washington to rally on the steps of the Capitol.[3]

Police political power trickled at first, but it soon became a torrent. Within a couple of decades, police had become well enough organized to be able to command resources and respect from Congress, the White House, and city halls and statehouses across the country. They did so without a single, national police union, though not for lack of trying. The balance of power within the profession shifted too. If chiefs and commanders wanted to survive, they had to accommodate or accede to rank-and-file power. Cops grew unafraid to wield this power openly, uproariously, and sometimes illegally.

After beginning to demonstrate, strike, and riot to obtain contracts in the 1960s and 1970s, police redeployed these same tactics in subsequent decades in response to perceived slights, including rare punishments for misconduct. Elected officials who tried to pacify angry police by affording them generous compensation as well as grievance procedures found that, once emboldened, police were not easily tamed. Their militancy reaped rewards from both municipal governments and Washington. Money was respect quantified. Respect was a proxy for power.

By the 1980s, police union leaders had learned that tough-on-crime rhetoric from politicians meant little if it was not backed by material support. Republican president Richard Nixon grew abstemious when it came to sharing federal revenue. Ronald Reagan was worse. Instead, it was a new generation of tough-on-crime Democrats like cop-turned-congressman Mario Biaggi and future president Joe Biden who most reliably turned police requests into legislation. In the 1990s, police union leaders were regularly meeting with officials in Bill Clinton's White House. When Congress passed the massive 1994 crime bill, Biden offered a simple explanation for how he determined what it should include: he "called the cops."[4]

Today, laws, departmental policies, and union contracts afford police incredible levels of insulation from investigation and punishment for wrongdoing. It is extremely difficult for departments to fire police officers for misconduct on the job or off. Individual cops are widely indemnified from responsibility for damages in civil lawsuits brought against police departments. Taxpayers shoulder the burden of paying settlements after police misconduct, which totaled $3.2 billion from 2010 to 2020, according to one study of just twenty-five departments. And cops are increasingly going so far as to sue protesters for inciting distress, misconduct complainants for causing reputational harm, arrestees for inflicting physical injury, and even those they shoot for emotional injuries they experience by "being forced" to discharge their firearms.[5]

The job of policing can be demanding, but not in the way television procedurals depict it. One cop aptly characterized police work as "basically 99 percent pure bullshit, because there is not that much going on," though "punctuated by one percent of just sheer terror." For this bullshit, police compensation includes a wide array of benefits and perks unavailable even to other unionized government employees. Police in big cities receive strong wages and cost-of-living increases, plus the overtime Jerome Dudzik had demanded, as well as pensions and other retirement benefits (sometimes after just twenty years), healthcare coverage, vacation and sick time, family funeral and bereavement leave, and many other allowances. Officers can earn bonuses for skills like a second language, paid time off on a birthday, and extra pay for working certain busy shifts. Unions help cops get insurance plans, low-cost loans, discounts on cell service and cable, and access to attorneys who help with wills, home purchases, and divorces. And police pay is often highest where street crime is lowest, in upper-class suburbs.[6]

For cops accused of misconduct, including brutality, protections are legion. These safeguards, which unions have seized, include legal representation, mandatory delays in interviews, sealing of prior records, and rapid expungement of disciplinary findings. Headlines record moments when police unions support their members for the high-pressure, high-stakes 1 percent of the job, but cops get as much support for the remaining 99 percent: stress, boredom, monotony, and frustration, which can lead to cynicism, burnout, substance abuse, physical health deterioration, and other challenges. These protections and benefits are nearly all less than fifty years old. They are the result of the political power police began to accrue in the 1960s.

Emergent police unions rode the coattails of the public sector union movement as it grew overall. The number of state and local employees covered by union contracts almost doubled from 1964 to 1972, reaching 1.1 million. These new unions reshaped governments and metropolitan economies across the country. Many public sector unions were militant, but police maintained this militancy long after it had crested among other public employees. Most public sector unions experienced setbacks or stasis beginning in the 1980s, but police unions continued to succeed. To this day, with around 7 million unionized public employees in the United States, it is difficult in most cities to consider other unions as part of the same movement as police unions—only one type of union representative approaches the bargaining table or meetings of a city's central labor council packing a pistol.[7]

This book is a biography not of a person but of a political force—Blue Power. It tells the history of how this political force coalesced, grew, and triumphed. The beginning was inchoate, with new police unions forged in rage during the 1960s and 1970s. Tutored in the ways of politics, police then refined their approaches, becoming entrepreneurial in the 1980s and 1990s. And they would be fired by new resentments in the twenty-five years after the 9/11 attack, continually radicalizing up to the present.

Though police organizations are fragmented by jurisdiction and geography, they have succeeded in fashioning themselves into a cohesive, collective political actor, constantly seizing the initiative on new terrain. Police gained self-interested political power first at the municipal level, then at the state level, and finally at the federal level. After notching a win at one scale, they redoubled the pressure at others, shrugging off losses by changing the venue for political contestation. When Dudzik threatened Congress with a national police strike in 1970, he was writing a check that police officers could not cash. The movement that he helped build, however, has made good on the threat of wielding collective strength, and it has done so with remarkable velocity. Our cities, our states, and our country are now governed by Blue Power.

What sets the police apart from other government agencies is their authorization to engage in violence. This is true everywhere. What makes the United States unique is the scale of its police violence, outpacing any other contender among rich countries. Police in the United States are responsible for over 13 percent of global police killings, though the country holds only 4 percent of the world's population.[8]

Many have rightly analyzed how police have enacted violence on the streets, but to explain how police in the United States became so much more lethal, better compensated, and less effective at crime control than cops elsewhere, *Blue Power* looks at how police developed political power. Less well understood than cops' authorization to engage in violence are their mundane methods of political organizing, familiar to many teachers and sanitation workers who belong to unions. Police have adopted these tools from organized labor but molded them to new ends.[9]

Power has two meanings in this story: operational power and the political power that shields it. Police operational power encompasses not just the authorization to engage in legal violence but also the ability to decide how to deploy violence. It is therefore defined by a key tool: discretion. Police discretion is an officer's ability to decide in the moment how to settle a given situation, sometimes checked by the direction of an incident commander or district sergeant, and guided by training, regulations, internal department culture, experience, instinct, mood, stereotype, snap judgment, and fear. A warning, a summons, a chase, an arrest, a gunshot, or no engagement at all: cops choose from this menu daily. Judicial processes come later, but everything hinges on the initial, irreversible decision cops make on the street, including whether to use lethal force. Although police often describe themselves as implementing the will of elected officials, they better resemble street-level lawmakers, actively resolving the law's ambiguities. This is the operational power of police.[10]

Police have great flexibility in their use of operational power. Cops on the street, outside the view of supervisors, claim significant autonomy in decision-making, trusting their partners and colleagues to back them up. When officer decisions harm their agencies' own legitimacy or invite new restrictions, however, police resort to political power. Through lobbying, campaign donations, political rallies, media blitzes, and other ordinary tools of politics, police have become extraordinarily effective at defending and maintaining their operational power. They have also at times augmented conventional political tactics with techniques pulled from their operational repertoire—bullying, deception, blackmail, and intimidation. What police do on the streets and what they do in city hall's backrooms are not the same. Over the past few decades, however, not only has the political work they do out of uniform supported the operational work they do in uniform, but their political tactics have also come to resemble operations.[11]

Blue Power explains how, beginning in the 1960s, the long-standing operational power of police became enveloped in an armature of raw political power—and what police have done with this power up to the present. Police are not simply arbiters of disputes, protectors of order, or enforcers of the law. Instead, through their professional organizations and unions, police are now self-interested, well-organized, highly motivated, and media-savvy political actors who have developed the ability to get the resources they want from legislatures and deference from courts.[12]

Understanding police as political actors illuminates important recent political transformations across the United States. It clarifies the fiscal austerity and privatization that have affected nearly every other aspect of governance since the 1980s, which police have often cheered as long as they can remain insulated from the cuts. It reveals why municipal governance often falters, as defiant police kneecap progressive elected officials, exerting a veto power over democracy. It helps us make better sense of both the persistence of macro-scale racial inequalities and the open growth of a vicious and paranoid far right, which, despite pledging fealty to law and order, is hostile to civil rights and democratic processes. Police, including sheriffs, Immigration and Customs Enforcement, and Border Patrol, have become essential contributors to Donald Trump's coalition, endorsing his culture-war positions as much as his authoritarianism. In their eagerness to blame each other for a frayed and coarsening society, liberal and conservative intellectuals alike have overlooked this key force shaping American politics at all levels.

The political power of police explains why the United States has developed a carceral state of aggressive law enforcement and mass incarceration, with almost 2 million people locked in cages, including almost half a million before conviction; 4.5 million more under some other form of punitive supervision; and as many as a quarter of all adults with an arrest on record. It also illuminates why committed movements to constrain, defund, and even abolish the operational power of police have foundered—by running up against the self-interested political power of police.[13]

Tracing the story of Blue Power's rise requires us to tease out the forces that competed for dominance within the movement. We must peer inside the notoriously opaque organizational structure of police agencies. Management and rank-and-file officers often vociferously disagree. Small-town police chiefs and big-city commissioners have dramatically different priorities. Elected sheriffs and appointed chiefs have little in common besides overlapping jurisdictions. We refer to "the police" as a unitary institution; that unity is not an illusion, but how police achieved it should be understood as a political project, born of political contestation.

Police do respond to criticism, however. When officers engage in abhorrent behavior or fail to stem crime, it can undermine their institutions and put elected officials at risk on election day. In response, liberals tend to look to police reform—better training, stricter standards, performance metrics, new technology—as a tool to reclaim legitimacy. Conservatives, in contrast, tend to reject reformism, arguing that it either will not achieve its stated goals or will restrict and weaken police, while claiming that criticism of the police sanctions lawlessness itself. These two positions roughly correspond to the perspectives held by organizations for commanders and rank-and-file officers, respectively. Commanders, answerable to mayors and city councils, have long urged professionalism and reform to improve their agencies. And patrol officers have long resented the controls on their work that they see reform to represent. Blue Power thus has two faces: the more reformist and professional commanding officers and the more recalcitrant and scrappy rank and file.

Over the decades, when elected officials have assented to Blue Power, Democrats have tended to cooperate with the commanders and Republicans with the rank and file. The most prominent exceptions were Joe Biden and Bill Clinton, who tried to bridge the factions. Yet the political power of police has grown so strong that although politicians may choose which segment to support, police do not need to offer anything in return. Instead, they can hold cities for ransom, extorting officials who do not go their way. In the middle of the twentieth century, good-government reformers tried to remove police from politics, overturning the old practices of political machines, which used cops as their pawns. But Blue

Power has reversed the situation. Now, politicians are more likely to be under the thumb of police.

Increasingly connected through national networks and organizations like the International Conference of Police Associations, tenacious rank-and-file police leaders first notched successes, gaining larger chunks of the municipal pie and impairing mayoralties, in major cities like Detroit, Baltimore, and San Francisco, as well as smaller ones like Milwaukee, Oakland, Stamford, and Elizabeth. Police leaders also learned how to leverage power in statehouses, allying with conservative legislators from outlying areas, far from the cities that would bear the brunt of Blue Power. And even as police from major metropolises like New York City found national media audiences and gained pull in Congress and the White House, their maneuvers remained most consequential in their home cities. Blue Power's strategic geography remains uneven, marked by asymmetric intensities, but tactically consistent across the country.

Police are notorious for dissembling when speaking to the public, but they are remarkably forthright about goals when speaking to each other, when exhorting each other to act. For that reason, to analyze police politics, this book draws heavily on police-produced sources, some hiding in plain sight, including a vast professional literature, testimony before legislatures, and evidence in lawsuits, as well as internal correspondence, FBI files released under the Freedom of Information Act, and other unpublished records in archives. Although police are record-keepers, they are not frequently record-sharers. They do, however, often brag about their successes and wail about their failures in their internally facing publications. To read these texts is to be sandblasted by their bravado. The crude tone and even the frequent inaccuracies contained in both public and internal police writing index the political culture they have created. Police accounts of their own goals in this bespoke archive therefore provide a remarkable window into how relentless they have been in trying to create a United States in their own image.

The political power of police may look immovable today, but it resulted from a recent process of police organizing to cohere as a political force. This book delaminates this force by following the rise of Blue Power to its apex and then its consolidation, acknowledging the gaps between bluster and reality, and examining cops' attempts to turn bluster into reality.

What emerges in this narrative is a massive, if not always smooth or coherent, effort by police to assemble themselves into an aggregate force in American politics at multiple scales. The consequences have been deleterious for liberalism, and for the very public safety and security that are to be democracy's police-enforced guarantors. Atop steady-state racism and economic exploitation that shape every aspect of our political system, police have become experts in bending that system even further to their will. Above all else, they have become experts in protecting and serving themselves.

CHAPTER 1

BLUE POWER'S MODEL CITY

Motor City was the model city.

Racially segregated, Detroit maintained a sizeable African American middle class in the mid-1960s, and white liberals in city hall worked with Washington to alleviate poverty among the more destitute Black population. From across the country, journalists, social scientists, and policymakers studied Detroit. It had once produced the Model T. Now the city itself was the model: promoting civil rights, overcoming ingrained social problems. As local and national press touted improvements in schools, revitalizing urban development initiatives, and surprisingly pacific "race relations," Mayor Jerome P. Cavanagh, elected at age thirty-three, seemed to be on a path toward the White House. The 1967 rebellion, that hot summer's most destructive, changed everything.[1]

Within a couple of years, Detroit instead became the model city for police. It showed that they could wage a multifront political war against police commanders, a liberal mayor, and mass Black militancy on the streets. And it served as an example to police across the country of what rank-and-file cops stood to win if they fought back.

"Everybody else can indulge in politics—every black group, every political party group, every church group," explained the president of the Detroit Police Officers Association, Carl Parsell, in 1969. "Why," he asked, "are police officers so different?"[2]

According to Coleman Young, Detroit's first African American mayor, who served from 1974 to 1994, the difference was simple: Parsell had turned the patrol officers' union into "the only armed political party in the country."[3]

COPS AT WAR

For much of the early history of formal police forces in the United States, there was no question about whether police were political actors. Throughout the late nineteenth century and the first half of the twentieth, police acted at the behest of two intertwined forces: local industry and the reigning local political party. Many cities—particularly east of the Rockies, where labor unions were strong—were home to a partisan machine, which fused politics and governing, doling out rewards to voters. Police were the foot soldiers of the machines, earning their jobs as patronage and enforcing the will of the machine bosses in their wards.

Under the machine, police work meant four things: enforcing the color line, fashioning a gendered social hierarchy, maintaining a ready and docile labor force by suppressing organized labor, and keeping the party in power. Most police activity accomplished all four at once, which meant that stifling the interpersonal and antisocial behaviors commonly labeled as crime was ancillary, unless cops could get in on the take. Corruption was not merely endemic to policing; it was constitutive.[4]

Turning the police into a more effective anticrime force became a widespread institutional imperative at the end of the Progressive Era, and it lasted for decades. This new orientation required disentangling police from politics, vanquishing the machines, and transforming governance into a more outwardly apolitical form of administration. These transformations occurred unevenly across the country, earlier in one city, later in another. But the goal was the same everywhere: creating politically independent or neutral police, whose primary mission was crime control. It meant at the very least upgrading standards for hiring, increasing training, rationalizing operations, and adopting new technologies. And police leaders eventually argued that a surefire way to ensure police competence and rectitude was to pay them handsomely. But this argument jelled because cops increasingly sought union protections.[5]

Detroit's department was already crawling toward political independence as war loomed. The city ended the spoils system, whereby appointments went to political supporters, with a 1939 voter-approved charter amendment establishing a Police Merit Board. But this board prevented civilian influence more generally, as it kept the police from coming under the city's civil service standards. Hiring and promotion, as well as discipline, would remain the prerogative of police command—for "the problems of discipline can never be fully understood by an outside agency." The higher-ups wanted the monopoly on hiring that a closed shop would afford, but without the power that a closed shop would offer to a union. Voters gave it to them.[6]

But the charter amendment could not stave off a unionizing drive. Detroit cops initially tried to unionize in October 1941, just a couple of months before the United States suddenly entered World War II. The American Federation of Labor (AFL), the Teamsters, and the Fraternal Order of Police all became involved, first through organizing campaigns, then by attacking police leadership in the press for their resistance, and eventually by taking the department to court. At the time, the International Association of Chiefs of Police (IACP) frowned upon rank-and-file unionization. How could cops be considered professional experts in public safety if they threw in their lot with every other labor union, from bricklayers to truck drivers? The IACP went so far as to equate union membership with membership in fascist or communist organizations, unacceptable during wartime. But the war had already come home.

Even as Detroit became the blast furnace powering the US war machine, a white population fearful of incremental Black advancement was itching to launch hostilities on the home front. White wildcat strikes and slowdowns in war plants, prompted by Ku Klux Klan agitation, broke out in response to promotion of Black workers, as well as Black demonstrations for desegregation and access to better jobs. White-versus-Black street affrays had been common for years across Detroit, and this violence went largely unmentioned in local media. Editors of competing newspapers all agreed, "Don't say anything about it, it'll go away." But it did not.[7]

In plants where communists were represented well, Black workers could count on support. But battles for the leadership of the United Auto Workers in the 1940s turned on who would be toughest on the communists in the rank-and-file caucus. Walter Reuther's virulent red-baiting approach won, hindering Black advancement in the plants but also strengthening many Black workers' ties to the primary outfit defending them, the Communist

Party. These ties only angered white workers who opposed the most insidious of all communist plots, integration of the shop floor. Yet war production had already begun to slacken in 1943, with the "heaviest weight of unemployment and part-time work," according to the Marxist economists of the Jefferson School of Social Science, "falling on the Negro workers."[8]

By April 1943, hundreds of police officers were signing up with the Fraternal Order of Police. Department leadership resisted this quasi-unionization effort. But that month, 10,000 white and Black workers rallied in Detroit against Jim Crow, including pervasive job discrimination in the plants. This political mobilization intensified white racial animus in the city, which changed the situation for the police unionists.[9]

On June 20, 1943, brawls among sunbathers spilled onto the bridge connecting Belle Isle to the shore, and then into the city. Both sides were emboldened and angered by ongoing labor agitation, and the fighting that evening was intense. Passels of Black looters roamed the streets of the Paradise Valley neighborhood on the first night, inflicting damage on commercial storefronts, particularly white- and Jewish-owned businesses.

The next evening a far larger riot commenced, as a white mob numbering in the tens of thousands, mostly people under age twenty-three, rampaged, "with lynch spirit running high," pulling Black passengers off trolleys or out of automobiles, to beat them and light their cars on fire.[10]

Cops took the white side. Instead of quelling the violence, many white officers left their posts to join mobs attacking Black crowds. Private security guards and watchmen working for the defense plants, frequently mistaken for city police, ignored beatings of "colored youth." They simply walked away instead of intervening. Cops who did not join the white marauders stood back and watched, cackling.[11]

Federal troops, National Guard, state police, and sheriffs intervened to pacify the city. The commanding Army officer was horrified by the "harsh and brutal" behavior of police, though intense police violence occurred after their military reinforcements arrived, when the risk of retaliation decreased. The toll was thirty-four dead and $2 million in damage (the equivalent of $37 million today), almost entirely in segregated Black areas. Police killed no white people and seventeen of the twenty-five Black people who died over the course of the rioting. Motor City's mini-Kristallnacht, incited by the "Gestapo in Detroit," in Thurgood Marshall's words, embarrassed the United States as it attempted to defeat fascism abroad. State police commissioner Oscar G. Olander, whose force performed no better than the city police during the riot, was rewarded at war's end with a position as a consultant in occupied Japan, where he was to introduce democracy to police. Illness and his death in 1947 prevented him from revealing whether he had any idea how.[12]

Detroit's explosion of white violence came while police were still trying to unionize in the city. Mayor Edward J. Jeffries attempted to mute criticism of the department. He did not want to antagonize officers and make himself a target of their ire. After the smoke cleared, his defense of the police department became stronger with each passing week, even with copious evidence that the police response had been reckless, racist, and reprehensible. Detroit's police commissioner also defended the rank and file, despite his turbulent relationship with them amid the unionization drive. The mayor grew incensed at dogged criticism from Black leaders after the riot, but he replaced the commissioner with a more socially liberal figure, John Ballenger, who had worked for the city's welfare agency. Cops were skeptical, worried Ballenger would turn them into "social workers."[13]

The war inspired people inside and outside the department to call for emulating the military model. Rank-and-file officers in the Arsenal of Democracy, however, believed police should be able to unionize, unlike soldiers. They even took the case to court, trying to gain clarity on whether city administrators could prohibit cops from joining a group like the Fraternal Order of Police. Courts in Michigan ultimately ruled against unionization after the 1943 riot, accepting the argument that cops were as essential as soldiers. The Fraternal Order of Police eventually pressed the case all the way to the Supreme Court, which declined to hear it. Ballenger gained cover to continue his predecessor's opposition. In Detroit as well as Lansing, the Fraternal Order of Police, with its national and state lodges, was outlawed.[14]

War veterans who joined the Detroit police force, however, chafed at sentimental invocations of armed service and police commanders' efforts to enforce military-style hierarchy and discipline. What police wanted was to be neither treated like soldiers nor asked to engage in social service provision. Less than a year after the riot, in March 1944, with organizers from a Congress of Industrial Organizations (CIO) affiliate attempting to organize the Detroit police, Ballenger made a small concession. He allowed the establishment of an organization to aid the "welfare" of the rank and file, though officers who joined a "labor union" were subject to "immediate dismissal." More than two-thirds of the 3,700 department members quickly joined the new Detroit Police Officers Association, which was independent from the CIO machinations. This enthusiasm inspired nearby cities like Chicago to rush to ban collective bargaining for police. Commanders retained the upper hand, and so this concession was insufficient to stem growing resentment among rank-and-file officers.[15]

TO PROTECT AND TO SERVE

Even as World War II stymied police unionization, there was one police organization that emerged ascendant. The IACP represented the interests of commanders rather than ordinary officers, and it welcomed a raft of new members as they returned from foreign deployments. Some spent time aiding the postwar occupations, helping to build new police forces in distant, defeated countries. This experience primed the IACP to share a consistent approach to policing, as applicable overseas as at home, which it would spread like gospel: professionalism.[16]

These chiefs dominated in the decades after World War II, guided by J. Edgar Hoover. They attained nearly complete control over policing. Not all police commanders were on board with the multifaceted project of reform, but the most powerful and media-savvy chiefs used their pulpit to make professionalization the centerpiece of what it meant to lead a police force.

One of the foremost professionalizers, Chief William H. Parker of the Los Angeles Police Department, enshrined a motto for the movement after a 1955 contest that invited the public to submit slogans for the department. One cop's teenage daughter came up with the winning entry: "To Protect and to Serve." She submitted it in the name of her dad, Joseph S. Dorobek, thinking it more likely to be adopted if it originated with a rank-and-file officer. She was right. The novel notion of the police officer as public servant—answerable to community standards but impartial in enforcement of the law—soon gained ground, and some variation of "protect and serve" is now emblazoned on police cars around the United States.[17]

The slogan "To Protect and to Serve" signaled the dawning of a new era, as professionalization brought about profound internal changes in police departments across the country. But it also mystified what was happening, making it seem that Parker wanted police to answer to regular people. In reality, he wanted to ensure that cops would answer to him, and that he, as chief, answered to no elected official. Parker is today long gone, but the professionalization movement he helped catalyze bore an unexpected fruit: by disentangling the police from local politics, it enabled police to become a new sort of political actor, answering to no one but themselves. Police associations capitalized on this shift. Police reformers at midcentury believed fraternal organizations might mount complaints about pay or pensions but would not interfere with the steady improvement of police capabilities that professionalization entailed.

After the failed attempt in 1919 to bring cops into the labor movement, police unions after World War II steered clear of organized labor, though many of their leaders continually flirted with labor leaders and occasionally hired union lawyers. Most police unions were originally "benevolent associations," created as fraternities and social clubs for police that provided entertainment and some aid, including insurance or credit unions, to officers and their families. Even the Detroit Police Officers Association remained mostly a "beer drinking social club" for two decades. With this origin story, rather than coming out of the labor movement proper, associations like this remained inward-looking, focused on the particularities of police officers' lifestyle. Over time, however, laws changed, allowing benevolent associations to obtain certain prerequisites that unions must have for collective bargaining. Most of the police unions that achieved collective bargaining rights in the decade after World War II were in the Midwest and Northeast, with Illinois and Connecticut predominating.[18]

Typically, labor unions do not include management, but some police associations that became unions did include most or all ranks below the chief.

The IACP, in contrast, was open primarily to chiefs and command-rank officers, but not patrol officers. The National Sheriffs' Association, founded in 1940, was a management organization, but it never had as much clout as the IACP, which was formalized in 1893 and counted the most important chiefs from across the country among its members. They spearheaded the key transformation for police of severing political machine control of officers. It was the foundation for professionalization.

The isolation of these organizations from both organized labor and political machines reflected but also strengthened the insularity of police departments. After spending years among cops, one writer observed, "Police officers live in a closed society—'hermetically sealed' might be a more accurate description—under incredible pressures from their peers and superior officers to conform." Police unionism became a vehicle for that peer-enforced conformity and provided a means of resisting pressure from superior officers. But the pressures of the job also created mistrust and suspicion, as well as the sense that anyone outside the force did not and could not sympathize with the police experience. Most cops socialized exclusively with other cops not just due to irregular or unpredictable schedules but also because they tended to feel, as an officer put it, "Nobody understands but another cop." The risks of the job and the feeling of being under siege, however, could not fully explain the desire of officers to be among their own. It was also cultivated. Veterans taught rookies to avoid civilians, who would only "hurt" a cop.[19]

The mores within police departments could fit uneasily with those instilled in the working-class neighborhoods cops called home. Police did tend to hail from the very same locales, schools, and churches as those they were arresting—at least on their own side of the color line. Loyalty and self-respect, suspicion of highfalutin book learning, discomfort with outsiders, and macho toughness were conducive to the discretionary despotism of police operations. These same values could also shape the cunning antiauthority wiles of the street-smart cad, confidence man, or crook. Both cops and crooks jealously guarded whatever meager boon they had obtained. Many cops exhibited the contradictions of proletarian values and cultural practices: hardworking but always looking to cut corners to get one over on the boss, charitable but skeptical of leeches, independent but susceptible to peer pressure, proud but defensive. The average cop was alert to scams and allergic to bullshit. He brought to the job a disposition that the job reinforced. Sociologists were perplexed. Were conservative and authoritarian young men drawn to policing, or did policing make them conservative and authoritarian?[20]

Police departments were defined by high internal loyalty among officers at the same rank, and they remain so. Cops were and are loyal to each other, and particularly to their partners, because of the discretionary character of their work. Differing combinations of rank hierarchy, discretion, and cohesion define most bureaucratic institutions. What makes the police unique is their high levels of both discretion and cohesion at the lower levels of rank. Police unionism grew both from this structural feature of policing and from increasing public rejection of the abuse that resulted from unbridled discretion.

Cohesiveness had cultural dimensions. Cops tended to share an attitude of animosity toward outsiders, which in Detroit in these decades extended mainly to African American men and women. Animosity toward immigrants, homosexuals, and reds bubbled up too. But internal cohesion or loyalty among officers is not necessarily about camaraderie, friendship, or even respect, though it may be. Instead, for cops, it is a structural imperative, a function of police discretion as officers engage in what one scholar has aptly called "violence work," distilling what is essential, rather than incidental, to the métier. Internal cohesion is about defending the discretionary choices your fellow officers make so that you know your own choices will be defended. It is about aiding your fellow officers when they are in need so that you know you will be aided when you are in need. It is about affirming and rewarding service in violence work, justifying the support you give your partner while he degrades or abuses an arrestee. And it is about hiding these mechanisms of internal cohesion from outsiders behind a veil of secrecy.[21]

Unity among police would be cultivated through training and departmental culture but also nurtured by these officer associations, which developed their own social halls with meals and drink, recreational activities and sports leagues, and eventually discounted opportunities for other forms of entertainment like cruise ship vacations and golf outings. Unions would grow to provide individual support in formal ways, like stress relief practices and suicide prevention, marriage counseling, and substance abuse and gambling assistance. They also offered more informal types of care, celebrating births of children, marriages, on-the-job milestones, and retirements, as well as mourning deaths of loved ones and highlighting historical trivia and remembrances of police exploits of the past. Unions even came to foster connections with businesses that donated or took out ads in their publications, and cops then developed loyalty to those businesses and came to expect hospitality. The routine perquisites that supplemented low pay under the old machine system returned in mutant form, now without the upward and outward tribute to political bosses. They were instead internalized, and the boons became less individualistic. Now they fed into the project of building police power and political sway.

But much of that was still in the future. Police associations needed to win their top priority of obtaining formal recognition, city by city. The Detroit Police Officers Association was not the first, but it set the national tone for what recognition could mean because Carl Parsell understood the new terrain better than most. He would lead it to strike the greatest blow against the dominance of the professionalizer chiefs.

IN AND AGAINST COMMAND IN DETROIT

In practice, the Detroit Police Officers Association, in its aspirations to become more union-like in the 1950s, mediated between rank-and-file prerogative to hold unlimited discretion and commanders' fantasies of military-like discipline, which limited that discretion. To commanders, police discretion was supposed to apply on the street, governing the stop, the search, the citation, and the arrest. Officers, however, desired the latitude to use their discretion to interpret and reshape command prerogatives: when, where, how, and how intensely to effect law enforcement. Each day was a new impasse, breached only when commanders, from the superintendent and sundry high-ranking officers to the inspectors in charge of precincts and bureaus, dispensed "rights at their pleasure," as Carl Parsell put it.[22]

Parsell was a consummate patrol officer who joined the force in 1947. With a nasally voice, an oblong face with a high hairline, and a perpetually furrowed but strong brow, Parsell looked more like an exasperated math teacher than the man who would soon cause observers to raise the "serious question" of whether civilian control of the Detroit police existed "in practice."[23]

Detroit's situation resembled that of many departments across the country after the war. Officers suffered "seemingly pointless manipulation" by commanders, whose purpose often seemed to be little more than "to make the officer's task on the street as difficult as possible," as the reformer Patrick Murphy put it. One officer summed up the beat cop's pervasive attitude: "Sergeants turn into shitheads pretty quick. Lieutenants are not too bad, but once you get above a captain, you can forget it. They no longer have anything to do with you. They're administrators."[24]

Under the cover of officer welfare, the Detroit Police Officers Association stiffened the spine of patrol officers. The association curried popular support for increased pay by arguing that police services were improving and should be rewarded with better compensation. Although the city did not budge on the pay increase amid fiscal difficulties, it granted the Detroit Police Officers Association a dues checkoff in 1956. The money would enable it to offer services to its members and charity to others. From Parsell's perspective, the city had created a "company union" because the association had no ability to advocate directly for its members.[25]

The department remained a top-down operation. Police command and rank and file disagreed about work routines, but the two sides found common ground on the central function of police power in the city: a "planned policy of containment and harassment of average Negro citizens." About a third of Detroit's 658,808 arrests from 1947 to 1956 were investigatory, meaning officers believed they would find a reason for a charge after detention, typically lasting three days. In the year the department granted the association its dues checkoff, cops arrested 33,186 people for investigation (45 percent of the total arrested that year), and only 6,490 were charged. The department's manual authorized this practice. In one week of an aggressive crime crackdown after a couple of high-profile murders of white women at the end of 1960, police arrested over 1,500 people for investigatory purposes, almost every one an African American man. A Black newspaper editorial called it a "police reign of terror."[26]

In 1961, the youthful Jerome Cavanagh upset the incumbent, Louis C. Miriani, to become the mayor of Detroit, thanks to support from, in the words of the establishment editors of the *Detroit Free Press*, "Detroit's Negroes, blue-collar workers and the unemployed."[27]

Cavanagh hired liberal commissioners but, beyond reducing reliance on investigatory arrests, there was little the commissioner could do to change the department. Each commissioner realized that the department's power center resided on "the third floor": with the superintendent and deputy superintendent, chief inspector, and chief of detectives. Conflicts with Cavanagh and his commissioners meant that the men in these roles changed. One fled to a more hospitable locale—South Vietnam—to become an advisor to police there. But the power they wielded over officers remained unchanged. Commanders abused officers, who abused Black Detroiters, and Cavanagh's commissioners fruitlessly tried to reconfigure operations.[28]

Detroit police grimaced at operational reforms, like the single-officer patrol car that was increasingly becoming managerial orthodoxy across the country. Detroit commonly deployed heavily armed four-officer patrols, in which a uniformed officer chauffeured three plainclothesmen around precincts to intimidate and often brutalize Black people. Generally, single-officer patrol stretched resources and enabled cost-cutting and operational flexibility. Statistics also showed that officers were more likely to be killed when in pairs. With single-officer patrol, the job became boring and lonely, but officers became less reckless and violent. Nevertheless, unions everywhere protested that officers were at greater risk when alone.[29]

By decade's end, cops in Detroit and elsewhere started demanding not only two-officer patrol but integrated pairs, thinking white cops were less likely to be attacked and killed if accompanied by a Black man in blue. In New York, cops called the integrated teams "salt and pepper." A former Detroit Black Panther relished the irony: armed self-defense campaigns and slogans like "Off the Pigs," not "nonviolent marching and singing," had actually "spurred the integration of the big city police departments."[30]

But integration of the Detroit police force was painfully slow. About 220 of the city's 4,400 police were African American by the summer of 1967, only three holding a rank above patrol. A paucity of trustworthy Black cops made it difficult to gather intelligence on Black revolutionaries before the 1967 rebellion, according to one commissioner. The city had grown to be almost 40 percent Black, up from 30 percent only a decade earlier, but the police force remained 95 percent white. When a Detroit police commissioner first tried to integrate scout cars in 1959, white cops staged the city's first slowdown, giving the Detroit Police Officers Association a newfound taste of power.[31]

Black cops had no say in the Detroit Police Officers Association, and their exclusion from groups like the Knights of Columbus gave them few reliable social ties to provide insider knowledge concerning promotions. The Detroit red squad surveilled Black cops who supported civil rights, and Detroit Police Officers Association cliques sometimes showed up at political events while off duty to observe their Black colleagues. In 1963, Black Detroit cops and Wayne County sheriff's deputies formed their own organization, the Guardians of Michigan. Isaiah "Ike" McKinnon, a Black officer who rose through the ranks and was appointed chief in 1993, recalled that when he became a cop in 1965, the Detroit Police Officers Association was still a "racist organization."[32]

Ray Girardin, Cavanagh's commissioner from December 1963 to July 1968, and his even more proactive predecessor, George Edwards, both pushed integration. That was the reason they were so unloved by both "old-line command officers" and the rank and file, 90 percent of whom Edwards believed to be "bigoted." Convincing white cops to accept Black colleagues was as difficult as getting them to change their behavior toward Black members of the public.[33]

White Detroit cops relished making Black colleagues so miserable that they would quit. If, as the National Association for the Advancement of Colored People (NAACP) observed, "every Negro arrested somehow fell down," and if when an African American man "walked in a police station to complain about a policeman he'd get the piss kicked out of him and get locked up," it could hardly surprise the commissioner that white officers refused to teach new Black colleagues proper procedures, requirements they resented anyway. The only time most white cops accepted standards of professional qualification was when they could use them to stymie Black promotion or recruitment. As a result, a large proportion of the Black cops hired both failed to adhere to the merit standards Girardin desired and indulged in brutality toward Black Detroiters, feeling they had to prove their worth or mettle to their white counterparts. Many Black cops enacted outward racism on the streets, a downstream effect of the inward racism they experienced in the precinct house. Less than six months before the rebellion, only 8.5 percent of Black Detroit felt that Black cops treated them better than white cops.[34]

Edwards, a former judge, and then Girardin, a former journalist, trusted police-community relations programs to fix these problems. So too did Cavanagh, who, as cops never forgot, had marched in the city alongside Martin Luther King Jr. in 1963. These community-oriented efforts were supposed to mitigate antagonisms while also collecting neighborhood-level anticipatory intelligence. Every precinct held quarterly community forums. Edwards also implemented "block clubs," dozens of nightly meetings hosted in Detroit living rooms, where neighbors gathered to speak to a local commanding officer. Further, federal funding allowed over 600 "problem" boys in each summer of 1966 and 1967 to get paid $1.25 an hour to perform minor service work for the department, like looking for lost children or reporting broken streetlights, while considering law enforcement as a career option. Cops got to know these boys.[35]

Detroit surpassed other cities in developing outreach efforts to Black youth and opening lines of communication between police and community leaders. These were accompanied by in-service training efforts in "human relations," intended to lessen bigotry and hostility among officers and explain what civil rights were all about. But their footprint was light, and they had little positive effect. In conjunction with Girardin's attempts at disciplining officers for mistreating Black people (via transfer or suspension), the programs often ended up compounding officers' resentments, both upward to command and downward to Black neighborhoods. The mayor's plan to use police-community relations, as well as social workers and other "citizen-sentries," to provide an "early warning system," alerting officials of probable unrest, was a flop.[36]

Police agencies in the Detroit metropolitan area, including the city's police department, did not exhibit great educational attainment even before in-service training in human relations. Almost 13 percent of cops in the area did not have a high school diploma as of 1966, and over 75 percent had never attended any college. Around 7 percent of officers had a college degree. Even as Cavanagh's Detroit remained in high esteem in Washington, researchers noticed problems, with education levels among officers a strong indicator that reform efforts both were necessary and had yet to take hold.[37]

Overall, Detroit police acted like "an army of occupation," meaning racist, ruthless, violent, unbound, and highly discretionary. The two-decade command effort to rationalize the force and control the rank and file by affording it informal organization had failed. Girardin ruefully reflected later, "These guys are hard to handle, they can screw you in 90 ways."[38]

LEGALIZING PUBLIC EMPLOYEE UNIONIZATION

The 1965 Michigan Public Employment Relations Act formalized Detroit's municipal police union. Public sector employees could now unionize across the state, with a proviso forbidding strikes. Michigan's new law empowered the Detroit Police Officers Association to challenge the mayor and his police commissioner while also weakening the mayor's position vis-à-vis the police. Members of the association elected Parsell, now a veteran officer, as union president that year—a job he would hold until 1972. He interpreted the new law as a warrant from the legislature to "get involved in politics," particularly because the law lacked a provision requiring arbitration, meaning that job actions to interfere with operations remained possible. The union could both orchestrate a political quid pro quo and exact political costs if it did not get its way.[39]

Against the nationwide backdrop of civil rights advances, the Detroit Police Officers Association became the tip of the spear in the fight against municipal leaders who accommodated the movement for Black rights and supported poverty alleviation. Cavanagh was the most prominent and promising of these leaders, and the new state law provided a rudimentary map, though not the actual treasure Parsell sought.

The pervasive but mundane social conflict of the 1960s has been called "the battle of the corner," an endless struggle between cops and Black people, especially the working class and those who were irregularly employed. Parsell's primary fight, in contrast, was for control of the department—call it the battle of the superintendent's office, or the battle of the third floor. To win the battle of the third floor, Parsell framed his demands in terms of controlling the corner, brooking no opposition to the way his officers policed Detroit.

Within the department, command and patrol officers alike rejected civil rights reforms that were gathering speed in the 1960s. Following Michigan's ratification of a new state constitution in 1963 that created a Civil Rights Commission with investigatory powers, the first of its kind in the country, only 5 of the 397 complaints the commission referred to the Detroit Police Department resulted in a trial board proceeding between January 1, 1964, and the outbreak of the rebellion on July 23, 1967. A single officer was dismissed for a civil rights violation.[40]

Instead, the vast majority of disciplinary proceedings against officers concerned infractions of departmental policy and procedure. Because the department employed no civilian labor relations administrators, it fell to the very commanders implementing disciplinary measures—for offenses like failing to write a report properly, neglecting duty, losing a radio, or damaging a scout car—to determine their fairness. These disciplinary measures irritated the rank and file and motivated the Detroit Police Officers Association's activism, as Parsell stoked hostility to command unilateralism.

Officers found that they could build outside support from conservative white voters and activists by portraying the threat of discipline as a Black and communist menace aiming to neutralize and hamstring police. But command had no such desire and reliably interfered with civil rights investigations. Practically speaking, the association fought for a "working agreement" that afforded officers Miranda-like rights and excluded self-incriminating board testimony from court proceedings. The Detroit Police Officers Association also began providing legal representation for officers under investigation. Later the association would take the Civil Rights Commission to court over how it publicized and investigated complaints against police officers, reaching a settlement in 1970 that benefited officers by expanding opportunities to participate in these cases. Cops in Detroit would win the battle of the corner by winning the battle of the third floor.[41]

All these fights within the department were but a prelude to the actions Parsell would organize in the first half of 1967, directly confronting Mayor

Cavanagh. Like many mayors, he trusted his police commissioners to keep things under control inside the station house and on the street. Police chiefs had made a name for themselves by promoting police reform, and they eagerly advocated what President Lyndon Johnson began calling a "war against crime." But their greatest antagonists were not the street hustlers and stick-up kids, or even protesters demanding equal rights. It was cops themselves who would raise the temperature from a simmer to a boil.

CHAPTER 2

ALL POWER TO THE CHIEFS

State by state, through the 1960s, legislatures were passing laws that favored unionization, and more and more police were drawn into organizing. At the national level, however, police chiefs, particularly those able to adopt the language of professionalism, held Washington's ear.

Washington had not always been so receptive. Although many chiefs in cities north and south sought outside help in accomplishing reforms during the 1950s and 1960s, these efforts usually relied on private consultants, university researchers, or the Federal Bureau of Investigation (FBI)—not Capitol Hill or the White House. Otherwise, police chiefs looked to their professional organization, the IACP, for guidance in attempting to modernize and keep up with social upheaval.

The IACP itself was going through changes too. Police chiefs tended to be instinctively wary of Washington, redoubt of stuffed shirts who might tell them what to do. Even reformist chiefs who expected more of their officers also felt that any externally imposed check on police prerogative was dangerous, especially in the context of the civil rights movement, Supreme Court decisions protecting defendants, and liberals running the Department of Justice (DOJ). The man who became director of the IACP in 1962, Quinn Tamm, tried to change chiefs' minds.[1]

Over the course of twenty-six years working for the FBI, Tamm rose to the rank of assistant director. He spent years working in the two FBI divisions that maintained the greatest contact with chiefs across the country, the laboratory and training operations. Beginning in the late 1950s, Tamm became J. Edgar Hoover's liaison to the IACP, where he always "insured that the best interests of the Bureau were protected." Tamm's responsibility behind closed doors was to make sure IACP staff and elected leadership remained Hoover's cat's-paws, empowering rural chiefs against nationally prominent big-city chiefs, like William H. Parker of Los Angeles, who might challenge Hoover. When Tamm retired from the FBI in early 1961 to become the director of the IACP Field Services Division, it was essentially a lateral move, continuing the same work upgrading and coordinating police departments he had performed as an agent. There was one crucial difference: he was no longer under J. Edgar Hoover's control.[2]

Though the IACP was a membership organization, the police chiefs elected as presidents were figureheads, switching off annually. With the help of the same backroom chicanery Hoover had taught him, Tamm deftly installed himself as executive director of the IACP and editor of its monthly magazine, *The Police Chief*, gaining exceptional power over the organization. Hoover had little chance of challenging his wayward protégé now.

Tamm was stubborn and difficult to intimidate. He was a "cop's cop." Tamm once told Atlanta police chief Herbert Jenkins, one of the nation's most well-respected police leaders and a close ally of Lyndon Johnson, that he would outlast Hoover. The director found out—and seethed. Hoover told his most trusted men that he wanted to see Tamm, a "rattlesnake," removed from the IACP. Clyde Tolson, Hoover's top deputy and closest friend, officially severed contact between the FBI and Tamm early in 1966. But the apostate outlasted the director, just as he had predicted.[3]

After turning his back on Hoover, Tamm was free to manipulate the IACP's internal democracy just as his mentor had trained him to do. Tamm aimed to convince small-town chiefs, overrepresented among members, to be less frightened of federal action. He believed that with Washington's help, there was an opportunity for the IACP, and its member police chiefs around the country, to accelerate the movement to professionalize policing.

As soon as Tamm started working for the IACP, the organization began seeking outside revenue sources. It already had one major source, a contract with the International Cooperation Administration, the predecessor to the

Agency for International Development, to train police from Third World countries in the United States. Although the contract was canceled in 1963, it helped whet Tamm's appetite for federal funding and gave him experience grappling with federal bureaucracies. Soon, under Tamm's leadership, the IACP had mastered the hustle of securing grants from federal agencies like the Bureau of Public Roads ($100,000) and the Department of Health, Education, and Welfare ($79,000), as well as private industry outfits like the American Trucking Association ($10,000) and philanthropies like the Ford Foundation ($400,000). It was just the beginning.[4]

Tamm also guided the IACP toward outright independence from the FBI. To this end, in 1962, he created the Institute for Police Management to gather data, provide technical assistance, and train police executives. Where Hoover had cultivated "blind obeisance" to divide and rule law enforcement, Tamm was working to forge solidarities among the chiefs. Aware an FBI agent was listening closely to his remarks, Tamm told an audience of IACP officers in 1964 that the organization had quickly become *the* source for professional advice, *the* font of reliable data, and *the* spokesman for law enforcement. Knowing he would have to report back to Hoover, the agent must have gasped at each "the."[5]

Police engage in calisthenics at the FBI National Academy. *U.S. News & World Report* Magazine Collection, Prints & Photographs Division, Library of Congress, LC-U9-26123, f 10.

THE CHIEFS AND THE WAR ON CRIME

The first great funding bonanza for police chiefs fell into their laps after Lyndon Johnson declared his war on crime in the fall of 1964. He signed the first major federal anticrime legislation early in 1965, creating the Office of Law Enforcement Assistance and kick-starting decades' worth of debate and transformation among police and their critics. Reforms cost money, but were taxpayers getting what they were paying for?

At first, most chiefs who belonged to the IACP were reticent to support the creation of this new agency in Washington. Ornery, irascible, insecure, and competitive, the chiefs rarely agreed with each other on the details of their mandate. A consensus on how to fight crime remained elusive; instinct, not science, was their guide. They also had to manage their own fractious rank-and-file officers. Commanders and line officers alike failed to disentangle new civil rights legislation, which seemed to impinge on local prerogative, from the assistance liberals in Washington wanted to provide. Worse, new Supreme Court decisions like *Mapp v. Ohio*, *Miranda v. Arizona*, and *Escobedo v. Illinois* that protected the rights of the accused threatened to undermine all familiar policing practices—and it felt like Washington liberals were to blame. IACP members even issued a resolution warning the federal government against "encroachment" on "state or local government in the law enforcement field," immediately after Congress issued new national road safety codes for recipients of federal highway aid.[6]

The IACP's warning was unnecessary. Neither Johnson nor powerful law and order senators like Nebraska Republican Roman Hruska and Arkansas Democrat John L. McClellan wanted Washington to control police at the local level. Combining conservative pressure to get tough on crime and a liberal technocratic faith in reformism, federal assistance was designed to pump dollars into police departments' budgets to stimulate innovation and professionalism. Admittedly, that was the last thing many cops wanted.

Tamm saw things differently than his organization's members. In the pages of *The Police Chief*, he rebuked the membership for its skepticism of federal-assistance legislation. Soon the Office of Law Enforcement Assistance awarded the IACP $800,000 in grants, with more to come. Tamm was certain he had made the right decision. The organization passed new resolutions in each of the next two years, changing its attitude. Now the IACP affirmed its desire to coordinate with the federal government and insisted on the necessity of federal assistance to law enforcement agencies at the state and city levels.[7]

Under Tamm's leadership, the IACP set about fleecing the feds. Three grants for the District of Columbia police alone totaled almost half a million dollars in 1966, with more than $154,000 of that dedicated to the IACP, plus another $81,000 soon to be awarded. These grants covered planning, in-service training, and technical consultancy on thwarting crimes like burglary and car theft. The IACP incurred "quite substantial" costs, though the organization was "very inactive." But the bureaucrats needed IACP support to expand, and they were loathe to admit that their agency was throwing good money after bad programs.[8]

Once suspicious of Washington, the police chiefs now had a real incentive to seek out and defend federal money for law enforcement. They became more organized, unified, and vocal. In 1965, reformers like Herbert Jenkins argued at the IACP annual meeting that chiefs needed more resources so they could replace the "dumb cop" and keep the "smart ones," capable of handling "difficulties compounded of sociological, economic and civic factors." Hiring better-educated officers not only required raising pay scales. It also meant affording these new cops the opportunity to rise in rank more quickly, something that more-senior officers resented.[9]

The chiefs quickly changed their tune amid social turmoil. By the next fall, the same leaders who had lamented rising costs, undereducated cops, and complex social problems were now proclaiming their own victimhood. Police were "the lonely, misunderstood victims of planned insurrection, crippling court rulings, and 'libelous' press." At the 1966 IACP annual meeting, Donald D. Pomerleau, a former IACP consultant who had just been installed as Baltimore's new police commissioner, detailed a community-relations program, receiving a cool response. In contrast, the speakers who preceded and followed him brought the chiefs to their feet, raucously applauding at exhortations to "stand and speak out." In July 1967, several weeks after a small uprising in Atlanta, the usually restrained Jenkins counseled, "Speak very kindly, walk very slowly, and carry a sawed-off shotgun."[10]

When Congress scaled back appropriations for the new law enforcement assistance program in 1966, Tamm publicly attacked legislators for their malfeasance. With a larger anticrime bill in the works in March 1967, Tamm then testified before Senator John L. McClellan's subcommittee, praising Congress for its support of putting resources in the hands of police. The IACP created a staff position to answer inquiries at any hour of the day or night from members of Congress about the police perspective on this and other legislation. Crucial to the bill's eventual shape, the subcommittee also included the segregationist Democrats James O. Eastland, Sam J. Ervin, and Strom Thurmond (a Republican as of 1964), plus northern liberal Democrats Ted Kennedy and Philip A. Hart, the last an early advocate of federal funding for anticrime measures. Tamm spoke to the subcommittee immediately after Ray Girardin, who used Detroit as an example of a city that, if it had better funding, would be able to "implement progressive police developments" to prevent crime and civil unrest. Girardin "unequivocally" supported a large federal anticrime bill.[11]

In speeches, media appearances, and his articles in *The Police Chief*, plus his testimony before Congress, Tamm showed his colleagues how to maintain message discipline, and why it was important to do so. Tamm also excelled at criticizing contenders for national prominence, whether in the FBI or the Fraternal Order of Police. Tamm was "hotheaded," Herbert Jenkins acknowledged, but as IACP director he did "a better job than anyone else." Even if the problems of crime and disorder that chiefs faced were the result of a combination of their own officers' incompetence and bigotry, or increasingly provocative and intransigent rank-and-file officer organizations, it was more effective to blame the timid liberals, including Supreme Court justices, who did not want to admit that without law and order, civilization hung in the balance. If that failed, Tamm blamed the commies.[12]

Each time an IACP grant application was rejected or a contract was terminated for failing to meet standards, Tamm would blow a gasket. Prideful and unable to weather criticism, Tamm's temper was so well-known in Washington that IACP staffers would warn officials to expect him to "forcefully" register his displeasure at any curtailment of funding. His vitriol kept the spigot open.[13]

Tamm's frequent rants about the fifth-column attack on police and widespread "contempt for law and order" gave the IACP a more militant veneer than it deserved. The IACP attained the legitimacy it sought and today upholds its legitimacy by keeping the lunatic fringe within policing at arm's length. But in the 1960s, though it was effective in Washington, the gospel of reformism that the IACP preached ended up backfiring in station houses when Tamm deployed it against unions.[14]

After Tamm criticized growing police unionism, on behalf of the IACP, for undercutting the authority of chiefs, the head of the Boston Police Patrolmen's Association groused, "The hell with Quinn Tamm. Who the hell is he?" He focused not on pay or benefits but on how Tamm's reformism represented the destruction of the craft of policing: "Let Quinn Tamm get a bunch of robots and wind them up and let them be your cops."[15]

Less than an hour from DC was the city that Tamm hoped to turn into a showcase for professional reform. But in a sign of shifting power dynamics, Baltimore, Maryland, would end up defying Tamm's brand of reformism—and mainline organized labor alike.

THE CHIEFS' CHIEF IN BALTIMORE

Crime in the city of Baltimore, Maryland, rose 22 percent in the month of January 1964, according to the police department. To put that spike in context, think about the spring of 2020. When the weather started to get warmer, after everyone had been locked inside for at least six weeks due to COVID-19, crime started to rise across the country. And after George Floyd's killing by police, it kept rising at an unprecedented rate. Increases in certain offenses, including homicide, occurred almost everywhere, leading to an increase of around 30 percent over the first year of the pandemic.

A single city recording a rapid, unexplained 22 percent jump in crime in January, a month that typically records lower crime due to colder weather, seemed suspicious back in 1964 to Richard Levine, an alert city reporter. He began investigating the police department's crime data. His research led to a series of articles outlining the flaws that led to this implausible crime spike. Levine found that, although opinions abounded, no one really knew for certain how much crime was occurring in Baltimore.[16]

Pressure mounted for officials to do something. By 1965, everyone in Baltimore, the nation's sixth-largest city, just behind Detroit, was becoming obsessed with the city's mediocre police department. To determine what was going wrong, five city and state groups conducted studies. One was the city comptroller's Committee to Raise Police Morale. Another was the Governor's Committee to Review the Operations of the Baltimore Police Department. Three private groups also weighed in, including the implacable United Baltimore City Police Wives' Association.[17]

This obsession peaked before crime itself did—at least according to the dubious statistics the Baltimore Police Department was releasing. They were so unreliable, in fact, that the FBI conferred an asterisk, meaning untrustworthy, on the city's 1965 data in its annual Uniform Crime Reports.[18]

Despite voluminous public interest in fixing the police department, stakeholders could not agree on a strategy. The disarray and disagreement among city elites left the governor's committee as the authoritative voice by statutory default, enabling it to seek outside help diagnosing the problem.

Three firms vied for a contract to conduct a survey of the department: a local consultancy, a large public administration advisor, and the International Association of Chiefs of Police. In February 1965 the contract went to the IACP, which hoped to turn Baltimore into a model city for the power of police reform to stop crime. The chiefs seized the moment.[19]

Conditions in Baltimore in the first half of the 1960s mirrored those in other segregated cities: an economic upswing for white people that many still believed was insufficient; stagnation for Black people, who were inspired politically by a national civil rights movement but kept in place geographically and socially by a bigoted and brutal police force. The city's Black population, however, grew dramatically in the two decades after World War II, nearly doubling. Though constituting 44 percent of the city's residents by 1965, Black people were confined to 16 percent of the city's land area. The city's white population, in contrast, had begun its steady, inexorable decline by 1960. Recognizing the shifting situation, Police Commissioner Bernard J. Schmidt made small strides to modernize the department, like appointing the first African American lieutenant, but Schmidt was not up to the task of major transformations.[20]

After ten months of research by a team of seven consultants, at a cost of $52,000, the IACP released its expansive, 600-page survey of the Baltimore police department on January 10, 1966. The IACP report called for organizational reform, new procedures, and upgrading personnel. It provided detailed guidelines for reconfiguring nearly every aspect of the organization's management and operations. Schmidt was already in poor health, and on the very day the IACP survey came out he announced his retirement.

The governor appointed an interim commissioner, Major General George M. Gelston. He was the adjutant general of the Maryland National Guard and had overseen the guard's deployment to Cambridge, Maryland, during civil rights protests and white rioting in 1963 and 1964. Although earlier sit-ins had desegregated some Baltimore drugstores and theaters, it was not until 1966, during Gelston's half-year in charge, that a militant civil rights campaign took hold in the city, organized by the Congress of Racial Equality (CORE), which also held its annual convention in Baltimore.

Meanwhile, Baltimore's police officers were increasingly rejecting control over their work routines. They flocked to sign union membership cards, with over a third of 2,700 eligible officers enrolling. The Patrolman's Organizing and Coordinating Committee had begun organizing in 1960 but accelerated its efforts in 1964. Linked with the American Federation of State, County and Municipal Employees (AFSCME), this organizing was occurring in the shadows in Baltimore, but officers were testifying in Annapolis and drumming up support. One cop, elated that unionization seemed popular among state legislators, declared, "A new day has dawned." These hopes were crushed, however, when the governor, upon advice of Maryland's attorney general, vetoed a bill to authorize the union. He placed the choice in the commissioner's hands. But Gelston simply upheld an old standing order prohibiting officer membership in employee organizations, leaving a decision on how to deal with the ongoing organizing among officers to his successor.[21]

At the same time that CORE staged rallies and pickets, a range of far-right groups, including the Klan and the National States' Rights Party, organized counterprotests and demonstrations. These frequently devolved into street melees. When white extremists from the city and outlying towns, bearing flags with Nazi insignias, appeared in Black neighborhoods, Baltimore officials often blamed local Black youth for any resulting brawls. But the Klan imitated the city's police by bringing a contingent of German Shepherd dogs to intimidate Black picketers. Lieutenant Colonel Frank Battaglia worked closely with Gelston "in handling these potential explosive situations," which led to his appointment as the new chief of patrol, the department's most important uniformed official. Gelston also began implementing some of the IACP's recommendations. He consolidated departmental operations into three bureaus, for instance, while a committee sought his permanent replacement. The committee settled on Donald Pomerleau. He was appointed commissioner on September 22, 1966, a couple of weeks before the Orioles swept the Dodgers in the World Series, thrilling the team's largely white fan base. Pomerleau's reign lasted fifteen years, until Battaglia replaced him in 1981.[22]

Originally from Montana, Pomerleau had been a military police officer in the Marine Corps for over two decades and Miami's director of public safety for a spell. He had attended the academies of the FBI, Border Patrol, and Federal Bureau of Narcotics. He was the first outsider appointed Baltimore's commissioner. Just before arriving in September 1966, Pomerleau had been working for the IACP's Field Service Division, sent as a police management consultant to Chicago, Dallas, Nashville, and other cities. He specialized in the implementation of recommendations, and he attended seminars with the Agency for International Development's public safety advisors, who conducted the same type of police consulting in Third World countries that US intelligence officials deemed at risk of communist revolution. Although Pomerleau was not listed as one of the IACP's Baltimore survey authors, he was the IACP's liaison to the city. One ex-reporter later joked that Pomerleau "wrote a report that suggested what Baltimore needed was a strong commissioner, possibly an ex-marine. He suggested the new commissioner be between 50 and 52 years of age. At the time, Don was 51."[23]

Soon after the IACP survey became public, the Maryland legislature passed a new Police Omnibus Act, which conferred "broad and far reaching" powers on the Baltimore police commissioner. The commissioner gained the ability to change any rule or regulation governing the department's operation, including those created by predecessors or by himself, and to implement any new rules or regulations he saw fit. Pomerleau would probe the limits of this empowering legislation as he followed the IACP recommendations like scripture, rebuilding the city's police department from the top down. But the report was silent on police unionism, Pomerleau's greatest obstacle.[24]

Pomerleau obtained a mandate to clean house in Baltimore. His new training requirements peeved many cops, at a time when it was still common for even top investigators to lack a high school diploma. Pay levels were haphazard, with new appointees earning what some veterans were taking home. Cops used sick leave liberally. Graft remained a persistent problem. Traffic safety, Schmidt's specialty, was terrible, with Baltimore officers themselves crashing police vehicles at high rates. And cops lacked a reliable complaint mechanism or grievance procedure until less than a month before Pomerleau's appointment, when Gelston created a Personnel Service Board, commonly called the grievance board, composed of elected representatives from the force.[25]

Inaccurate crime data were a major concern for the IACP survey team. Inefficient deployment of personnel was both cause and effect of bad data. The IACP prescription was for all department operations to be shaped by crime's actual incidence, but bad data meant headquarters remained uncertain when and where crime was occurring. The city was already spending more per capita than every large city other than Chicago and Washington, DC, and it employed more police per 1,000 residents than any other city save Washington. But the department had little to show for its expenditures.

Pomerleau attempted to deploy police resources both in a cost-effective manner and according to actual need, which meant new activity reporting procedures for officers, plus increasing automotive patrol. Like many other cities then, patrol staffing was evenly spread across three eight-hour shifts, and officers were allocated to standard beats without regard to need, leaving some cops busy and some bored. Further, many officers obtained plum assignments patrolling the city's hospitals or hotels, while others were assigned to patrol absurdly large beats on foot. These differences fueled resentment within the ranks. After Pomerleau's reforms, cops came to resent the new paperwork they had to fill out, but they disliked new patrol allocations even more. These reconfigurations took officers from familiar beats and placed them in different areas, at new times of day, where and when the department's number crunchers anticipated crime would occur.

The department was still segregated at the time of Pomerleau's appointment. Black officers were relegated to foot patrol only in Black neighborhoods. Pomerleau immediately ordered operations officially desegregated and instituted training on "Negro history" to improve police attitudes toward Black Baltimore. Change was slow, however, as the department was only 3 percent nonwhite when he started, rising to 15 percent in seven years. The African American population of the city possessed no clear avenue of complaint after suffering police abuses, like warrantless raids conducted on 230 "mostly colored" homes in the city after two officers were shot soon before Pomerleau's appointment. The new commissioner claimed to be committed to improving police-community relations, though his undercover officers would soon spy on the uniformed officers tasked with meeting with African American community groups. Early on, he did fire probationary officers accused of hurling racial slurs. He also convinced one African American cop, Edward Woods, who had resigned because of his colleagues' bigotry, to return to the force; in July 1989, Woods would be appointed commissioner himself.[26]

But Baltimore awakens every morning with an antebellum hangover. Thanks to legislation in 1860 intended to allow Democrats to preempt the Know-Nothing Party's political grip on Baltimore and to quell gang violence, the city's police department remained technically under state control until legislative changes in 2022 and 2024. The police budget nevertheless drew from municipal coffers. As in St. Louis, the other big city with a similar system, the basic premise was to deny the city's small population of white Republicans and comparatively large population of free Black people direct control of the police.[27]

Police commissioners were appointed by the governor, a nineteenth-century system that left the governor with outsized control over whether a reformist or outsider would take charge of the department. Pomerleau believed that such a system had the benefit of allowing the appointee to stay above the fray of local politics.[28]

In fact, local politics would define the future of policing all over the country. It was in Detroit that a progressive reform program would run into its most angry and intransigent challenge.

CHAPTER 3

BLUE POWER RISING

Over the course of the late 1960s, police came to fear and loathe the movement they knew as Black Power. Police understood figures like H. Rap Brown (Jamil Al-Amin), Stokely Carmichael (Kwame Ture), Eldridge Cleaver, Angela Y. Davis, Gloria Richardson, and many more as advocates of lawlessness and wanton violence against police. Surprise attacks targeting police did occur, though not on a scale commensurate with the attention they received. It was far more common for police to initiate the incidents that led to them getting hurt.

Police tended to tar any and all critics as members of an extreme and even Moscow-directed subversive conspiracy. After an investigation into police misconduct in Chicago, cops suggested its findings must have been the work of either communists or Supreme Court justices, who were equivalent. In explaining what cops were up against, one police chief characteristically condemned radical "literature, if you can call it that," which "attacks obscenely every facet of American life." Even worse, radicals had "launched a semantic attack," calling police "animal names." But cops also repurposed terms like "pig," advocating "Pig Power" during a police strike in Milwaukee—"Bring home more bacon" went the appeal—or rebranding the epithet as an honorific: "Join the P.I.G.S. (Proud Intelligent Guardians of Society)."[1]

"Blue Power" was the response to Black Power. The term circulated quietly among cops initially. Carl Parsell was among the first cops to popularize it in an interview with a local journalist. Observers of labor politics noticed it too. Blue Power was, for cops, "the political force by which radicalism,

Milwaukee police picket city hall during a four-day strike in January 1971. Sherman A. Gessert Jr., © *Milwaukee Sentinel*, USA Today Network via Imagn Images.

student demonstrations, and Black Power can be blocked," in the words of one 1968 assessment.[2]

Police enacted retribution on Black political activists who criticized policing practices—false arrests, trumped-up charges, harassment, threats, and violence—in Baltimore, Chicago, Detroit, Houston, Los Angeles, San Francisco, and elsewhere. In a Brooklyn, New York, courthouse, off-duty cops calling themselves the Law Enforcement Group brutalized supporters of Black Panthers who were on trial in 1968; the cops chanted "White power!" and "White tigers eat Black Panthers!" Not every city with Black militancy also had a burgeoning police unionization movement, but they often inflamed each other. Organizations ranging from the Nation of Islam to the Communist Party USA to the Black Panther Party all antagonized cops with explicit critiques of the primary vehicles of Blue Power, local police unions. But police were far more powerful. And at the same time that police ratcheted up their repression of Black Power activists and others on the left, they were trying to achieve gains in compensation and working conditions, as well as impunity for wrongdoing. Extremist factions within police unions like the Law Enforcement Group pushed these already conservative organizations even further to the right.[3]

Black Power and Blue Power were not mirror images. Blue Power pushed against an open door, while Black Power encountered racism and an unyielding political establishment, or else co-optation. But by virtue of proximity to the civil rights movement's social and political changes, police who organized for Blue Power fused their demands for better working conditions with rebarbative reaction against social-movement and legal pressure for equal treatment under the law. The rank and file mustered internal strength and organization from the bottom up, along with outside support, by opposing civil rights. They would reject, delay, and diminish both top-down power by commanders and efforts by outsiders to restrain racist abuse.

Liberal elected officials who supported civil rights tended to support public sector unionism as well, and they made concessions to police unionization demands in this spirit. Some commentators were optimistic that exposing cops to the "liberal social viewpoint of the labor movement" could reduce bigotry and increase humane attitudes and protections of civil liberties, while also minimizing both corruption and abuse of officers by commanders. Such hope was strong in Michigan, which was home to the great unions that supported the Johnson administration, particularly on civil rights. But Detroit was also a locus of Black Power, as well as home to a host of left-wing radicals and countercultural kids. Cops knew the enemy. They took advantage of Mayor Cavanagh's belief in the ameliorative possibilities of unionization, while refusing to entertain the social liberalism that was supposed to accompany it.[4]

THE ELUSIVE BENEFITS OF UNION RECOGNITION IN DETROIT

After Michigan allowed public sector bargaining, Detroit's police pressed their case for unionization with the mayor. Cavanagh had recognized the Detroit Police Officers Association, but the benefits seemed elusive in the absence of formal contract negotiations. Conferring with Cavanagh, the civil service commission, and other Detroit municipal representatives amounted to, for Carl Parsell, "collective begging." From city hall's perspective, recognition of the Detroit Police Officers Association deflected the possibility of it affiliating with the Teamsters or another major labor union. However hollow, this threat posed a greater danger than recognizing the unaffiliated fraternal group. Cavanagh did not believe recognition would dramatically change anything. Parsell turned proving Cavanagh's assumptions wrong into a sport.[5]

The Detroit Police Officers Association began its negotiations by demanding a substantial pay increase for fiscal year 1966–1967, raising the maximum base salary by $1,665 to $9,000. Negotiations proceeded slowly, and the adopted city budget did not include the requested increase. But police pay did still rise, with all city employees receiving $312 more and police and firefighters an additional $688, for a total increase of $1,000. In fact, Cavanagh had gained approval from most police when he first ran for mayor in 1961 because cops thought Miriani, the incumbent, was unwilling to compensate them well. In the two years before Parsell became Detroit Police Officers Association president in 1965, under Cavanagh, police pay was already rising faster than ever before.[6]

Parsell was not satisfied with the 1966 raise, however. The Detroit Police Officers Association moved the goalposts, now requesting a maximum base salary of $10,000 for the next fiscal year, 1967–1968. This salary increase was consistent with the fresh recommendations of the President's Commission on Law Enforcement and Administration of Justice, led by Attorney General Nicholas Katzenbach. To attract competent, college-educated cops, police salaries should ideally start at $7,000–$10,000 and range as high as $15,000. But a more realistic range was $6,000–$9,000 and a maximum of $12,000.[7]

Across the country, reformist chiefs were willing to earmark new expenditures, but they tended to focus on new training and technologies rather than the salaries their officers desired. The Katzenbach Commission similarly codified new benchmarks of police professionalism while mostly ignoring the simmering rank-and-file rebellion and union activity. Its only published discussion of police unions actually concerned Detroit. A subsidiary task force on policing echoed the findings of the Michigan Civil Rights Commission, which heard complaints from the Detroit Police Officers Association that disciplinary actions taken against police did not match the severity of their offenses. The report concurred. It particularly noted that Detroit police officers almost never received more than a written reprimand for civil rights violations.[8]

Behind the scenes, the Katzenbach Commission had briefly communicated with Parsell on issues of compensation. In the spring of 1966, Parsell sent a telegram to Lyndon Johnson, seeking the president's aid. Parsell asked

Johnson to contact the mayor's office directly to convey his support for better pay and increased numbers of officers in Detroit. The union head sensed that a solution to the impasse might come from outside the city. James Vorenberg, the commission's newly appointed executive director, responded. The commission, he noted, was interested in "establishing a realistic level of police compensation." But he cautioned that no "direct assistance" on the request would be forthcoming. Parsell's union was on its own.[9]

When it came to wages, officers around the country focused on maximum civil service salary levels. Because of the rank structure, raising the ceiling at each rank seemed to be cops' best option. Most departments were marked by limited opportunities for promotion due to strong competition for few openings. And many officers never attempted to rise up the ranks. Professionalizers like the Katzenbach Commission urged the adoption of lateral transfer, which would allow skilled and well-trained police to change departments into a higher rank through open examination processes. Not only would it foster more universal standards, but it could overcome "provincialism" and the "lifetime of personal debts, friendships, animosities" that accrued while policing one jurisdiction. But police were "still too bound by traditionalism to accept the idea too readily." One study of 493 police agencies at the time found only four chiefs, three detectives, one sergeant, and one lieutenant who had moved laterally to another department. Only about a third of agencies reported having accepted any lateral transfers, and mostly at the lowest rank. Cops tended to stay put once they reached upper salary bands.[10]

From World War II into the 1960s, unionized factory wages increased at almost double the rate of police wages. From 1961 to 1966, a period of dramatic economic expansion throughout the country, police salaries did not increase as quickly as salaries for comparable types of public employment. Federal government employees saw an increase of 23 percent, local transit operators 35 percent. For police the figure was 18 percent.[11]

The average maximum police salary was $7,327 in big cities—too low to feed a family of four, cops insisted—when Detroit police latched on to the symbolism of the $10,000 figure. City officials worried that declining revenues would make such a pay increase impossible, particularly as public schools were swelling. An additional 10,000 students had enrolled in the past decade, requiring a projected $63 million to be spent on hiring new teachers and building new facilities. The city pivoted its budget toward austerity, clipping $700,059 from police operations. Parsell charged Cavanagh with pleading poverty while spending money frivolously: the zoo's new $1 million penguin cage especially galled police. Parsell accused the mayor of refusing to seek creative ways to cover higher police salaries. In 1966, in fact, Cavanagh asked Congress for $15 billion in federal funds for poverty alleviation and "urban renewal" over the next decade, but at that time, the prospect of Washington funding city police salaries was anathema.[12]

The buck was not always the source of friction, however. In the first round of negotiations, police commanders showed up in uniform and demanded that officers do so too, making it impossible to negotiate as equal parties at the table, outside the rank hierarchy. Relations only deteriorated in the next round, as the Detroit Police Officers Association gained confidence in manipulating appearances to shape the negotiations. Police across the city proclaimed how offended they were when, at a city labor mediation board hearing in November 1966, a city lawyer insulted Parsell, calling him a "well-meaning dolt" and threatening that he would "ream" him a "new asshole with a dull blade." Negotiations stalled. Aggrieved cops were already scheming.[13]

Beyond daily harassment, Detroit police staged confrontations with activist and subcultural youth on Kercheval Avenue on August 6, 1966, and again on Belle Isle on April 30, 1967. They were trying to gin up racial antagonism, drawing on information gathered by the red squad and FBI surveillance. The cost of such intimidation seemed low.

But Detroit's civic and police leaders took the wrong lessons. The so-called Kercheval incident in 1966 was widely called "the riot that didn't happen" because unrest began but quickly dissipated after officers attacked a group of activists in a desperately poor Black part of the city. They were likely trying to instigate an incident that would provide a pretext for arrests and destroy a Black Power organization in the process. Fights broke out but were contained. In the aftermath, the department attributed the peaceful end to tensions and street melees to its intelligence-gathering, outreach to community leaders, and strict adherence to its recently updated riot manual.

What actually halted the spread of unrest was a torrential downpour on the first night. Police commanders grew confident that the city would be able to handle any political provocations. They were looking at Black Power, while ignoring the Blue Power threat.[14]

CRIME INSTRUMENTALIZED

As tensions rose, an arcane statistical alteration prompted a consequential shift in the politics of crime rates. Across the country in the 1960s, many police departments changed how they recorded crime statistics. Detroit joined its peers in adopting FBI standards—leaving scholars then and today to debate endlessly how much of the reported crime increases were statistical artifacts and how much reflected real changes on the ground. According to the FBI's numbers, violent crime increased 49 percent nationally from 1960 to 1966, and burglaries, larcenies of $50 or more, and auto theft increased 64 percent in the same period. Not every city recorded crime the same way, meaning that although Detroit was definitely the country's fifth-largest city, it may not have actually ranked fourth in incidence of crime overall and third in serious crime. And no statistical measure existed to account for the assaults police committed, or deaths by police gunfire.[15]

For Detroit's white right, increasing crime indicated that the police were unsupported and the mayor's liberalism was bankrupt.

For Cavanagh's administration, increasing crime might have poked holes in the reputation it had built, signaling that all was not what it seemed in the model city. But Cavanagh believed his own hype: Great Society liberalism was meeting the challenges that modern urban life was producing, and the gains of the civil rights movement were alleviating the civic alienation and economic disenfranchisement that had plagued the Black quarters of the city. Journalists from around the country visited Detroit to learn about Cavanagh's good works, but knowledgeable locals knew things were not right economically.

The past two decades had been the nation's greatest period of macroeconomic growth on record. Yet during that time Black Detroit experienced only modest improvements. Black workers' most significant advances occurred in the automobile industry, the city's major employer. They had made inroads at some auto plants by the 1960s, though the United Auto Workers was more interested in supporting the national civil rights movement than in advocating specifically for Black workers on the shop floor. Integration of auto plants was uneven, with several counting 30 percent of their employees as African American and others fewer than 5 percent. Black employees still tended to be relegated to less skilled and more hazardous positions. And many Black autoworkers experienced vicious bigotry and abuse on the job. They tended to be the group at the greatest risk of layoffs, whether due to short-term downturns or the secular automation trend.

Other industries in the city were even less hospitable to Black employees, though public employment, including in schools, was one sector that saw consistent growth for Black people. Shut out of many domains of formal employment, numerous Black men sought erratic and degrading day labor, meaning that a Black man looking for work could appear to a white observer like someone loitering, trespassing, or otherwise causing trouble. Cops responded accordingly.[16]

Detroit insiders also suspected there were deep problems in the police department that spanned the rank hierarchy. In 1966, cops became embroiled in a bribery scandal centering on the Grecian Gardens restaurant, known as much for its lamb chops as for the likelihood of spotting a Detroit Lion gambling in the back. Around forty officers were linked to organized crime upon the discovery of a list of names in the joint, just a couple of blocks from police headquarters. Ultimately, a grand jury indicted twenty-one officers, most for lying in the subsequent investigation. Thirteen would be suspended. Another five faced a trial board, with four punished. It was a notable number in a city where cops were accustomed to impunity, but the details of what exactly had transpired in Greektown remained murky.

Rumors implicating Commissioner Girardin himself circulated. At the very least, he was less aggressive in pursuing crime syndicates than his predecessor. Girardin tried to be tough, transferring implicated cops whom he did not suspend. But the more oxygen Girardin gave the scandal, the more he risked a backdraft. In one broadcast interview, Girardin seemed evasive, frequently coughing between words. A morning radio host, Dick Purtan, then staged a call-in contest: Who could best imitate Ray Girardin's cough? The commissioner himself dialed in and hacked an entry.[17]

The Grecian Gardens scandal tainted the whole force. Inside the department, it fed tensions between line officers and command. The episode ruined the career of the chief of detectives, who had authorized the investigation into the Grecian Gardens. He became persona non grata among his officers. Girardin came to despise him for making it look like the commissioner was leading a crooked force. Outside the department, cops on the beat bristled when passersby accused them of taking bribes. The thousands of cops who were uninvolved got a bad rap, and it was easy for the man on the street to point a finger. But the man on the street also knew that many more cops were dirty than the headline-grabbing episode revealed. The man on the street perceived what Parsell pursued: cops wanted a payoff.

BLUE FLU IN DETROIT

As early as October 1966, Detroit police had begun planning a ticket-writing slowdown to threaten the city's fiscal solvency. The planning began after the Kercheval incident, and it commenced May 16, 1967, just weeks after the confrontation on Belle Isle, when police blitzkrieged a love-in held at the park where the white riot had broken out in 1943. Wayne Kramer, guitarist of the rock band MC5, who performed that day, his nineteenth birthday, recalled how the love-in turned into a hate-in: "The sun went down and the Detroit Police department decided we weren't clearing out quickly enough. They started bum rushing every-one off Belle Isle.... We were a bunch of stoned-out weirdos and Budweiser-buzzed factory rats enjoying a free concert. What we didn't realize was the first pass by La Policia set the stage for the massacre to come."[18]

First came the ticketing slowdown, however. Parsell himself, who had worked traffic duty before becoming Detroit Police Officers Association president, usually set up on Grand River Avenue, on the west side. From his daily perch, he could watch white commuters flee to their new homes in the suburbs, the racial transition on display every rush hour.

A slowdown was a counterintuitive tactic for the union while it was arguing that the city could afford to pay cops more money. Suddenly strangling the otherwise dependable revenue stream generated by minor citations was risky. The city deposited fines into the general fund, from which police salary increases would be drawn. But the slowdown was designed to attack the department's command imperatives.

Commanders required officers to write 100 tickets per three-shift car each month, or risk transfer to undesirable beats. Cops hated this quota system, and when the city's 1967 budget proposal increased expectations for ticket revenue by $1 million to $7.2 million (of an estimated $300 million in total revenue) without delivering pay raises to officers, cops rebelled. The slowdown, quickly throttling fine-based revenue by two-thirds, suggested that issues of status and respect, as well as individual discretion, mattered more than the mechanics of a pay raise. And many cops never believed Cavanagh's claim that there was not a cent to spare in the budget.

The Detroit Police Officers Association was determined to prove how unhappy rank-and-file officers were. Cops picketed an advertising agency commissioned by the Greater Detroit Board of Commerce to assist in recruitment. The firm had released findings of a survey that dubiously purported police morale to be high. Parsell released his own survey results, finding the opposite. Picketers' signs impugned the survey's methodology: IT'S TOO LATE TO SURVEY THE 230 MEN WHO QUIT. Police claimed pay was not high enough to prevent "manpower" losses, as they were called, while commanders and city leaders feared that manpower shortages could lead to disorder. By mid-1967, the force was 400 officers short of its target size. Police unions often pointed to difficulties in hiring and retention as the clearest proxy for morale, but officers typically cared less about aggregate size than functional manpower questions like the number of officers per cruiser or per night shift.

A few days into the slowdown, the city council, then called the Common Council, adopted a budget that contained no pay increases for city employees. Police continued to stop motorists, giving warnings instead of citations. Ordinarily, commanders had little truck with such expressions of officer discretion. But they worried about a Detroit Police Officers Association tactical shift; instead of warnings, officers could suddenly begin citing any and every possible violation, rankling taxpayers. Detroit cops brandished their discretion like a protest placard.[19]

Police appealed to the numerous powerful unions in the region for solidarity, and received it. The United Auto Workers, the Teamsters, Detroit's AFSCME chapter, and others pledged support. Mayor Cavanagh caviled to Girardin about insubordination. Publicly, he stuck to the script of highlighting successes in Detroit's war on poverty. He even lauded his police department's effectiveness on television on May 17, desperate to nip the day-old ticket slowdown in the bud. It did not matter.[20]

Ticket revenue declined by as much as $15,000 per day, around 80 percent. Command officers retaliated, threatening future promotions and forcing Parsell back out on a patrol tour. Commissioner Girardin ordered resumption of the "norm" in traffic citations (not a quota, he insisted). The Detroit Police Officers Association claimed that by ignoring revenue-generating quotas, cops were now able to engage in substantive enforcement. The union wanted to relocate operational decision-making to the rank and file, sneering at the brass. To break the job action, the department transferred veteran officers who had not been writing tickets to foot patrol. "If the mayor wants war, war he will get," announced the Detroit Police Officers Association. The monthlong slowdown, which cost the city $583,000 in anticipated revenue, was only one campaign in the battle.[21]

Inspired by a police job action in Pontiac, Michigan, the prior year, where officers decided to use accumulated leave time en masse, Detroit officers started to call in sick on Thursday, June 15. It was a tactic that became known as the "blue flu." The police officer association's lawyers predicted 1,000 officers would not show up for work on Monday, June 19, in what appeared to be a technically legal maneuver. Absent officers were risking suspension if they claimed to be ill while healthy. Thus, many performed invisible ailments like headaches or back pain for department physicians. The waiting room, one observer recalled, was like the battlefield at Antietam, full of groaning lads begging for God's mercy. Some cops who doubted their own skills as thespians claimed that family members were gravely ill; they sought emergency leave to tend to relatives who could not be subjected to a departmental medical exam. The city sued the Detroit Police Officers Association, sought a permanent injunction, requested $1 million in punitive damages and $50,000 per day in compensatory damages, and suspended dozens of officers immediately. Cavanagh had an announcement prepared for roll call, threatening officers with jail time if they failed to show up. Strikers, of course, could only read about it in the papers and chuckle.[22]

Parsell's blue flu tactic dared the mayor to risk an outbreak of street crime or unrest, like what had occurred in Boston half a century earlier. Detroit police commanders forced nonstriking officers to work longer shifts. The department switched from three 8-hour shifts to two 12-hour shifts, meaning that more cops were on the street at any given moment. Desk jockeys and detectives hit the pavement. Police coverage may have been better than normal, though not by the most disgruntled and motivated officers. The militants among the rank and file were not on the streets. Those who were patrolling exercised caution.

The mayor trusted that his administration's strides in mitigating social alienation and poverty would keep the peace. But Cavanagh would emphasize that the "fierce militancy" of the Detroit Police Officers Association challenged the "social renewal" that his administration sought, by undermining baseline "respect and faith in law and order." After a few days, outside support for the cops began eroding. Other unions broke with the Detroit Police Officers Association, and newspapers began criticizing the police for unlawfulness.[23]

The blue flu's timing put Cavanagh in a tight spot. As a rising star, the Jack Kennedy of municipal governance, he was scheduled to give a speech in Hawai'i to the US Conference of Mayors. Cavanagh struck a tentative deal to resume talks with the Detroit Police Officers Association, ending the blue flu on Sunday, June 18. He immediately hopped on a plane to Honolulu, only to learn that the deal fell apart an hour after he landed when officers on the 4 p.m. shift failed to show. At that conference, AFSCME's president, Jerry Wurf, harangued the nation's mayors. They were, he intoned, "our perpetual prod of militancy" and "our assurance of continued growth."[24]

Back in Detroit, increasing numbers of cops failed to report for duty on Monday. Cavanagh's blue flu inoculation failed, though he had promised to begin negotiating. On June 19, 3,000 cops' wives and children picketed city hall, demanding Cavanagh be recalled. Many also joined picket lines surrounding station houses. The Detroit Police Officers Association intentionally made Cavanagh look like a fool, jetting to the middle of the Pacific Ocean while his city was in disarray. He later reflected that the Detroit Police Officers Association acted like it was "sort of a joke." The union's negotiators believed city negotiators had been acting in bad faith all along, particularly by prematurely claiming the budget to be "closed." Cops wanted to penalize the mayor. By Tuesday, June 20, over one-third of the patrol force had called in sick, taken emergency leave, or been suspended. The mayor caved. Cavanagh withdrew the lawsuits, handing victory to Carl Parsell and the Detroit Police Officers Association.[25]

CITY HALL FORCED TO NEGOTIATE

Despite the drumbeat of ugly crime statistics leading up to the blue flu, crime failed to rise during the time cops stayed off the job, weakening the Detroit Police Officers Association's argument that they deserved improved compensation because they kept the city safe. The automobile accident rate even seemed to decline during the ticket slowdown. "A good side effect of the 80% reduction in writing tickets," concluded a columnist in the radical rag *Fifth Estate*, "was that there were fewer police contacts with the Negro community." Girardin himself noted fewer citizen complaints about police during the period of the ticket slowdown and the blue flu.[26]

With these job actions, Detroit officers revealed a paradox that the political project of police cannot escape. Police invariably argue that they are indispensable to a livable society, the thin blue line between order and chaos. In such a view, the most radical tactic police can employ is to withdraw their labor, whether by slowing down enforcement or striking outright. Yet by withdrawing, they permit a controlled experiment, testing just how essential they really are. As it turned out, crime did not skyrocket during the blue flu. In fact, Black Detroit felt for the first time in years that it could breathe.

Nevertheless, Cavanagh agreed to negotiate with the Detroit Police Officers Association, putting everything on the table. Between June 20 and July 10, the two parties hashed out noneconomic agreements, including officer discipline and grievance procedures. These mattered greatly in a department that had been marked by arbitrary and imperious commanders who insisted they never be questioned. The Detroit Police Officers Association won the right for officers to confer with counsel privately and wait twenty-four hours before making a statement about an incident, as well as the right to wait ten days before appearing before the department's internal Citizens Complaint Bureau. It also won union steward representation or legal counsel at all disciplinary proceedings and right of appeal concerning the severity of trial board decisions. Misconduct hearings in Detroit came to be "legalistic," guided by a neutral legal scholar as an advisor and marked by consistent punishments, rather than the previously arbitrary and variable punitive recommendations.[27]

Through its insurgency, the Detroit Police Officers Association ensured it would gain the upper hand in disciplinary proceedings by enabling appeal to arbitration, rather than allowing the commissioner final say. Further, the association focused on managerial quotas for enforcement, the other face of command pressure on the rank and file.

Parsell recalled that "the green flag"—economic issues—went barely mentioned in the initial discussions after the blue flu. All that mattered was making "the job better." Ultimately, negotiations quashed the expectation that officers write a certain number of traffic tickets, along with a city residency requirement for officers. Economic negotiations proved more difficult, however, and Parsell's mistrust of Cavanagh grew. Arbitration was the only way forward.[28]

Initial fanfare over the agreement to negotiate—"the first agreement of its kind," Cavanagh reported—ended quickly. Next came an announcement that official fact-finding, a typical labor negotiation tool, would be necessary to determine how to deal with the economic issues. The city could use this tool to delay resolution; the Detroit Police Officers Association believed a fact-finding panel would support a pay raise and wanted its recommendations to be binding. But fact-finding would take some time. Detroit cops accelerated the tempo by changing the facts on the ground.[29]

CHAPTER 4

COLLECTIVE BARGAINING BY RIOT

During the June 1967 blue flu, cops had disappeared from Detroit's Twelfth Street corridor, the city's centrally located Black working-class area—and a good deal of crime had disappeared with them. When cops returned, the petty harassment and arrests that typified everyday Black life in the area resumed. What Cavanagh called "the usual inherent antipathy" that Black people felt toward police would hang like a pall over the west side. Just a month after the end of the blue flu, as the city and the police officers' association stalemated, the Detroit rebellion kicked off.[1]

The spark of the Detroit unrest was an aggressive nighttime police raid on a Black social club, a "blind pig," the type of after-hours, unregulated drinking den that was the product of decades of exclusion of Black people from white establishments. At 3:45 a.m., the police infiltrated the United Community League for Civic Action's blind pig, one floor up from Economy Printing, at Twelfth Street and Clairmount, in a zone packed with illegal bars. It was just one of five raids across town that night. The task force was wearing a new style of uniform that made observers suspicious that the bust signaled an intensification of police operations in the area. Meant to be the final raid of Saturday, July 22, by the time two Black undercover officers were able to get inside, they found eighty-two patrons celebrating the return of two servicemen from Vietnam. There were only 44 cops on duty in the area by that hour of Sunday morning, and 193 across the whole city. Nevertheless, the squad decided to arrest all the people inside the bar. One young man shouted, "Black Power, don't let them take our people away." Ill-prepared cops took almost an hour to load the arrestees into paddy wagons. A crowd gathered on the dreadfully hot and muggy streets. Mayhem ensued.[2]

The raid extended the earlier police provocations and job actions. It was as much a raid on Black Detroit as it was a spotlight on the contradictions of public policy in the city: the idea that crime control, police-community relations, fiscal constraint, and police command prerogatives could coexist. If commanders required officers to hit quotas, then cops would do so by repeatedly attempting to raid the same joint—nine times in the preceding year at this blind pig, twice leading to arrests. And if the owners wanted the raids to stop, they would have to pay a bribe. One way or another, cops were going to get paid. The raid was a declaration that the police department ruled the All-American City. But the officers overestimated their ability to keep the lid on the anger they unleashed.[3]

The unionization effort was not incidental to the uprising—the union's success was possible only after Detroit had gone up in flames. Afterward, the city's government was eager to calm white fears of Black violence. The police gained "leverage" by presenting themselves as professional guardians of order.[4]

Any account of US history in this period would include the Detroit rebellion as a turning point, ushering in the end of the ameliorative promise of the Great Society and spurring white reaction against civil rights in the name of law and order. The efforts of the Detroit Police Officers Association to bring about this shift, however, must be added to our understanding. Police not only took advantage of the rebellion's destructive consequences but also created the conditions for it to occur, attacking Cavanagh and the liberalism he embodied. Most importantly, however, in light of the officer association's two-decade effort to gain control, the Detroit rebellion must be seen as the juncture when police operations yielded significant political results. The union could not have known what to expect, but Parsell grasped how to use bedlam for political gain.

As the raid unfolded in the predawn hours of July 23, officers found themselves outnumbered. They withdrew from a situation they knew they could not win. The son of an owner of the blind pig remembered, "For the first time in our lives we felt free."[5]

On July 24, the fiery Monday of the rebellion, there were 1,289 criminal offenses reported to police, and 617 fire alarms. The actual toll of the mayhem was far greater. The first day's exultation and expropriation were followed first by an erratic police response, then by a second day of massive, wanton destruction.[6]

Police racism, and the disgust it engendered among Black people, was the fundamental cause of the Detroit rebellion. According to all subsequent analyses, the city was a tinderbox. Yet even among the most violently racist cops, like Ronald August, who executed nineteen-year-old Auburey Pollard Jr. at the Algiers Motel during the rebellion, there was no sense that "racial problems" were any worse than usual. The steady state was awful. Rather than "race relations," what was different in July 1967, however, was labor relations: police views of their management. August himself recalled that police morale was "very low."[7]

The Detroit rebellion was the most destructive, costly, and deadly Black uprising of the decade. Over 4,800 Army and 8,200 National Guard troops helped to quell the Detroit rebellion, and in the process 43 people were killed, nearly 1,200 injured, and over 7,200 arrested (one-quarter for misdemeanors). The police, Army, and National Guard were directly responsible for thirty of the deaths. Damages due to fire and looting were $45 million (in adjusted dollars, roughly equivalent to 2025 expenditures on the Detroit police).

Subsequent understandings among police officers of what spurred the rebellion were bifurcated, with patrol officers, sergeants, and lieutenants holding similar views but commanders offering notably different interpretations. The slowdown and blue flu had already widened this gap across the ranks. Compared to patrol officers, twice as many commanders believed the cause of the rebellion was political, based on frustration at the socioeconomic situation for African Americans. Compared to any other cause, more patrol officers attributed the rebellion to abstract reasons like inspiration from unrest in other cities or a lack of respect for authority, though many officers blamed agitators and militants too. One expert drily suggested that among the patrol, "There was also a striking lack of appreciation of the role police played in contributing to riot etiology."[8]

But in the eyes of many Detroit cops, the rebellion was the fault of the commanders, and above all Girardin and Cavanagh. From the first smashed windows, around ninety minutes after the raid, orders stood: no gunfire without explicit command approval. But cops interpreted this as a directive to back down. Parsell amplified this complaint, arguing that his men were hamstrung by command during the rebellion and urged to allow looting, which earned him plaudits on the segregationist far right. His words fed into conspiracy theories about Black communist subversives in league with liberal do-gooders.[9]

Yet the brass in Detroit had studied the unrest in Harlem in 1964 and Watts in 1965, learning that police had inflamed the situation by firing their weapons at crowds, moving cars, and buildings. The 1967 uprising in Newark, which unfolded mere days earlier, had also been marked by wanton, indiscriminate gunfire by police and National Guard. Detroit's police leadership wanted to avoid this dynamic.

But over a few days and nights, Detroit experienced enough police and National Guard gunfire to kill more civilians than in any of the other episodes of unrest that decade. Cavanagh reckoned that the trigger-happy Guardsmen, deployed to the turbulent west side, were white country boys who "would be frightened to death on any night walking down a main street in Detroit." The more disciplined Army ended up on the calmer east side. Military intelligence units relayed locations of suspected snipers from Detroit to an Army post at Fort Holabird on Baltimore's southeastern edge and then to the Pentagon so that "generals in the war room . . . might discuss how best to remove gunmen from buildings they had never seen." Most of the men with guns in Detroit were firing blind.[10]

As the rank and file grasped it, commanders worsened the situation by tying cops' hands, while the mayor fruitlessly hoped his community relations efforts might calm the streets. Cops insisted that a few dead looters early on would have scared everyone else into lawfulness. In fact, the police first shot a suspected looter less than twenty-four hours into the unrest, at 10:15 p.m. on July 23. Moreover, the department's new riot procedures allowed even sergeants to approve gunfire.[11]

Over the week of unrest, as large swaths of the city burned and people looted businesses during both day and night, police and National Guard protected public utilities like waterworks and government buildings far from any unrest, remaining unmolested for the duration. Meanwhile, rumors spread that Detroit police themselves were involved in looting and lighting fires.[12]

Soldiers and cops pursued easy targets and old grudges during the rebellion. White officers pulled over a Mustang driven by Ike McKinnon on the first night. After McKinnon identified himself as a cop, a white officer pulled his gun on McKinnon and threatened, "You're going to die tonight, n——." McKinnon leapt onto the floor of the car and fled, pressing the gas pedal with his hand as shots rang out behind him. On an Army tip, police raided a pad near Wayne State University, leading to the arrest of seven, including Wayne Kramer of MC5. Six were released without charges—a few with contusions, however. The pretext? A telescope in the apartment's window might have been used by the mysterious sniper army. On a police tip, the National Guard tear-gassed the offices of *Fifth Estate*, rendering them unusable for over a week. The pretext? Snipers again.[13]

Mass arrests overwhelmed the courts, leading to arraignments without counsel, while police reports often amounted to little more than a Polaroid of an arrestee beside piled booty. With precinct houses and the county jail overflowing, one cop had the idea of returning to Belle Isle. He proposed turning the island's bathhouse into a temporary detention center. Belle Isle became "Belcatraz," at last briefly desegregrating the white redoubt of the Detroit Yacht Club.[14]

For his part, Parsell departed Detroit on July 26, while the unrest was still intensifying, to address the annual meeting of the International Conference of Police Associations. Cavanagh did not publicly point out the irony. The Detroit Police Officers Association itself had been instrumental in forming this "association of associations" in 1954, aiming for cooperation among police organizations on labor issues, rather than only operational ones. By 1967, it was a loose confederation of over 100 police unions, representing more than 100,000 cops.[15]

At that 1967 meeting of the International Conference of Police Associations, while the city was still on fire, Parsell blamed both Cavanagh and Governor George Romney for ineffective responses to the unrest, arguing that each was seeking partisan advantage over the other, kneecapping the mobilization of resources. He also insisted the city had covered up the extent of the destruction and how many cops had been shot since the raid on the blind pig. In 1970, Parsell became president of the International Conference, at the same time as members endorsed a resolution favoring "superior" weaponry for police against attacks with rocks and bottles as well as guns, and threatening "on-the-street justice" if judges did not get tougher on those who menaced police.[16]

The Detroit Police Officers Association took full advantage of the unrest. The union capitalized on a situation it shaped and conditions it helped stage: a tense city on the verge of a maelstrom that only the police could contain. And by benefiting from unrest in 1967, the union repeated a pattern from 1943, when an earlier bout of destruction occurred during a Detroit police organizing campaign. Success at the bargaining table occurred not because the police were protectors of order but because they could prompt disorder.

After the rebellion, police got what they wanted: formal recognition by the city government plus improved pay and working conditions. The cops suspended for the blue flu were reinstated and given back pay. The police rebuked Jerome Cavanagh, a young, liberal mayor who had campaigned on bridging "the river of hate" between Detroit's Black population and its police. The tragedy was that the police were willing to sacrifice the city itself in the process.[17]

Detroit police made good on Parsell's threat of street justice. And then they asked for more.

BLUE POWER'S FIRST TRIUMPH

Police in Detroit got their way not because of their authorized capacity for violence, which distinguished them from other workers, but because they exceeded their authorization. In 1952, the British social historian Eric Hobsbawm devised the term "collective bargaining by riot" to describe how early modern workers won concessions from factory owners through tactics of political contention that, on their face, seemed chaotic, like breaking a loom. The point was that collective action might not look like an orderly picket line, and the working class might not all hail from the same constituencies and agree on how to win. It was not their tactics but instead their goals that fed these workers into the grand historical stream of working-class militancy, transforming rowdy tactics into collective pressure, forging the "essential solidarity of the workers" in the process.[18]

The Detroit rebellion was unquestionably a groundswell of Black political militancy, but the city's police union at the time cannot be left out of the story. The rebellion came on the heels of the blue flu and the desultory initial attempts to agree on a police union contract. In this light, police activity that summer can be appreciated as its own form of collective bargaining. Yet the self-interested police activism was anything but solidaristic—rather, it strained and fissured the laboring classes, traducing principles of solidarity and heightening the already intense levels of white racism in the city and state.

The alienation of police from the union movement after the Boston police strike, which cops blamed on the AFL, led to the rise of more right-wing,

Carl Parsell, president of the Detroit Police Officers Association from 1965 to 1972, in May 1971. Hugh Grannum.

rascal, unaffiliated organizations, like the Detroit Police Officers Association. That sordid experience left striking cops permanently out of work, while boosting the career of the antiunion governor of Massachusetts, Calvin Coolidge. Parsell's organization set the new precedent: police successfully used a riot to gain formal bargaining rights.[19]

The Detroit Police Officers Association ratified its new contract in August 1967, right after the rebellion. That contract did not cover economic issues. Six months later, on February 27, 1968, the fact-finders hired to assist the negotiations between the city and the Detroit Police Officers Association at last recommended Detroit police be paid $10,000 maximum. At the time, base pay was $7,424 for recruits. It would now rise to $7,500, and the maximum of $10,000 would be reachable in four years. In contrast, New York's pay after three years was $9,383, but it included, for example, a uniform allowance and required work on eleven paid holidays. Boston and Birmingham alike had significantly lower base pay rates. Comparisons of compensation for police in different cities were difficult because the ingredients of each package differed, but the fact-finders believed Detroit's new ceiling to be the highest in the nation.[20]

Plenitude for police meant cost-cutting for the rest of the municipal workforce. Although city revenues threatened to fall short of expenditures, Cavanagh refused to break the parity regulation that afforded cops and firefighters the same pay. He worried that losing the votes of the firefighters would be more costly to his political career than the pay increase would be to the city's fiscal solvency. The Detroit Police Officers Association responded to Cavanagh's worries about the budget by recommending that "city services which do not have the priority of the demands for an adequate police department" be cut, including public concerts, swimming pools, skating rinks, small museums, and arboreal pest control: "amenities" that "make the city livable" to taxpayers. A resentful union official later grumbled, "Apparently it's more important to the city to have picnic tables and trolley cars than police officers." Not merely unsympathetic to the impossible position the mayor and city council were in, the Detroit Police Officers Association aimed to tighten the vise: asking the city to raise expenditures even as they threatened both revenues and the governing legitimacy that might secure or stabilize revenues.[21]

On the very day the fact-finders' salary recommendation became public, the Detroit police commenced a "riot sale." The department offered unclaimed goods that police had confiscated during the previous summer's rebellion—or that sheepish looters had turned in, no questions asked. The department acquired "gymnasiums and garages full of stolen property, everything from 16th century broadswords to modern day washing machines," the deputy superintendent recalled.[22]

Furniture and linens became available on February 27; televisions and stereos went on sale the following week. All sales were final, paid in full in cash. Hundreds packed the basement of police headquarters to pay inflated prices for mementos of the rebellion. The city's general fund netted $5,934 the first day. Buyers thereby funded a few officers' pay bumps. A reporter noted that rifles and shotguns, also confiscated during the rebellion, were on display in baskets. But cops held these back from sale.[23]

The contract went into effect July 1, 1968, with the maximum pay set at $10,300. The Detroit Police Officers Association's success with fact-finding, resulting in a significant pay increase, set a tone, soon replicated in several other cities where police unions successfully rolled the fact-finding dice. By 1969, police salaries nationally had risen 38 percent over five years.[24]

But salaries were only one component of police compensation. One of Cavanagh's first successes as mayor had been to repair the city's police pension problems. Officers were retiring early, and unfunded liabilities had soared beginning in the mid-1950s. Upon election in 1961, Cavanagh faced a $35 million budget deficit. Almost half of the total was owed to the pension plan. Cavanagh instituted a new income tax. It quickly zeroed out the shortfall. Yet he could not change the fact that cops were retiring early. The city's fire and police pension fund remained in the black for only a moment, as unfunded liabilities again skyrocketed to $188 million, over $31,000 per officer, on the eve of the rebellion.[25]

There were twice as many other active city employees as there were cops and firefighters. But the cost for public safety pensions was twice as high as for the others, amounting to 50 percent of payroll. Facing the restive rank and file, Girardin's proposal was to improve pension benefits and lower costs to officers.

In 1968, Cavanagh instead demanded pension reforms to lower costs to city hall, not to officers. Retirement should be based on years of service, with vesting after twenty-five years on the job. And retirees should get a standard cost-of-living adjustment annually, whereas payments had been pegged to active-duty salaries. The city charter held that such pension eligibility reforms would have to go before the voters, which gave the Detroit Police Officers Association and the firefighter union the opportunity to organize against the amendment.

The Detroit Police Officers Association used every tool at its disposal to fight pension reform, spending $250,000 on the campaign. It collected a special assessment of $10 a month from patrol officers to fund its effort. Officers handed out leaflets door-to-door, reaching a quarter million households, and slapped bumper stickers on their scout cars: VOTE NO, AMENDMENT A. Parsell and others formed the Citizens Committee for Responsible Detroit Government, by which they meant the opposite. They took to the airwaves with their campaign, as well as buying newspaper and billboard ads. The police and firefighter line was that the city's safety was at stake as job losses loomed. Cavanagh's modest pension reforms, they claimed, would mean qualified candidates would choose to work elsewhere.

Ultimately, neither voters, civic leaders, nor newspaper editors bought the argument Parsell and his cronies made. The pension amendment succeeded at the ballot box, powered by the city's Black voters, who turned out to vote against Nixon. About 26,000 more voters approved the measure than rejected it, despite credible evidence that the union had engaged in illegal campaigning. After the blow to the pension demands of the Detroit Police Officers Association, the union filed a complaint that the city had been bargaining with it in bad faith prior to the election. That complaint progressed to the state supreme court. The union lost there too in 1974.

By then, the first year of Coleman Young's two-decade reign as mayor, it was already clear that Cavanagh's modest reforms had been insufficient. The city could not avoid a desperate fiscal situation. Although the force peaked under Young at 5,900 sworn personnel, he would ultimately cut around 2,000 positions in the police department (while increasing the number of Black cops significantly). With the pension plan largely intact, the result was that retired white cops, many of whose positions were subsequently eliminated, could live far outside Detroit and collect checks funded by the increasingly tax-burdened remaining Black residents of the city, whom they hated anyway.[26]

Cops who fled the city were the vanguard of the broader transformation that afflicted Detroit and other cities like it, a story whose broad contours are so familiar they risk being overlooked.

Upwardly mobile white families, aided by a growing economy and federal incentives in lending and education, left cities for new municipalities springing up beyond the city limits. Five of eight major metropolitan areas lost population for the first time during Nixon's first term. Many of the 114,000 people who left Detroit justified their departure with their fears of rising crime and faltering services. In leaving, they made the city government less able to afford to eliminate the behaviors that registered as crime through better education or employment opportunities. Abandoned and derelict housing gave city blocks the feeling of danger and disregard.

Left behind were African Americans and new immigrants, whose numbers were continually increasing after the mid-1960s, as well as working-class white people who stayed, believing the bosses would not shutter their factories. City leaders in Detroit even offered General Motors and Chrysler tax abatements to open new plants, a proactive move. However, the firms simply consolidated manufacturing operations, moving employees around but not hiring many new ones. And eventually numerous factories did close, taking revenues that city hall needed to address the problems that had been building for generations.[27]

Big-city mayors like Young who looked to Washington for help received little support. The Nixon and Ford administrations had little interest in saving cities. In his first four years, Nixon vetoed appropriations by Congress on health, education, and welfare three times, with two vetoes upheld. Beyond spending cuts, both administrations increasingly relied on a new fiscal architecture of federal support that distributed money to the states, allowing governors and legislatures instead of urban leaders to determine how to spend the funds. Instead of the more targeted "categorical" funding stream favored by the Johnson administration for its War on Poverty, Nixon's New Federalism created a warrant for undermining the social welfare system by redirecting targeted funding. Block grants, first tested in law enforcement through the Law

Enforcement Assistance Administration (LEAA), seemed designed to miss. They created the self-fulfilling prophecy of government inefficiency.[28]

Police departments were engulfed by the three-pronged crisis of the 1970s that afflicted city governments across the country: declining revenues, increasing expenditures, and a deficit of legitimacy due to ineffective services. Chiefs were at the center, tugged by irreconcilable demands. "I'm just trying to survive" was their perpetual refrain. The rank-and-file rebellion against the rule of the chiefs was the flywheel of the crisis.[29]

I WILL PROTECT

Thanks to Parsell, the police union movement, as if out of nowhere, suddenly started to command national headlines and attract the attention of policing experts. Parsell gamely answered calls from out-of-town reporters, but he knew his power was greatest at the municipal and county levels, as well as in Lansing.

His union was increasingly dedicated to engaging in political organizing—and increasingly ungovernable. In June 1969, two years after the blue flu, two Black vice officers demanded that a twenty-one-year-old Black woman sex worker sleep with them in exchange for letting her off without an arrest. She refused, and the officers raped and stabbed her. The police department was willing to sacrifice these officers for their heinous and illegal act: they were suspended and faced criminal charges. But the Detroit Police Officers Association paid the victim a $5,000 bribe to withdraw a civil suit and to cease cooperating with prosecutors, on the condition the officers resign. She reported that the union's attorney told her its goal was to show that it would "stick up for the colored officers." Protecting these Black men accused of sexual violence would illustrate what type of fraternity the police union could be: macho, colorblind, and willing to support cops no matter what.

More generally, the Detroit police department was out for revenge in the years after the July uprising. The Michigan Civil Rights Commission and the NAACP, along with more radical organizations, recorded, investigated, and denounced numerous police abuses. The Black Panther Party, League of Revolutionary Black Workers, and Republic of New Afrika all were outspoken critics of the department. In turn, they experienced confrontations and attacks by police. The civil rights commission was staid. It strove for a thorough and unimpeachable approach. But that did not protect it. The commission's director, a fifty-year-old white man, was murdered in March 1970. At this moment, police union members were openly refusing to testify in the commission's inquiries. One NAACP official labeled the killing a "political assassination." Some speculated that a member of the police union committed the crime, and the police department made little effort to investigate it. The crime was never solved. Although the commission obtained a consent decree that compelled police to testify, the agreement also vested all ability to punish officers for wrongdoing in the department's trial board and the commissioner, reaffirming the terms of the collective bargaining agreement.[30]

In Parsell's vision, aggressive political action was intended to protect the police. Through door-knocking and donations, the Detroit Police Officers Association worked to become a "quasi-official campaign organization for candidates it endorsed" in the city. It was not always successful, but it learned from its shortcomings. Parsell even believed Cavanagh's victory in the pension reform battle to be Pyrrhic, as 200,000 Detroit voters took the union side of the dispute, which lost by only 20,000, signaling strong support for the rank and file.[31]

The Detroit Police Officers Association honed its political tactics by learning how to persuade voters. Although Parsell never wavered in his commitment to his officers, he came to believe that the best way to help them was to focus on white fears of Black crime and political radicalism, rather than the policeman's lot. He framed the choice as simple: support the Detroit police or support those "at war with our society," particularly the Black Panthers. "The Policemen of the City of Detroit do not intend to be shot down in cold blood," he announced. "We will protect ourselves and our fellow Officers by any and all means necessary."[32]

Carl Parsell left the Detroit Police Officers Association in 1972, seeking a bigger canvas. He spent the remainder of his working days helming the statewide fraternity of police unions, the Michigan Police Officers Association, which he had founded, and as an officer of the International Conference of Police Associations. Today, a $1,000 college scholarship for children of police, firefighters, and other public employees bears Parsell's name, as does an annual union golf outing. The scholarship's announcement reminds applicants why it memorializes him: Parsell was "the architect of modern-day police labor relations."[33]

For a decade after Parsell became president of the Detroit Police Officers Association, the union's member magazine was replete with crime stories, attacks on "women libbers," and criticisms of the mayor and the police commissioner as well as the press, frequently in Parsell's own monthly column. The magazine was called *Tuebor*, after the Michigan state slogan, usually translated as "I will defend," but which the union rendered as "I will protect."[34]

The magazine's name deserved to be changed, however, to reflect how Parsell had reshaped the police union movement. It should have become *Me Tuebor*: "I will protect myself."

Detroit's police union was no outlier at first. Its 1960s activation came in the context of broader public sector militancy. And what drove the rank and file to demand job protections was the common behavior of police commanders everywhere: capricious, imperious, and unforgiving. But the Detroit Police Officers Association learned how to suture its anger about departmental management to white racial animus and the rejection of Black civil rights. If managers demanded control, then the union, whose purpose otherwise was to battle management, would simply argue that managerial policies stood in the way of law and order. The police union movement gained popular support for its internal battle with management, which aroused little outside support, by framing this fight as against the excesses of urban liberalism and civil rights.

The Detroit Police Officers Association discovered a potent concoction. Black radical thinker James Boggs diagnosed the national precedent these officers in his city had set: "All over the country today the police are organizing themselves into independent political organizations, outside the control of elected civilian officials, and challenging the right of civilian administrations and the public, whom they are allegedly employed to protect, to control them."[35]

CHAPTER 5

LABOR POWER OR BLUE POWER?

Spiro Agnew became governor of Maryland in January 1967. Nineteen months later, Richard Nixon chose him as his running mate, but only after the governor had reinvented himself, abandoning his tepid support for civil rights and adopting the blunt mien of the opponent he had beaten in 1966 to become governor, conservative Democrat George Mahoney. When Black Baltimore rose up after the assassination of Martin Luther King Jr. in April 1968, Agnew did not hesitate to summon state police, Army and Air National Guard, and Army regulars to quash the revolt. And in an angry speech to Baltimore's Black civic leaders days later, Agnew castigated his audience of moderates for failing to denounce militants like Stokely Carmichael, out of "a perverted concept of race loyalty." It turned out to be a successful audition for a national political career, hailing a constituency of white voters who would vocalize their own race loyalty in terms of law and order. In the words of Agnew's gubernatorial successor, Baltimore native Marvin Mandel, the city had experienced something new: a "riot resulting in a vice president." Baltimore police officers should have been direct beneficiaries of this new political posture, but the department was tearing itself apart over the question of whether to join hands with organized labor.[1]

When he came into office, Agnew urged Pomerleau to accept the ongoing unionization efforts. Pomerleau was resistant—after all, he had been appointed to demonstrate what a powerful police executive could achieve. He did not want to cede any authority. The governor could not be easily ignored, however. Pomerleau begrudgingly permitted the Fraternal Order of Police Maryland Lodge #3 and the AFL-CIO–affiliated AFSCME Local 1195 to begin organizing openly in the spring of 1967, allowing a paycheck deduction for dues. He quietly favored the fraternal order but hoped the competition for members would exhaust the two groups. What ensued was a triangular battle between the commissioner, the lodge, and the local.

BALTIMORE'S INSURGENT FRATERNAL ORDER OF POLICE LODGE

When Pomerleau arrived in Baltimore, no one could have predicted what was to come: a tiny group of arrivistes formed a proto-union that would eventually sign a collective bargaining agreement with the city. It would defeat both the long-serving and supremely powerful police commissioner and the public sector union movement that had finally, after years of trying, succeeded in organizing cops in a major city. It prevailed because of two key tactics.

The Fraternal Order of Police's first tactic was claiming to speak for every cop while blaming deficiencies on their superiors. This messaging it learned from the labor movement. But the Fraternal Order of Police effected a subtle but consequential shift in target. Whereas AFSCME often attacked the commissioner and departmental leaders who shaped job routines, the Fraternal Order of Police trained its sights on elected officials, particularly African Americans, who criticized police abuses but had no practical supervisory or statutory say over the city's police.

The second tactic was convincing white voters in a hypersegregated city that crimes unlikely to occur anywhere near where they lived were their most important political problem. The Fraternal Order of Police figured out, first, how to bastardize the principle of labor solidarity and, second, how to weaponize it as white racial solidarity.

An organization with little practical political experience but strong local ties and a surfeit of moxie, the Baltimore Fraternal Order of Police lodge succeeded, and shaped the national position of the organization, first as a parasite on the broader labor movement and then by disavowing any fellowship with it. Baltimore's history of police politics is one that matched the perpetual underdog of a city: the losers won, through legalistic maneuvers, perseverance, grit, subterfuge, and a willingness to use police powers to obtain political power.

For decades, cops in the United States had asserted how they were different from the labor movement. They amplified labor's ties to the far left and relished their role breaking strikes, disrupting political organizations, and denouncing communist subversion. But it was in Baltimore that cops confronted a stark choice, either to join the broader labor movement or to protect and serve themselves. Baltimore's squabble between the AFSCME union and the Fraternal Order of Police, which initially shared overlapping memberships, refined police combat tactics for years to come, affecting everyday life in the city, politics in the state, and the fortunes of organized labor across the country.[2]

What catalyzed change in Baltimore was the fear of a civilian review board. Coalitions of progressives, civil rights and African American organizations, and civil libertarians began pushing for external review of complaints against police forces through the 1960s. They succeeded only in Rochester and Philadelphia at first, with New York City to follow in 1966. Police in Baltimore took note. To Pomerleau, external review meant external influence, and it signaled that cops could not be trusted to oversee themselves. Putting civilians in charge of officer discipline, one of his deputies quipped, made as much sense as "asking a committee of civilians to solve bank robberies." Still, he did not intend to ignore public pressure for civilian review. He attempted to find a middle path by announcing a strengthened internal investigation unit within the department, which answered directly to him and made a civilian review board redundant. Rank-and-file Baltimore cops bristled, as Pomerleau's new investigation unit still entailed greater oversight of officers, not less.[3]

Into this climate stepped the head of the Fraternal Order of Police's Grand Lodge, John Harrington, early in 1966. Harrington was a plainspoken firebrand, a leader of conservative revanchism among rank-and-file cops. He rose to prominence in an extended battle over civilian review in Philadelphia. Through lawsuits and public appeals, Harrington successfully paralyzed that city's independent review board. And he translated that victory into national leadership of the Fraternal Order of Police for a decade.[4]

Invited by the United Baltimore City Police Wives' Association, Harrington visited Baltimore to denounce civilian review, attract attention for the Fraternal Order of Police among officers, and obtain support in the city. To Deputy Commissioner Ralph G. Murdy, a former FBI agent who vocally opposed civilian review because it impinged on professional autonomy like the old political machines had, the Fraternal Order of Police appeared "to be a compromise between a union and no outside affiliation by police officers." Nevertheless, Commissioner Gelston pleaded with the Fraternal Order of Police to cease and desist. Harrington was becoming the outside agitator he constantly decried, taking advantage of local conditions to push his political agenda.[5]

Harrington's appearance forced the AFSCME group to go public and become official. For AFSCME, Baltimore was a prize: a large city on the border of the South, where union leaders hoped to make new inroads. Some of the cops who pressed for unionization had worked in unionized jobs prior to joining the force and believed in the benefits of union representation. They noted that firefighters in the city were unionized, and police wage levels followed the firefighters' contracts. AFSCME, the largest public sector union, appealed to cops in Baltimore not because of its stance on big issues like civil rights but because it promised to improve their working conditions.

Nationally, AFSCME was not a big player among police departments, however. It represented only around 8,000 or 2 percent of the country's police by the early 1970s. Over ten times as many were represented by the Fraternal Order of Police. From 1960 to 1976, the number of local lodges across the country more than doubled, to 1,100. AFSCME was recruiting 1,000 workers weekly by 1974, though few cops. But even as AFSCME was trying to unionize Baltimore's police, the AFL-CIO was increasingly out of step politically with working-class white precincts in the city, which voted against a progressive, union-backed candidate in the 1966 Democratic gubernatorial primary, instead preferring the conservative George Mahoney, who claimed that from the governor's office he would tell cops to "hit first, fire first."[6]

Twenty-seven Baltimore cops sensed the shifting winds. They formed Baltimore Fraternal Order of Police Lodge #3, Maryland's first, in May 1966, on Harrington's recommendation, officially incorporating in August. Eastern District patrol officer Richard Allen "Dick" Simmons became the lodge president, and narcotics officer Earl Kratsch the treasurer. Simmons and Kratsch had connected through a shared antipathy toward the ongoing, furtive organizing effort by officers supported by AFSCME. Whereas many officers dreaded the implementation of civilian review, the ones who formed the nucleus of the Baltimore Fraternal Order of Police channeled this fear to their own ends of opposing organized labor. The threat of civilian review cemented their desire to form a lodge, the primary unit of the Fraternal Order of Police's organization.[7]

The Fraternal Order of Police lodge was not popular in the department. The same month it incorporated, not one of its candidates won election to the grievance board, while the union's candidates all succeeded. To gain members, lodge-affiliated cops knew they would be confronting the many officers who had signed up with AFSCME. Opposition to civilian review was their reliable plank. Charging half as much as AFSCME in dues was an incentive. Manipulation of departmental rules was their primary tactic. For instance, when the officers held early meetings of the lodge, they obtained Gelston's permission, even after he had fruitlessly asked them to stop. Gelston then demanded that the meetings not be announced at roll call, but officers announced them anyway, later claiming a misunderstanding of Gelston's rule. The rule-abiding AFSCME union leader could only stew.[8]

The Fraternal Order of Police distinguished itself from unions. Nationally, its members were forbidden from striking as a coercive measure to change departments. The Fraternal Order of Police instead argued that legislatures should approve police reforms. Unlike a public sector union, the Fraternal Order of Police was open to police officers primarily but sometimes conferred membership on concerned civilians. Unlike some of the police benevolent associations, the Fraternal Order of Police was open to all cops regardless of rank, plus retirees. Local lodges wrote their own bylaws and set their own dues rates, without control from headquarters, Harrington's Grand Lodge. Only two cents of every dues dollar went to the Grand Lodge. "Each local lodge is autonomous and pledges allegiance to the community it serves," read a Fraternal Order of Police notification to Baltimore officials. The message was clear, if not always stated aloud: it was impossible to know whether communists were secretly infiltrating either civilian review boards or organized labor, but police could trust the fraternal order because it was steered by cops.[9]

Less than two months after Pomerleau became commissioner, four AFSCME officials visited headquarters for a sit-down meeting. They asked the commissioner to recognize their union. His reply was a simple no. And he showed them the door. The conversation lasted eight minutes. After this meeting, Pomerleau began to suggest that if he were to allow officers official representation, it would be by the Fraternal Order of Police, not organized labor. AFSCME was persistent, however. And it found a friend in the statehouse, an increasingly rare figure, a pro-labor Republican. The governor's name was Spiro Agnew.[10]

Yet the Fraternal Order of Police was growing across the state, thanks to the incorporation of Baltimore City's lodge. Once three local lodges existed, Fraternal Order of Police rules permitted the formation of a state lodge, composed of the local lodges. Harrington presided over the creation of the state lodge, arguing that the police could accomplish more if they banded together. Harrington asked Dick Simmons to become the first president of the newly formed state lodge, but, according to Simmons's sidekick Earl Kratsch, he declined. Left with two other local lodge presidents, Harrington tossed a coin to install the first temporary president of the state lodge. Once the new organization held its first conference, the leader of the Prince George's County lodge was elected as state president. Simmons became the organization's national trustee, representing Maryland to the broader Fraternal Order of Police. And Kratsch became the treasurer, a position he has held ever since. As Kratsch put it, upon its creation, the state organization's primary goal was "expansion."[11]

As it grew in Maryland, the Fraternal Order of Police ingratiated itself with powerbrokers, local residents, and cops, including sergeants and lieutenants. It sold ads in its journal and sent copies to every business that advertised, "putting police and F.O.P. right into the business community." The Baltimore lodge sponsored a Little League team and a Boy Scout troop. It took out ads on billboards, as well as radio and television, and leaders like Simmons made themselves available for interviews with journalists. Its appeal to Baltimore cops was simple: although AFSCME had experience in labor negotiations, it lacked cop knowledge. "Both the State and Grand Lodges have a stored wealth of administrative tactical knowledge built up through years of fighting for the rights of policemen," including "lobbying activities" at all levels of government and "more than 55 years of innumerable courtroom battles."

The Fraternal Order of Police of Baltimore embodied the contradictions of the time. Its slogan was "individual rights through collective unity." It would organize cops against organized labor. It would mobilize an everyman anticommunism to expand what it believed was rightfully owed to the underdog, workaday cop, who was misunderstood and mistreated by the public and the press. It would cooperate with the brass, including even Pomerleau, to aid the rank and file, in avowed opposition to the "adversary principles" of unions toward management. The group first consisted of a militant minority. Its greatest enemy was militant minorities. The organization touted its early successes, when its attorneys defended cops accused of illegally killing Black Baltimoreans and violating their civil rights. The Fraternal Order of Police, the Baltimore lodge announced, "is republicanism and democracy in living action."[12]

Pomerleau, however, still held the upper hand. The department remained in a shambles, and he was unrelenting in trying to impose discipline. In Baltimore, as across the country, the Fraternal Order of Police's accommodating stance toward management appealed to some cops, but others sought open confrontation.

The Fraternal Order of Police joined AFSCME in trying to go over Pomerleau's head, seeking legislation guaranteeing the right of public sector workers to unionize. But the two groups split the legislators and ended up with two competing measures. The AFSCME bill would have allowed officers a vote on representation; the Fraternal Order of Police's would have designated it the cops' representative. Neither bill succeeded. Pomerleau instructed detectives to collect photographs of officers who appealed to legislators.[13]

The local and the lodge continued to weaken each other by squabbling. In 1968, both visited Annapolis once more, trying to get a bill passed that would change personnel policies. Meeting with legislators, the two organizations spent more of the session attacking each other than advocating for the bill. Frustrated and furious, the chair of the Baltimore City delegation "literally ripped the bill into little pieces." No personnel policies would be changed by legislators or the union. Pomerleau succeeded by default once again.[14]

If Commissioner Pomerleau had been terminated at this point, he would today be counted as one of the many minor chiefs of the late 1960s whose careers were derailed by Black insurgency and white fears of crime. But Pomerleau survived, becoming the most powerful police executive of the era. On the radar of the DOJ and Quinn Tamm's IACP, he had both federal funding and the backing of the most powerful professional association to thank for his power, not to mention enthusiastic cooperation among Army intelligence, FBI, state police, and his own red squad in the city, which attacked and dismantled grassroots mobilizations coming from the left. But times were changing, and the Blue Power movement had him in its sights. Even his formidable apparatus of supporters and collaborators would struggle to defeat the labor movement brewing among his own officers.

POMERLEAU'S POWER

At the 1969 annual meeting of the IACP, after Local 1195 had spent two years pushing for him to be fired, Pomerleau railed from a lectern that unions represented "the greatest deterrent to the professionalization of law enforcement." But he also conceded that unions were not going away. Chiefs would have to work with them. Pomerleau's highest priority was ensuring, whatever economic benefits he had to give over to a union, that a police chief "*never* be placed in a position that compromises his control."[15]

Pomerleau's stern demeanor and reform mandate were supposed to defuse tensions. But officers found him aloof. They did not trust him, and he did not seem to trust them. Early on, he created a unit to investigate and monitor officers under the banner of "quality control," but he was reluctant to travel around the city and meet officers face-to-face. He rejected the old methods of promotion, which mainly depended on favoritism, but refused to eliminate the possibility that he could promote men at his own discretion. When it came to public meetings that concerned police business, including with elected officials, Pomerleau tried to bar officers from attending. Because he answered to the governor, Pomerleau also at times refused to answer queries from the city council, and he sparred openly with the mayor, particularly Thomas D'Alesandro III, who followed his father's footsteps into city hall in December 1967.[16]

Cutting a tall and burly figure, with jowls, thick-framed eyeglasses, and a high forehead, Pomerleau was born to intimidate. He molded operations accordingly. The department's intelligence unit answered directly to Pomerleau. In under a decade, it spied on 125 local organizations, plus colleges and universities, journalists, and elected officials at all levels. The unit was not designed to develop evidence for prosecutions that needed to hold up in court, allowing it to indulge in unlawful techniques.[17]

Baltimore's mini-FBI was called the Inspectional Services Division—ISD, or I Serve Donald. It gave Pomerleau formidable power. When meeting with elected officials or members of advocacy organizations, he often boasted about how much he knew about them. He would hint at his clandestine monitoring: "I know where you meet, when you are going to meet before you meet, what you do," and so forth. He testified about these tactics: "It is not intimidation, it is cooperation." When the State of Maryland convened an investigation, akin to a miniature Church Committee, into Pomerleau's secretive intelligence operations, he ordered his officers to destroy the massive file collection they had developed. The investigatory committee, chartered by the state senate, was not convinced by Pomerleau's nonchalance, pronouncing his actions "abominable." One gubernatorial aide remarked that Pomerleau "may not be so good as a human being, but he's a good cop."[18]

Baltimore cops and Baltimore Black Panthers were sworn enemies. The city's chapter was founded by an undercover officer and riddled with informants even though, as one sergeant later noted, the Baltimore Panthers were "more interested in community service programs" than in "committing crimes or provoking the police." Many cops and many Panthers alike believed Pomerleau was a dictator, inching toward full-blown fascist. Both, it turned out, called Pomerleau "Donald Duck," a silly sobriquet that failed to match the hostile underlying sentiment. Pomerleau did not help himself when, confronted by a journalist trying to verify whether his intelligence unit spied on elected officials, Pomerleau asserted: "Just the blacks. Just the blacks. Just the blacks." African Americans were not the unit's only targets, but they were its most prominent ones. Police spied on Congressman Parren J. Mitchell and State's Attorney Milton B. Allen, each the first Black Baltimorean elected to his position. Pomerleau's intelligence unit kept Mitchell under twenty-four-hour surveillance and relied on illegal bugs and informers who infiltrated his campaign operations.[19]

Still, Pomerleau maintained support among those who mattered politically to him, primarily the governors: Millard Tawes, who appointed him; Spiro Agnew, who briefly mediated between him and organized labor; and Marvin Mandel, who reappointed him and supported him in a moment of crisis. Some speculated that Pomerleau stayed in Mandel's good graces for years because his intelligence unit had gathered dirt on the governor, who did eventually get locked up on esoteric corruption charges. But after President Ronald Reagan commuted Mandel's three-year sentence, Pomerleau joined Mandel's family to greet him at the airport upon his return to Maryland.[20]

Pomerleau looked both upward and downward to ensure his own longevity. Although the commissioner knew that he served at the governor's pleasure, he also believed he could earn officers' loyalty through their wallets. When a municipal order exempted fire and police from time-and-a-half overtime pay that other city employees could earn, the commissioner defended his officers and forced city hall to change course (the Fraternal Order of Police took credit). Pomerleau argued vociferously for increasing the department's budget, first to buy new vehicles and other hardware, then to hire new officers, and finally to raise pay and pension funding. And he focused on acquiring federal funds to facilitate his reform program.[21]

Quinn Tamm lamented that in 1966 when Pomerleau took over, the force was one of the country's worst. But some of Pomerleau's changes had quick and palpable effects. Vacancies among the ranks declined. Entry-level salaries quickly increased from $5,604 to $6,780, to rank fifteenth nationally, and each year after that they increased further. Beyond overtime pay, Pomerleau also introduced a five-day workweek and a thirty-minute lunch break, which had been a sticking point among officers. The department purchased 200 new automobiles in Pomerleau's first year and 300 more in the next couple. The fleet was repainted to symbolize the dawning of a new day, marked now by increased motorized patrol. Officers also began copious new training, provided by the IACP, FBI, and Marine Corps, Pomerleau's own launchpads. He encountered a force dominated by men without high school diplomas, but officers began earning equivalency degrees and college credits, largely via courses taught by commanding officers at local universities, thanks to his initiatives. Quinn Tamm predicted that Pomerleau's educational efforts and recruitment of more Black cops would prevent unrest from breaking out in the city. He issued this forecast to a prominent columnist on April 6, 1968, before news spread that an uprising had begun and city and state authorities imposed a curfew. Still, by 1969, Tamm declared Baltimore's police force to be among the country's best.[22]

Although Pomerleau was supposed to root out corruption, he stumbled into a scandal of his own in his first year. Using materials purchased by the department, cops painted Pomerleau's house, in the 4000 block of Keswick Road—situated, like the commissioner's position itself, at the boundary of upper-class and working-class white Baltimore. Police unionists likely tipped off a reporter about the paint job, but an investigation discovered that the maintenance supervisor was storing department-purchased paint at his home and paying suppliers for paint the department never used. Invoices included exotic tints like "Persian Pink." No criminal charges were filed, but the governor censured Pomerleau. Afterward, activists continually raised this scandal. At a rally in the Western District six years later, protest signs read SHOULD POLICEMEN PAINT OR PATROL?[23]

The painting scandal revealed a broader problem beyond the routine rewards afforded to commanding officers. It had been normal practice for cops to paint buildings around the city. In fact, city police engaged in many non-police-related activities while on the clock. One of Pomerleau's major reforms then became stripping police of duties related to maintenance, sanitation, towing, or health inspections. But the cops who had been doing this work now had to engage in crime control duties, which were much more challenging. Some had been painting walls for so many years they couldn't remember how to write a ticket.[24]

NEW ARROWS IN BLUE POWER'S QUIVER

Baltimore police officers did not appreciate Pomerleau's changes to operations, like new patrol routes, or his imperious approach to discipline and rooting out graft. They also resented commanders' continual foot-dragging and obstruction of their attempts to gain collective representation. This combination came to a head soon after the 1968 uprising.

One year after being named Baltimore's policeman of the year for 1967, Officer Eugene C. Brukiewa managed to insult Commissioner Pomerleau so egregiously and publicly that the Maryland Court of Appeals would have to decide whether a cop really had the right to call his boss incompetent on television.[25]

Not only a thirteen-year veteran, Brukiewa was also president of Local 1195, which in 1968 issued a report lambasting the IACP and the commissioner. The miscellany of complaints criticized changes to uniforms, reporting forms, training texts, and patrol routines. It declared that officer morale was "at its lowest ebb."

Around the same time, a fellow officer, Gary Woodcock, who had been on the force for nine years, filed "the most detailed grievance ever received from the union." Woodcock was a member of Local 1195's executive board. Working a canine detail, he had been assigned to patrol a "hot area" of the Sandtown neighborhood of West Baltimore (a few blocks away from where Freddie Gray would be arrested in 2015). His complaint was that, in the month following the April 1968 civil unrest, a commanding officer demanded that Tactical Unit members arrest every inebriate, "roving" gang member, and loiterer they saw on a corner. Woodcock believed the order to arrest "everyone" was an inappropriate restriction on the Tactical Unit's discretion, based on "unreliable" information. Though superior officers worried about further vandalism, looting, and arson, Woodcock claimed that shopkeepers did not share their concern. (A sergeant later could find no evidence that Woodcock had actually canvassed shopkeepers.) This four-page grievance and Local 1195's fourteen-page jeremiad resulted in an invitation for Woodcock and Brukiewa to be interviewed on television.[26]

Christopher Gaul, a reporter for Baltimore's WJZ, asked the officers bluntly, "Do you think Commissioner Pomerleau is a competent, effective administrator?"

Woodcock hesitated: "Ah . . . ," then replied with a terse "No."

Gaul turned to Brukiewa. He asked whether it was appropriate for the union to criticize department policy so openly.

"Well," Brukiewa responded, "we feel that it's gotten to a point where definitely we have to start criticizing police policy, due to the fact we have tried to get together with Commissioner Pomerleau to explain problems that still exist with patrolmen, the reporting system, other issues, to try to help him to make us a good department, but Mr. Pomerleau just has a mind of his own, he sticks strictly to the IACP report and we feel definitely that this is nothing to this city."

Unsurprisingly, the department's disciplinary board found that the two officers had violated rules that explicitly banned public criticism or ridicule of the department or any member of it. The board recommended Woodcock and Brukiewa be dismissed for conduct unbecoming an officer, but they were allowed to remain on the force, working only night shifts for six months—a sentence Pomerleau extended to a full year.[27]

The two officers sued, and they ran together on a slate for president and vice president of Local 1195. Woodcock fell short of winning the election, then dropped out of the lawsuit, but Brukiewa won his race and stuck with *Brukiewa v. Police Commissioner of Baltimore City*. In the end, the appeals court eventually determined that his words did not imperil departmental operations.[28]

IACP officials were alarmed that an officer could go on television and insult a high-profile member of the organization who was instituting one of its signature reform plans. Tucson's chief urged Pomerleau to press the case all the way to the Supreme Court. But the Baltimore ruling followed similar judgments in Chicago and New Orleans, enshrining the speech rights of officers to appeal to the public with a rejection of top-down reformism.[29]

The legal setback was a sign of Pomerleau's compounding difficulties as the 1970s began. No matter how successful he might have been at raising the department's benchmarks and enacting the IACP blueprint for reform, his own popularity among the force and the department's popularity among Baltimoreans continued to decline.

An effective police force, at least as measured by arrests, was an intrusive police force. One reform that Commissioner Pomerleau instituted in

Baltimore was called the Total Officer Concept. It was designed to attack the problem of narcotics by giving responsibility for enforcing drug violations to all patrol officers, instead of reserving this responsibility for the narcotics squad. As a result, by the beginning of 1972, the patrol division was making over 90 percent of narcotics arrests, as compared to 50 percent when Pomerleau arrived in Baltimore. The annual number of drug arrests exploded, from 430 in 1966 to 4,617 in 1972, changing the daily character of police work, and dramatically increasing the amount of unwelcome police contact with city residents. At the level of Baltimoreans' everyday experience, widespread arrests for suspected drug possession were little more than a new excuse for harassing Black Baltimore.[30]

Outside funds that the Baltimore Police Department raised, from the Law Enforcement Assistance Administration, Ford Foundation, Department of Transportation, and elsewhere, did not clearly reduce crime. But they changed life in the city. The most prominent transformation was the introduction of helicopter patrol in October 1970, thanks to $100,000 from the LEAA. To this day, the helicopter is still called Foxtrot, as it was in 1970. Although the aircraft is now far more advanced, it operates with similar capabilities: cameras, high-intensity lighting, and loudspeakers.[31]

The experiment with helicopter patrol exemplified the type of help the feds provided to cities under the terms of the 1968 Omnibus Crime Control and Safe Streets Act, which created the LEAA. Funding was apportioned to states largely by population, and it came with few strings attached or oversight from Washington. But the money was not supposed to cover personnel salaries, recurring equipment costs, or land purchases and construction of regular facilities, which were law enforcement's three major expenses. Congress crafted the legislation to stimulate new efforts, not substitute for local expenditures. Yet salaries, retirement, and other benefits amounted to 85–99 percent of police budgets at the time.[32]

Meant to reward innovators with resources, the LEAA had the peculiar effect of hollowing the promise of reform by failing to attach reform ideas to the bureaucratic and fiscal capacity to help them last. Instead, experimentation was the focus, with little planning for how to make the findings stick. In the aftermath of the uprisings of 1967, the Kerner Commission proposed massive spending on cities. It never came. Instead, an even greater fiscal need emerged as the 1970s dawned. Detroit mayor Coleman Young complained that "the only answer" mayors like him received from the federal government "to the problems in our cities" was the "millions and billions of dollars of aid to the police force" via the LEAA.[33]

The LEAA funded police, courts, and corrections, with the balance tilted toward police throughout the agency's existence. In 1969, police received over two-thirds of LEAA block grant awards; by 1977 this proportion had declined to 41 percent but remained the largest tranche. Corrections rose from 13 percent to one-third in the same period, while courts rose from 8 percent to one-quarter. Police were garnering most of their resources from appropriations closer to home, even as the federal portion of total expenditures on law enforcement rose to 13 percent by the mid-1970s. Overall, the LEAA spent $7.5 billion from 1968 to 1982, making it the fastest-growing federal agency in that period.[34]

At the outset of his War on Crime, Lyndon Johnson had pledged "not only to reduce crime but to banish it," but by the 1970s, LEAA expenditures had not succeeded in bringing crime under control. Persistent urban crime trends stoked law and order politics. A frustrated Nixon administration decided to bypass the clunky state-level planning bureaucracy of the LEAA to funnel money directly to eight cities in 1972, including Baltimore.[35]

The High Impact program was supposed to reduce murder, rape, aggravated assault, robbery, and burglary by 20 percent in five years. The rate of these index crimes in Baltimore decreased from 4,190 per 100,000 in 1970 to 4,082.5 in 1974—in other words, barely at all. Nevertheless, Pomerleau's commanders were happy to take the $3.8 million in federal funds, though they were unwilling to relinquish authority to the LEAA, or even communicate with the feds. Pomerleau managed to allocate over $2 million of the funding to developing new foot patrol positions, finally acceding to a persistent union demand. These "intensive" new patrols, plus plainclothes units, however, simply displaced criminalized activities into surrounding areas adjacent to the new footposts. The High Impact program in Baltimore was, according to an in-depth review, a "failure" that simply added money to the department's already swollen budget.[36]

By the early 1970s, Pomerleau's department had escalated its repression of Black political organizations in the city, as well as New Left and antiwar groups. Whatever Spiro Agnew's 1968 scolding of Black moderates had done to convince white voters nationally to depart the Democratic Party and support Nixon, militancy had only intensified among Baltimore's Black residents in the years that followed. Pomerleau aimed to stop it in its tracks. His officers already routinely beat Black protesters after arresting them, shocking one veteran CORE field organizer who arrived in Baltimore after campaigns in cities like New York. More insidiously, Pomerleau's intelligence unit worked in league with the FBI and Army intelligence, headquartered at Fort Holabird, to harass, undermine, and fracture Black organizations. After a "so-called round-up . . . by pig Commissioner Pomerleau's evil pimps of brutality and terror," in the words of Lil' Masai (Steve McCutchen), a Baltimore Black Panther, more than twenty party members either were incarcerated or became fugitives by the spring of 1970. Baltimore Panthers still paid close attention to the police department's internal politics, even announcing a provocative plan: if Eugene Brukiewa returned to full duty, the party would open a new headquarters on his beat.[37]

Pomerleau's campaign of political repression increased public cynicism about the department, which only worsened his officers' us-versus-them mentality. In 1971, over 100 Black leaders demanded that the governor fire Pomerleau, but Governor Mandel reappointed him to a second six-year term around the time Mayor Thomas D'Alesandro III decided not to seek reelection after a single four-year term. Representative Parren Mitchell was particularly outspoken against Pomerleau. The city's Fraternal Order of Police president, Dick Simmons, responded: "He's not anti-white. He's not anti-black. He's anti-blue."[38]

By now, Pomerleau had become so detested by his own officers that some plotted to use Black public opinion against him. White officers conspired to use the mistreatment of African American officers to enrage Black Baltimore into toppling the commissioner. One clique of officers falsely blamed one of the highest-ranking Black officers, Major Clarence Roy, for an episode of brutality. Then, when the first Black commander of the Western District, Captain Dennis Mello, retired, the mostly white

John Clark, Baltimore Black Panther Party, 1970. H. Christoph, ullstein bild, Getty Images.

officers of the district demanded a white replacement. Mello was far from congenial, and he had a reputation for accepting payoffs. Even so, a group of Black police wives rallied to demand that another Black officer succeed him, certain that the heart of Black Baltimore, as well as their husbands on the beat within it, would be safer with one of their own at the helm. One protest sign read: WESTERN DISTRICT POPULATED BY BLACKS, POLICED BY WHITES. Another targeted Pomerleau: BALTIMORE NEEDS A NEW POLICE HEAD TO IMPROVE THE FOOT PATROL. Pomerleau's reputation continued to falter, but he remained steadfast, continually calibrating his control of the department.[39]

The union believed it had the best answer to a domineering boss, and thousands of Baltimore cops agreed.

CHAPTER 6

ORGANIZED LABOR'S GREATEST ADVANCE AMONG POLICE

While Pomerleau weathered bad press, Local 1195 and the Fraternal Order of Police Lodge #3 continued to organize cops in Baltimore. As of October 1970, the union counted almost four times as many members as the Fraternal Order of Police, but less than a year later, the lodge had more than doubled its membership, from around 400 to almost 900. Among the reasons the lodge appealed to the rank and file was its habit of needling the commissioner over operations. For instance, the Fraternal Order of Police requested installation of sirens on all departmental vehicles. It also consistently advocated granting officers greater firepower on duty, including shotguns and the chemical munition CS (tear gas), as well as small revolvers for off-duty use.[1]

Besides competing for members within the city, both the union and Fraternal Order of Police eyed an expansion into Baltimore County, a much larger landmass that clutches the city like a gnarled white claw. To give county cops a safe outlet for political expression, the Fraternal Order of Police incorporated Lodge #4 in 1971. To achieve successes on the street and at headquarters, these cops needed to get organized.

As competition escalated, the union touted improved benefits it had won legislatively, including more holidays, as well as overtime and vacation pay. Pomerleau was shocked when the union successfully circumvented him and demonstrated the depth of its support among legislators with these wins. He became more conciliatory toward the union after this point. This only emboldened the Fraternal Order of Police, which started to take credit for gains that the union had achieved.[2]

At Christmastime in 1970, AFSCME circulated a letter among Baltimore County officers that denounced the "phonies" and "back stabbers" who joined the union only to spy on it, and it attacked the "credit grabbers" in Lodge #3, a "do nothing group." The accusations elicited a formal Fraternal Order of Police rebuttal. Sure enough, the union missive also made its way to Pomerleau's desk through intelligence unit channels. The officer who obtained it from a county source was Earl Kratsch, Lodge #3's treasurer, now working in the Inspectional Services Division, supervised by a former FBI agent. Sending inflammatory "poison pen" letters was a common FBI counterintelligence tactic in this period, primarily used to foment rifts among Black radical groups. An open letter could not be forged in the same way, but this ambitious member of the red squad must have relished his find. Putting it in the hands of city Fraternal Order of Police members had the same incendiary effect.[3]

Yet even Pomerleau and his nearly omniscient ISD could not control the roiling anger among police. He had to make concessions.

CONCESSIONS TO COPS

With both the Fraternal Order of Police and the union consolidating support, Pomerleau tried to stave off the inevitable next push for formal union recognition in the city by asking the city council to raise salaries. The top-level patrol salary increased to $10,732 in 1972. Fortunes for workers across the city were not improving as much as they were for cops. In the preceding five years, over 16,000 industrial jobs disappeared from Baltimore, and 159 plants shut down. Although police salaries had not been keeping up with inflation, year to year they came closer than the average industrial wage did.[4]

In this period, the department amplified Fraternal Order of Police arguments about dangers that officers faced, as a rejoinder to public complaints about brutality by officers and internal complaints about overzealous discipline. Pomerleau was not above playing games with data. Whereas the Baltimore police department told the LEAA that it could not generate "hard statistical evidence" linking drug use to major crimes, Pomerleau circulated a precise complement of statistics testifying to "the fact that citizens in increasing numbers have been attacking police officers."[5]

Pomerleau conceded a revision to the department's grievance procedure, but he tried to maintain personal control over it. He continued to investigate and discipline officers, relying on hated lie detector tests. He initiated a crusade against corruption after $140,000 in cash and thousands of bags of heroin went missing from the Evidence Control Unit in 1972 and early 1973. In February 1973, eight officers and eighteen civilian police employees were arrested, shortly after the shooting death of a "known drug dealer" linked to the theft. Pomerleau cultivated an informant on a federal grand jury and hired an outside private firm to investigate low-ranking officers in response. Many cops felt these drastic measures to eliminate corruption unnecessarily tarred the reputations of the innocent. Cops had begged the department to let them patrol on foot, not in cars, as Pomerleau preferred, but his corruption probes meant they had to listen to Baltimoreans call them dirty.[6]

Scandals like these erupted frequently across the country in this period, coloring public perceptions of police. Management tried to use them to stifle the power of the rank and file, but most officers, in turn, resented the implication they were on the take and rejected the measures taken to stamp out corruption. Blue Power's cogs kept turning.

In September 1973, Pomerleau finally allowed an election for officer representation. Although he had long preferred the Fraternal Order of Police due to his antipathy for organized labor and AFSCME leadership's strident criticisms of him, Pomerleau had started to see Lodge #3 as a problem too. The increasingly confident Fraternal Order of Police was making noise about departmental operations and policies that the commissioner believed it should not and could not direct. The Fraternal Order of Police also declared "war" on the District Court of Maryland, succeeding in intimidating judges into limiting pretrial release. AFSCME, in contrast, had over the years softened its public criticisms of the commissioner and focused its organizing mainly on bread-and-butter issues.[7]

Fraternal Order of Police Lodge #3 lost the November election to AFSCME Local 1195, defeated by the financial resources and organizing experience the rapidly growing public sector union was able to marshal. Already granted a dues checkoff and a grievance procedure, the union was poised to complete the crucial trinity of union representation by collective bargaining. Pomerleau recognized Local 1195, hoping to neutralize officer dissatisfaction. He wanted to restrict what was bargainable and preserve his prerogative. The commissioner maintained one overarching condition: strikes were prohibited. The city's public sector workers pushed the police to challenge Pomerleau's prohibition.

ORGANIZED LABOR STRIKES IN BALTIMORE

The first half of 1974 brought economic tumult to the United States. Three years of wage and price controls ceased in April, and inflation began to spike, swiftly adjusting prices upward as if controls had never existed. Municipal budgets were stretched to their limit, according to city hall authorities and bond-rating agencies. To cope with rising costs, government workers across the country pressed for higher wages. A rank-and-file rebellion hit cities, counties, and states, with sanitation workers, prison guards, and bus drivers striking. It was AFSCME's moment to shine. A decade of relentless organizing would finally bear fruit.[8]

About forty miles from Washington, where Nixon's lawyers were arguing to the Supreme Court that whatever the president did was legal, Baltimore police officers would test the limits of their own legal protections when they tentatively began a job action that same Monday, July 8. Eight years of discontent with Commissioner Donald Pomerleau had come to a head.

Three thousand other AFSCME workers in the city were already on strike, after up to 90 percent of city teachers had walked out for a month in February. AFSCME by then represented 12,500 laborers in Baltimore, from dogcatchers to zookeepers, but the majority worked in maintenance and sanitation. Most were underpaid. Outside the police department, most were Black. Comparing Baltimore to thirty other large cities, only six had a lower starting hourly wage for sanitation workers ($3.18). They were all southern cities. And only six cities offered a lower maximum wage in sanitation; Baltimore's top hourly wage was more than a dollar lower than Detroit's minimum. As local CORE leader Walter P. Carter observed in late 1968, Baltimore did not have a Black unemployment problem—not yet, at least—but most of the jobs open to Black people were menial, underpaid, and void of opportunities for advancement. Not much had changed in five years.[9]

A wildcat strike among blue-collar city workers began on Monday, July 1. A thousand sanitation workers, or "sanitmen," spearheaded the wildcat. Their union, Local 44, had ratified a new contract, but many workers were displeased with the pay increase of 6.2 percent plus fringe benefits, amounting to twenty cents an hour over a year. Another pressing concern was a punitive program for reducing "absenteeism" that city departments had unveiled earlier that spring, which the contract did not eliminate. Sanitmen and highway workers surprised union officials by refusing to don their green uniforms and work. Local 44's members proved they could muster strength and cohesion. As their slogan said: Green Power.[10]

Topping the pop charts that week was "Rock the Boat" by the Hues Corporation. Why, asked this soul disco track, would someone in a long-standing relationship of "love and devotion" suddenly rock the boat? Heralding a summer of wildcat strikes, you could hear the tune blaring from just about every passing Pinto.

Union officials tried in vain to sit down with representatives from the striking maintenance and sanitation yards. The unfolding walkout was "unquestionably hurting our efforts," an aide reported to Jerry Wurf, national president of AFSCME. Yet when union officials attempted to set up meetings with the striking sanitmen, most of the workers were blotto. They had spent the first day of the strike drinking and carousing.

The unauthorized strike would extend at least another day, and union leaders felt obligated to support it. Wurf, after all, had made his name backing Black sanitation workers in Memphis. He had helped form the Memphis local whose strike Martin Luther King Jr. was supporting when he was assassinated.[11]

The same scorching summer Sunday that Local 44 ratified its contract, the police union rejected its own new contract. But while the disgruntled sanitmen walked out the next day, the cops watched and waited. After city hall indicated it would not budge, cops voted on July 6 to begin a job action, with plans for a work stoppage if the department penalized union members.[12]

With negotiations stalled, the police commenced a job action. Cops worked to rule, a parody of Pomerleau's rules-obsessed program. Officers began a ticket-writing blitz, increasing the number of citations, some officers reckoned by 1,000 percent. Even the mayor's limousine received a parking ticket (fine: $12) and a citation for illegally changing lanes (fine: $15).

The next day, in addition to writing tickets, officers began clogging the evidence control system. They would turn in any lost "objects of value" they encountered, filing a report. With the sanitation strike entering its second week across the city, "lost" property was piling up in the streets. Cops who spotted a penny on the sidewalk would turn it in and file a report.

But working to rule did not satisfy every cop. Officers started to block roadways with their personal vehicles, as if to throw AFSCME's budgetary analysis into stark relief. Union officials believed Baltimore was spending too much on "postponable capital construction projects" like highways, when the city council could be spending that money instead on salary increases. Yet local code did not distinguish between capital and non-capital budgets, making the budgetary transfer union officials desired a fantasy.

Pomerleau was in a pickle. How far would officers go to get what they wanted? Would punishing them end their job action? Should the city defer maintenance on school buildings and other capital projects to pay police salaries, as union officials intimated? While the Maoist Revolutionary Union proposed dumping even more trash in the streets, Lyndon LaRouche's National Caucus of Labor Committees suggested another solution: stop paying the city's debts.[13]

The police would have their say one way or another. A cop stopped and raised his car's hood in the left lane of the still-incomplete Jones Falls Expressway—a gash down the city's spine that rockets white commuters from the suburbs downtown and back while encountering nary a Black face. For his fictitious engine trouble, the officer faced suspension. Although the department quickly backed down, harsh disciplinary measures were the union's agreed-upon trigger for a strike.[14]

Behind closed doors, Pomerleau, in fact, seemed to initially support a job action demanding better wages, provided it remained within legal bounds. But police were not just going to work to rule. They planned a 500-car caravan to snarl traffic in the city, and commanders spread the message that if any cop, or any cop's spouse or children, participated in an automobile protest, they'd face arrest. Officers could not get the brass to budge. Threats of punishment mounted. Union members decided to join the ongoing wildcat by other AFSCME workers in the city. Although the police strike had its own causes, its coincidence with other union action realized Pomerleau's greatest fears.

At 8 p.m. on Thursday, July 11, officers began walking off the job in the Southwestern District. Captains immediately suspended the striking officers. The suspensions went to the heart of the rank-and-file complaint: command, and especially Pomerleau, had too much power.

Soon, officers were not only walking out. Some also tried to prevent their colleagues from continuing to work by holding the microphone open to prevent others from using the radio frequency, mixing up squad car keys in the motor pool, and blocking buses that were delivering reinforcements. Officers "exhorted or coerced" others to strike. Worst of all, according to Pomerleau's PR shop, strikers spat on cops who kept working.[15]

The day before officers walked out, the Baltimore Promotion Council inaugurated a new ad campaign, meant to woo tourist dollars. It dubbed Baltimore "Charm City, USA."[16]

The IACP condemned the strike. Quinn Tamm even debated Jerry Wurf in the pages of the *Baltimore Sun* newspaper. Tamm noted that unions and organizations like the IACP could agree on improving police salaries and benefits. But strikes and slowdowns were beyond the pale. It was nothing short of a miracle that Baltimore had not fallen into utter chaos when officers walked off the job, Tamm suggested.[17]

The police strike lasted five days, ultimately involving 36 percent of the force. Guards in the city jail joined the striking cops, and an uprising broke out in the city's juvenile detention facility. Young rebels even took jailhouse hostages for a brief period. Pomerleau claimed crime rose by a third during the strike, but it was mostly vandalism. Trash fires were the greatest nuisance. Vacant houses burned too. Someone set fire to a block of formerly dilapidated rowhouses that had been a signature municipal revitalization program, one of the mayor's "pet projects." The midnight arsonist was never discovered. Whether it was a cop is uncertain, but the target seemed designed to pose a question to city hall about priorities: Urban homesteaders or the officers who could protect their property?[18]

Officers eventually ratified a two-year contract, negotiated by municipal officials. But it was not much different from the one they had rejected before the strike. Pay after five years increased to $13,500, while starting pay rose to $10,000 by July 1, 1975. The union claimed the city had proposed a 5.5 percent increase, while the contract won a 21 percent increase. In fact, the 5.5 percent raise was for the current year, with the 21 percent raise effective at the top of the pay scale years later. As ever, cops saved face with fuzzy math.[19]

However much economic demands mattered, Pomerleau did not oppose giving officers a raise. Yet the contract also contained little to shape what working under him would be like on a daily basis. He set out to prove his authority by breaking the governor's promise that there would be no retaliation against strikers. Striking officers' reactions, one journalist reported, "were largely unprintable."[20]

At roll call in the Southwestern District just after the strike concluded, the commanding officer also used largely unprintable language. He upbraided his men as "scums, SOBs, and deserters." He advised them to quit the "God damn union." But Pomerleau did not want to give them a choice.

In the end, Pomerleau suspended all of Local 1195's officers and even banned them from entering police headquarters without his permission. He dismissed eighty-two probationary officers for striking, ending their careers as cops. He also demoted eighteen police agents, a specialized position he had created for college-educated cops. To manage resulting manpower deficits, punishments included extra work hours. Pomerleau also reassigned all of the LEAA-funded High Impact officers to other roles, effectively terminating that program. After trial board proceedings, seventy-five officers lost their jobs, fifty-five of whom then lost lawsuits trying to get reinstated. Ninety officers resigned. In total, 901 officers received some kind of official penalty, though two-thirds were only reprimanded. Pomerleau's most severe response, however, was to strip Local 1195 of recognition and cancel dues collection. The AFSCME international tried in vain to get the governor to overrule the commissioner, but Mandel would not budge. Local 1195 ceased to exist by the middle of the summer of 1974, around the time Baltimore became a majority-Black city.[21]

The greatest inroads organized labor had made into a big-city police department vanished overnight. The Fraternal Order of Police was poised to welcome disgruntled officers.

TO PUNISH LABOR AND REWARD THE FRATERNAL ORDER OF POLICE

In the wake of the Baltimore strike, Governor Marvin Mandel frequently repeated a story about Jerry Wurf. Mandel claimed Wurf threatened him: Baltimore would burn if AFSCME's demands were not met. After arson and trash fires did occur, this threat became fodder for right-wing denunciations of public sector unionism. Ralph de Toledano, a cofounder of *National Review*, titled a shrill 1975 book about this Big Labor blight on politics *Let Our Cities Burn*. Far-right senator Jesse Helms contributed a foreword. In succeeding years, as small lenders shriveled and credit dried up, cities did burn, but many arsonists were landlords seeking insurance payouts or replacement tenants.[22]

Wurf denied that he ever made the threat to Mandel. It is impossible to know what words the two exchanged behind closed doors. But AFSCME filed a lawsuit against the governor containing suggestive evidence, corroborated in testimony later given in a departmental disciplinary hearing of the union's president. The union wanted to secure an injunction preventing the department from firing the striking cops or ceasing recognition. The suit alleged that the threat to burn Baltimore came not from Wurf but from a cop, Edward Crowder, assigned to the Inspectional Services Division. Crowder was a member of the Local 1195 bargaining committee, but the city council president believed him to be Pomerleau's inside man, a provocateur. The court filing claimed that Crowder declared the city would burn. And it alleged he spoke at the direction of both Mandel and Pomerleau. It was unlikely the governor played such an instigating role, but Pomerleau relied on the department's intelligence unit to spy on the union and monitor the strike. His officers informed on one another, taped meetings, and photographed picketers. Crowder even advocated and voted in favor of the strike. Pomerleau alone could not have provoked the strike, but in its aftermath, he got what he wanted: a halt to the spread of organized labor's militancy among his police.[23]

Despite public polls in Maryland showing that after the strike, the union, particularly the suspended officers, was more popular than Mandel, AFSCME was chastened. It lost its lawsuit against the governor in 1977, and twenty of the fired officers in turn sued AFSCME for misleading them about the possibility of losing their jobs. Nationally, the union would never again organize a big city's police.

Wurf's decade of militancy in the public sector began to unravel as well. Six years later, a heart attack killed him at age sixty-two, just four months after Ronald Reagan fired 11,345 air traffic controllers for illegally striking. Reagan also decertified their union, crystallizing growing national scorn for organized labor.[24]

In Baltimore, the firings and suspension of the union, followed by retirements and resignations, depressed police morale. The fallout eliminated some of the more labor-oriented members of the police department, shrinking the already attenuated range of political ideas available among most Baltimore cops to varieties of conservatism.

Less than two months after the strike, State's Attorney Milton B. Allen lost in a low-turnout primary election, right as the Klan was mounting a resurgent campaign in the white northern Baltimore enclave of Hampden. Allen, the incumbent, was the only elected African American state's attorney in the country. He did not see eye to eye with Pomerleau or the city's police union militants. He had been well respected across Black Baltimore until he prosecuted Sherman Dobson, the son of a prominent minister, for assassinating James "Turk" Scott, a state delegate under federal indictment for trafficking heroin. (Dobson walked.) Allen's successful opponent, William A. Swisher, had run a television ad that referred to the city as a "jungle" while sirens wailed in the background. It played endlessly. A self-described anti-intellectual who urged Baltimoreans to arm themselves against criminals, Swisher's law and order campaign proved that placing blame for crime on a Black prosecutor won votes in the city. Swisher would eventually be charged with corruption, leading the *Afro-American* newspaper to quip that it was "shedding no tears" for him.[25]

Pomerleau granted the Fraternal Order of Police its dues checkoff in September 1976. The group had 1,850 members by then, a bit more than it claimed during the 1973 election but still fewer than Local 1195 counted when it won recognition. It was not until after Pomerleau resigned and Frank Battaglia succeeded him as commissioner that the Fraternal Order of Police was able to bargain for a contract with the city. The Fraternal Order of Police was never more popular than the union, but it won because Pomerleau had eliminated its competition.[26]

The Fraternal Order of Police had always been riding the union's coattails. Whereas the union started from nothing among Baltimore cops, the Fraternal Order of Police organizing that restarted after the strike built on everything the union had previously achieved: good pay and benefits, workplace protections, connections in Annapolis, and public approbation. The Fraternal Order of Police claimed all of these as its boon, disavowing organized labor's success in garnering them.

Baltimore's police strike marked a turning point in the development of Blue Power. Unlike in New York or Detroit, where there was no competition among organizations to represent the police, Baltimore's cops had a choice. They voted to align themselves with organized labor, and they even expressed a mote of solidarity with other public sector workers by striking when the sanitmen struck. But the commissioner responded by ejecting organized labor from the field of contention for police unionism in the city. At a crossroads, Blue Power was both pushed and pulled away from organized labor.

In the summer of 1974, a few days into the sanitation walkout that preceded the Baltimore police strike, city residents began carting their own trash to municipal landfill sites. The mayor had ordered four of them to remain open 24/7. With the city handing out thousands of plastic trash bags, local youth were making good money hauling garbage, scabbing. On Monument Street in East Baltimore, striking sanitmen formed a picket line, blocking the landfill's entrance. They were not about to let Baltimoreans solve the mounting trash problem themselves. Piles of refuse stinking in the July heat were the strikers' best weapon, as rats reveled.

On Friday, July 5, AFSCME leaders descended on Monument Street to join the picket. As police officers parted the line each time a driver approached to drop off their garbage, Jerry Wurf led his colleagues in breaking the police line, dashing toward cars that neared the landfill entrance. Opened the previous year, the Monument Street site was in a Black neighborhood, picketed by mainly Black sanitmen, whose courage the white union leaders hoped to gird.

Wurf and his colleagues tried to reestablish the picket as cops waved drivers through. Officers then ordered picketers to make way. After a couple of rounds of this dance, one cop got fed up. He cuffed Wurf, along with his secretary-treasurer and a Maryland union representative, for disobeying a police order and blocking a thoroughfare. The arresting officer was Gary Woodcock, formerly of Local 1195's executive board, who had called Pomerleau incompetent on TV.[27]

This onetime police union militant arrested one of the country's most prominent labor leaders. It was the ultimate abrogation of the principle of solidarity. Woodcock's arrest of Wurf was a puckered answer to the old labor question: Which side are you on?

In the years after Woodcock and Brukiewa excoriated Pomerleau on TV, Woodcock did not turn his back entirely on the idea of collective action, however. Woodcock had switched his allegiance, becoming a Fraternal Order of Police official. He had a vision of the future of police unionization, and it was not with organized labor.[28]

CHAPTER 7

A COLORBLIND COUNTERREVOLUTION

The Kerner Commission, appointed by President Johnson, found that rough and abusive encounters between white police and Black residents spurred the unrest of 1967 in Newark, Detroit, and elsewhere. It thus endorsed recruiting and promoting African American officers in its groundbreaking 1968 report: "Negro officers should be so assigned as to ensure that the police department is fully and visibly integrated." Putting more Black cops on patrol in still-segregated Black neighborhoods was supposed to ease tensions and ameliorate relationships between police and Black populations, preventing further civil disorder. Moreover, Black officers, better able to work undercover among their own kind, could also provide sharper intelligence than white ones.[1]

Detroit had in fact been one of the first northern cities to appoint an African American cop, in 1893. New York City followed suit in 1911. Baltimore commissioned its first Black officer, a woman named Violet Hill Whyte, in 1937, but she was not permitted to carry a gun; the city's first Black officer promoted to sergeant came a decade later. In Atlanta, where being a cop required Klan membership in the early part of the century, the first Black officer was hired in 1948 and the first Black sergeant in 1961. Black Americans, particularly business and religious leaders, sought the appointment of their own to the police force as a means of social advancement, by demonstrating adherence to "the economic, social, and sexual norms" associated with "good order."[2]

Early Black officers were typically "morally indignant about the high rate of Negro crime." Many earned a reputation for strict and uncompromising enforcement, making headlines in the country's leading Black newspapers when their arrest statistics outpaced those of their white counterparts. "In the case of the black policeman and the black offender," observed a writer in *Freedomways*, the intellectual journal of the Black Freedom Movement, "the policeman must prove that he is not partial to blacks, thus, he too, is quick with the club and his trigger finger."[3]

Police departments across the country did begin to integrate more thoroughly, if reluctantly, at the end of the 1960s. There were programs aimed at recruiting Black, Latino, and other minority candidates in about a third of county and municipal police agencies and 55 percent of state agencies by 1973. Conservative police leaders like the Fraternal Order of Police's John Harrington worried that these programs enabled "infiltration" of departments by Black Power radicals. Harrington identified "dissension" between white and Black cops within departments as a new phenomenon, attributing

A member of the Guardian Civic League at a demonstration in Philadelphia in 1968. Leif Skoogfors, Corbis Historical, Getty Images.

it to "activists." But discrimination, bullying, chauvinism, stereotyping, harassment, and name-calling were not new, and affirmative action programs did not quell racism. In many cities, they invigorated a crude and defensive posture among white-led police unions.[4]

In contrast, young Black recruits tended to be more politically aggressive, unwilling to accede to bigotry in the station house. Whether calling each other "brother," reading Black nationalist literature while on duty, wearing dashikis while off duty, or pulling a service weapon on a white colleague spouting bigotry, the new Black officers sought a fresh covenant with their white peers and superior officers. They also sought to change the relationship between police and the policed. Militant organizations like the Black Panther Party were skeptical. Was the Guardian Civic League, the fraternal organization for Black police in Philadelphia founded in 1956, merely, as the local party branch suggested, "a tool to try to control the community, exploit the community resources, and make niggas suffer peacefully"? Whether Black cops would patrol the streets differently was the key issue for critics outside police departments, but it was often overshadowed on the inside by the bigotry and hierarchy Black cops experienced.[5]

The civil rights aspiration was that integrating police forces would result in fair treatment of Black people. This aspiration never disappeared, but battling racism within the station house quickly pushed operational questions to the margins for Black police groups. Collective energy would be expended on equal employment opportunity issues; individual energy might go, if a Black cop could bear the frustration, toward fixing his partner's behavior. Integration thus helped police forces to appear more legitimate and forward-looking, heeding liberal recommendations like those the Kerner Commission produced, but its practical consequences were limited.

Liberals and conservatives outside police departments largely agreed upon the abstract goal of hiring more Black cops, but they disagreed on how. Conservative activists mobilized their constituencies to respond as the feds tried to answer that question. When the Equal Employment Opportunity Commission issued new voluntary guidelines on affirmative action, it solicited feedback. The public response was overwhelmingly negative, with 95 percent of comments by mail objecting to "remedial" practices.[6]

In turn, fraternal associations comprising the growing cohort of African American cops dedicated copious resources to supporting affirmative action programs and finding answers to the "how" question that favored their members. These included numerous local outfits, as well as the National Black Police Officers Association and the National Organization of Black Law Enforcement Executives, which the privately funded Police Foundation helped charter. Even the most militant of these organizations, Chicago's Afro-American Patrolmen's League, established to eliminate racist police brutality rather than to advocate for Black police employment alone, found itself pulling the minute levers of equal employment opportunity law by the mid-1970s.[7]

Though police unions tended to oppose affirmative action, some police administrators were sympathetic to the goals. Impeding their efforts were promotion policies that required a certain number of years of experience at a lower rank, which candidates who were Black and Latino or white women could rarely meet. A secondary problem was that when the courts forced police departments to develop new policies and testing programs, they had to prove that they would not unlawfully discriminate. The LEAA pitched in, spending hundreds of thousands of dollars on research to create nondiscriminatory examinations.[8]

Yet as departments attempted to raise standards, by requiring college degrees or upgraded writing exams, these new standards became further barriers to recruitment of Black and Latino cops. A scandal rocked Atlanta when, in an apparent effort to prevent litigation by the city's Black police fraternity, examiners helped Black cops who belonged to the group to cheat on newly designed promotional exams. These new exams had themselves been created to reduce existing hurdles to Black advancement. On the cusp of the 1980s, one sergeant wrote, "With respect to the law of equal employment opportunity, then, police administrators' most pressing task is not to ascertain whether affirmative action is legal—it is. The task is to design and adopt affirmative action plans matching those that have withstood legal attacks."[9]

Nevertheless, a common refrain reverberated across station houses and union halls: "reverse discrimination." The notion was, according to the Black Panther Party, "reactionary-chic." They heard it as "the mournful cry

Detroit Concerned Police Officers for Equal Justice picket the headquarters of the Detroit Police Officers Association, while President Gary Lee looks on, July 1974. Steve Thompson © *Detroit Free Press*, USA Today Network via Imagn Images.

emanating from racist Whites when they discover that they can't have the *whole* pie, only 99 per cent." As in other professions, white police union members labeled impatient and frustrated Black officers the actual racists. Cops in Boston and Detroit, for instance, sued for reverse discrimination after efforts to redress these departments' racial disparities. The Detroit Police Officers Association's opposition to affirmative action spurred Black cops to protest its leadership on multiple occasions. White cops picketed after a judge ordered Coleman Young not to lay off newly hired Black officers when the city faced a budget deficit. One held a sign saying REAL AFFIRMATIVE ACTION, FIRE THE MAYOR; white cops beat up a Black colleague counterprotesting, as one pointed a gun at the outnumbered Black cop.[10]

Courts ordered Fraternal Order of Police lodges to allow membership by Black officers, but newcomers found the reception less than welcoming. A Pittsburgh Fraternal Order of Police picnic devolved into a gun-wielding melee when a Black male cop danced with a white woman after the band switched from polka to soul. Two hundred white cops attacked twenty Black cops and their wives, as well as officers from the municipality hosting the picnic who arrived to break up the fight. Almost every Black officer immediately quit Pittsburgh's Fraternal Order of Police lodge, a pattern repeated across the country after other racist incidents.[11]

Some lodges ousted Black members who complained about bigotry. One in Cleveland tried to expel three Black cops who sued it for spending $10,000 on political ads targeting the city's first Black mayor, Carl Stokes, without member approval and in violation of the city charter.[12]

Police hostility to affirmative action drained time and resources from its advocates. Having opposed the goals of the civil rights movement in the streets with truncheons and dogs, police now took to the courts to battle equal opportunity law. What began as a demand for rights, equality, and freedom became a narrow, legalistic game of numbers and aptitude criteria. Police departments were not the only employers whose defiant employees forced affirmative action to be diluted, but because integration of police forces had a higher goal than just employment opportunity, this resistance was doubly deleterious.[13]

Those who resisted integration of police agencies could not hold the line forever. Particularly in cities with declining white populations and growing numbers of Black elected officials, total segregation could not last. Nevertheless, these battles over affirmative action and integration sharpened the blade of Blue Power. They afforded police organizations experience with litigation, both as plaintiff and defendant, and opportunities to mobilize external support. Each new campaign was an opportunity to forge solidarity among white cops who otherwise may have disagreed about operations or other aspects of the job or, far less frequently, among white and Black cops who favored a so-called colorblind approach that eliminated favoritism in the name of fairness.

These local battles over equal employment opportunity were also national fights. Washington was slow to realize how much energy police chiefs and mayors would have to expend on affirmative action; nor did lawmakers or the bureaucrats of the DOJ much appreciate that the end result would be disempowered chiefs and a pugilistic, mobilized, and unrestrained rank and file, battle-tested as much in the fight against crime on the street as in the courtroom and the chambers of police commissions and city councils.

FROM PATRONAGE TO QUALIFICATION

Unlike the white male police union leadership in Detroit and Baltimore, an integrated group of young male officers renovated the San Francisco

Police Officers' Association at the beginning of the 1970s. They took the helm pledging fairness and equal opportunity for advancement. Previously, leadership of the association had long been the preserve of plainclothes officers, who gained their higher ranks based on "who they knew" in city hall. The association's membership thus blurred management and rank and file. But several brash uniformed cops, calling themselves the Bluecoat Committee, set out to transform the association into a bona fide labor union.

Until this point, the San Francisco Police Officers' Association had been a fraternal group that advocated on behalf of police officers and engaged in charity. Originally, the organization operated mainly as a credit union. Membership was not compulsory, and all ranks were included. The association lacked automatic dues collection, collective bargaining rights, and standard grievance procedures. It was anything but a labor union in 1968 when California began to allow municipal authorities to "meet and confer" with representatives of employee organizations. Collective bargaining was still not mandatory. There was no clear way for employees to force governments to sign binding contracts. The Bluecoat agenda was to change this situation for police not only in San Francisco but across the state as well.

In Baltimore, the question of unionizing police turned on a debate about whether management prerogative might be better constrained through affiliation with either a police-only national organization, the Fraternal Order of Police, or organized labor, via AFSCME. On the other side of the country, by contrast, San Francisco's officers' association started out fully independent. The Bluecoats capitalized on lingering resentment of the city's old patronage system. But as that system was dissolving, the increasingly strident efforts by Black cops to obtain equal opportunities for employment and promotion became targets for a new wave of political mobilization. Commanders who supported affirmative action, and particularly quotas, attracted rank-and-file ire, though the anger was not always explicitly bigoted. Although a bitter fight and lengthy legal battle ensued in San Francisco, it was this colorblind approach to political empowerment, rather than the more obstreperously exclusionary tack adopted by most departments, that ultimately won out nationally. But that took decades.

Some Bluecoats were liberal, even opposing the US war in Vietnam, while others were more conservative. They disarmed skeptics with race-neutral appeals. Describing the group's membership, one Black member, "Crazy" Joe Pierce, quipped: "Hey, we don't give a shit... as long as he's a 'blue coat.'" This attitude allowed the Bluecoats to forge a series of alliances that proved critical to their success. Among their elected allies was a young member of the city's board of supervisors, Dianne Feinstein, at the outset of what would become one of the longest and most distinguished careers in contemporary American politics.[14]

The Bluecoats were able to smash vestiges of the patronage system that kept them out of power in the police department—with Feinstein's blessing. Her own politics of cautious, colorblind centrism-as-principle would be forged in a city gripped by a tireless Blue insurgency. And that experience guided her quixotic quest for consensus, and by extension the Democratic Party's, for decades.[15]

The crucial support Feinstein lent the Bluecoats was to ensure that a charter amendment about supervisory credentials appeared on the municipal ballot in November 1971 as Proposition E. Feinstein invited the first Bluecoat president of the Police Officers' Association, Jerry D'Arcy, to her home to collaborate on drafting the ballot text. It asked voters whether a civil service examination should be necessary for a police officer to enter the plainclothes Bureau of Inspectors, and, therefore, whether a supervisor should hold an equal or higher civil service rank than his supervisees. Proposition E posed a relatively specific and arcane question of bureaucratic rules. But for Feinstein, it was a way to depart from cronyism and "old-style politics." Among rank-and-file cops, the ballot asked: Should better-paid cops be better qualified, or should they be well-connected "juice boys," chosen by city hall?[16]

The city's African American police organization, Officers for Justice Peace Officers Association, had already attempted something similar. When the Police Officers' Association's leaders had refused to support Black officers charged with an off-duty violation, Officers for Justice confronted the leadership of the organization, and the department, by proposing a referendum. The proposal combined improvements to overtime pay with a provision that would elevate a Black officer to a position of authority equivalent to the head of the homicide unit.

The Black cops hoped the pay initiative would be popular among the rank and file, and could therefore discredit the association's crusty old white leaders. Sure enough, those leaders refused to support a Black-led proposal, and it failed, but it was the Bluecoats who then managed to topple the leadership in the association's internal election.[17]

Voters narrowly supported the Bluecoats' proposition. This victory meant that patronage would give way to qualification, and the Bluecoats heralded the win as "the first Equal Opportunity Charter change." In point of fact, it departed from the civil rights spirit of equal opportunity by focusing on individual merit as the means of advancement, rather than considering how institutions and prevailing political power impeded collective advancement. The result was to make the mechanics of racial hierarchy and harm invisible within a broader triumphal story of reform. The Bluecoats charted a path to reform that would appear meritocratic, while Officers for Justice launched a new campaign against discrimination by filing a lawsuit against the city's civil service and police commissions.[18]

AFFIRMATIVE ACTION FIGHTS

Unlike many other US cities, San Francisco was home to approximately equal Black, Latino, and Asian populations, constituting just under half the total population. But only about 10 percent of the police force was nonwhite as the 1970s dawned. Washington Garner was the lone African American member of the police commission. Though an older conservative man, he was explicit: the department was "full of racism." Ceremonial photos of Garner posted in station houses were stolen and vandalized on a weekly basis. A young white woman, Sandra Silva, who became a clerk in the department in 1972, was a dedicated member of the American Nazi Party, notorious for condemning busing at school board meetings while wearing a swastika armband. Silva had decided to take a job with the San Francisco police because "there you get a better class of people," meaning "no blacks or Jews."[19]

Though Proposition E mandated that an examination would now be the means for advancement in the department, no robust testing standard existed. Officers for Justice sued because the new civil service system seemed to be keeping Black cops out of supervisory roles, which they had previously been able to access through patronage. The lawsuit presented data to show that 54 percent of white applicants passed the entrance exam, while only 4 percent of Black applicants did. Latino and Asian applicants fared only somewhat better. When it came to promotion, in 1971, zero Black officers and 18 percent of white officers passed a sergeant-level promotion exam. The lawsuit demanded that existing promotion exams be halted and new exams be developed, with strict monitoring to ensure no further discrimination and racial quotas to be imposed on hiring and promotion.[20]

The lawsuit surprised and angered the Bluecoats. Severing their previous ties with Officers for Justice, they called the suit "political blackmail" and correctly predicted "a long and bitter battle." In today's parlance, they immediately doxxed the eleven complainants, printing their personal information in the *San Francisco Policeman* newsletter.[21]

By suing, Officers for Justice helped to unify the "notoriously divided and bickering" Police Officers' Association, which paid for its attorneys by assessing active members $50 each. For the association, the case held broad implications, far beyond the city: "The surrender of City Administration to well funded minority activists throughout the country will stop here in San Francisco." But less than six months later, aided by supportive affidavits from progressive police leaders, Officers for Justice got exactly what they wanted. District Court Judge Robert Peckham prohibited the use of extant written tests for patrol officer and sergeant and instituted a quota system for hiring at these ranks keyed to the goal of attaining 30 percent minority representation.[22]

The city stopped hiring cops for twenty months. Officers for Justice engaged in an intensive tutoring program to help aid the recruitment of minority cops, while the city developed a new entrance exam. The results for male applicants satisfied Peckham. He canceled his quota. Yet at the outset of the litigation, there were thirteen white female cops and no non-white female cops on the San Francisco force. Peckham introduced a new quota system in 1975 to increase this number. Then, despite decent results in promotion at lower ranks, the judge found flaws in the promotion exam for assistant inspector, with only 4 percent of Black candidates passing. Despite the relative effectiveness of both court oversight and the active efforts of Officers for Justice, the Police Officers' Association remained staunchly opposed to each of the district court's revisions. As one member wrote, the lawsuit presented "conflicting goals": raising standards in police operations versus hiring additional "minority group members" on the force. Both goals were valid in his estimation, but the union's stance was that quotas could not resolve the conflict.[23]

Such antagonism between largely white police associations and Black fraternal organizations was common across the country. Black cops favored independent organizations that allowed them to form alliances with cops in other jurisdictions. In Maryland, for instance, the relatively small number of African American cops in Baltimore allied with others in surrounding areas to form the Vanguard Justice Society in 1971 under the leadership of Sergeant Melvin Freeman. Within two years, the group had filed complaints of discrimination against Donald Pomerleau's department with the Equal Employment Opportunity Commission. At the end of a series of lengthy and complex legal proceedings, the court ruled in favor of the Vanguard plaintiffs, forcing the department to promote more than fifty male Black cops and three female white cops.[24]

At critical junctures, Black police organizations could also ally with unions. In Baltimore, given the choice between the Fraternal Order of Police and AFSCME, the Vanguard Justice Society chose the labor movement. Before the police union election in Baltimore, wary of the gains Lodge #3 was making in organizing cops, the Vanguard Justice Society joined Local 1195 in a formal relationship. The goal was to convince Black cops to vote against the Fraternal Order of Police. The deal, arranged by Freeman, would put two Vanguard Justice Society officers on the local's executive board and one on the negotiating committee. The local would also pay for a Vanguard Justice Society member to attend a national AFSCME convention in Hawai'i in 1974. For the first time, Black rank-and-file officers might have a say in overall departmental issues without resorting to the courts.

The arrangement faltered, however, after Local 1195 won the right to represent the department's officers. The local reneged on sending a Vanguard member to Hawai'i, pleading that it was sending six of its own members and that it could not afford travel costs for a seventh. The AFSCME international quickly realized that whatever the "internal politics" were, as vaguely explained by local president George Hoyt, the optics of failing to support the Black delegate's attendance were ugly. But Local 1195 had chosen its fate. White Baltimore cops' bigotry and disregard for their Black colleagues weakened the organization at a key moment: immediately before ratification of the union's first contract. When the union's members disapproved of the contract, the ensuing strike would bring about Local 1195's destruction. It would also dash hopes for a strong bond between Black police and labor, as that alliance was quickly sundered. The persistence of prejudice in the police department ensured that the Vanguard Justice Society would outlast the labor union in Baltimore.[25]

EQUAL EMPLOYMENT LAW VERSUS RACIST DEPARTMENTS

Employment discrimination occurred in police departments across the country, leading to lawsuits and complaints to federal bureaucrats. In most cities, the most politically active police did not adhere to the Bluecoats' colorblindness. Again and again, Black officers failed to advance in departments—or faced retaliation—and Black recruitment levels remained abysmal. Further, when budgets dried up amid urban fiscal crises, the last hired were the first fired.

Police leaders began to accept that affirmative action could make police departments more representative, with proportions of Black and other nonwhite cops approaching a given city's population distribution. But many administrators and union leaders resisted, asking a misdirecting question: How were these levels to be measured, particularly as white flight was rapidly changing urban demographics? Consulting firms popped up to address the challenges and provide remedies. Applied Urbanetics of Washington, DC, for example, offered police departments computer-generated packages that would sift and clarify the data, producing clear goals and timetables, to help chiefs discover whether they were sitting on an "EEO time bomb." But the best delay tactic was to use old data, from when the white-Black ratio of city residents tilted more heavily white.[26]

Adherence to equal employment opportunity law became imperative as the LEAA and the Nixon administration's Office of Revenue Sharing began to take note of noncompliance. They conditioned federal funds on grantees' ability to demonstrate that the money was not used "for a discriminatory purpose." Aggrieved Black cops found it cheaper to bring complaints to these bureaucrats than to the courts. Because the federal government had little direct say over local policing, the threat of damming these funding streams was one of the only ways to ensure compliance with civil rights law.

The LEAA did suspend funding to at least six state and city police agencies due to discrimination, later restoring it after remediation. The National Black Police Association believed this small number was inadequate given the size of the problem. Joining a dozen police and police recruits, it sued individual LEAA administrators for failing to cut off funds to agencies that discriminated. Supported by several elected officials, including Congressman Ronald Dellums of Oakland, California, this lawsuit signaled a new battle front for Black rights, and it received significant attention from the Black Panther Party. The law book had always accompanied the gun for the Panthers, but now that the Oakland branch had lowered its rifles, targeting individual officials with lawsuits appeared a viable option.[27]

After a tortuous journey through the courts, the litigation ended up confirming the obligation of federal agencies to cut off funds to grantees that violated equal opportunity law. But a far more common remedy was a negotiated agreement between the LEAA and law enforcement agencies. After more than 1,000 complaints, 660 such agreements to ensure affirmative action were signed by 1980. Whether a police force discriminated in its operations, however, was outside the purview of the civil rights bureaus of the LEAA or the Office of Revenue Sharing. The point of desegregating the station house was to alleviate police racism on the streets. Federal bureaucrats trusted the correlation between desegregation of the police and protection of the civil rights of the policed to hold even as they separated the two in their oversight.[28]

The DOJ had obtained the power to investigate a pattern or practice of discrimination in matters of "general public importance" through the 1968 Fair Housing Act. Yet almost thirty years passed before the department overcame a strict and conservative reading of this power as excluding police operations. The 1994 Violent Crime Control and Law Enforcement Act would finally grant the specific ability to investigate a pattern or practice of discrimination in policing on the street.

Nevertheless, incidents of police violence toward Black residents could motivate a city's Black cops to push for further Black hiring, even as their very presence on the force was often a response to prior racist police violence. Milwaukee, a city with about the same population as San Francisco but a larger police force, was home to a confident, uncompromising, rules-obsessed chief, the "borderline fascist" Harold A. Breier. The chief terrorized Milwaukee officers, and they, in turn, terrorized the city's Black residents. Police killed a young Black man, Daniel Bell, touching off the city's civil rights movement in 1958. Black activists who took part experienced police harassment well into the 1970s. One recalled learning about police in the Deep South while traveling; he ruefully remarked, "They wasn't nothing compared to Harold Breier."[29]

With the support of conservative local business elites and a lifetime appointment, Breier survived two days of unrest in the city in 1967 and national attention for his officers' brutal response. He also weathered a lengthy campaign organized by the local chapter of the Black Panther Party and other activists for a citywide police oversight board. Controlling information about his department was key. Breier forbade his officers from speaking to Johns Hopkins University researchers funded by the Ford Foundation who were following up on the Kerner Commission's findings. He was uninterested in actively desegregating the force, reluctant to share data on the force's racial composition, and unwilling to elevate the few Black officers to command positions.[30]

In 1973, Wisconsin's own state planning agency for criminal justice, which was responsible for allocating LEAA grants, urged the feds to defund the Milwaukee Police Department by denying a $400,000 grant. Obstinate and imperious, Breier had refused to disclose officer demographic data to the agency's civil rights compliance official. Instead, the chief reluctantly forwarded the information straight to Washington, bypassing the state agency. The LEAA, however, tipped off the DOJ's Civil Rights Division that the

Milwaukee Police Department reported dreadful rates of minority employment. Washington threatened to withhold not only LEAA funds but also all revenue-sharing funds, totaling over $16.3 million, of which around 40 percent went to public safety. The threat pushed the department to introduce new recruitment efforts, as Black officers appealed to the local office of the Equal Employment Opportunity Commission and to the courts.[31]

To remedy employment discrimination, a district court judge imposed a consent decree in 1974 and a hiring quota in 1975 on the Milwaukee Police Department. These measures tripled the number of Black cops by the outset of the 1980s. But this increase barely raised the proportion of Black officers to around 10 percent, which was less than half the city's proportion of Black residents. Unlike some chiefs who begrudgingly accepted affirmative action in order to alleviate tensions on the streets, with Black elected officials, and among testy Black cops, Breier was cavalier in a deposition when confronted with evidence of discrimination. He denied knowledge of Title VII of the Civil Rights Act and insisted there was no bias in the department. For its part, the Milwaukee chapter of the Black Panther Party publicized a plan to decentralize the city's police department, as a way to break Breier's control and empower the few cops "dedicated to the people's needs" in the city. Breier did admit that some of the city's police districts had no Black officers assigned to them.[32]

After the Equal Employment Opportunity Commission found unlawful discrimination, frustrated Black officers also went straight to the Civil Rights Division of the Office of Revenue Sharing. They believed that bureaucrats holding the purse strings might be more threatening than a federal judge. White candidates were passing the sergeant's exam at more than double the rate Black, Latino, and Native candidates were. But even these data were deceptive: only four of the minority candidates passed the exam for promotion, while ninety-six white candidates did. And there was still only one Black officer ranking higher than sergeant.[33]

In addition to an authoritarian chief, Milwaukee was home to a frustrated but militant police union, the Professional Policemen's Protective Association of Milwaukee, later renamed the Milwaukee Police Association. Its leaders, including Jerome Dudzik, had eagerly complained on Capitol Hill about the plight of police officers, but the organization did not lend much support to the city's Black cops. More than fifty self-identified minority officers sent an open letter to Robert Kliesmet, the association's president, imploring the union to help fix the situation: "The Milwaukee police department has made its stand clear. Minorities are not wanted in command positions. We are qualified, we have the experience and seniority yet we are constantly being thrown to the bottom of the list." They convinced Kliesmet to appeal to Chief Breier. On behalf of the minority officers, Kliesmet asked for an explanation of what criteria were used, other than examination scores, to determine eligibility for promotion. He wanted to know if discrimination was to blame for the lack of Black commanders. But he also suggested that perhaps Breier could prove discrimination had nothing to do with it.[34]

This message to the chief from the Milwaukee Police Association's president was an ineffectual intervention. A gentle letter stood in stark contrast to the union's willingness to take departmental disciplinary cases to court. The union was then spending more than three-quarters of its $330,000 annual budget on legal fees. Kliesmet had once told *Newsweek* that cops were "the new n——s of the world." He meant that cops lacked rights all others had obtained, but it is no surprise he refused to see Black cops as equally deserving as white cops.[35]

The Office of Revenue Sharing threatened Milwaukee, but it chose not to cut off the $13.9 million in funds it controlled. It recommended that local citizens monitor the situation and work with Black cops. The local NAACP chapter took on this responsibility and soon filed another complaint with the feds. But when this route failed to change the department's practices, a group of plaintiffs, led by an organization of Black cops in the city, the League of Martin, filed a class-action discrimination suit against the department, the police and fire commission, and Breier. The otherwise litigious Kliesmet denounced this lawsuit, saying the city's Black cops had gone "berserk."[36]

The League of Martin lawsuit came on the heels of the police killing of Ernie Lacy. This twenty-two-year-old Black man died in circumstances that combined the recent killings of George Floyd and Freddie Gray: Milwaukee police officers kneeled on his neck and then tossed him in a van. He arrived at the station fifteen minutes later, dead. An activist had a ready label for the incident: "police van instant death syndrome." Around 10,000 people, both white and Black, rallied in the streets that summer, protesting Breier's police force for its brutality. Activists staged sit-ins and boycotts of local retailers. The chief dismissed them all as "pinkos." His own investigation found "no wrongdoing" in the Lacy incident.[37]

But the Fire and Police Commission fired one of Lacy's arresting officers. It suspended four others without pay. Kliesmet denounced the commission's actions, protesting that "historically, they never disciplined members for the kinds of things they do now," like when a cop once shot a woman who was holding a knife after her husband attacked her, or a member of the Outlaws motorcycle club died of head trauma in a paddy wagon. The League of Martin eventually won a favorable settlement to its lawsuit. And after more than two decades, a federal jury finally awarded $1.8 million to the family of Daniel Bell, slain by police back in 1958, finding that the cop who killed him had used racial epithets, planted a knife, and lied about his actions. Shared outrage over these legal decisions tempered the friction between the Milwaukee Police Association and Chief Breier. They finally found common cause. The union organized a fundraising rally in defense of the five officers punished for Lacy's death. They received a standing ovation. And for the rank and file he had domineered for two decades, Breier was now the "undisputed star of the evening."[38]

Outside pressure to eliminate racist police operations brought the warring chief and police association together. But collaborations to actively exclude Black, Latino, Asian, and Native officer candidates from hiring or promotion were becoming rarer, in part because evidence was growing, with more Black cops on the force, that nonwhite cops were willing and able to police Black people just as vigorously as white cops. Colorblindness in the station house, as the Bluecoats in San Francisco preached, could sanction racist brutality on the street.

CHAPTER 8

A COP IN CONGRESS

Mario Biaggi was the most decorated member of the New York Police Department when he retired in 1965. He had been a cop for over two decades, reaching the rank of detective lieutenant. Cited multiple times for valor, Biaggi was wounded eleven times, including a leg injury caused by a runaway horse. It left him with a lifelong limp. Biaggi also shot and killed multiple suspects during his career, including one who tried, but failed, to carjack him. In 1968, Biaggi was elected to Congress as a Democrat, flipping a Republican stronghold in the Bronx. His ascent in national politics symbolized the waxing of Blue Power. If rank-and-file cops were ineffective on the national stage when he entered Congress, his achievement would be their effectiveness when he left it.

Biaggi was a new breed of tough-on-crime northern Democrat. He spent his political career championing the cause of police on Capitol Hill, often choreographing lobbying efforts by cops who were neophytes in Washington. In committee hearings, Biaggi reliably provided the police officer's perspective, invoking his own experiences. "He was recognized as the guy to go to if you had a concern about law enforcement," his aide Craig W. Floyd recalled. Ultimately, Biaggi's major legislative accomplishments included death benefits for families of slain police officers, a ban on armor-piercing bullets, and the founding of the National Law Enforcement Officers Memorial Fund, which Floyd would supervise for decades.[1]

Biaggi also championed a federal law enforcement officers' bill of rights, which would, as one police unionist put it, "once and for all outline the basic rights of policemen, nationwide." Biaggi claimed it would increase officer morale and thus effectiveness. He first introduced a federal version of the bill of rights in 1971. The next year, he gathered 125 cosponsors, and it received a Judiciary Committee hearing in 1973. He lined up an impressive roster of union support, including John Harrington, on behalf of the Fraternal Order of Police; Ed Kiernan, on behalf of the International Conference of Police Associations (he had recently succeeded Carl Parsell of Detroit as president); John Cassese, on behalf of the fledgling National Union of Police Officers, recently affiliated with the Service Employees International Union; and Jerry Wurf, on behalf of AFSCME. Both Kiernan and Cassese had cut their teeth leading New York's Patrolmen's Benevolent Association. Kiernan would continue to collaborate with Biaggi on versions of the bill for years to come.[2]

The bill of rights did not pass in Congress. Biaggi reintroduced it annually, even though it consistently failed in committee, never earning a floor vote in the House or the Senate. The IACP opposed the bill, arguing it would constrain chiefs. The National Sheriffs' Association also opposed it, even passing a resolution that such a bill "would abrogate the management prerogative of sheriffs."[3]

But the bill's repeated failure had its uses. According to Floyd, "it was important to rank-and-file law enforcement especially." By consistently putting the bill before Congress, Biaggi was able to present a "model" for police officers, and particularly their unions, who had more clout locally than in Congress. They could point to persistent congressional inaction and demand that a state-level bill or a union contract instead enact the protections they desired, which Biaggi's bill delineated. "If we hadn't been promoting it at the federal level," argued Floyd, "there's a good chance we wouldn't have seen the states and localities enact their own versions."[4]

The emergence of the law enforcement officers' bill of rights was part of a shift in the balance of power within the police writ large, away from command, toward the rank and file. Throughout the era when chiefs like Parker in Los Angeles, Breier in Milwaukee, and Pomerleau in Baltimore tried to rule with an iron fist, rank-and-file officers despised top-down implementation of new work routines. And many police felt that disciplinary measures, also coming from the top, were harsh, unpredictable, secretive, and capricious. Officers resented being treated by their commanders as if they were ordinary criminal suspects. Cops wanted the due process, access to lawyers, and benefit of the doubt that they only reluctantly afforded people they arrested.

The LEAA provided funding to answer the long-standing call for professionalizing reforms, but many of its most vocal advocates were exhausted and approaching retirement. Worse, fights over the operations of the byzantine LEAA sapped the attention of federal law enforcement leaders. Crime bedeviled municipal leaders and social scientists alike. And cops in city after city seemed to be on the take. The dawn of the 1970s was a frustrating moment for those at the top of law enforcement. In contrast, the push for an officers' bill of rights, led by tough-on-crime Democratic legislators like Biaggi, gave rank-and-file officers a reliable cause to rally around, in defiance of management. It was energizing.

INTERNAL AFFAIRS

Formal internal affairs investigations did not become widespread until the 1970s. They aimed primarily at ferreting out and preventing corruption and malfeasance. In Biaggi's own former force, the New York Police Department, corruption was a "department-wide phenomenon," according to one prominent legal expert, "indulged in to some degree by a sizable majority of those on the force and protected by a code of silence on the part of those who remained honest." During his stint as commissioner in New York City, leading professionalizer Patrick Murphy griped to an audience of fellow chiefs convened by the LEAA that civil service regulations made weeding out corruption difficult. And police unions "fail to support administrators and condemn wrongdoing by policemen."[5]

Pressure to develop official internal affairs investigatory capabilities originated with Lyndon Johnson's President's Commission on Law Enforcement and Administration of Justice, which was inspired by the IACP's investigation into the Baltimore Police Department. A 1967 Supreme Court decision, *Garrity v. New Jersey*, however, ruled that statements police were compelled to give in disciplinary hearings could not be used in criminal trials. This ruling fortified police resolve to defy investigations that would remain internal, which were usually decided according to a chief's prerogative.[6]

By the outset of the 1970s, complaints from members of the public had begun to occupy increasing proportions of formal investigative units' attention. The emerging tacit division of labor in police oversight held civilian review as an antidote to public complaints of racist abuse and internal affairs investigations as an antidote to corruption and graft, which commanders understood as separate and unrelated, to the degree they admitted either existed. Intensive inquiries, whether by distinguished appointed commissions or journalists, would repeatedly challenge this separation, finding that the two went hand in hand then and still do today.[7]

Eventually, all large departments created internal affairs units. They were unloved. Officers scorned them, and many administrators tended to look upon them as a regrettable necessity. Dealing with internal affairs investigators meant dealing with "rats, headhunters, the chief's men, shooflies, rubbershoes, gumshoes, stool pigeons, snitches, traitors, and finks." Meanwhile, police used collective bargaining, as well as lobbying, to neutralize their investigatory abilities, even as resistance to civilian review widened their ambit to include civil rights complaints. But many cops had little to fear. The internal affairs unit of the Louisville Police Department, for instance, was "not fair, not equitable and not impartial." It mainly acted "against black citizen complaints and black police officer defendants," according to a 1976 federal inquiry.[8]

Biaggi's law enforcement officers' bill of rights sought to stymie these kinds of investigations. The bill's major provisions included the establishment of statewide grievance committees to hear, investigate, and adjudicate complaints by police, as well as a requirement that states explicitly outline the rights and privileges of police facing investigations. It ensured that police officers had the right to bring civil suit if their rights were violated, and it also guaranteed police officers the right to engage in political activity while off duty. And it worked by conditioning LEAA funding on state compliance with these provisions.

Supporters mounted two main arguments for the bill of rights. First, it would check superior officers who "conduct themselves in arrogant, ruthless, and improper fashion." This justification was consistent with common justifications for police unionism. But Biaggi rallied a cohort of white legislators and police unionists, almost all men, who also framed the bill as a needed complement to civil rights legislation, even cynically arguing that the bill's opponents echoed opposition to civil rights guarantees for Black Americans.[9]

The bill of rights did duplicate existing protections, Biaggi acknowledged, including the right to representation by a lawyer in a criminal proceeding. But the Civil Rights Act and Voting Rights Act also guaranteed already existing constitutional protections. They simply created a more direct enforcement mechanism. In hearings on the Hill, Biaggi hammered this comparison, circling back repeatedly to civil rights law.

On his first day in office in 1972, Attorney General Richard Kleindienst, a staunch conservative who had been Barry Goldwater's presidential campaign manager, objected to the bill. He argued it represented a federal intrusion into state and local government affairs. Biaggi caviled: "This argument probably sounds very familiar. It is the same argument used against the Civil Rights Acts." Further, he argued that because state and local governments failed to protect civil rights, the federal government had been compelled to act—for instance, by ordering children to be bused across cities to desegregate schools. "Why then," Biaggi asked, "is it so difficult to place a similar requirement on the States to assure the rights of law enforcement officers?" He scolded his colleagues for their impassivity, which he contrasted with their willingness to extend civil rights laws in the recent past. Would police be forced to "conduct marches in the streets, engage in civil disobedience or conduct riots? Is violence the only force that will move Congress?"[10]

In fact, police marches helped convince New York City's leaders to implement the original blueprint for Biaggi's officers' bill of rights in the first place. In the mid-1960s, Mayor Robert Wagner, wary of antagonizing already restive municipal employees, had resisted calls for a beefed-up external review board for a couple of years (the department had implemented an internal board in 1953). But after unrest in Harlem and Bedford-Stuyvesant in 1964, the mayor started to show interest in the idea. Public demands for external review were also increasing. But cops were not having it. In June 1965, 5,000 off-duty officers flocked to Lower Manhattan to picket city hall, denouncing Wagner's plans for the civilian review board. Cops threatened a small gathering of CORE counterprotesters, shouting at them to get on home or ship off to Vietnam. Wagner decided not to run for a fourth term.[11]

Wagner's successor, John Lindsay, ultimately created a new review board in 1966, consisting of seven appointees, four named by the mayor and three by the police commissioner. It had no formal power, however, and could not even interact with accused officers or make specific disciplinary recommendations. But the Patrolmen's Benevolent Association, led by John Cassese, successfully argued that the mayor had overstepped his authority. The board had to be put to a referendum before voters. Conservative leader William F. Buckley Jr. collected over 40,000 signatures, added on to the more than 50,000 that Cassese's men collected, to ensure that the referendum made it on the ballot. One former police lieutenant argued that the campaign was not really about the power of the commissioner or mayor but was "a fight for PBA power, police power, and perhaps the Conservative Party power."[12]

Once the referendum was on the ballot, the Patrolmen's Benevolent Association mounted a vociferous red-baiting media campaign against civilian review, including billboards and television commercials. One depicted a white woman walking alone from a subway exit to a darkened city street. The message was that external review would leave her unsafe. Civilian review supporters faced police harassment, including frequent arrests on charges of disorderly conduct. The association sponsored a truck tour through Brooklyn, featuring on the back of the truck go-go dancers who shimmied to Jewish folk songs while loudspeakers denounced the mayor and civilian review. Voters soon struck down New York's review board, marking, according to one historian, the beginning of the end of the Black–Jewish civil rights coalition in the city.[13]

In the fallout, the New York Police Department strengthened its police-only review board and created an internal affairs investigatory division, which officers hated only slightly less than civilian review. At the same time, the union managed to institute a bill of rights, authorized by departmental order in 1967, that contained specific requirements for how officers were to be treated in potential disciplinary situations.

Its ten guidelines for departmental investigations stipulated that officers should be interrogated only during the daytime, afforded rest periods and meals, and compensated for time lost due to interrogation. They were to be "informed of the nature of the investigation before any interrogation commences, including the name of the complainant." Investigators could not employ "offensive language," nor could they threaten an officer with "transfer, dismissal, other disciplinary punishment." No "off-the-record" interrogation was allowed, and investigators had to Mirandize officers in advance of arrest or if the officer became a target of a criminal investigation. Biaggi saw to it that his federal bill replicated these provisions, and many contractual bills of rights that police unions negotiated followed suit.[14]

But New York's patrol union was not finished. In time, the union came to celebrate a "tremendously expedited" grievance procedure that would take effect if the enumerated rights it granted officers were violated. This special process required a meeting of the department's grievance board within two working days, a decision within another day, and a review by the commissioner's office within another two days. Only an arbitrator, who would issue a binding ruling, could hear an appeal. In contrast, protections for New York police officers questioned by superiors came to slow the process, with a forty-eight-hour "adjournment" after an incident. Officers would be afforded representation by a union confederate, the right to an attorney, and specific limitations on the types of questions that could be asked. It came to be nearly impossible to discipline a cop with all these protections in place.[15]

In New York City, the success of the campaign against civilian review and the expansion of protections for officers meant that Biaggi's law and order rhetoric attracted imitators among Democrats. In the words of a writer for the *International Socialist Review*, "The idea was to upstage Republican Governor Nelson Rockefeller, the Attica murderer, in his call for more cops, more judges, more jails, and longer sentences." After throwing his hat briefly in the ring for the Democratic mayoral ticket in 1973, Biaggi found that every contender was adopting his approach. "All the other candidates are talking more about law and order than I am."[16]

But it would not be New York state, or Congress for that matter, that instituted the first bill of rights for police officers. It was Maryland, where Pomerleau and the plucky union were at each other's throats, even as the struggle between Black Baltimoreans and the city's police was reaching a crescendo of its own.

THE FIRST STATEWIDE LAW ENFORCEMENT OFFICERS' BILL OF RIGHTS

In the early 1970s, the fledgling Baltimore Fraternal Order of Police chapter had begun making political endorsements in Baltimore elections, based on, for example, candidates' positions regarding civilian review. In races between white and Black candidates, Lodge #3 reliably endorsed the white one. But the Fraternal Order of Police also followed the lead of one specific elected official, John J. Gallagher. A white Democratic legislator from northeast Baltimore, Gallagher became a great advocate for the city's rank-and-file officers after his election to the state House of Delegates in 1971.

A onetime high-school track star and a consistent ball of energy, Gallagher was "ultra-conservative." He rejected anything he saw as a communist conspiracy, including the counterculture, racial integration, public opinion polling, and financial disclosures from elected officials. Gallagher supported Commissioner Pomerleau's repression of the left but opposed his disciplinary measures for police. A fan of the LEAA when its funding came with few strings attached, he criticized any move by Pomerleau, judges, or wardens that risked decreasing federal funds for local law enforcement. Forgotten today in Baltimore, Gallagher distilled the essence of actually existing American conservatism: big government when it came to controlling Black people, small government when it came to aiding them.[17]

By trade, Gallagher was an ad man. He believed that legislating had much more to do with selling a product than with fine-tuning social policy. He openly admitted that the audience for his product was the conservative white residents of more-rural Maryland counties, and he helped Baltimore's police reorient themselves accordingly. Gallagher embroidered his advocacy with threats if he did not get his way, such as "The white American has within him the seeds of violent reaction"—a rhetorical flourish attractive to police because they could make good on it.[18]

Although John Gallagher had no medals of valor pinned to his chest, he had moxie. Whereas Mario Biaggi needed to cultivate alliances on the Hill, Gallagher was shameless and opportunistic. Angered by Pomerleau's increasingly imperious behavior toward the rank and file, and in alliance with the Fraternal Order of Police, Gallagher drew from the New York Police Department model to craft what he considered "an absolutely flawless piece of legislation." The bill was explicitly designed to limit Pomerleau's power, and police elsewhere in Maryland were initially skeptical. Reading more like a union contract than a piece of state legislation when first enrolled, the bill of rights codified protections for officers, both against complaints of wrongdoing by the public and against discipline and retaliation by commanders.[19]

AFSCME Local 1195, Fraternal Order of Police Lodge #3, and the United Baltimore City Police Wives' Association all supported the bill in Annapolis. Cops testified in favor, and no one testified against it. Local 1195 even published photographs of Gallagher and four dozen cosponsors of the bill in its newsletter. The bill passed the House of Delegates in 1973 and was signed into law the next year, but it received virtually no media coverage until after the Baltimore police strike. The effect of the new state law on Pomerleau's dismissal of striking officers was nil. But it would protect cops who abused or killed civilians in the street for decades.[20]

The Law Enforcement Officers' Bill of Rights became a superordinate tool to protect officers. Birthed in a struggle within the Baltimore department, it would insulate cops from outside scrutiny or punishment for their actions on the street. The legislation, more than the strike, would symbolize the end of the era of the authoritarian professionalizer chief.

Thanks to Biaggi's persistence, at least fifteen other states would go on to institute replicas of Maryland's bill. Florida was first. Its enacted version had a broader scope than Maryland's and enumerated ten protected rights for officers facing interrogation. Legislators would continually fortify these protections over time—for instance, extending Maryland's adjournment period after a "use-of-force" incident to ten days, based on the spurious claim that the extension enhanced an officer's memory.[21]

And Gallagher took to the road. He testified about the importance of a police bill of rights in other state legislatures, including Wisconsin's, joining Ed Kiernan of the International Conference of Police Associations. Together, their effort formed the chrysalis of an interstate network of politically inclined police powerbrokers. It inspired police unions to imitate what Gallagher had achieved in Maryland. San Francisco's Bluecoats were eager to bring a police bill of rights to California, as their rank-and-file police movement and the resulting lawsuit over racial discrimination were reshaping politics in the city and the state.[22]

CHAPTER 9

FROM CITY HALL TO THE STATE CAPITAL

The legacy of San Francisco's Bluecoats was a colorblind ideology, but ideology did not dictate the tactics needed for political gains. The first two Bluecoat leaders of the San Francisco Police Officers' Association were, however, sharp political tacticians. They understood the local landscape well, but they also developed a repertoire that operated at multiple scales. Although Baltimore's police militants attempted to gain a foothold in the state capital, San Francisco's Bluecoats were far more successful in vaulting from municipal terrain to state-level politicking and back again, even dabbling in national politics in Washington. The use of these scalar shifts to the advantage of Blue Power was their great innovation.

Jerry D'Arcy was an original San Francisco Bluecoat. He gained citywide prominence when he organized a police protest in Civic Center Plaza on November 18, 1970. Called Black Wednesday, the rally and march honored slain police officers, but it also signaled a new orientation for the rank and file. The initial payoff was D'Arcy's election to lead the association in January 1971, after having become second vice president the prior year. But the bigger prize was the passage of Proposition E a year later. The proposition meant that supporting the mayor and board of supervisors would no longer be enough to ensure promotion. Police officers could therefore be much more critical of elected leaders. They could make demands. D'Arcy was prescient. He realized a memorial for cops killed in the line of duty would be a potent organizing tool.[1]

Early in 1971, the Bluecoats modified the Police Officers' Association constitution to allow it to make political endorsements. D'Arcy had become president by promising transformation. "No longer can we function as a police social club." Instead, "the Association is embarking on an *era of involvement*"—involvement in politics. A fast-learning, fierce operator, D'Arcy used his new mandate to issue the association's endorsement of the incumbent mayor, Joseph Alioto.[2]

Although no great friend to organized labor, Alioto repaid the association for its "precedent-shattering" support when he handily beat Dianne Feinstein in the November election. First, he signed a detailed memorandum of understanding (MOU), which the Bluecoats championed as their Magna Carta. Although the agreement outlawed strikes, it was not a union contract: neither collectively bargained nor ratified by membership, it did not change police compensation. But it did contain protections for police; in effect, it amounted to a law enforcement officers' bill of rights—guaranteeing, for instance, that officers under internal investigation be shielded from press inquiries. Their names were kept private, but they were also to receive any complainants' names and addresses.[3]

Robert Kliesmet, the police union leader from Milwaukee, inspired Jerry D'Arcy to push for these protections. Kliesmet was then working with Biaggi to pass the federal law enforcement officers' bill of rights, which provided the "skeleton" for San Francisco's MOU. Kliesmet joined Carl Parsell, Robert Gordon, and Ed Kiernan as the cantankerous, outspoken leaders of the International Conference of Police Associations at the time. The fractious association by then claimed to represent over 150,000 officers, and San Francisco's officers' association became one of its anchors, along with the Detroit Police Officers Association and the New York Patrolmen's Benevolent Association. Based on his experience in the New York City trenches, Kiernan took D'Arcy under his wing, becoming his mentor, while Kliesmet guided him through Washington corridors as they worked together on federal legislation.[4]

Back home, D'Arcy was urging San Francisco cops to write letters to their own members of Congress, asking them to back Biaggi's bill. But he warned his officers to watch out for the "guy who wears a big American flag pin and a 'support your local police' bumper sticker on his auto" and who proclaims he "supports law and order" but "who would go into hysterics if they thought a Cop would even think of going on strike."[5]

For these police officials, the litmus test was whether a representative in Washington supported Biaggi's bill of rights or the Sacramento version of it. The San Francisco Police Officers' Association proved ready to endorse candidates who backed the bill. One who passed the Bluecoat test was John Burton, scion of a Democratic machine family and native of the city. By endorsing Burton, the association developed links with a powerful clique, including John's brother, Congressman Philip Burton. Sala Galante Burton, who represented San Francisco in Congress after the death of her husband, Philip, would name a successor from her own deathbed: the sister-in-law of a former president of the board of supervisors and daughter of Baltimore mayor Thomas D'Alesandro Jr.—a Democratic Party activist named Nancy Pelosi.[6]

Over the next few years, the Bluecoats gained power in the association, while department commanders who opposed them fell out of favor. Mayor Alioto forced city police chief Thomas J. Cahill to resign in 1970. Cahill had been in charge since 1958, and Alioto recognized that he could seem tough on crime while departing from Cahill's hidebound and elitist racial conservatism by siding with the rank and file.

Alioto replaced Cahill with Alfred "Snooky" Nelder, a lifelong cop who worked his way up the ranks (after a brief stint playing baseball for the Cincinnati Reds). But once the association endorsed Alioto, Nelder recognized his place between the rock of professionalism and the hard place of rank-and-file activism. After only a year, he bailed—though not before angering the city's gay community with a moralistic approach to nightlife, enforced by his cadre of "priests in a blue uniform," as *The Gay Crusader*, an underground newspaper, called them.[7]

Once Alioto won reelection, he replaced Snooky Nelder with Donald M. Scott. His soft touch effectively put the Bluecoats in charge. Rewarded with a weak chief, the Bluecoats became unquenchable. Although not all association members agreed with the Bluecoats, the upstarts took it upon themselves to convince any dissenters that unity was essential—and they were not going to back down. One of their changes was to rename the association's newsletter *San Francisco Policeman* to make it seem to represent every officer—even as it was increasingly a Bluecoat mouthpiece. Although the newsletter would publish contributions by any current or retired department member, Bluecoat positions received the most space.

The Bluecoats did not represent all cops in the city. But they wanted all cops to see things from their point of view. This required making their position the successful one, earning tangible gains. If Baltimore's AFSCME chapter erred by assuming the path to victory for cops was the one pursued by other public sector unions, the Bluecoats learned how to chart a path specific to police.

THE SOCIAL COMPOSITION OF BLUE POWER

One of D'Arcy's most important projects was a formal study of the attitudes and working conditions of the full complement of officers in the department. With the blessing of Alioto and Nelder, the association hired a professional research firm to produce a survey, though it was never meant to be impartial. The firm introduced the results as follows: "In this period of great social change and a growing disrespect for moral and man-made law, largely obscured from the public has been the viewpoint of the men upon whom they depend for the prevention of crime and law enforcement." It was true that the attitudes and social demographics of police officers remained both underanalyzed and stereotyped.

The firm did not portray the officers of an increasingly militant police department as a monolith. The city's "social atmosphere," as evidenced by street protests, and its racial demographics were shifting, with fewer white and more Black and Asian, as well as "Spanish-surname," residents. Cop attitudes were changing too. Before donning the uniform each day, young cops and veterans brought divergent understandings of society to the station house. Yet police operations would amalgamate them into a singular product.

The survey provided a remarkable window into a police department in the throes of upheaval, and the Bluecoats used its findings to support their campaign for Blue Power. All members of the police department could answer the fifteen-page survey questionnaire—even those who refused to join the Police Officers' Association—and anonymity was guaranteed. Officers for Justice refused to turn over its mailing list, however. Instead, the survey firm provided the necessary stack of forty questionnaires for the organization to distribute to its members. But the members refused to participate, meaning that few Black cops were included in the survey findings. The survey excluded the most politically savvy and engaged Black officers. Mistrust was too great, and Black officers felt their unique position would not be appreciated among everyone else's responses, which ultimately totaled 1,258, for a participation rate of 65.5 percent.

The report synthesized a composite average San Francisco beat cop. He was 36.4 years old and had entered the force at age twenty-one. He had three kids and was married (of the 20 percent unmarried, many were divorced). His wife worked if the kids were in school, and he supplemented his income through off-duty employment. He had a high school diploma and two years of college, studying criminology, police science, or law, usually after a stint in the Army or Navy. Few spoke a foreign language fluently, but young officers tended to be more conversant, particularly in Spanish or Italian; a few spoke Chinese or Thai. Promotion to sergeant took at least thirteen years (for the 200 who managed to achieve it), and mandatory retirement loomed at age sixty-five.

The survey split cops into three age groups. Cops in their mid-forties and older had experienced a department structured in all aspects by patronage. Career advancement that required "book knowledge" was of little interest to them. "Despite a certain amount of callousness arising from years of abrasion, those in the older age brackets display... highly practical knowledge." Cynicism and "gripes" were common.

Cops in their thirties were often military veterans, which meant they adhered to standards of professionalism and strict discipline. Becoming a cop at a moment of economic expansion was a choice, and it meant certain financial sacrifices. But these cops also believed that they could advance their careers through study and "demonstrated ability."

Finally, the youngest cops and cadets, in their twenties, "are a product of the same environment in which so many youths have been in rebellion against the 'establishment.'" As one cop put it, "My age group believes the police are oppressors." But young officers were usually altruistic and understood the "social ills" behind the "problems they will face." Sensitivity to unfairness translated into suspicion: a representative young officer felt "minorities have a better advantage" in promotions.

Despite these differences among cops at different stages of life, the survey found unanimity favoring a salary increase. Further, "an inauguration of 'fringe benefits' would go far" and "be a tremendous 'morale' booster." A third of the respondents had at some point been a union member, but San Francisco's force differed from those on the East Coast, as only 8 percent had a relative who was a cop. Respondents at all ages wanted political patronage, "nepotism," "political pull," and "favoritism" to become extinct, and saw Alioto and Nelder as making positive strides in that direction.

Cops, the survey found, were frustrated professionally, sexually, and otherwise. One cop suggested the survey should inquire into "divorce, alcoholism, infidelity, sexual problems," essentially the "complications arising in an officer's home life because of uncertainty about overtime and days off." Most cops did not like working a second job, but the pay was too low for it to be avoided for half of respondents, who believed their living expenses outstripped their pay. Many nevertheless reported choosing to be a cop because it was a secure job. In fact, it was too secure, according to some, who believed professionalism required the department to "suspend and fire the men who refuse to put in a day's work for a day's pay." Professionalism also required that "the fact of race or color should have no bearing" on hiring or promotion, though 85 percent thought there was no racial discrimination in the department. But cops also by and large did not want residency requirements or pay parity with the fire department. They hated the idea of lateral entry.

Officers' answers to the survey were not all coherent, but the Bluecoats took them as a question of political organizing. The survey did not dictate what the association should do. It dictated how cops' attitudes might need to be reshaped. Cops mostly wanted paid medical insurance, with fewer desiring dental coverage and time-and-a-half overtime. Night differential pay was not hugely popular. Around 85 percent of cops thought the union was aggressive enough. But the 10 percent who thought it needed to be more aggressive energized the Bluecoats. One cop said the association should be "more militant and not afraid to step on toes." And many cops approved of the new leadership that D'Arcy represented, though younger officers were more vociferous in their support of his tone. Still, on the whole cops did not support the right to strike, even as unions in the private sector were seen to aid their members, with the Teamsters as the most popular. Most ignored a question that asked if job actions like a blue flu were acceptable. The survey firm concluded that San Francisco cops "look to their Association to be their spokesman, with a mandate for action," including "obtaining benefits; eliminating favoritism; righting wrongs; increasing efficiency; and winning public confidence." The survey ordained recommendations not for the department but for officers to act collectively: appeal to legislators, change the city charter, express displeasure with the courts, and abandon the "role of bystander" in politics.[8]

D'Arcy's time leading the association was limited, and he was lured away to a post as a motorcycle lieutenant in 1972. An officer's ability to transfer to a position of choice was one of the boons of the MOU, so D'Arcy reaped the benefit he had helped to earn. He had also become frustrated at the complacency of his fellow officers. For instance, the association was able to get a proposition on the ballot allowing negotiation with the board of supervisors over fringe benefits, only to lose: "We only campaign several weeks prior to an election," he observed. Winning unions, in contrast, "campaign 365 days a year, every year."[9]

D'Arcy picked his replacement as president: Jerry Crowley, who had been the association's secretary, responsible for successfully guiding the Proposition F machinations. Though he remains largely forgotten outside San Francisco, no single cop had a greater impact on politics in California than Crowley. In part, he was in the right place at the right time, but he also recognized that for police to win in politics, they needed to choose the battlefield first, the enemy second. D'Arcy's trips to Washington, however exciting, were not greatly consequential back in San Francisco. Because of his courage, D'Arcy was, in Crowley's words, "our shield against political reprisal." But Crowley knew that no single man could shield the whole force. To get the protections his men needed, the brash cop had to trek no further than Sacramento.[10]

POLITICAL ACTION

Jerry Crowley, according to fellow Bluecoat Paul Chignell, began nearly every sentence not with "I," but with two words: "The Association." It was "his life." But to ensure that the San Francisco Police Officers' Association could succeed, two other words were always on his lips: "political action." With long, graying sideburns, a perpetually arched and furrowed brow, and a lantern chin, Crowley exuded a cool intensity, a coiled fearlessness, acquired when he trained as a boxer in high school and college. As the Bluecoats took over the union, they sometimes met the fists of the old guard, unwilling to relinquish its power. But over and over again, the Bluecoats prevailed.[11]

Under Crowley's leadership, the association began experimenting with new ways of making its voice heard and engaging its membership. One example was printing preaddressed form letters in its newsletter, which members could then clip and send to the mayor and the supervisors. In addition, the association identified a range of activities for members, including retirees, to help support its agenda, including posting signs, making financial contributions, speaking to civic groups, and urging friends to vote. At the end of the 1970s, one of Crowley's colleagues reflected on their many successes, and the variety of tactics they had needed to use: "Political considerations, pressure on politicians, talking, influencing, supporting, opposing politicians is what got the work done." Simply put, over and over, "our answer was politics."[12]

For several years, Crowley was peerless. The Bluecoats, under his leadership, formed a tactical alliance with liberal local activists and civil libertarians who opposed consolidation of police operations and closure of station houses in a few neighborhoods, including Park Station near Haight-Ashbury, where a number of original Bluecoats had walked the beat. From 1950 to 1970, not only had the once white neighborhood become a centerpiece of the hippie counterculture, but its population grew to be about one-third Black, while another quarter comprised Latino and Asian American people. Working-class Black newcomers and white professionals and hippies alike tended to oppose centralized authority. Their communitarian and localist argument that police should be closely acquainted with the neighborhoods they policed complemented the Bluecoat desire to maintain dispersed authority within the department, rather than allowing greater top-down control, as during Cahill's reign. The board of supervisors, wary of Alioto's attempts to wrestle away its influence, supported a Bluecoat-endorsed ballot proposition to reopen closed police stations and require board approval for future closures. It narrowly won. Although Park Station reopened, its softball team, the Golden Gate Porkers, always a playoff contender in the departmental league, never returned. Energies would be expended elsewhere.[13]

Crowley realized that he would be most effective at consolidating police by cultivating the ability to pivot and jump scales. He leapt from the station house to the Civic Center to Sacramento, continually balancing his strengths and his association's needs across these different venues. He maintained local goals, like perpetually enhancing police compensation, though the department's officers already received the state's highest cop wages. Local success sometimes proved more challenging, however, than goals pitched at a higher scale.

THE ARMY OF LEGISLATIVE LOBBYISTS

In Sacramento, Crowley concentrated on two distinct objectives. His priority was to institute statewide collective bargaining for police, superseding the existing framework that required only that public workers and governing bodies "meet and confer" over wages and terms of employment. Second, he wanted to institute a statewide law enforcement officers' bill of rights. That work required that he mobilize beyond San Francisco itself.

Crowley helped to found COPS, the California Organization of Police and Sheriffs. With its creation, Crowley announced: "We are saying publicly for the first time that we are political and that our potential strength demands respect." COPS was like the International Conference of Police Associations in miniature, a California-based association of associations designed to press for cop-friendly legislation in the statehouse. As one retired officer argued, "Whether we like it or not, we are in politics. It also follows that the stronger and more vocal we are the more the politicians will listen." COPS was the vehicle for this new voice.[14]

Originally called the Peace Officers Political Action Council or POPAC, the founding "nucleus" of COPS included officers from across the state, though they were concentrated in Southern California. Representatives joined from police officers' associations in Beverly Hills, Burbank, Compton, Glendale, Los Angeles, and Long Beach, as well as Alameda, San Diego, and Ventura County sheriffs, among others. In an open letter to other police, inviting them to join the effort, Crowley acknowledged that "the courage needed to politically pursue those goals common to all police organizations is not the same courage needed to lay down your life in protection of life and property," but noted that this effort would nevertheless require "time, sweat, and people" if police were to "achieve those rights and benefits traditionally denied fragmented law enforcement groups."[15]

But COPS was not the first statewide effort. When Crowley became the president of the San Francisco Police Officers' Association, there were already eleven statewide police associations, beyond those in individual counties or cities like the one he was now leading. The most militant was the Peace Officers Research Association of California (PORAC), whose name POPAC arrogantly parodied. PORAC began its work by collecting and disseminating information about compensation levels. But it established an office in Sacramento and employed full-time lobbying staff. And it came to represent city police in places like San Diego in their bargaining efforts. When police and firefighters in Vallejo walked out in 1969, for example, striking for five days, a PORAC lawyer helped them to win concessions on standard and overtime pay. The strike was also a "test case" for PORAC. Although Governor Ronald Reagan called the strike illegal, the state's lack of a collective bargaining law created an ambiguity. No penalty resulted, even though a court ordered the strikers back to work. Observers suggested that PORAC resembled the Fraternal Order of Police, which had a much stronger base back east, because it was more aggressive than the other associations. But it also resembled the Fraternal Order of Police by making no clear distinction between command and rank and file.[16]

At first, because of its assistance to militant police officers, Crowley supported PORAC. But he soon began to question how effective the organization was politically, and he began to needle PORAC in the San Francisco Police Officers' Association newsletter. How was PORAC spending its money? Where were the results?

Three crucial bills came before the state legislature in 1973. The first was to concretize collective bargaining rights for police and firefighters statewide, superseding the framework of the 1968 Meyers-Milias-Brown Act, which allowed local jurisdictions to decide whether to grant bargaining rights for public employees. The other bills would abolish police residency requirements and secure statewide retirement benefits for police. When the legislative session came and went without any advances on these issues, Crowley was infuriated. PORAC had achieved nothing. He worked with political fixer John Burton, who was on the verge of leaving the state assembly for a seat in Congress, to help incorporate COPS, dropping the name POPAC.

"The thrust of COPS is ACTION, Political Action," one union official announced. Its agenda included the three stuck pieces of legislation, plus the statewide law enforcement officers' bill of rights. Now Crowley was at the peak of his influence. His association had just signed a new MOU with Mayor Alioto, now promising collective bargaining and binding arbitration for police in San Francisco, along with a grievance procedure—though Crowley still believed these hinged on changes to state law that COPS demanded. The MOU, which contained a strict bill of rights, also enshrined officers' right to engage in off-duty political activity, which enabled Crowley to work for the association full-time, exempting him from patrol duties.[17]

COPS did not immediately gain the buy-in from police across the state that PORAC had enjoyed. But its member organizations included what Bluecoat Paul Chignell called "those extremely active medium and small" associations across the state, rather than the "politically naïve" associations that were "controlled by strong authoritarian chiefs of police." Furthermore, COPS formed to take advantage of a fortuitous moment: every elected official in the state was up for reelection, from the governor to members of Congress to state legislators—and districts had recently been redrawn. New campaign finance laws constraining big donations also leveled the playing field somewhat. The moment was "a historical and monumental opportunity." If COPS did not seize it, Crowley intoned, "our former isolation, our apathy, and our paranoia" would return.[18]

While COPS worked in Sacramento, Crowley urged San Francisco police to register to vote and pay attention to ballot measures. He followed the lessons of Kiernan's International Conference of Police Associations, but he was also studying in multiday seminars on political action organized by Jerry Wurf's AFSCME. These seminars taught the Bluecoats the "finer points of campaigning," including "targeting precincts, voter registration, get out the vote drives, precinct walking," and more.[19]

When speaking on behalf of both COPS and the San Francisco police union, Crowley was blunt. He never failed to make his position clear, even as some union members wondered why he was so focused on statewide issues. Some even found his political involvement unseemly. But he was honest about whether he succeeded or failed. For instance, after the November 1974 election, *San Francisco Policeman* tabulated the results, showing which COPS-endorsed candidates had won. Over 84 percent of the candidates COPS endorsed were successful, including Jerry Brown, who personally thanked Crowley and his second-in-command, association secretary Bill Hemby, for their support. Transparent about his motivations, Crowley trumpeted his results.[20]

In contrast, according to Hemby, PORAC took secret positions behind closed doors. He was shocked to learn that PORAC's lobbyist had interfered with a state legislative survey on police retirement benefits, in order to prevent the legislation from advancing, after PORAC publicly claimed it took no position on the bill. With the machine politician Burton no longer in the state legislature, COPS was unable to maneuver behind the scenes to support the bill, and Hemby was left to call out PORAC's duplicity in public. Soon the noisome Bluecoats were attacking "weak, traditional" PORAC more than any other opponent. It had become "a police disgrace," in the words of Paul Chignell.

COPS was ascendant, securing a lengthy meeting with Governor Brown, attended by Crowley, Hemby, the organization's full-time lobbyist, and other members from Long Beach and Los Angeles. They pressed the governor to support the California law enforcement officers' bill of rights, as well as a new labor relations bill. Crowley and his comrades also advocated crime prevention programs that rank-and-file officers preferred, including restoring foot patrol in California's cities. They wanted control over their working conditions, as well as over police operations themselves.[21]

Ultimately, COPS successfully shepherded the police bill of rights through the state legislature in 1976. According to Chignell, PORAC was inconsequential and clueless in these efforts. When the bill came up for a final vote in the state senate, Chignell could be seen sprinting through the halls of the legislature, rounding up votes. PORAC's chief lobbyist stopped him and asked why he was so frenzied. Chignell told his PORAC counterpart, breathlessly, that this bill that rank-and-file cops were demanding was now up for a vote; the PORAC lobbyist had had no idea. PORAC, Chignell charged, was being "increasingly exposed as a band of incompetents." Despite its apparent initial militancy, PORAC now represented management's interests, unlike COPS. Still, from the outside, COPS and PORAC together seemed to constitute "one of the most potent lobbies in Sacramento." They were able, by decade's end, to see nearly every bill they endorsed through to passage.[22]

The new police bill of rights marked the end of what Chignell called the "days of autocratic, gestapo tactics by certain police administrators," including even the "liberal" and "humanistic" chief of the San Francisco Police Department appointed by Mayor George Moscone in 1975, Charles Gain. The new chief argued that if officers had nothing to hide, they had nothing to fear in internal investigations. That was not good enough for Crowley.[23]

At the state level, COPS notched wins that were proving impossible within San Francisco itself. For instance, the organization endorsed a statewide proposition to eliminate residency requirements for police and other municipal employees. Just a few years earlier, the San Francisco board of supervisors had revised the city's existing residency rule. Whereas cops previously had to live within a thirty-mile radius, this new change required them to reside within the city limits. D'Arcy, Crowley, and Chignell all testified against the change, without success, and the association filed suit.

Though the leaders hoped to convince other city employee unions to sign on, these groups saw no benefit to a rule that would allow members to live outside the jurisdiction. Dianne Feinstein, then president of the San Francisco board of supervisors, the position awarded to the highest vote-getter in the preceding election, similarly opposed eliminating the residency requirement. Unable to gather other plaintiffs, the association eventually dropped the litigation. Other police unions around the country were also challenging residency requirements, including the Detroit Police Officers Association, but success was elusive, especially after the Supreme Court deemed them constitutional in 1976. Many cops chose simply to lie about where they lived. The scrimmage over residency requirements highlighted the peculiar power configuration of police unions: they leveraged a mismatch between their geographic base of support and the site where they wielded their operational power.[24]

After dropping the lawsuit, COPS returned to a familiar Bluecoat tactic: a ballot referendum. Voters across the state supported the COPS-endorsed proposition. Instead of forcing employees to live within city limits, now the law required they live within "a reasonable and specific distance," opening the possibility of future battles over what that distance would be.

If Crowley's Police Officers' Association had been forced to rely on local political influence to win this new regulation, it likely would have failed. But by uniting with police across the state, Crowley was able to command greater support. In Sacramento, he and Chignell "had a friendly politician introduce the bill, testified before committees, twisted politicians' arms, cuddled up to the 'terrible' politicians and got the 2/3 votes of the Senate and Assembly to place the amendment on the ballot." Crowley's position was locally unpopular with voters and other public employee unions but crucial to his members, who were increasingly uninterested in living within the city limits. He would soon learn, however, that Feinstein's direct power over the police department could not be easily circumvented by relying on friends in Sacramento.[25]

The dawn of Blue Power was not a series of unalloyed successes. Nor was it always obvious what tactics would succeed where. The well-timed jump from one scale to another, trading in municipal concerns for state-level power, though powerful, did not solve every problem. Even as the rapid ascent of the Bluecoats gave Crowley great confidence, cities across the country were facing increasingly precarious fiscal situations, San Francisco among them. In the middle of the 1970s, the question municipal leaders would confront was whether it was possible to give everyone what they wanted. Police, however, had a unique capability to pressure elected officials by organizing chaos.

CHAPTER 10

WELCOME TO FEAR CITY

New York was the city that President Gerald Ford told to "drop dead," according to a famous *Daily News* headline. But the city's police played a more active role in its fiscal calamity than the White House. And the city's police budget was a national bellwether: from 1965 to 1972, total expenditures on police had increased 210 percent, with 36 percent of the increase due to inflation but 26 percent due to real increases attributable to union strength and collective bargaining or arbitration awards.[1]

In June 1975, with city hall threatening to lay off 11,000 cops, New York Patrolmen's Benevolent Association president Ken McFeeley orchestrated the "Welcome to Fear City" campaign. McFeeley was a chain-smoking militant elected the prior year as part of an insurgent slate. In response to the layoff threat, he attempted to distribute thousands of pamphlets, *Welcome to Fear City: A Survival Guide to the City of New York*, at Kennedy Airport and bus and train stations. They warned tourists to avoid walking the streets, avoid public transit, avoid leaving Manhattan to travel to the outer boroughs, like the Bronx or Brooklyn, and avoid the dark because the cash-strapped police could provide no protection from burglars, rapists, robbers, and murderers. "Good luck," the pamphlet read, beside a grim reaper's skull. Less of a quisling than McFeeley believed, a furious Mayor Abe Beame obtained a restraining order to block the pamphlet distribution plan.

And Beame did not back down from thinning the police ranks. Ultimately, a bit more than 5,000 cops received a pink slip, effective at 24:00 on June 30. The next day hundreds of young, drunk, off-duty cops occupied the Brooklyn Bridge and brawled with veteran officers who had kept their

The New York City Patrolmen's Benevolent Association stages its "Welcome to Fear City" protest at an airport in June 1975. Wide World Photos, *Police Magazine*, September 1978.

jobs. It was a five-hour rage carnival. McFeeley's goal was not only to prevent layoffs but also to break police-fire pay parity in the city. He failed, and in the process he also shredded a new coalition of police, fire, and other peace officer unions that he had just helped launch. It was supposed to push for bargaining with the city together, but separately from the larger Municipal Labor Committee, which included unions for most of the city's employees. McFeeley lasted less than one term as president of the Patrolmen's Benevolent Association. Facing a disgruntled membership, he resigned early, just a few months after assuring a reporter, "The only way to stop me is to kill me." McFeeley died of lung cancer about a decade later at age forty-seven. He spent the final months of his life recording public service announcements for cops, warning them that cigarettes were more dangerous than assailants' bullets.[2]

The "Fear City" campaign is justifiably remembered as a tense collision of police militancy and fiscal austerity, but in the vast sweep of the history of New York City's 1970s crisis, the episode did not have direct political consequences because of the mayor's firm response. For that reason, it appears a curio, emblematic of a dark moment. In contrast, in San Francisco, the Bluecoats mounted a far more successful campaign to insulate police in a parallel dire fiscal moment. Unlike in New York, on the West Coast police figured out how to calibrate political threat against economic threat.

"DON'T THREATEN US"

San Francisco's financial mess in the summer of 1975 included rising costs and debt burdens, declining tax revenues, bond issuances that elicited no buyers, and little help forthcoming from Washington. But the political situation that summer was even more volatile. The Golden City was facing restive public employee unions while also on the cusp of an election that threatened to end the careers of multiple incumbents. There were eleven members of the board of supervisors. Two were running for mayor, Dianne Feinstein and her conservative nemesis John Barbagelata, trying to succeed the term-limited Joseph Alioto. Six others were also up for reelection. And the tax assessor had just released new property assessments, raising taxes 100 percent on some homeowners.[3]

In this context, San Francisco Police Officers' Association president Jerry Crowley asked simply that police be granted the raise that the laws on the books since 1952 would allow. It was supposed to be 13.05 percent after four years of service, pinned to the pay level of the highest-paid cops in other jurisdictions around the state. Feinstein was in her second term as president of the board of supervisors. Presented with the police raise formula, she said no.

It was the first time that the board rejected the formula raise. Police could not help but notice that the formula raises for tradespeople employed by San Francisco, including gardeners and plumbers, meant they took home more money than cops. And now the supervisors were planning to break the formula. Alioto's second MOU, moreover, promised binding arbitration, but it was not a contract, as Sacramento still had not mandated collective bargaining for unionized public employees. Thus, in the summer of 1975, cops found themselves with little recourse.

Accepting less than the formula raise meant that obtaining other forms of improved compensation would be difficult. "A blessing to City Hall perhaps, but a burden to you for many, many years to come," one Police Officers' Association member warned his colleagues. Angry cops began signaling they were ready to strike if the board of supervisors offered an increase below the formula sum of 13.05 percent. Alioto threatened in response: "Any policeman who strikes will be fired." But over 90 percent of the rank and file were prepared to strike anyway, according to internal data Crowley collected. Milwaukee's Kliesmet summarized the sentiment: "If cities want 'good' cops, they'll have to pay for the privilege. We're through being n——ed."[4]

Alioto claimed the cops were bluffing, though he also offered to mediate the dispute. Chief Donald Scott felt that at least 50 percent of his men would stay on duty, though the Bluecoats taunted him, pointing out that he had no evidence to back up the sunny prediction. Crowley gathered off-duty association members at city hall to respond to the board of supervisors' vote. He warned that if the formula raise was rejected at 2:02 p.m., then "we'll go out at 2:03 p.m." On Monday, August 18, 1975, Dianne Feinstein opened the hearing, and the board quickly voted unanimously, save one abstention, to grant a raise of 6.5 percent, half the formula. No audience member spoke, and no debate preceded the vote. Crowley strode to the rostrum and asked for permission to speak. Feinstein followed the rules. She asked whether anyone on the board would make a motion to recognize the speaker. The room was silent until Feinstein said, simply, "Sorry."

If Crowley was embarrassed to be momentarily cut down to size when Feinstein did not blink, this insult made no difference. The board's salary increase offer made the strike certain. None of the supervisors budged—but neither did Crowley. Officers in the room whooped "Strike!" and "Shut it down!" Soon a picket formed outside city hall, and officers walked out across San Francisco.

Within a few hours, drunken cops were shooting out streetlights. Opportunistic young expropriators smashed and grabbed. Television and newspaper reporters covered incidents like the looting of $10,000 worth of coats from North Beach Leathers and the masked teenagers who robbed patrons at gunpoint at restaurants like The Hippo and the Far East Café. But in the words of one police officer's wife, "The real crime is that this city has for so long kept on its books a pay formula that allows for the POSSIBILITY of a police strike."[5]

At 2 a.m. on the strike's second night, a pipe bomb exploded outside Mayor Alioto's house, severely damaging the door and vestibule. A note left behind referenced Alioto's failed attempts to prevent the strike: "Don't threaten us." Despite the implication, the mayor blamed "that white crowd over in Berkeley," rather than cops, for the bombing. A perfunctory investigation turned up no concrete leads beyond a description of a getaway car. Cops did not seem very interested in getting to the bottom of it.[6]

More than 1,000 of the department's 1,800 officers struck for four days beginning that Monday afternoon. Cops sparred with other cops during the strike. Vandalism at police stations was rampant. Most of the damage was to police vehicles, as well as officers' private vehicles: tires slashed, keys stolen, spark plugs removed, windows shattered, antennas broken. Cops opposed to the strike committed some of this destruction, as well as physical violence. But strikers were behind much of it, focused on patrol and commanding officers who refused to walk out. Somebody even broke into one sergeant's locker and stole his paycheck.[7]

But most of the strike activity consisted of unruly pickets. A judge ordered police not to carry their guns while picketing, but many officers ignored the court order and brandished their weapons. Alioto began to recognize that the police were ungovernable. "Who," he asked, "is going to uphold this order?" Alioto realized he needed to quash this paroxysm. The mayor admitted he could not fire all the striking officers. But he would now have to deal with them. As a lame duck, he was the only person who could or would mediate between the pugnacious Police Officers' Association and the supervisors.[8]

Feinstein looked outward, mindful of the precedent she could set: "Everybody is watching us. Every major city in the U.S. is facing a severe fiscal situation and every city is going to have to learn to say no and make it stick." Privately, she knew that continuing to stand up to the police was not going to make the city more governable, especially if she became mayor. Projecting calm and relying on sensible technocratic solutions got her only so far while business owners were ranting about robberies and looting. She did, however, quietly lead the supervisors in waiving the deadline for new ballot propositions, signaling the steps that would follow the strike's resolution. Almost immediately, Feinstein's conservative rival, Supervisor John Barbagelata, introduced a new proposition to make police and fire strikes illegal, and another to cut the pay formula.[9]

Alioto and Crowley negotiated over the coming days. Robert Gordon of the International Conference of Police Associations joined the negotiations, and via telegram his colleague Ed Kiernan prodded Alioto to concede. On the third day, city firefighters also struck, forcing the San Francisco Airport, among the country's busiest, to conscript emergency "volunteers" from its staff. Air traffic controllers were forced to radio incoming pilots to change course.[10]

At points, Alioto attempted to engage the supervisors. Late on the strike's third night, he convened a meeting to apprise them of the negotiations. Several supervisors were drunkenly rambling and "hysterical." They wanted the governor to intervene, but Alioto refused to sanction any appeal to Jerry Brown. Flabbergasted, according to a reporter, Feinstein declared herself "so angry I can't speak." She had lost her first campaign for mayor against Alioto three years earlier, in part because she was seen as the candidate who would raise taxes. Now, just months before an election he would sit out, Alioto was poised to saddle the city with an expensive wage burden.[11]

On the afternoon of the strike's fourth day, the board rejected a settlement Alioto had crafted with the Police Officers' Association, which included amnesty for striking officers. Enraged, he invoked an obscure emergency power to suspend the board's oversight and unanimously adopt the settlement, including the proposed raise, ending the strike. The board of supervisors became a nonentity. Throughout her career in the city, Feinstein had presented herself as interested in modernizing governance, breaking away from old habits and backroom influences in the city. Her stance would benefit downtown business interests eager for redevelopment. But the strike could not be forced to a conclusion by anything besides raw power, and unlike Alioto, she was not interested in wielding such power publicly. Feinstein's revenge would come later, in cold and calculating technocratic terms, just like her initial assistance to the Bluecoats on Proposition E. First, however, her eyes were on the 1975 mayoral election.[12]

The strike catapulted the campaign of John Barbagelata forward; he blamed Feinstein for it all coming to this. To her left ran George Moscone, a state senator. The victor was the liberal Moscone. In a polarized city, the far-right candidate pulled votes from the centrist, and Feinstein came in third, a humiliating defeat that burnished her commitment to hew to a position between left and right. The trauma stayed with her for years to come—but Blue Power's revenge was only getting started.

POLICE ANTAGONIZING VOTERS

The day after the November election, police engaged in a ticketing blitz. Cops issued three times the normal number of traffic citations, retaliating against voters for supporting Barbagelata's Proposition P to cut police wages. Crowley recognized that angering the public in this way was not a good idea, but he had cultivated a belligerent and reactionary rank and file. They could not be held back. For her part, after the strike, Feinstein led the board of supervisors in rescinding the 1974 MOU, Crowley's crowning achievement in the city. The supervisors' argument was that the police had violated its terms by striking. The police commission made the same argument, to which the association's lawyer replied that the decision should fall to the supervisors. But this attempt to circumvent the commission did not save the agreement. Alioto opposed the cancellation of the MOU, but the supervisors overrode his veto.[13]

Crowley and his association's lawyer quarreled with the police commission after the strike. Washington Garner, the lone African American commissioner, regretted the "many manpower hours" he had "wasted" on the MOU, time that could have been better spent attending to patients—and getting paid—in his career as a doctor. "I think what happened is, our understanding was different" from the association's, he explained, with exasperation. "We understood one thing," but the association reinterpreted that meaning and put it "into whatever form they wanted to put it in." Crowley ultimately returned to uniform duty in December 1975, while the Police Officers' Association bled members, particularly inspectors, many of whom had opposed the strike.[14]

If Moscone's win could not directly be attributed to the strike, Feinstein's loss, as well as the passage of four ballot propositions, signaled that voters were angry. Most importantly, Proposition P rejiggered the police pay formula (as well as pay for other city employees). Whereas cops in San Francisco had previously been paid at the state's highest rate, now the rate would be pegged to a mean of city police salaries across the state. Feinstein had wanted to shrink expenditures, which meant that the Police Officers' Association blamed her, as well as Moscone, rather than the conservative Barbagelata, for the prospect of smaller future raises.[15]

Crowley insisted the labor action had been worth it, but the San Francisco police strike of 1975 marked a turning point. Conservative columnist William Safire called the strike "extortion" and "kidnapping." During the strike, KRON-TV broadcast ongoing public hearings. Outraged homeowners shook their white-haired heads at increasing tax assessments. And the channel's man-on-the-street interviewees blamed "the system" as well as the supervisors, who "won't listen to reason." But unlike the Baltimore strike the prior year, this one soured public opinion. Voters continued to punish the San Francisco police and firefighters in 1976, raising pension contributions and decreasing pension payouts.[16]

California voters, at the vanguard of the Reagan Revolution, were on the brink of joining a tax revolt. San Francisco's voters primed themselves for this posture by years of voting down ballot initiatives for bond sales to improve parks and public schools, particularly in the predominantly Black neighborhood of Hunters Point. In 1978, fueled by disgust at supposed government profligacy, the state's voters passed Proposition 13 three years after Crowley led the walkout, capping property tax rates in the state. The San Francisco police strike lit the match, and the ensuing fire burned public employees for generations to come. In the meantime, with ally Alioto out of office, police in the city confronted the new liberal leadership.[17]

CHAPTER 11

A STRIKE'S AFTERMATH

George Moscone's victory in the 1975 San Francisco mayoral race ushered in an era of reformism within the police department. The liberal chief he hired, Charles Gain, had been in command across the Bay in Oakland. Though Gain was unpopular with the rank and file for his new rules, including a ban on drinking alcohol while in uniform, he had the mayor's support. And the mayor had been elected on a campaign that promised a new era, bringing together disparate activist and ethnic groups into a precarious localist coalition. Different objectives cohabited under the premise of communitarianism and local input. But the police strike introduced an abrasive undercurrent to city politics that would not easily wane.[1]

Bluecoat dissatisfaction with Gain was intense, and police were collectively loath to cede any more ground after their largely unsuccessful strike. Seeking to return the department to its old top-down ways, Gain pressed for reforms and sought to tamp down the insurgency roiling the rank and file. The San Francisco Police Officers' Association reacted by placing television and radio ads highlighting the "devastating" crime rate. Its leaders testified before the board of supervisors against Gain's reformism. Infuriated, the chief complained to reporters about the union's public airing of internal departmental matters. The association shot back that Gain was more concerned about silencing criticism from the rank and file than about addressing crime.[2]

Around this time, sex worker advocate Margo St. James began receiving dishy phone calls from a police officer she had known decades earlier. She called him Joe the Pig. His compulsive phone calls mixed gossip with frightening updates on what was unfolding among the rank and file. During one of his calls in 1977, he explained that right-wing cops were planning to assassinate Chief Gain. St. James dutifully warned the chief, who began taking precautions. Around a year later, Joe the Pig noted that while no attempt on Gain's life had taken place, some of the same cops were now aiming higher, planning to off the mayor, even though his first budget cut the police department much less than the fire department and the arts festival. Again, St. James passed along the intel, and Moscone quietly appointed a bodyguard.[3]

While rank-and-file cops jeered at Moscone in print—"Moscone Must Go," blared one article advocating a voter recall, by Bluecoat Paul Chignell—Crowley's support was evaporating. He ultimately lost reelection as president of the union in 1979. Still, the rank and file could at least count on one of their own on the board of supervisors, Dan White, a former San Francisco cop and firefighter elected in 1977, who told reporters on the campaign trail, "Crime is number one with me."[4]

Also elected that year to the board of supervisors was Harvey Milk, the first openly gay elected official in a city that was home to a growing and increasingly organized and militant gay population. Gay men and lesbians constituted almost a fifth of the city's population by the late 1970s. For many gay men, Milk, a self-identified "gay liberationist" first and foremost, was a hero. But by his own account, his support was "broad-based," including some traditionally conservative labor unions.[5]

Under Chief Gain, the police department began recruiting gay police officers. The goals were two-sided. Gain wanted the department to reflect the community and address the demands of constituents, but he also sought more effective control of the city's raucous nightlife and the rough trade. The San Francisco County sheriff had first pressed for hiring gay deputies in 1972, and by 1979, Bob Barry, who succeeded Crowley as president of the association, was supportive of gay cops, provided they were "qualified to be a police officer" and they didn't "let his or her sexuality get involved in the job." In contrast to the Bluecoats' antidiscrimination stance, neither for nor against recruiting gay officers, the IACP opposed recruitment efforts like Gain's. As long as homosexuality remained unacceptable to the "general public," a spokesman argued, police officers should present what the association considered a morally untarnished public image.[6]

Gain's support for gay cops further discredited him in the eyes of many officers. Even among more liberal cops, most were wary of change. How would rising numbers of uncloseted gay officers change the department? One motorcycle officer grumbled, "I've had to handle enough queers on my job. I feel like they're kind of infiltrating us by working in the Department." Tellingly, after Gain invited gay cops already on the force to come out, for three years none did.[7]

Particularly after a 1976 charter amendment traded at-large elections for a district system, the position of supervisor in a rapidly changing city was a difficult one. Supervisor Quentin Kopp complained about "our own immediate, searing problems." He argued, "We're a city which is now reaping the disadvantages of almost a decade of lassitude in management." While at-large elections had forced supervisors to accommodate diverse interests, the district system pushed officials to focus much more narrowly. What might have appealed to a larger constituency of voters a few years earlier no longer was guaranteed to work in a given district, and vice versa. This new system also made supervisors more vulnerable to police pique, as their responsiveness to crime in a district could make or break a supervisor's electoral viability. Plus, the supervisor position did not pay well. The annual salary was around $9,600, as board duties were considered half-time, though requiring long hours. Feinstein did not have to worry much about money, even after the death of her husband, Bert Feinstein, in 1978. (She later married Richard Blum, a wealthy investor.) Other supervisors had shallower pockets. Dan White, forced to resign his position as a firefighter upon election, took a $30,000 pay cut to become a supervisor.[8]

White was a macho conservative repelled by the growing homosexual population in the city. A key plank in his campaign had been to block the construction of a Catholic psychiatric treatment center for teenagers in his district. But the board approved the plan, overriding the local-control ethos shaping many of its other decisions. He also voted against an ordinance that outlawed discrimination based on sexual preference early in his term, only to watch as it passed anyway. White felt humiliated. The job of legislating required compromise, anathema to his uncompromising persona.[9]

Though no longer a cop, White embodied the all-or-nothing police approach to politics. Without a significant caucus, this approach left him lonely on the board. White soon became withdrawn, either sulking or becoming irate over small matters. He tried to focus on a new business venture, a fast-food stand called Hot Potato, but it only added to his money woes.

After less than a year in office, White decided to resign from the board of supervisors in November 1978, effective immediately. The San Francisco Police Officers' Association, which considered him one of its own, however, was counting on his vote against a prospective settlement in the Officers for Justice discrimination lawsuit. Real estate lobbyists also pressured him to change his mind. His reliable vote was crucial to preserving the slim conservative majority on the board. Quickly, White tried to rescind his resignation. He appeared alongside officials from the police union at a press conference to announce his decision to return. His remarks came across as angry, though he had only himself to blame.[10]

Moscone was willing to welcome White back, but Harvey Milk and other liberals in the city saw White's departure as an opportunity. They urged Moscone to appoint someone more progressive than White, while the city's attorney ruled that the decision was Moscone's alone. White could not force the mayor to act, nor could the other supervisors intervene. Ultimately, Moscone decided not to reappoint White, instead choosing a Filipino community activist who would tilt the board's balance leftward.

On Monday, November 27, as Moscone prepared public remarks announcing his new appointment, Dan White climbed through a city hall window, circumvented a magnetometer, evaded the mayor's security detail, and entered the mayor's chambers. The two talked briefly. Moscone conveyed formally what White had already learned, that he would not be reappointed. The mayor offered White a drink and asked him what he would do next. Instead of answering, White pulled out a .38 revolver and shot Moscone in the chest and shoulder. While the mayor lay on the ground, White shot him twice more, killing him.

White sped out of the mayor's office, with additional bullets jangling in his coat pocket, in search of Harvey Milk. "Harv, can I see you a minute?" White asked Milk when he found him, inviting him into his own office. Milk crossed the hall from his office into White's. The former cop slammed the door behind Milk. The supervisor's last words were "Oh no." White shot him three times in the upper torso and twice in the head. Feinstein heard the first shot and assumed White had killed himself. After the next four, she knew that was not what had transpired. Then she saw White run out of his office.

Almost immediately after the initial commotion, a scrum of reporters appeared. Feinstein, shaking with fright and with Milk's blood on her skirt, decided it was up to her to address the public. With Chief Gain at her side, the ashen supervisor, in a tone that indicated she could barely believe her own words, announced, "As president of the board of supervisors, it is my duty to inform you that both Mayor Moscone and Supervisor Harvey Milk have been shot and killed." Members of the crowd shrieked and gasped. Footage of this announcement would appear in political ads that Feinstein ran for years to come.[11]

White fled. He phoned his wife, who was at Pier 39, where Hot Potato was located. She met up with him, and the two walked to the police department's Northern Station. There, to turn himself in, he sought out Paul Chignell, author of "Moscone Must Go." Chignell was his "close friend," according to Milk's biographer. He was someone "I could trust," White soon remarked, someone who he knew "would do things properly." In the station, White recognized other officers. "I know most of them, I've worked with most of them," he later reported. They frisked him, took the gun and his wallet, and placed him under arrest. A few officers patted him on the back, expressing support and condolences for his predicament. At headquarters, some warned, "Gain's next."[12]

Rather than express regret or contrition about one of their own murdering the most prominent gay man in the city, the department went on the offensive, spending the next six months attacking gay establishments and harassing their patrons. Some officers even raised money for White's defense. Cops hawked "Free Dan White" shirts.[13]

White would eventually be found guilty of voluntary manslaughter on May 21, 1979, after his attorneys argued that he had lost his wits and acted rashly in a moment of passion. A psychiatrist suggested on the stand that White's excessive consumption of junk food contributed to depression and mental instability. Amplified by the press, it was what came to be known as the "Twinkie defense," scrubbing the politics of the assassinations away entirely, erasing the common view that he was a "classic homophobe." Feinstein, called as a witness by the prosecution, confirmed that the job of supervisor was "frustrating" and even indicated that White was not the "type of man that would have shot two people." When the verdict was announced, carrying a maximum sentence of seven years and eight months, police officers sang "Danny Boy" over the radio, rejoicing. The response of gay men and lesbians in San Francisco, who had been subject to increasing police persecution after Moscone and Milk's killing, was different. Rather than celebrating White's conviction, they rose up.

Crowds immediately gathered in the Castro, the neighborhood at the center of gay social life. They chanted, "Out of the bars! Into the streets!" Thousands congregated in front of city hall, which soon became a target for all manner of aerial attacks, as protesters threw uprooted parking meters, garbage cans, and newspaper racks at the building. Gain ordered officers not to disperse the crowd at first, but their patience wore out quickly as chants of "Kill Dan White" and "Dan White, Hitman for the New Right" rippled across the plaza. A progressive supervisor, Carol Ruth Silver, attempting to pacify the crowd, took a rock to the face, receiving a bloody gash. And tear gas that police unleashed floated through broken windows on the first and second floors of city hall, forcing Feinstein to evacuate from her own office.[14]

The "White Night" riots in the verdict's aftermath pitted cops against San Francisco's gay movement and its supporters. According to one movement leader, "they," the police, "started the riot, not us." But police bore the brunt of the damage. As many as sixteen police cars were set alight, while crowds rained rocks on the tactical squads trying to break up their gatherings in front of city hall. Over 100 officers were injured. This retaliation, which combined pent-up fury at intensifying harassment of gay men and lesbians alike, as well as despondence at the seemingly light criminal penalty that White would face, galvanized the city's gay movement. Even after crowds dissipated from the area around city hall, police chased gay San Franciscans in the Castro, far from the melee, deep into the night. Although the movement had lost a unifying leader, its unifying antagonist was clear. "Never again," shouted one spokesman to a crowd as the smoke cleared, "will our people stand by and let Dan White's people rule the day."[15]

The political forces collided that night: the gay movement and the police. "A lot of energy has come out of it," commented transgender punk rock columnist Ginger Coyote, "some good, some bad, but one thing that's clear is that people from all walks of life are willing to fight for justice to be upheld." A flyer soon circulated in the city, raising money for defendants arrested in the riots. It depicted a burning police car and proposed a defense like White's: "Revolution Is the Poor People's Crime of Passion."[16]

Feinstein, two-time loser of mayoral races, was appointed mayor after Moscone's murder, winning a vote among the board of supervisors. The appointment suspended her between the two political forces. The movement proved it was unafraid, though not all agreed with the confrontational approach that exploded on the cathartic night of unrest. The next evening, which would have been Milk's forty-ninth birthday, a more subdued crowd gathered in the Castro. Some mourners wore shirts that read NO VIOLENCE, PLEASE.[17]

The police department was also in turmoil in the aftermath of the unrest. Neither the street violence nor White's killings could diminish the power of the Police Officers' Association. Members voted "no confidence" in Chief Gain; it was an overwhelming sentiment among the rank and file, with 1,081 cops in favor and 22 opposed. Association president Bob Barry demanded that Gain be removed. After antagonizing the city's white police with his support for quotas in the Officers for Justice lawsuit, he had never achieved much popularity among the rank and file. The no-confidence vote helped convince Feinstein to ask Gain to resign after the White Night (only the police commission could fire him), but she specified that the resignation should not be effective until the end of what would have been the full length of Moscone's original term, in January 1980. Thus, he would not be the next mayor's chief. The Police Officers' Association took credit for his removal: "This action was sheer political power."[18]

As Feinstein served out Moscone's term, she and her new husband, Richard Blum, courted Washington. Jimmy Carter visited the city, and Feinstein began her inexorable ascent to the national and even international stages.

She took a trip to China in June 1979, right after the unrest. At home, Feinstein look-alikes were ascending to the stage in gay bars. Dianne Feinstein drag contests were all the rage. They were not exactly complimentary. After the mayor proved unable to rein in police harassment of gay San Franciscans, DUMP DIANNE T-shirts became a frequent sight in the Castro.[19]

Yet Feinstein was still able to win the mayor's race in November 1979, largely due to the gay vote. She defeated a runoff challenge from Quentin Kopp. He had bitterly attacked Feinstein, blaming her for the city's rising crime rate. But the Police Officers' Association backed Feinstein on her promise of a new MOU. Kopp relished campaigning, slinging arrows at Feinstein from dawn to dusk. She, in contrast, hated to campaign. But Feinstein focused her attention on governing, chastened by the White Night. Kopp charged that she was hiding from voters, but she turned the attack back on him, arguing that while she was managing the city, all he was doing was bloviating.

Feinstein also fended off another challenger, Jello Biafra, the caterwauling front man of hardcore punk band Dead Kennedys. The band's first album, *Fresh Fruit for Rotting Vegetables*, would depict a line of burning police cars, a photo taken during the White Night. Biafra's campaign for mayor was mostly a "tongue-in-cheek" stunt, but it had serious undertones. He opened his candidate's statement by arguing against both Kopp's fearmongering about crime and Feinstein's tourist-focused development plans: "I don't want to see San Francisco's spirit muzzled in the name of law and order and tourist dollars." But his supporters believed his campaign was mainly about "embarrassing Dianne."[20]

Biafra's absurdist antics pressed buttons in a city still on edge. When Feinstein orchestrated a photo op that had her pushing a broom to clean up the city streets, Biafra showed up at her house with a vacuum. He called on the city to erect statues of Dan White and supply residents with stones, eggs, and tomatoes to throw at them. He proposed that city workers who lost jobs due to Proposition 13 cuts should be rehired as panhandlers, with city hall garnering a hefty cut. Biafra also suggested that city police officers ought to be elected by voters in the neighborhoods they patrolled, rather than appointed by the commission. Voters could vote "yes" or "no confidence."

In this way, Biafra apotheosized the localist communitarianism that had shaped the city over the previous few years, while also lampooning the Police Officers' Association's no-confidence vote in Chief Gain. Although Feinstein and Kopp commanded the great majority of votes, Biafra came in fourth, with 6,591. His campaign cost around $400.[21]

At the outset of her new term as mayor, Feinstein appointed a new police chief who had worked in the department for twenty-seven years. The Police Officers' Association supported his appointment, grateful that Feinstein had ousted Gain. But after she earned the union's support in November 1979, she balked at signing a new MOU. Each time she recoiled from giving the union what its leaders wanted, usually in the name of walking a centrist line, she turned a ratchet, tensioning the spring powering the union's political demands. She would back away, but the union never backed down.[22]

Harvey Milk would become a national hero to progressive and queer people, lionized in an Oscar-winning film in 2008. For his part, Dan White would also remain a hero in grubbier quarters, such as young Republicans' yearbook captions. Future Fox News nabob Tucker Carlson reported membership in the fictional Dan White Society in 1991.

White's killing of Milk and Moscone is not usually remembered as a story about the history of the police, even less about police political power. Yet after the strike, the assassinations, and the White Night unrest, the Police Officers' Association managed to remain strong, against all odds. Every setback was a foundation for a new campaign, and the association's leaders were tireless. The Officers for Justice lawsuit, which tested the resilience of the Bluecoats' colorblind approach, however, remained to be resolved.

THE PERSISTENCE OF THE OLD REGIME

In the end, the Officers for Justice legal case in San Francisco concluded without much street protest. After the assassinations, Judge Peckham believed he could ease tensions in the city by developing a consent decree and ending the litigation. The Department of Justice had also joined the plaintiffs, threatening to deny San Francisco $21 million in LEAA and revenue-sharing funds. When Washington signed on, it made the case unwinnable in the eyes of the Police Officers' Association. Negotiations among the association and municipal and federal officials over the final terms of the consent decree nevertheless proved arduous. Consent was elusive.[23]

When the parties finally reached an agreement, the consent decree entailed a decade of monitoring for compliance. At least half of new recruits were to be minorities and 20 percent women. Peckham also awarded a settlement of $1.2 million, of which $500,000 was allocated to minority recruitment, testing, and retention. And $400,000 was set aside for paying out individual discrimination suits, though the judge capped the award any claimant could receive at $3,500.

The Police Officers' Association called the consent decree "total capitulation," but it trumpeted its negotiating savvy in rendering the baseline decree as agreeable as possible. The association was able to whittle the required overall proportion of minority police to 45 percent, down from the proposed 60 percent. And, correctly anticipating white flight, it insisted on using 1970 census figures for calculating representative percentages of the population going forward, rather than the data that would be enumerated the next year. The association also managed to retain written exams, though the plaintiffs requested only oral exams.[24]

In support of the Officers for Justice lawsuit, the DOJ rebuked the department as "a safe and hospitable sanctuary for... infantile and often socially destructive racial baiting and harassment of minority officers." A decade after Officers for Justice had formed, pictures of monkeys still appeared on bulletin boards. A dead skunk turned up in the car of an Asian cop. Changing this culture of animosity proved challenging.

The discrimination lawsuit inspired both command and rank-and-file officers to be more aggressive. One Black officer and one Mexican American officer received departmental discipline for criticizing San Francisco police practices as racist, for example. These two members of Officers for Justice then sued after they were formally reprimanded. Unlike with the Brukiewa case in Baltimore, these officers encountered unsympathetic judges. Whereas Eugene Brukiewa, who was white, lambasted his commissioner, these two officers of color criticized police tactics. They even made the same comparison to the Gestapo that the Bluecoats had made in criticizing Chief Gain's internal affairs investigations. But the Ninth Circuit declared that an employee did not have "an unqualified right to abuse his employer in public while remaining on the payroll." It upheld their reprimand. The Supreme Court declined to hear the case. The "Gestapo-like tactics" in question received no further comment.[25]

The San Francisco Police Officers' Association also lashed out at Black critics outside the force. In November 1978, it filed a lawsuit for slander against the NAACP and the local Bayview–Hunters Point Foundation. The suit named the president of the San Francisco chapter of the NAACP, Joseph Hall, who allegedly had declared that "San Francisco police are engaged in a systematic, sadistic and criminal program" in their treatment of Black people in the city. Further, his organization's meetings with the police chief were fruitless because, Hall claimed, the chief "has struck a compromise with the Police Officers Association to protect his men." Although, in point of fact, the association maintained contentious relations with the chief, these statements, the lawsuit charged, would "lower the esteem of the P.O.A. in the eyes of the general public." The association asked for $50 million, $10 million for reputational damage and "hurt feelings," the remainder punitive.[26]

The lawsuit was spurious. Lawyers for the NAACP patiently explained why in motions. Hall even denied using much of the alleged abrasive language. But the association refused to drop the suit. In fact, it consistently extended the litigation through delays, motions, and "dilatory tactics." Lawyers personally recommended that the association drop the suit, as it was unwinnable. The American Civil Liberties Union argued that the "controversy is fundamentally a political one" that had nothing to do with defamation. The association feinted, allowing dismissal documents to be produced, only to withdraw them. In the end, the suit dragged on for seven years, into 1985, until a court of appeals affirmed a summary judgment of dismissal. The "frivolous" lawsuit proved that the Police Officers' Association was willing to engage in a form of sedulous, systematic harassment of Black organizations, trading court filings for batons.[27]

The Police Officers' Association and Officers for Justice remained at loggerheads into the 1980s. Each minute revision to departmental practice within the terms of the consent decree led to a scrum. The association demanded, for example, cutoff scores on exams crafted to exclude Black candidates. Officers for Justice demanded scores that would include them. The organization's Black president, Rodney Williams, remarked that these seemingly small changes "may not mean much on the surface but when you examine it closely it forms a rather ugly picture." The Police Officers' Association continuously revealed itself not to be as colorblind as the Bluecoats had promised.[28]

The association still asked Black cops for their support in the political arena. It put two propositions on the ballot in 1983, one concerning retirement benefits, the other concerning the city's standard salary formula. Officers for Justice officially supported them, as both were likely to benefit Black cops. But it did not throw its weight behind them and organize, whereas the association sent out eight separate direct-mail appeals in support of revising the pay formula. Ultimately, the retirement proposition succeeded, while the pay formula proposition failed. Williams observed, with chagrin, that "Black and minority" districts voted in favor of both propositions. "I believe that the P.O.A. feels that no matter what, third world people will forever support them. And it appears that they may be right." Perhaps these voters recognized that public employment remained a route, however gnarled and winding, to economic stability.[29]

The rocky trajectory of Officers for Justice mirrored the vicissitudes of Black police organizing after the 1960s. An initial burst of militancy and anger over racism on the streets and bigotry in the station house was canalized into narrow and legalistic questions of eligibility in employment law. Bad behavior by white cops never disappeared, and the more general function of policing to maintain the unequal status quo of race and class in American cities remained unchanged. But the battles in court tested the resolve of police unions. Antiracist challenges perfected the machine of Blue Power. Indeed, the Bluecoats originally had claimed that the only thing they desired was fairness. This argument was still just as potent more than a decade after their insurrection began, and it gained coast-to-coast reach in the years ahead as cops fought to channel their bottom-up movement into a single national organization representing Blue Power.

CHAPTER 12

ONE BIG POLICE UNION

Police officers were gaining the upper hand over managerial disciplinary measures. And a national standard was emerging: officers would be protected from departmental punishment, as well as legal proceedings, by union-paid lawyers, counselors, expert witnesses, and other representatives. Yet despite a host of state-level successes, rank-and-file officers still lacked a national organization to coordinate their campaigns and carry them forward to Washington, DC. It was not for lack of trying.

Throughout the 1970s, a small cohort of police unionists harbored hopes that they could construct a single national vehicle for police representation. But the questions were whether and how organized labor should be involved. After all, since 1918, firefighters had been represented by the International Association of Fire Fighters, which AFL president Samuel Gompers helped to charter. (Today, 85 percent of all firefighters are members.) With the AFSCME debacle in Baltimore, police activists concluded that whatever they gained from linking with organized labor, wins could be jeopardized by the expectation that police would support other public sector workers in their own labor struggles. Instead, in the view of Robert Gordon, Ed Kiernan, and Robert Kliesmet, police needed to organize with other police, while finding a way to siphon the resources of the labor movement. They hoped to use the International Conference of Police Associations for this purpose.

Kiernan, a tall and imposing veteran officer and union president from New York City, and Gordon, an eager cop from a small seaside town on Long Island, were unapologetically political. In 1969 and again in 1972, the

International Conference of Police Associations increased its member dues to support lobbying efforts in Washington, trying to wrest legislators' attention back from the managerial voices of the IACP.

Kiernan and Gordon rejuvenated the International Conference of Police Associations' magazine, *The Law Officer*, in 1975. Their first issue bore the cover headline "Police and Politics." The "Political Cop," they insisted, was an idea "whose time has come." Other than politicians, proclaimed Kiernan, no "element" of society was "more inherently politically oriented than police officers." And he believed that legislatures and departments should not restrict off-duty activities of police, including ringing doorbells, driving voters to polls, stuffing envelopes, and joining political rallies.[1]

Yet geography was an obstacle to a unified voice inside and among the different police associations. They were not evenly distributed across the country, and each was loath to give up its home field advantage. The Fraternal Order of Police was largely confined to the Midwest and Northeast, as was the International Conference of Police Associations, which also included some of the feistier groups in California like Crowley's San Francisco Police Officers' Association. The smaller International Brotherhood of Police Officers, in contrast, gained big pockets of membership in the District of Columbia, Florida, and Texas, as well as in New England, where it began. Others were more widely dispersed.

These geographic fractures were a function of even more widespread fragmentation in the profession, which has grown rather than abated over time. Urban and rural forces differ greatly in resources, training, and even responsibilities. City police answer to appointed chiefs or commissioners, while county police often answer to elected sheriffs and typically operate jails. There are also fast-growing federal law enforcement agencies with gargantuan budgets, including Immigration and Customs Enforcement and Customs and Border Protection created in 2003. And special-purpose police agencies have increased massively in recent decades: a local water department, parks department, public school system, university, airport, and train system may all have their own police departments.

The structural impediments to organizational unification of police were significant. Many of these police agencies did have their own benevolent associations, Fraternal Order of Police lodges, or other unions, loosely grouped together in statewide or other conferences, but not typically organized according to the international/regional/local arrangement of the industrial labor unions.

A greater impediment, however, was ideological: most cops hated organized labor. Through the 1970s, after the agonies of unionization in Detroit, Baltimore, San Francisco, and elsewhere, it had become clear that Blue Power appropriated US trade unionism's trinity—dues collection, collectively bargained contracts, and grievance procedures—because of the effectiveness of these tools at winning benefits for cops, not out of any great sympathy with the labor movement.

Once the local pattern for achieving collective bargaining rights was set, police activists like Kiernan and Gordon aimed their sights higher. They believed that national-level success would be within reach only by organizing rank-and-file police into a single sectoral outfit that would mount a unified program in Washington and challenge the dominance of the International Association of Chiefs of Police. Gordon even appeared before the chiefs at their 1975 annual meeting. "Your problems are just beginning," he threatened. "You haven't seen anything yet." Otherwise, cops were doomed to competition, as had occurred in Baltimore—or else mere incremental and local gains. It would require a larger political transformation, and a Democratic president keen to align himself with police interests, to make good on their aspirations. In the meantime, Blue Power's trailblazers would struggle to convince their labor-averse colleagues of what they stood to gain together.[2]

NATIONAL DALLIANCES WITH ORGANIZED LABOR

New York's John Cassese first broached the idea of one big cop union in 1969 when he attempted to create a new National Union of Police Officers by affiliating the International Brotherhood of Police Officers with the AFL-CIO. This ambitious initiative came on the heels of one of his final acts as president of the New York Patrolmen's Benevolent Association, which also involved an attempt to affiliate with the AFL-CIO. The grander plan aimed to unify all police and improve wages and working conditions across the country. It also included a national no-strike pledge. At first, George Meany, the powerful leader of the labor federation, signaled interest and endorsed an exploratory committee.

It was not the first time a proposal for a police union had crossed Meany's desk. A clutch of police unions within AFSCME schemed to form their own international, akin to the International Association of Fire Fighters, in the 1950s. Meany ruled that the decision should fall to a vote within AFSCME. But members declined to advance the proposal.

Meany ultimately backed away from the audacious Cassese proposal. He recognized that the International Brotherhood of Police Officers was "largely a paper organization." Meany was also skeptical that police and organized labor could overcome their history of conflict. He was quoted as saying, "You have been kicking our members' butts on the picket line all these years," bringing the preliminary negotiations to an end.[3]

Skepticism of a shotgun marriage between organized labor and police was not confined to the bigwigs of the labor movement. In traditional homes of powerful labor unions, like Detroit, the police and the major unions were antagonists. In 1969, Parsell's Detroit Police Officers Association joined the Boston Police Patrolmen's Association in opposing the creation of a new national police union after Cassese's initial affiliation scheme. The unions sent letters to police groups in 100 cities urging them not to affiliate. One justification was technical: the AFL-CIO did not favor a police right to strike, though this became moot when AFSCME, under Jerry Wurf's leadership, resolved to drop a no-strike provision for police from its constitution in 1970. Wurf's aggressiveness was a boon to police unions, turning up the heat on municipal governments everywhere at once, even as rank-and-file militancy surpassed Wurf's ability to control it. The other reason Parsell opposed a national union was more directly political: he argued that affiliation with a national organization would weaken a police union's ability to shape local politics and mobilize local constituencies on its behalf.[4]

There was one exception to the rancor and mistrust between police unions and the AFL-CIO: the National Border Patrol Council, representing US Border Patrol agents. It developed a tentative blueprint for national action. Originally an association composed of six regional lodges, it adopted the moniker National Border Patrol Council and became a union in 1965. It affiliated with the American Federation of Government Employees, an AFL member, riding the wave of federal-employee unionization that the Kennedy administration unleashed. The union president in the early 1970s, James R. Dorcy, was proud that most Border Patrol agents—"a majority of whom," he admitted, were "basically not too much in sympathy with the union philosophy"—had signed membership cards within just a few years.[5]

This union's creation coincided with the passage of the Immigration and Nationality Act, which transformed immigration law away from the restrictive, quota-based national origins formula. But, pertinent for the Border Patrol, housed in the Immigration and Naturalization Service, the new law also inaugurated a numerical limit on immigration from Mexico and the rest of Latin America. The National Border Patrol Council obtained recognition by the DOJ two years later, in 1967, to little fanfare or public notice. And unionization initially had little effect on the working conditions for patrollers, which could be highly variable but often difficult due to inhospitable terrain in the desert Southwest. Because of this, the contracts signed by the different locals themselves could vary significantly, a situation that persisted until members ratified a collective bargaining agreement covering all sixteen locals and raising the floor among them—in 2019.[6]

Like other police unions, the National Border Patrol Council first found its voice amid the Nixon-era law and order fervor. It demonstrated to other police unions how to blame its own failures to reduce crime—in this case, "illegal immigration"—on management, even the biggest manager of them all, the president. Nixon's Operation Intercept used the Border Patrol to effectively close the southern US border for several weeks in the early autumn of 1969. This tough-on-drugs ploy strained the organization and put it in the spotlight. Union officials began to argue they had no say in the Border Patrol's mission, which contributed to low morale among agents. Dorcy complained that if a private corporation were run like the Immigration and Naturalization Service, it "would be doomed to early bankruptcy." Policies "shackled" patrollers, and administrators "subverted" operations.[7]

Within a few years, a wide corruption investigation called Operation Clean Sweep focused on the Immigration and Naturalization Service. The National

Border Patrol Council originally supported the investigation, hoping it would reveal agency mismanagement. But after the effort ensnared a number of patrollers, the union's president was disappointed to see the investigation stall. In his view, when it started to indicate that corruption might extend up the bureaucratic hierarchy, Operation Clean Sweep fizzled. "When you work as a law enforcement officer, it is a chore to keep from souring on the world," a veteran of the Border Patrol, Buck Newsome, reflected in a memoir around this time. He believed patrollers acted with honor and courage amid an endless onslaught. "You need a good sense of humor to survive in dealing with the sordid side of life. In the Border Patrol, your customers are plain wetbacks, smugglers, dope peddlers, rapists, murderers, whores, thieves, burglars, procurers, robbers, gunmen, pimps, addicts, drunks, bums, homosexuals, politicians, and every other kind of god-damn riff-raff on earth."[8]

In addition to demanding that more agents be hired to confront this riff-raff, union officials directed their energies to pressing for new legislation that would outlaw or penalize hiring undocumented workers, even if at the municipal or county level, as well as to spreading the word to Republican Party donors about "the silent invasion" occurring at the border, which augured a "fractured culture." Due to "illegal immigration," a union spokesperson cried, it would "take generations" before "a sense of national identity" could be restored. "The laws we enforce are never popular," Dorcy told a House subcommittee, "but we believe our mission is essential to the security and well-being of our country." After retiring from the federal government, Dorcy became a Washington lobbyist for the Federation for American Immigration Reform, an extremist anti-immigrant organization.[9]

Although the Border Patrol primarily operated along the border from Texas to California, with a few northern outposts, it did not yet play a direct role in local politics in borderland towns. Instead, it attempted to infuse the peculiarities of the borderlands into national politics, while turning the local politics of the border into a national issue. As anti-immigrant sentiment coalesced in the ensuing decades, the union would realize that it had already concocted a winning strategy.

In contrast, John Cassese understood the importance of wielding police union power locally. He was the president of the New York City Patrolmen's

Benevolent Association for just over a decade. He ran it in a "highly autocratic" fashion. But Cassese departed this leadership role at the very moment when broader conditions for public sector unionism around the country, and within the city, were changing. Even though cops were tasked with tamping down the insurgencies of the 1960s, they were not immune to them. Whercas Cassese had been able to steer his organization through the turbulence of New York City politics for many years, successors would find themselves tossed by the waves. The first warning came when members rejected the final contract Cassese negotiated in 1968. Linking with organized labor was one way to respond to increasingly unpredictable rank-and-file militancy.[10]

Ed Kiernan succeeded Cassese, and after failing to support a wildcat strike led by young officers in a pay dispute, he faced a rank-and-file rebellion of his own. The strike began in the Bronx, then spread to Manhattan and Brooklyn, ultimately involving 21,000 officers. When union delegates voted to quell the wildcat, rank-and-file strikers attending the meeting focused their ire on the union president, shouting, "Kill Kiernan." The wildcat lasted six days. One Trotskyist faction reported that this cop militancy "symbolizes a change which is occurring in the labor movement."

Officers jeer delegates and President Ed Kiernan of the Patrolmen's Benevolent Association in January 1971 after a wildcat strike. AP Photo/Marty Lederhandler.

Workers' Action, a more incendiary Trotskyist rank-and-file paper, mocked this approval of police militancy. It argued that the strike was "fundamentally an *anti-labor* action," a "*political* strike by a police force that has become dangerously conscious of its social role as the armed defenders of the social system of big business." But, reporting the "Kill Kiernan" exclamations, *Workers' Action* did note that, "frankly, we would not grieve of the loss of Patrolman Kiernan."[11]

The strike caused Kiernan to resign from his leadership post before his term was up, but it also led him to think in nationwide terms about police unionism. While even more militant caucuses like the 3100 Club and Patrolmen's Rank & File formed in the benevolent association, Kiernan followed in Cassese's footsteps onto the national stage.

THE FRACTIOUS FRATERNAL ORDER OF POLICE

As president of the International Conference of Police Associations, Kiernan joined a picket of a Chicago hotel where the National Conference of Legislators was meeting. The demonstrators' demand was collective bargaining for police across the country, as well as in the Windy City. Although some Chicago cops joined the picket, the local district commander ordered arrests of anyone demonstrating in front of the hotel itself. Kiernan and a Chicago police union organizer, plus three cops from Kliesmet's Milwaukee police union, disobeyed police orders and ended up in the clink. They were charged with disorderly conduct and traffic violations. The ranking officer displayed "hostility and hysteria" when he refused to let the arrestees out on bail until they cleaned up cigarette butts on the floor of the police station, after holding them for five hours without Mirandizing them. He treated the picketing cops like common reds. Isolated pickets could go only so far, especially with police still antagonistic toward the tactical bread and butter of labor unions.[12]

Even the chiefs, who had overcome divisions of their own decades earlier, recognized that there would be some value in rank-and-file cops minimizing divisions. The IACP tried to forge some commonalities among the Fraternal Order of Police and independent benevolent associations by issuing standard contract language and recommending negotiating standards. They recognized that fully taming the insurgency seemed impossible, but these guidelines could ease the difficulties police chiefs faced. Tempestuous relationships among police associations nevertheless persisted. As a result, one observer noted in 1978 that police unionism still did not have much of a consistent voice in Congress or even many state legislatures. Instead, a journalist confirmed that the "most audible national voice in the police field" remained "that of a management organization," the IACP.[13]

The fractious Fraternal Order of Police was the main contender that the International Conference of Police Associations faced in vying for national leadership among police. The Fraternal Order of Police nevertheless branded itself as the "only national police organization," and it often behaved as if it represented all the nation's rank-and-file cops. But its bylaws forbade joining or being "controlled by" a labor union. It was the greatest institutional obstacle to a national labor union for police.[14]

From 1965 to 1975, the Fraternal Order of Police's president, John Harrington, was ruthless, boisterously complaining about slights, such as when Nixon's attorney general, John Mitchell, failed to invite him to a gathering of police leaders. He also flexed organizational muscle, bringing 3,500 officers to rally on the steps of the Capitol in 1970 to denounce the Black Panther Party and American Civil Liberties Union for promoting violence against police and the Supreme Court for coddling criminals. A year later, he returned, bringing over 6,000 officers to demand greater federal investment from "an administration which cried law and order so loudly."[15]

Kiernan and Gordon, as president and secretary-treasurer, respectively, of the International Conference of Police Associations, had the good sense to play nice in public with figures like Harrington, including by sharing endorsements of legislation, like a bill to make assaulting a cop a federal offense. The two international conference officials had much to gain from sharing the stage with the Fraternal Order of Police; Harrington had little to lose. When one of Harrington's main rivals on the Fraternal Order of Police's executive board once tried to humiliate him by falsely claiming Harrington wanted to merge the fraternal order with the International Conference of Police Associations, Harrington maneuvered to consolidate his power and eliminate any rival from the board.[16]

Police rally on the steps of the Capitol in October 1970. *U.S. News & World Report* Magazine Collection, Prints & Photographs Division, Library of Congress, LC-U9-22342, f 8A.

Kiernan was careful to distinguish his International Conference of Police Associations from the Fraternal Order of Police, particularly after he took up Cassese's interest in affiliating with the AFL-CIO, over the objection of some longtime members. "The Fraternal Order of Police," he remarked, "is an association of individuals," while "the Conference is an association of Associations." The distinction was important because although police associations could poll their members on affiliation with a particular union, the associations themselves would have a single vote, making it seemingly easier for Kiernan to press ahead. Yet Kiernan's opponents in the conference, including Detroit's Carl Parsell, worked with Harrington to form a Joint Council that was in favor of uniting and professionalizing police officers in the United States and Canada but took a neutral position on labor unions, neither for nor against.[17]

Harrington and Kiernan came together to meet with President Nixon in the Oval Office in September 1972, during his reelection campaign. It was not the cantankerous Harrington's first trip to the White House; Kiernan, in contrast, had never visited officially. Still, despite Harrington's previous meetings with Lyndon Johnson and Vice Presidents Hubert Humphrey and Spiro Agnew, the Fraternal Order of Police had endorsed the segregationist third-party candidate George Wallace in the prior election, causing the immediate resignation of 600 Black Fraternal Order of Police members. In 1972, both the Fraternal Order of Police and the International Conference of Police Associations endorsed Nixon. Presidential endorsements, however, meant little at the bargaining table. And without engaging in union activities, Kiernan's group could not justify big membership fees, forcing it to raise money by writing LEAA grants and selling children's booklets like *My Daddy Is a Policeman*.[18]

THE INTIMIDATING INTERNATIONAL BROTHERHOOD OF TEAMSTERS

Besides the AFL-CIO, the main suitor for labor-curious police was the International Brotherhood of Teamsters. When the AFL expelled them in 1958, Teamsters president Jimmy Hoffa announced he would organize the police next. He mounted a tentative campaign in New York City, but the commissioner stopped it in its tracks. Polling showed low public support for the campaign, and the commissioner argued that Hoffa's unionization proposal, particularly its grievance procedure, would undermine discipline among police and lead to corruption.[19]

Legislators in a dozen statehouses and Congress quickly threatened to ban Teamster representation of police. They feared that Hoffa's alleged ties to organized crime would undermine the integrity of police departments. Hoffa retreated, grousing he wished he had never raised the issue. The Teamsters did accrue as many as 15,000 police as members by the late 1970s. But police unions did not need to be linked to any mobbed-up labor shop to indulge in the territorialism, backslapping seniority structures, and kickback-laden investment practices that had come to pervade the labor movement. If organized labor largely capitulated to undemocratic anticommunism beginning with the first red scare, cops were eager adherents.[20]

Beyond corruption, criminologists and police administrators fretted that amalgamating cops with the traditional labor movement could put police in a difficult spot. Even police unionists worried. The president of the Ohio Union of Patrolmen Associations argued that it was "absolutely inevitable" that police would someday "confront a picket line of Teamsters." Membership in the same union would cause problems for the police trying to quell labor unrest. He mused, "The Teamsters would say, 'Hey, you can't do that to us. We're your union brothers!'" This police leader believed cops should express solidarity with other cops first and foremost.[21]

But these fears of labor solidarity were misplaced. More than actual membership in the International Brotherhood, the threat of affiliation or even of taking advice from the Teamsters proved to be a valuable tool for police. They used it either to get to the negotiating table or as leverage once seated around the table. As one FBI special agent tasked with analyzing police labor relations noted, affiliation with a powerful labor union could be intimidating. These organizations had copious bargaining experience to share, as well as financial resources, accrued through steep dues. Even when independent police unions had no intention of affiliating with the Teamsters, lest their local power be diluted, union leaders could unnerve city officials by claiming that these organizations were sniffing around.[22]

Cops in St. Petersburg, Florida, for instance, were able to convince the city's stone-faced negotiators to budge by threatening to join the Teamsters in 1977. The threat was effective because the Teamsters had a reputation for both uncompromising negotiating strategies and a tendency not to play by the rules. But it was not clear the Teamsters were much interested in deepening their ties to police, other than as a public relations effort. Cop unions got headlines, which could benefit the other sectors the Teamsters represented. Carl Parsell, a police union militant who opposed organized labor, was cynical about the Teamsters in particular. He believed they were using police to slither toward the larger prize of the other public sector workers who were likely to join the AFL-CIO otherwise. But every police union election held a potential reward. After San Diego police did elect to join the Teamsters, some cops were surprised that the dues were around twice what the standard-bearing San Francisco Police Officers'

Association levied. They soon moved to sever ties with the International Brotherhood.[23]

THE VOICE OF CONCERNED POLICE

Navigating this difficult terrain in the middle of the decade, Kiernan and Gordon took up the task of trying to increase the reach of the International Conference of Police Associations. They believed it could become "The One Voice" of "concerned" police across the country, heard in statehouses and also able, when needed, to "shake every chandelier on Capitol Hill." To convince cops to join, they first exaggerated their own influence. Kiernan claimed that elected officials in Washington listened primarily to their organization, not others, now recognizing that "the police of the United States are no longer a splintered body seeking a head." In fact, he crowed, by 1976, the "head" was now the International Conference of Police Associations.[24]

The organization set up a subsidiary called the Interested Committee on Political Action (adopting the same initials). It would be funded separately from the association's dues to avoid running afoul of campaign laws. San Francisco's Jerry Crowley chaired it initially. And the association assiduously recorded in its magazine how each member of Congress voted on legislation, such as a bill to provide emergency assistance to cities that had to lay off police due to budget cuts. (It passed the House but snagged in a Senate committee.) Crowley had previously urged cops to create a quid pro quo relationship with elected officials: help get them elected, then get something in return. Now, in the election year of 1976, Crowley's "dream came true." The International Conference of Police Associations sponsored a national convention specifically focused on endorsing candidates for federal office. It took place in Chicago in October, coordinated by Crowley, Kliesmet, and a few other police union heads. Fewer than 200 police from thirteen states attended, revealing the organization's limited geographic reach. Neither President Ford nor candidate Jimmy Carter attended. Both sent messages of regret and best wishes, as did Carter's running mate, Walter Mondale. The convention endorsed Ford almost three to one. He lost in November. But around 85 percent of the 200 House and Senate candidates these police endorsed won. The majority were Democrats, mostly in the Midwest and

Northeast, as well as California. The organization did not have much reach across the Sunbelt, the New Right's incubator.[25]

These political endorsements did not reap immediate benefits. No significant bills pertaining to police advanced in the Ninety-Fifth Congress. With competition among police organizations persisting rather than diminishing, it seemed that a single organization for all cops was infeasible. Kiernan and Gordon needed a different type of leverage. Linking the International Conference of Police Associations with organized labor seemed to be the best way to expand police political power.

In 1979, when the conference was at its greatest size, purportedly with 175,000 members, Kiernan and Gordon tied its fortunes to the AFL-CIO. Although, as a journalist observed, Kiernan "used to swing a club in the same neighborhood where his friend Meany once swung a plumber's monkey wrench," the AFL-CIO affiliation for cops finally became a reality only as George Meany was facing retirement. The conference had the support of his longtime right-hand man and replacement, Lane Kirkland, who was also to Meany's right politically, notoriously supporting the US war in Vietnam. Many police officers in the conference, however, objected to joining with organized labor. Kiernan himself cast the deciding executive vote in favor, leading members to object on substantive and procedural grounds. Kiernan believed affiliation with the AFL-CIO but independence as its cop-only shop to be a compromise between joining a union like AFSCME that had nonpolice members and remaining fully independent of organized labor like the benevolent associations.[26]

Robert Gordon insisted affiliation would lead to significant growth in the number of police organizations under the International Conference of Police Associations umbrella. But several associations immediately pulled out. Others threatened to quit. Some were bound by state law prohibiting police from affiliating with outside unions, which the association could not control.

A few public sector labor leaders within the AFL-CIO hoped affiliation by police might help tame continual police job actions. Public employees had unjustly earned a reputation for rampant work stoppages, though police were primarily to blame, argued George Hardy, president of the Service

Employees International Union. In several cities, police had begun trying to wriggle out of the rules and guidelines set by civil service commissions, and labor councils were fracturing, as police tried to ride the rising tide of public sector militancy but remain unaffected by its ebb.[27]

After the initial close vote to affiliate, the International Conference of Police Associations needed to raise money to convince the AFL-CIO it was serious. The only way was to increase individual membership dues. They would quadruple to $12, with $2.67 of the new revenue going to the AFL-CIO. But members had to approve such an increase, and Kiernan failed to rally the votes. Hailing from labor-heavy New York, Kiernan and Gordon had misjudged the profession's interest in organized labor nationally. They resigned, initiating the organization's dissolution.

The very same day, Kiernan created the rump International Union of Police Associations. It had one-third the number of members but pursued active ties to the labor movement. Some police unions carried their membership over from the old organization to this new one, like the San Francisco Police Officers' Association. Kliesmet's Milwaukee Police Association was among the first to newly join the organization. But, signaling low enthusiasm, the turnout among Milwaukee cops was pathetic. Only 270 members of the 1,800-member unit approved the new affiliation; 139 voted against it. The International Union of Police Associations, chartered as an AFL-CIO member, then held its first annual meeting in San Francisco in July 1979. Bluecoat leader Jerry Crowley and his successor Bob Barry joined Governor Brown, entertainer Ed McMahon, Kiernan, and Gordon on the stage to celebrate this new organization.[28]

But most police organizations that supported the avowedly politicized orientation of the International Conference of Police Associations did not support or desire affiliation with organized labor—they disdained it. Thus, the two-thirds of the organization's membership who wanted independence from the labor movement formed the new National Association of Police Organizations when Kiernan created the International Union of Police Associations. Detroit Police Officers Association vice president Robert Scully suggested this new outfit would "become what the ICPA was supposed to be." He was elected the organization's president in 1983 and later became its executive director. The philosophy behind the National Association of Police Organizations was to leave collective bargaining to state and municipal outfits, while focusing its lobbying and public relations efforts on Congress. Kiernan's flamboyant efforts to get himself arrested on picket lines and Gordon's appearances in negotiating sessions of member unions had no place in this new organization. Instead, it mostly used its bargain-rate membership dues to pay a professional Washington lobbyist. The National Association of Police Organizations initially had no office or employees of its own, relying instead on volunteers.[29]

Kiernan, Gordon, and Kliesmet were proud to lobby directly in Washington, as cops, rather than hiring specialists. And they took credit for any and every legislative initiative that they had advocated. From the outset, the International Union of Police Associations supported bills sponsored in Congress by legislators on both sides of the aisle. Mario Biaggi's law enforcement officers' bill of rights remained a perennial goal, along with further expanding death benefits and changing tax regulations on police retirement benefits. They had long demanded that Congress pass a law specifically guaranteeing police a right to bargain collectively. The union also backed the creation of the Federal Protective Service, a bill sponsored by Baltimore's Black congressman Parren Mitchell, whose working-class constituents stood to benefit from new sources of federal employment. The organization also supported a bill introduced by Ohio Republican Tennyson Guyer, a former circus clown later called the "King of Corn" by his constituents, that would outlaw federal enforcement of racial quotas in employment. But the International Union of Police Associations could not claim many substantive victories for its members. The bill of rights and the collective bargaining bill stalled.[30]

In the end, rather than coalescing into a national police union movement, cops ended the decade even more fragmented than they had begun it. And the most right-wing outfit of the bunch, the Fraternal Order of Police, continued to claim the greatest number of members nationally. It recognized that solidarity among cops was a rhetorical device, a cudgel. Solidarity did not extend to material issues like standardizing compensation. Fear of the local ceiling falling outweighed interest in raising the national floor. As the president of New York City's Sergeants Benevolent Association observed, "Although police officers in California may respond emotionally to attacks upon officers in Ohio," they were unlikely "to cast their lot with the other officers where the determination of wages, hours and working conditions is concerned."[31]

The Fraternal Order of Police's consistent pledges that it was not a labor union, as well as its decentralized structure, allowed lodges to engage in behavior that affiliates of organized labor would rarely tolerate. In Washington, DC, in 1981, the Fraternal Order of Police raided the rank and file, which had chosen to link with the International Brotherhood of Police Officers after the city obtained home rule in late 1973. The local had recently won a contract with raises of 20 percent over three years, improving on a far inferior previous agreement. The improved contract relied on the union's connections to experienced negotiators. But the local also maintained close ties to Marion Barry, the veteran civil rights activist who had been elected mayor. Around half the local's members were African American cops, matching the department as a whole. The Fraternal Order of Police, in contrast, was mostly white. Its leaders hated Barry, and its main operation, the union claimed, was a "sleazy," white-only bar. Nevertheless, the Fraternal Order of Police won in a high-turnout election, replacing the union local as the bargaining agent for the Metropolitan Police Department. As late as 2019, the Washington, DC, Fraternal Order of Police lodge was still funding itself through liquor sales, now online, in violation of federal law.[32]

John Cassese, who had jump-started the campaign for a national police union, turned back to the local scene he knew best after several years of frustration while organizing on a grander scale. He returned to New York's Patrolmen's Benevolent Association in 1975, where he spearheaded a political education committee, teaching cops how to identify allies and enemies among elected officials. But no matter how politically engaged it became, the Patrolmen's Benevolent Association was struggling to maintain cohesion. Over 2,800 detectives fled in 1979, saving each one $100 annually in dues.[33]

Some cops still sought the formal counsel of organized labor. The International Brotherhood of Police Officers affiliated with the National Alliance of

Government Employees. Then the Service Employees International Union, a massive member of the AFL-CIO, absorbed this public employee union in 1983, though it retained its nominal independence. Kiernan, in a bid to expand his International Union of Police Associations, then proposed merging with the International Brotherhood of Police Officers. But because the latter was now part of the Service Employees International Union, the goal of maintaining a police-only union would be negated. Kiernan's old buddy Bob Kliesmet threatened to remove the diehard Milwaukee Police Association from the organization. As research director for the International Union of Police Associations, he felt that promises of independence from the Service Employees International Union were "snake oil." Kiernan's argument all along had been that "cops ought to be with cops." Now, desperate to expand the organization and fund a staff, lobbyists, and office space, he reneged. In the end, this merger never took place, and Kliesmet went on to succeed Kiernan as president of the International Union of Police Associations. In the meantime, the San Francisco Police Officers' Association, whose Bluecoat militancy Kiernan had helped shape and prod, left the union, accusing Kiernan of mismanagement.[34]

Kliesmet never dispensed with the dream of a single national police union. He believed that membership in the AFL-CIO was key, due to its contacts and its "clout." Unlike Kiernan, he was less interested in maintaining staff, lobbyists, and office space independent of the AFL-CIO's, which cut costs and streamlined the operation. But the union hemorrhaged members, and Kliesmet could not convince AFL-CIO member unions to stop competing to sign up new police shops, nor to release existing shops to his union.

Conflicts between Milwaukee's domineering chief, Harold Breier, and its police union helped Kliesmet hone a pugnacious attitude. And he could not let it go, even after he was arrested and fired from the department for what he considered union activities (overturned on appeal). This aggressive approach characterized so many would-be national leaders of police and caused endless factionalism and bickering in the profession throughout the period of ascendant Blue Power. In the mid-1980s, Kliesmet was keeping alive Kiernan's old beef with the Fraternal Order of Police, saying that it "leeched off of organized labor." Moreover, "that whole bunch of crap about being professional that the FOP spits out," he remarked, "I'm just not impressed by it." But working with the AFL-CIO meant that, as president, now he was faced with the question of the relationship between the International Union of Police Associations and other public employees in the federation. Merger possibilities with the American Federation of Government Employees, AFSCME, or the International Brotherhood of Police Officers remained on the table, and he had to entertain them. By 1985, his deteriorating outfit's membership had dwindled to 13,000, about 587,000 officers short of representing the entire nation's men and women in blue.[35]

Kliesmet finally resigned from the leadership of the International Union of Police Associations in 1995. The National Association of Police Organizations grew and thrived while his organization withered. Kliesmet pivoted away from organizing to begin an intellectual collaboration with researcher George L. Kelling. They wrote about how police unionism might improve the profession from below. Kliesmet thus continued to reject top-down professionalization and reform efforts. But he and Kelling also downplayed the evidence that unions were uninterested in progressing "beyond their traditional concerns" to "develop enthusiasm for improving the quality of American policing." At the international union, Kliesmet successor, who remains president of the organization to this day, was Sam A. Cabral, a detective from an Ohio town called Defiance. Where else?[36]

In practice, the International Union of Police Associations, as the one cop-only union within the AFL-CIO, chose to remain largely separate from the wider labor movement, drawing on its resources and expertise but dodging any accountability to organized labor more generally. That accountability and solidarity also largely elude the other AFL-CIO locals that today represent cops alongside many other types of workers, including AFSCME. Police participation in these other unions presses them to take more conservative positions, meaning police often benefit from their membership more than other union members do. And the International Union of Police Associations today is as likely to raise money via telemarketing through its offshoot the National Police and Troopers Association as from dues-paying members.[37]

The IACP, a management organization, the National Sheriffs' Association, another management organization, and the Fraternal Order of Police, which combines management and rank and file, would remain the most influential police associations in years to come. None is a labor union by tax designation or even has any ties to organized labor. Yet each represents a different strain of police politics, with the IACP on the center right, the National Sheriffs' Association on the far right, and the Fraternal Order of Police somewhere in between the two, though it is so decentralized by design that its Grand Lodge has little say over its local lodges. It is unlikely a national police union could have pushed police politics leftward, but the zero-sum approach that police have taken toward politics and especially toward municipal expenditures has resulted in police sacrificing potential allies rather than engaging in solidarity with them.

The first decade of rank-and-file rebellion would end without a single national vehicle for Blue Power. Yet at the local level, police were gaining the benefits and protections of collectively bargained contracts, despite the strains on fiscal capacity in many locales that characterized the 1970s. Without any centralized control or democratic mechanisms for input from officers at the national level, media-savvy entrepreneurs like Kliesmet were able to dominate conversations about law enforcement without being held responsible for the lack of significant advances for cops in Congress. Blue Power's approach was, by default, acephalous.

Kiernan and Gordon's instruction that cops should get involved politically would obtain everywhere. The question was what would result from activists in any and every police department across the country seizing the opportunity to prod the limits of their collectively bargained protections.

CHAPTER 13

GRIEVANCES, ARBITRATORS, AND MORE GRIEVANCES

In Washington, DC, in 1976, a Metropolitan Police Department helicopter careened onto a tree-lined residential street in the nation's capital. The pilot survived but lost his job when the brass determined that his negligence had led the Bell 47 to run out of fuel, causing the crash. When a vacancy in the Helicopter Branch later opened, the former pilot reapplied but was not selected. With the help of the International Brotherhood of Police Officers, he filed a grievance. Because the department did not choose him for the vacant position, he argued, it was imposing an additional disciplinary measure. Although the city's lawyers believed it was well within the police department's rights to "forever" exclude a pilot who had already crashed a helicopter, an arbitrator ruled in the officer's favor, against the city, compelling the department to create a new selection process and eligibility list for the vacancy.[1]

A news story like this one—"Police Pilot Must Be Considered for New Position Despite Crash," read the headline—could provoke a head shake or a cynical guffaw. But it was not an isolated incident. During the 1970s and into the 1980s, officers were chalking up surprising wins against their own departments, overriding their chiefs. The fervor for law and order among the broader public may have been abating, heard now less often during political campaigns, but police power was only growing.

The era of the omnipotent, imperious police chief who adjudicated grievances, instituted disciplinary measures, and controlled promotions was waning. Instead, new tools to disperse these decisions were emerging, crafted for each department's legal and bureaucratic ecosystem. Power was relocated from the chief's hands. The facts of each decision were unique, but the methods for winning change were similar, as police unions joined the rest of the labor movement in relying on third-party grievance arbitration to enforce contract terms and adjudicate whether disciplinary measures were taken for "just cause." Together, these pointillist achievements by individual police unions decisively transformed power relations within police departments—and between police and the American public. Stepping back, a pattern of rank-and-file cops gaining the upper hand was emerging even as police struggled to create a cohesive national-level organization that could advance a single Blue Power strategy.

Police unions that relied on third-party arbitration to referee grievances or "rights disputes" started to find positive results for officers. Because complaints against officers often emerged from outside departments, including from legislators or other powerbrokers, but could also arise through internal investigations, disciplinary processes were complex and tended to result in grievances. Chiefs often made decisions under political pressure, without regard to contract stipulations. With union aid, officers demanded due process in disciplinary investigations and appealed penalties they claimed were unfairly harsh, improperly or unequally applied, or otherwise unjust.

Arbitration successes frequently offered protections for police officers who engaged in bad behavior based on the premise that rules had to be enforced equally and in accordance with the contract. If an arbitrator found that the standard of "just cause" was not reached, overturning a decision or reducing a penalty was likely. To many outside observers, these decisions seemed to enshrine impunity.

But arbitration decisions additionally set precedents, including simply the precedent that arbitrators, not police management, should review and then decide whether a cop could be disciplined, and how. Police quickly found that arbitrators and courts often sided with union members, against unilateral decision-making by management, in part because they deployed their resources to press the most egregious cases of maladministration. The more police used arbitration, the more they accumulated precedents that guided statewide officer associations, as independent bargaining units within them weakened disciplinary processes and won improved protections for cops.[2]

In some cases, arbitrators confirmed that police malfeasance and abuse had occurred, but they rejected the disciplinary measures that departments chose. For instance, an officer who physically struck detainees should not have been fired, according to one arbitrator, because although he had used excessive force and abused his discretion, he had an otherwise unblemished record. Instead of termination, the arbitrator recommended reinstatement and "progressive discipline," meaning a "corrective and educational opportunity." It might allow him to resume his good behavior and help discourage others from "overreacting so quickly in the future." Arbitrators were eager to factor officers' records into their evaluation of punishment, ruling that first offenses should not result in severe reprimands. But punitive measures and disciplinary records often were new routines. Departments had long ignored misbehavior, and they were now rushing to rein it in. Yet years of turning a blind eye meant that factoring in misreported prior behavior necessarily lessened punishment.[3]

The distinction between departmental discipline and criminal punishment became fodder for numerous arbitrators' decisions. In rural northwest Michigan, a sheriff's office discovered during a stakeout that a thief regularly siphoning off the county's supply of gasoline was one of its own deputies. The sheriff held off on disciplining him because he was charged with a criminal count of larceny. But at trial he was acquitted. The sheriff then fired him. His union, a Teamsters local, filed a grievance, but an arbitrator ruled that he could still be discharged. It also ruled, however, that the sheriff should not have waited until the outcome of the criminal trial. The arbitrator awarded the thieving deputy four months of back pay due to the delay in the boss's decision to fire him. The guideline here was simple: departmental discipline and criminal punishment were separate and independent. In fact, the arbitrator cautioned that criminal conviction need not guarantee discipline, while departmental discipline could be applied without any criminal offense occurring.[4]

Arbitrators aided officers in other ways amid the rapid labor relations changes affecting the police profession in the 1970s. Even as many white police were cool toward antidiscrimination measures, arbitrators were finding that imposing physical fitness standards violated contracts. One of the ways that women and Latino and Asian men experienced more hidden barriers to police employment was through fitness standards, including height minimums. In many cities, San Francisco among them, to remove discriminatory hurdles, these standards had to be modified or removed. Yet unions rarely asked arbitrators to intervene in these situations; cases originated with affected candidates. Still, outside of cases that edged toward discrimination against protected classes of people, arbitrators protected individual cops. One department in a small town in Connecticut suspended an officer who weighed 339 pounds, more than 100 pounds over his weight when he was hired. Although he tried to slim down, he could not, and he was removed from the streets. Yet after a grievance, the arbitrator determined that, given his stellar record and his good-faith effort to comply with the department's prod to begin dieting, the officer was to be reinstated.[5]

Small grievance decisions could also affect officer compensation. A canine officer in a suburb of Detroit received extra compensatory hours as well as some money for the extra duties that caring for the dog entailed. The town's union contract stipulated these conditions. But when the police dog required an emergency visit to the veterinarian, the handler requested time-and-a-half overtime payment for this excursion. City hall balked at paying him extra, and he filed a grievance, with the union also demanding punitive damages. The arbitrator ruled in the officer's favor, awarding the overtime payment, but rejecting the punitive award. In this case, the city's interest in the dog's health was the arbitrator's primary concern, deciding that overtime costs were worthwhile if they would ensure that the dog received the care it required. The judiciousness of the arbitrator still redounded in the officer's favor.[6]

Even as arbitrators across the country were deciding in favor of the rank and file in grievances, police administrators attempted to maintain their own discretion and authority, and chiefs sometimes managed to claw back some power through arbitration decisions. The tug-of-war over the scope of contracts was constant. For instance, an arbitrator in Toledo, Ohio, determined that traffic officers could be punished if they refused to follow a command order to increase the number of citations they issued as the city grappled with a rash of fatal crashes. The union contract in Toledo contained a "management rights" clause, which allowed commanders to implement changes to police tactics. The arbitrator rejected the argument that such changes should be decided at the bargaining table; he also disagreed with the claim, designed to embarrass police commanders, that increased enforcement amounted to a ticket quota.[7]

STILL CATCHING THE BLUE FLU

In addition to relying on third-party arbitration to resolve grievances, as all unions do, in the 1970s police unions also began to take advantage of third-party "interest" arbitration for setting the terms of a contract when the union and representatives of the government could not agree on what it should contain. Throughout the public sector, when an impasse arose during negotiations, arbitrators would evaluate the situation and determine a plan that would bind both the union and the governing officials (or departmental leadership). Only one state had a compulsory arbitration law on the books in 1965. By 1978, at least seventeen did. These provisions were separate from those in contracts for arbitration when officers wished to challenge management's disciplinary authority.[8]

For its part, the International Conference of Police Associations favored interest arbitration clauses as a way of neutralizing "anti-union" mayors who might reject the results of collective bargaining. And lawmakers approved of binding arbitration in principle because it promised to curb strikes and lockouts, but the consequences for municipal budgets could be ruinous.[9]

Cities with aggressive police unions, particularly ones that had already engaged in a blue flu or other illegal job action, were more likely to institute arbitration policies, as legislators hoped to pacify, or at least mollify, Blue Power. Detroit mayor Coleman Young came to rue his prior support for binding arbitration as a state senator when, from 1977 to 1981, arbitration decisions led police and fire salaries to increase by 36 percent, as compared to an increase of 13 percent for other city employees. This major bump led to a budget shortfall of $132 million, of which $80 million was attributable to arbitration awards for Detroit cops and firefighters. Ballooning compensation led to insolvency. It only worsened as the police union used its power to impede capital spending projects that city leaders believed would rejuvenate the local economy. In the unironic words of the president of the Detroit Police Officers Association, the city was "operating on a Cadillac budget when it should have been a Chevy."[10]

When negotiations, grievances, or even interest arbitration did not go the way rank-and-file officers desired, they were often perfectly willing to disrupt operations in response. Some officer resistance to command looked more like juvenile pranks, like the southern Brooklyn precinct house where the chairs kept going missing from the captain's office. Others amounted to convoluted workarounds to skirt the law—for instance, when officers claimed that they were both on duty *and* on strike simultaneously. "There is a type of officer," a Memphis commander lamented, speaking of jejune younger recruits, "who in my opinion is unwilling to accept authority and does not appreciate the incumbent responsibility that goes with his oath of office."[11]

In a few cities, cops seemed to relish breaking the law. In Toledo, the arbitrator's intervention in the traffic citation dispute was followed by a painful strike the following year. Officers turned on the flashing lights of their squad cars and locked the doors before walking out, causing the batteries to drain. In Newark, New Jersey, cops vandalized squad cars, smashing windows in forty-six of them, and sabotaged traffic signals across the city, all to protest layoffs due to a budgetary shortfall. If frequent police strikes continued, Patrick Murphy wondered, might National Guard units need new training to take the place of striking cops? Who else could intervene? Binding arbitration failed to be the antidote that lawmakers and police chiefs had sought to unlawful job actions like the blue flu, but one inexhaustive study found that only five of eighty-one police strikes in the 1970s occurred in cities with binding arbitration to resolve impasses in contract negotiations.[12]

Even without breaking the law, cops innovated. In Des Moines, Iowa, officers appealed directly to the public for assistance when police representatives and city officials could not agree on wages as a contract was expiring. The police wanted an increase of 12.5 percent, more than double what the city was offering. Cops took out ads in newspapers, imploring those who supported improved compensation to contact the mayor and members of the city council. The ads included the officials' phone numbers and mailing addresses. At least 550 people sent letters, while many others picked up the phone. This response was not immediately effective, and off-duty cops and police wives still staged demonstrations outside city hall when it seemed likely that binding arbitration would ensue. But taking the case directly to voters and asking them to contact elected officials on behalf of police became part of the police union toolkit—though the textbook on successful police unionism points out that newsprint ads should be "the last alternative," after television, radio, and direct mail. Moreover, "to reach the most voters," intones *Police Association Power, Politics, and Confrontation: A Guide for the Successful Police Labor Leader*, "you should request that the ad be placed in the metro or city section of the paper, or in the sports page."[13]

By protecting the status quo, police unions interfered with reform programs and encouraged corrupt and violent practices to continue. Even if they achieved only moderate successes at the bargaining table, unions both expressed and shaped departmental culture, and union leaders set a tone. These intangible factors often overshadowed the formal and legalistic provisions of a contract, particularly when union leaders maintained closer political ties than jet-setting chiefs. When Victor I. Cizanckas arrived in Stamford, Connecticut, in 1977, to become the new police chief, the city was receiving more public complaints about police practices than any other in the state. He confronted both corruption and an intransigent police association, led by Salvatore Ladestro.

Cizanckas was a nationally known reformer, perhaps the most progressive police executive in the country at the time. He had initiated a program to "demilitarize" police in Menlo Park, California, by introducing more casual uniforms. Cops now would dress like "mods," wearing ties and blazers that hid their guns and handcuffs. Cizanckas also shifted the departmental hierarchy away from military-style ranks to functional titles. Sergeants became "operations directors" and lieutenants "police operations managers." In Stamford, however, Cizanckas did not demilitarize, but he cut down on leave and overtime abuse, developed an internal affairs unit, instituted merit-based promotions, and oversaw construction of a new police headquarters. These reform efforts came under fire from Stamford police officers.

Organized by the Stamford Police Association, with the support of a few local officials, rank-and-file police repeatedly challenged Cizanckas. After multiple officers were indicted for links to organized crime, Cizanckas was misquoted in a magazine as saying that 9 percent of the force was "honest," instead of 90 percent. But his correction did not mollify the cops. Officers attended a police commission meeting, where they demanded that the chief "start dealing with the personal feelings" of officers he had offended, including when he used terms like "hip-shooter" and "dishonorable." The truculent Ladestro organized a poll of union members that revealed a majority had "no confidence" in Cizanckas. But these tactics did not lead to his removal.

Stamford cops tried new and unorthodox methods to hinder the reform program. Officers began picketing headquarters while off duty, interfering with the new facility's construction. And this battle over changing departmental routines became personal. Someone, likely an officer, broke into the chief's office, for instance. Ladestro sued the department after he was charged with dereliction of duty for a scheme to avoid responding to calls, which he claimed was to allow him to conduct union business. Most egregiously, officers blew the cover of an undercover investigation into political corruption in a vindictive attempt to frame the investigation itself as evidence of corruption on the part of the chief. Though appointed to a term that was supposed to last until he was sixty-five, Cizanckas died of a heart attack at only forty-three, around three years after arriving in Stamford, just as his reforms began to bear fruit. Ladestro outlasted him and lobbied for his replacement to be drawn from the department, rather than outside. It took decades to eradicate corruption in Stamford.[14]

BOUND BY LAW

Still lacking a voice for the rank and file in Washington, obstreperous police unions across the country closed out the 1970s with continued labor unrest, from Southern California to Utah to Ohio. Nearly every officer across the Hawaiian archipelago walked off the job in July 1979. With two separate strikes, cops forced the cancellation of the annual Mardi Gras festival in New Orleans for the first time since World War II, humiliating the city's first Black mayor, who had promised local business leaders a lucrative tourist boom during the raucous carnival season.[15]

These rank-and-file mobilizations were now yielding diminishing returns, however. Courts and commanders were growing more aggressive in squashing these actions; for example, in Passaic, New Jersey, a judge issued a bench warrant for the arrest of an officer who participated in a three-day blue flu action but refused to be examined by a physician. For both sides, a commitment to binding interest arbitration only increased.[16]

The public was also souring on rank-and-file mobilizations. Early in 1978, Gallup found that only 33 percent of people across 300 communities believed that police should have the right to strike. In contrast, a larger proportion (43 percent) believed teachers should have the right to strike, while approval of labor unions generally stood at 59 percent. By August 1981, another poll found that only 26 percent of people believed police (and firefighters) should be allowed to strike, as compared to 39 percent for teachers and 28 percent for air traffic controllers, who were then on strike.[17]

Still, the labor situation among police was difficult for the public to perceive and parse. Crime went up or down independent of police enforcement tactics, and news coverage provided little help. The shift toward interest arbitration worried elected officials who feared loss of control over their municipal budgets, but for most people, these changes were all but invisible. Who could name or blame the unelected arbitrator who was determining—in lengthy legalese—how expenditures on police would change?

Emboldened, police also began turning to civil courts for remedy, both when accused of misconduct and when injured on the job. The small but energetic nonprofit research agency Americans for Effective Law Enforcement found that one in thirty-four cops had been sued in the five years from 1967 to 1971. It operated a legal defense shop, providing police with some forms of assistance when they were sued. Cops tended to win these cases; plaintiffs lost more than 80 percent of suits against police. The agency also endorsed individual liability insurance, which some police associations, like the National Sheriffs' Association, had begun offering.

The void formed by the absence of a national union for cops would be filled by a strategy both chiefs and rank-and-file officers could agree upon: sue or get sued. The International Conference of Police Associations and the National Sheriffs' Association, guided by Americans for Effective Law Enforcement, urged members to sue civilians who caused line-of-duty injuries. The International Association of Chiefs of Police helped provide leadership for Americans for Effective Law Enforcement, including advisors like Donald Pomerleau and Chief Thomas Reddin of Los Angeles, as well as leading police educators like Arthur F. Brandstatter and conservative commentators like Fred E. Inbau and Eugene H. Methvin. Rather than pausing to inquire whether a high rate of litigation was justified by police actions, these experts went on the offensive. Local police associations followed the lead of national organizations. The Los Angeles Police Protective League, for example, sued the Progressive Labor Party, a communist organization, for $2 million in 1978 after nine police suffered injuries controlling a demonstration. The executive director of Americans for Effective Law Enforcement remarked proudly that his work helped police realize "they don't have to be punching bags anymore."[18]

CHAPTER 14

BLUE POWER IN THE RED

As the 1980s dawned, police union leaders were confident that the local gains of the 1970s were durable. But protests of police abuse were continuing, while intellectuals threw up their hands at the persistence of crime. Washington also was losing interest in supporting the chiefs. All was not well.

When it came to violence committed by police, the decade of Blue Power's entrenchment ended much as it began, with African Americans significantly overrepresented among those killed (59.6 percent). But trends were unclear, and data frequently unreliable, with the decade's police killings underreported by as much as half. Still, as many as 3.6 percent of all homicides nationally may have been committed by police. Each of five calendar years during the decade saw an increase from the prior one in "justifiable homicide" by cops. In some cities, like New York, police killings peaked at the beginning of the decade, while in others the carnage peaked toward the middle or end. The year New York City police killed eighty-seven people was also the year Ed Kiernan, as president of the Patrolmen's Benevolent Association, urged his officers to purchase unauthorized shotguns and "shoot to kill" because it was "all-out war."[1]

As episodes of police brutality eroded public support, police violence increasingly targeted recent immigrants from Latin America and the Pacific Rim. Police beatings and shootings were growing more common in "the new immigrant ghettos," as a lengthy feature in *Police Magazine* labeled them. To police eyes, this new urban terrain turned out to be much like the old immigrant ghettos: inscrutable, distrustful, hostile, "unnerving," and brimming with vice. The new immigrants, primarily from areas where the Cold War had flared, found themselves experiencing what generations of immigrants from Europe had experienced. Like those immigrants, they quickly learned how to leverage voting power in Washington.

The administration responded with a tactic that would become more common a decade and a half later, opening DOJ investigations into police brutality and suing departments for misconduct. In 1978, Attorney General Griffin Bell angered cops by ordering an investigation into abuse of Latinos, spurred by the new Congressional Hispanic Caucus. President Jimmy Carter himself condemned a "particularly disturbing case" of the shooting of a handcuffed Chicano boy in the back of a squad car. And when Houston cops brutally beat and drowned a Mexican American veteran, José "Joe" Campos Torres, three were convicted on federal civil rights charges, though their punishment was minimal.[2]

Court decisions and arbitration awards served as placeholders for a real national strategy for rank-and-file police officers, but competition among police organizations for dominance of the profession meant that gains were not easily universalized. Exactly whom the changes of the past decade protected and served remained an open question. One subculture spat out an answer.

HOUSTON POLICE ASSOCIATION VERSUS PUNK ROCK

As hardcore punk detonated across the cities and then the suburbs of the United States at the dawn of the Reagan regime, it became obligatory for every set to include at least one ripper decrying cops:

"Police Story"
"Police Truck"
"Teaching You the Fear"
"Youngster on the Force"
"Killa Poe Leese"
"Pigs Run Wild"
"Cops Are Out"
"Violent Arrest"
"On Whom They Beat"

Black Flag's "Police Story" summed up the prevailing sentiment: "Fuckin' city is run by pigs / They take the rights away from all the kids." Of course, not all the claims of abuse shouted from the stage by shaven-headed white-boy malcontents stood up to scrutiny. Yet there was one song that stood out from all the rest. If the charts had tracked which single had most enraged the police, "The Badge Means You Suck," by Houston's AK-47, would have reigned supreme. Its release led to a frenzied investigation and civil suit by the Houston Police Officers Association.[3]

Houston cops became notorious during the mid-1970s for killing or injuring twenty-five people in just three years, without a single officer facing charges. Protests gave way to arrests and more brutality, setting the stage for an out-and-out revolt in 1978, complete with fires and looting. To help repair the reputation of the embattled Houston Police Department, a local ad agency crafted a slogan: "The Badge Means You Care."

The recently formed local band AK-47 repurposed the slogan on the cover of its debut 45. The band crossed out "Care," replacing it with the word "Suck," and then listed the names of nine people killed by the department in the past decade, including Carl Hampton, a charismatic Black political leader, and Joe Torres.

AK-47 picture sleeve, 1980. Jimmy Bryan, courtesy of Harry Leverette.

Up-tempo and driving, "The Badge Means You Suck" snarled out the names of these victims and the stories of how police had killed them. "Murder doesn't bother to whisper / In this fucking town it roars," spat vocalist Tim Phlegm. "The killers of Milton Glover / Might be pulling you over tonight / And if you happen to get shot / Well I guess you started the fight." Phlegm was a local journalist who had a lot to lose, and he joined the other band members in hiding his identity behind a pseudonym. That proved to be a wise decision.

Stung by the punk effrontery, the officers' association filed suit against the band for libel and defamation in 1981. Local record shops shied away from distributing the 45, meaning that, as one reporter noted, "most police probably haven't heard all the lyrics." Nor did they know the identities of the band members: the lawsuit could offer only fake names to the court. Cops had a hard time even finding the band's gigs to serve the lawsuit to the band. But the officers' association was not wrong that the record was made "with actual malice."

The case ultimately went nowhere. Three of the members, including Phlegm, had quit by the time the lawsuit was discharged in 1985. The record, however, became a coveted collectible, and the song remains an incandescent piece of American political art. It signaled the disrepute and opposition that big-city police forces engendered going into the 1980s, the disorder characterizing the profession in the wake of the blue insurgency. "Gonna coin me a new slogan / The badge means you're fucked / the badge means you suck."[4]

THE TICKING TIME BOMB

Punk rockers were not the only ones expressing frustration with cops. While campaigning for president, Jimmy Carter condemned bureaucratic inefficiency and wastefulness, and his prime example of this Washington plague was the LEAA. The congressional authorization for the LEAA peaked at $1.25 billion in 1976, with the amount actually disbursed peaking the prior year at $895 million. But it was never enough.[5]

The greatest expense for police departments across the country was compensation. LEAA funds bought tens of thousands of radios for police, for instance, but that hardly made a dent in the fiscal need. Manpower funding was available for new positions or deployments only if they adhered to the ambiguous criterion of innovation. And once LEAA funds dried up, municipalities were on the hook to keep paying these officers. As the LEAA budget grew, state and local expenditures increased considerably, almost doubling from 1969 to 1973 and tripling by the mid-1980s. Although LEAA leaders optimistically projected that Washington would cover 20 percent of expenses, the actual amount was closer to 4 percent of what states and localities were spending.[6]

The need for money was only increasing. The otherwise sober Advisory Commission on Intergovernmental Relations considered police to be responsible for setting a "time bomb." Cop pensions were set to explode.[7]

As inflation continued upward, cost-of-living adjustments in compensation, particularly for retirees, were swallowing budgets. It did not matter whether retirement benefits had been won through generous union contracts and arbitration awards or offered as recompense by voters and civic leaders out of a sense of gratitude. Either way, they had become a problem, in part because they were less predictable than salaries. Insolvency loomed.

Tax revolts and inflation tightened the straitjacket. But police had manufactured it. Cities cut back on other services in order to fund police pensions. Reducing social services, however, was itself criminogenic. City leaders then felt the pressure to invest in public safety as disorder seemed to increase, causing a spiral of increasing costs in some cities or a binge and purge of police hiring and firing according to a given year's accounting tables.

Police (and firefighters) were uniquely positioned in the pension schema, often because their retirement costs were largely borne by cities, whereas retirement costs for other government employees like teachers were the responsibility of states. Cops also retired young, whether due to the imposition of age limits because of demanding job requirements or because pensions made it easy to afford to do so. And, in comparison to other public sector jobs like teacher or librarian, many more cops sustained or claimed to sustain injuries at work, making them eligible for disability benefits. Although police accounted for a relatively small number of overall government employees, their pension costs were disproportionately high. Some police unionists even argued that the unique character of police pensions meant they should not affiliate with organized labor, which was ill-equipped to assist.[8]

The salary-to-pension ratio kept shifting for most municipalities, as more and more officers moved from active duty on the streets to retirement. Detroit by the late 1970s had four pension beneficiaries for every five active officers, accounting for more than the city spent on parks or sanitation, around 10 percent of the city's expenditures. San Francisco counted nine retired cops for every ten active ones. New York City had more pension or disability beneficiaries than active officers. In 1982, right before voters raised the minimum, the average retirement age for Los Angeles cops at full pension was forty-three. And soon retired members accounted for large and growing portions of police union membership rolls.[9]

Convincing cops not to care that they were bankrupting cities became an organizing goal. Ed Kiernan modeled the snide approach to this "basic entitlement": "It is too damned bad that cities haven't set aside enough money to pay their police when they retire. My heart goes out to city fathers like these."[10]

Rick Helms, the director of the Los Angeles Police Protective League, the city's police union, argued that small caps on cost-of-living adjustments would not aid the taxpayer because any surplus would be spent on fixing potholes or keeping the library open. That was the point of the caps, according to a city council staffer, Charles Britton: substitute a "Mercedes" plan for a "Rolls" plan—still pretty good for retired cops—and use the savings to provide other services. But the police union's head saw things differently. Helms theorized that "cities were created for protection," not "to provide water and power and street maintenance." Britton encapsulated city hall's exasperation: "Jesus, they can't have everything they want. They've gone too far."[11]

Kiernan recommended that unions not negotiate pensions at the bargaining table, where they might be subject to "trade-offs." Instead, police unions should obtain pension protections in state legislatures. He further urged cops to press state legislatures and city councils to fund pensions fully, rather than continue to let unfunded liabilities balloon. But departing from the usual pay-as-you-go approach would have spelled disaster. Small towns could see their liabilities double with the retirement of a single officer, but the dollar amounts in bigger cities were staggering. With a force comprising 823 officers, Minneapolis owed $100,000 each in unfunded liabilities in 1976, more than five times the top annual salary for a patrol officer.[12]

Although Congress enacted legislation to protect pensions in 1974, the Employee Retirement Income Security Act, state and local governments successfully lobbied for exemptions, to the annoyance of officials leading police associations. Instead, Congress decided to study the issue. It found that unfunded liabilities were massive, up to $175 billion in 1975. A lack of transparency made accounting difficult, however, and the actual amount was probably a lot higher. Moreover, nearly half of public employee pension programs did not adequately inform future beneficiaries about their plans. Conservatives increasingly emphasized devolving fiscal responsibility to states, counties, and municipalities for everything from transportation to food stamps to education. Reduced tax receipts and continued shrinkage of transfers from Washington meant that fully funding pensions was impossible.[13]

When labor management consultants, actuaries, and legislatures proposed disarming the ticking time bomb on the recipient side, a few common tactics emerged. First was raising the retirement age or modifying job responsibilities based on age to allow older officers to keep working in less strenuous positions. Another was changing pension benefits away from cash payments toward educational stipends or other incentives to allow a second career. Reducing the way pension payments were calculated was the third, as either using the last and highest salary to determine retiree payments or pinning retiree payments to current employee salaries proved challenging. Recalibrating the ratio of employer contributions to employee contributions was also common. Yet many police unions refused to go along with these measures, turbo-boosting municipal pension liabilities even if other unions made concessions. When states eventually moved toward 401(k) retirement plans for employees, police pension plans remained untouched. Michigan was a prime example due to the intransigence of the Detroit Police Officers Association.[14]

Kiernan believed that Proposition 13's revenue cuts in California could boost his efforts to create a nationwide police union by convincing some otherwise reluctant police to see the value of unionization. "In the old days, they didn't want to have anything to do with labor unions for their security. But with Proposition 13 out on the West Coast, they know goddamn well they are in trouble." The flaw in his argument, however, was that the police unions were as responsible for the squeeze as the antitax voters, and truculent police unions had only stoked antitax attitudes.[15]

THE END OF THE ERA

Jimmy Carter did not prioritize the fight against crime. The LEAA was the only major agency Carter originally left with interim leadership, and he ordered layoffs of a quarter of DOJ employees, while also choosing not to stage meetings with representatives of police agencies. After convening a study group on the LEAA that failed to find consensus, Carter nevertheless committed to doing something. In December 1979, he finally signed the Justice System Improvement Act, which dramatically simplified the LEAA's grant-making process, while also shrinking its operations and delegating some responsibilities, like data collection and research, to new agencies within the DOJ. Homer F. Broome Jr. received Senate confirmation to become the first African American administrator of the LEAA in May 1980, just as the organization was on its last legs.[16]

That was the same month that the majority-Black Liberty City section of Miami exploded with rage after four white Dade County cops were acquitted in the beating death of Arthur McDuffie, a Black executive. It was the most destructive uprising since 1968, with eighteen killed and dozens of businesses looted and charred, after a woefully underprepared Miami Police Department failed to mitigate the rebellion. Another uprising broke out in a housing project in Liberty City in July of that year, leading to the wounding of five officers, as well as further looting and fires, and still more Black uprisings lay ahead in Orlando and Chattanooga.

In November 1979, the day before students in Tehran stormed the US embassy, police did not intervene in Greensboro, North Carolina, as members of the Klan and the National Socialist Party shot and stabbed demonstrators at an antiracist rally organized by the Workers Viewpoint Organization, which had recently christened itself the Communist Workers

Party. Four communists died at the site of the rally, and one died in the hospital days later. Twelve people were wounded, including Nelson Johnson, the city's most prominent Black activist and likely the top target of the violence. Although the full extent of police, FBI, and Bureau of Alcohol, Tobacco, and Firearms collaboration with the white supremacists remains unknown, a Truth and Reconciliation Commission found evidence of police complicity in the violence twenty-five years later.[17]

As ever, apparent police failures became a warrant for capital-intensive reforms. For fiscal year 1981, with the election looming, Carter's budget recommended increasing the LEAA's funding by 17 percent. But Congress slashed its budget by 90 percent instead, down to $50 million. The IACP led an effort to reverse the cuts before the final vote. Its president, Joseph Dominelli, pleaded with Carter, while lobbying groups for governors, county executives, and district attorneys banded together with a "coordinated strategy" asking Congress to give the LEAA $500 million instead of the proposed $50 million. Even morose LEAA officials, who suspected the end was near, were impressed by this unified effort. But a precarious attempt in Congress to keep defense spending high while fighting inflation with a balanced budget meant that House leadership categorized the LEAA budget as social welfare spending, which made voting to increase it anathema.[18]

At the municipal level, city councils tried to develop new revenue streams to replace the funds that measures such as Proposition 13 had taken away. In Oakland, California, voters rejected a ballot measure, the Anti-Crime Act of 1981, better known as Measure A, that was supposed to raise over $37 million for the police department through new taxes on homeowners and businesses. A coalition of labor unions, local Democratic Party and community organizations, and left-wing groups including communist cliques and the deteriorating Oakland core of the Black Panther Party collaborated to oppose what they called a "police tax." Avowed Leninists held their noses to engage in vanilla electoralism because they believed they could inject antipolice sentiment into the coalition's organizing while launching a wider anticapitalist program. Oakland's police chief, George T. Hart, who had succeeded Charles Gain, gravely warned that without the new revenue needed to hire eighty-eight new officers, the department could not be held responsible for whatever mayhem might descend. But Oakland officers had killed nine Black men in 1979, already crippling relations between the Black populace and the department.[19]

All but one member of the Oakland city council supported the measure. They urged their constituents to vote in favor. The lone opponent, Wilson Riles Jr., argued that the demand for new money for police was consistent with Washington's approach to foreign affairs: "They are beefing up the militaristic police force locally, while Reagan is beefing up the military—as if this is the answer!" He argued, "Those who are victims of inflation and crime are those with the heaviest burden to pay under these plans." The city's poorest neighborhoods did vote against the tax. Yet the police department itself was keen to note that inflation was hurting it too. The measure's defeat dismayed officials in other cities across the state. But the city council levied a small new tax to fund pensions anyway, which survived a court challenge.[20]

As police unions refused to budge, departments across the country scaled back on hiring and changed operations to fit thinner ranks. Patrolling and responding to emergency calls would be prioritized, particularly as the brass believed these activities most directly affected public perceptions of police effectiveness. But if a 911 call seemed less than urgent, a caller might hear a recording, rather than speaking to a dispatcher. Investigations into lesser crimes like burglary all but ceased, police complained in Detroit and Oakland.[21]

Worried about costs, police racism, and operational ineffectiveness, Oakland's first Black mayor, Lionel Wilson, then attempted to gain some control over the police department, which was under the supervision of a city manager. Wilson had received support from the Black Panther Party while campaigning, and his plan for stronger mayoral control of the police department retained some of the flavor of prior Panther demands for community control of police. His proposal also coincided with a departmental initiative to hire more Black cops. The Oakland Police Officers' Association rejected both. White cops marched on city hall in protest and threatened to strike. City council members intervened to restore order by appeasing the police union. The council tossed out the hiring plan in a racially divided vote. Wilson's effort to arrogate oversight of the police department to the mayor's office also failed.[22]

This episode of police asserting their political power, coming in the early 1980s, was just one of many in that decade and the next, after most observers of the labor movement assumed that the collectively bargained contract, the dues checkoff, and the grievance procedure would have pacified the rank and file.[23]

The zenith had not passed, however. In cities across the country, the political power of police was entrenched, but the turbulence did not fade. Instead, rank-and-file police worked to consolidate their gains by refusing to back down. Management discovered, to its dismay, that concessions made to militant police early on, including bills of rights for officers in disciplinary cases, "stymied" attempts to regain control, while police unions continued to expand their interest in bargaining over "decisions that were once thought to be the sole prerogative of management." And new power bases emerged, kindling new national strategies.[24]

CHAPTER 15

PASSING THE TORCH TO THE SHERIFFS

The International Association of Chiefs of Police entered the 1980s bruised by a rank-and-file rebellion that would ultimately remake the profession from bottom to top. The professionalizers who had helmed the organization in the 1960s had been remarkably successful in steering funding from municipal budgets and foundations to police forces across the country, but their time was passing. Across the country, cops were fed up with the priorities of the older generations. Upstarts vied with older, reform-minded leaders like Quinn Tamm and Patrick Murphy for power. Those chiefs who remained stuck in their ways would find themselves left behind by the transformations the Reagan era unlocked.

Cops across the country greeted Ronald Reagan's election with hope. He brought a "hardline law-enforcement philosophy" when he spoke before an enthusiastic audience of chiefs at the IACP's annual meeting in 1981. Reagan was passionate about denying bail in the name of "preventive detention," expanding the death penalty, and eroding the exclusionary rule that disallowed evidence from trials if obtained in violation of the Fourth Amendment.[1]

This rhetoric differed starkly from what the progressive chiefs leading the professionalization movement had been offering until recently. As president of the Police Foundation, Patrick Murphy had spent years advocating for new standards and training to lessen the use of "deadly force." By the 1980s, the appetite for these reforms was disappearing. Not only did IACP members reject his proposals, but they adopted a resolution opposing restrictions on police use of deadly force. The International Union of Police Associations went even further, demanding Murphy's ouster from leadership of the Police Foundation and recommending that its members boycott any organization with ties to the foundation. Within a few years, Murphy had been expelled from the IACP altogether.[2]

Several big-city chiefs, as well as leaders of organizations like the International City Managers' Association, criticized the IACP's actions. Instead of professionalism, one member complained, too many chiefs had "chosen to revert to the easy comfort of the past, when our actions and inactions were unquestioned." But the episode revealed just how thoroughly professionalizers like Murphy had lost their grip on the profession in the wake of the blue insurgency. Quinn Tamm spoke up in Murphy's defense, decrying the attempt to impose "conformity" among IACP members as "outrageous." But he had done the very same thing a decade and a half earlier in the effort to push passage of federal anticrime legislation. Murphy and Tamm had long believed that greater resources would lead to public respect for the police, as well as unity in the profession. Unity remained out of reach, however, and rank-and-file police were brandishing the respect they had earned like a pistol in a stickup.[3]

In the meantime, even as they were being shown the door, the professionalizers' skills at securing funding were needed more than ever. Reagan's speech before the IACP evinced his fondness for punitive crime policy, but it also revealed the aversion to domestic government expenditures that characterized his presidency. Though most chiefs shared Reagan's conviction that it was time to let go of the belief that social "deprivation and want" spurred crime, his eagerness to close the government's purse posed a new problem. To cash-strapped police holding out their hands, the visionary behind Reagan's ideologically fervid but fiscally penurious anticrime approach, Rudolph Giuliani, rasped, "Maybe they should stop crying," because after billions spent on the LEAA, "the crime rate hasn't gone down."[4]

Momentarily pausing its infighting, the IACP used its annual meeting in 1982 to renew its call for greater federal spending. The chiefs' efforts, they believed, had already been successful at transforming the public's perceptions of the profession—in the words of one IACP member, "We used to be 'no good, rotten pigs.'" The new esteem cops garnered was the result of their professionalism. But now they needed money more than legitimacy.[5]

The LEAA, however, finally shut its doors in April 1982. The legislators who had overseen the LEAA's birth could not keep it from expiring. Senator McClellan had died in 1977, after Hruska retired in 1976. When the Violent Crime and Drug Enforcement Improvements Act of 1982 landed on Reagan's desk, he killed it with a pocket veto, ensuring that LEAA funds would not be replaced. For now, Washington would disburse no new funds to police.[6]

Former federal law enforcement officials, who watched appropriations decline after they left Washington, pleaded with Reagan to let his budget requests match his "tough-sounding" crime talk. But his administration prioritized austerity and bureaucratic culling. For all the efforts of legislators and police organizers and lobbyists, Reagan would remain an obstacle to the Blue Power movement for the duration of his two terms.[7]

In every election year from 1982 to 1996, members of Congress voted on a crime bill. Not all of them became law, but those that did enacted tougher penalties and more proactive federal drug policies that activated and invested in federal agencies like the Drug Enforcement Administration, while relying on the Pentagon as much as small-town cops to reduce crime. With almost clock-like regularity, Congress attempted to get tough on crime with big legislation when voters might be paying attention. The Republicans repeatedly pulled skeptical Democrats toward law and order, while battles within the Democratic Party for supremacy would consistently be decided in favor of legislators who got tough. The elected officials who took over the party during these years were the ones who made a point of listening to cops.

In the meantime, the balance in law enforcement was shifting. The chiefs were declining in stature. During the 1980s, no chief bent the ear of members of Congress as frequently as one older police sergeant. The bombastic John Harrington, retired and out of the limelight, took up a quiet weekly residency on Capitol Hill. Every Tuesday the former cop would ride the train from Philadelphia to Washington. He would stop by Mario Biaggi's office and ask Biaggi's aide Craig Floyd which members of Congress he should buttonhole that day. Harrington was no longer the president of the Fraternal Order of Police, or even paid by the organization. He became a plainclothes volunteer police lobbyist on the Hill.[8]

Yet it was not Harrington's rank-and-file rebels who were ascendant. Instead, it was the country's sheriffs. They belonged to the National Sheriffs' Association, long a sleepy operation that commanded little influence during the years of the IACP's reign in the profession. The organization had watched the rapid rise and slow demise of Johnson's War on Crime mostly from the sidelines. But it saw the disarray among the chiefs and rank-and-file cops at the beginning of Reagan's first term as an opportunity to seize a leadership role among police.

THE NATIONAL SHERIFFS' ASSOCIATION AWAKENS

Sheriffs love their history. They invoke it as ironclad tradition, even as they have transformed more than any other type of law enforcement since the 1980s. The first "shire-reeves," or sheriffs, took office in England in AD 993. Bearing this tradition in mind, rather than the more native traditions of slave-catching and westward territorial expansion, leaders of the National Sheriffs' Association insisted a thousand years later that their members correct anyone who referred to a sheriff's "department" in the United States. The politics of identity they outlined was antediluvian. Sheriffs occupy offices; they are not department heads. Sheriffs are not subordinate to another authority, whether mayor or governor, that sets budget priorities. Sheriffs are largely elected, with the office named in thirty-three state constitutions and responsibilities outlined by statute in thirteen states. And if sheriffs could work together, these totals might grow. But working together has always been the tricky part.[9]

In their own sovereignties, sheriffs are both politically powerful and politically sensitive, particularly when campaigning for reelection. Yet they are not formally part of municipal, state, or federal governments. Instead, sheriffs are attached mainly to counties and usually afforded state jurisdiction. They personify an ideological localism, and there had been little reason to look beyond the county line for most of their history.

Nor was there much apparent reason for anyone in national politics to take sheriffs seriously as a potential constituency. They had remained on the sidelines during much of the debate about law and order in the late 1960s, too closely associated with southern white reaction to possess much credibility during the waves of urban unrest and Black protest in the North. By the 1980s, during what Richard Nixon hailed as Reagan's revolution against the long reign of Democrats in Congress, sheriffs sniffed an opening. The new executive director of the National Sheriffs' Association, L. Cary Bittick, helped develop a national political strategy and aspired for sheriffs to become the "dominating influence on all law enforcement legislation at the national level." With the IACP mired in a federal investigation due to misallocation of grant monies, Bittick and the sheriffs focused on superseding the chiefs.[10]

The urban fiscal crisis helped. From the mid-1970s to the mid-1980s, growth in municipal spending on police lagged, while county spending, largely on sheriffs, increased 146 percent. By 1985, counties were dedicating a greater percentage of their expenditures to law enforcement than states or municipalities.[11]

The National Sheriffs' Association did not have much to show for the lengthy history of the office. J. Edgar Hoover kept the association at arm's length, lest Klan members among the southern sheriffs be linked to the FBI, tarnishing its reputation for remaining above the fray. The association's greatest public initiative was the Neighborhood Watch program, encouraging regular people to adopt an informal but pinpointed and proactive stance toward assisting law enforcement. Its emblem, inscribed on rusting street signs throughout middle-class neighborhoods, was often installed in first-ring suburbs that have since shifted from the all-white demographic makeup the signs quietly affirmed.

The 1982 retirement of the long-standing executive director of the sheriffs' association opened the door to a new generation of leadership. Bittick, who had once been the youngest sheriff in his home state of Georgia and still retained the boyish handsomeness of a prep school class president at age fifty, was joined by Lauren "Jack" Goin and Thomas Finn. They were Washington insiders with deep knowledge of the law enforcement landscape that they gained while working for the US Office of Public Safety, training and assisting police from across the globe at the height of the Cold War. They brought to the funding-averse Reagan years one key article of faith: bromides about law and order are meaningless without a budgetary commitment.

Reagan's belief that appearing tough on crime would win him reelection dovetailed with Bittick's goal of winning a central role for the National Sheriffs' Association on the national stage. Reagan addressed the association's annual gathering for the first time in 1984, raising its stock overnight.

With his western cowboy air and embrace of the white South, the Gipper delighted the crowd of sheriffs. He reminded them that he had once played a foolhardy sheriff, a man who "thought he could do the job without a gun." That sheriff ended up dead before the television program's half-hour was up. But before Reagan now sat a group with no illusions. "Throughout the Nation, there's a new consensus on the crime issue, which you've helped form," he suggested. "It's a consensus that utterly rejects the counsels of leniency toward criminals and the liberal philosophy that fostered it." It was a familiar tone for Reagan, but he seemed more willing to listen to those tasked with solving the crime problem. What he heard were more pleas for money, now coming from behind the sheriff's badge.[12]

THE SHERIFFS IN THE CAPITAL

For Bittick's reorientation of the National Sheriffs' Association to succeed, its members needed to start paying attention to what was happening in Washington, to look beyond their own jurisdictions. *The National Sheriff*, the association's magazine, printed the names of every member of the House and Senate Judiciary Committees, urging "personal communication with key decisionmakers in Congress." Bittick hired another Washington insider as special legislative counsel: Courtney A. Evans, a former FBI assistant director who, like Quinn Tamm, had been a close subordinate of J. Edgar Hoover in the 1950s. To help take what Bittick called "a proactive stance on legislation," the association also appointed a Law and Legislative Committee, composed of member sheriffs, to craft its official positions on new bills and circulate model legislation, such as tougher drug laws, for sheriffs to promote locally. This committee grew rapidly from an initial membership roster of three sheriffs in 1984 to fifty-eight members a decade later. It became the association's largest standing committee, indexing its attractiveness to members.[13]

While the sheriffs remade their capacity to influence national politics, Congress was changing too, as a set of young, tough-on-crime Democrats entered the scene. Getting any crime bill through the Republican-led Senate would require striking a deal with archconservative segregationist Strom Thurmond, who headed the Judiciary Committee. After an apprenticeship under Thurmond as the committee's ranking minority member, Delaware's Joe Biden emerged as the Democratic Party's foremost negotiator on crime legislation. Biden had won election to the Senate in 1972 against a liberal Republican, J. Caleb Boggs, by arguing that the incumbent was out of touch. Although Boggs initially came into office as a cold warrior hoping to protect the country from Joseph Stalin, today the real threat was street crime, argued the thirty-year-old challenger. In this race, only Joe Biden understood "the new crime problem in this country."[14]

Keen to resuscitate an LEAA-style funding regime for state and local police, Biden promised more police officers, improved training and equipment, better prisons, an overhauled court system, new streetlights, and "an all-out attack on drugs." With a mixture of surprise and admiration, a Delaware newspaper called Biden an "iconoclast" for this stance. Years later, he reflected that Democrats responded to Nixon's law and order pledges with promises of "justice, whatever that meant." In contrast, Biden won simply by declaring, "Lock the SOBs up."[15]

Biden was not the only Democrat eager to snatch the Republicans' mantle of law and order. In the spring of 1984, Senator Arlen Specter, Republican of Pennsylvania (though he had been a Democrat until 1965), and Congressman Richard Hughes, Democrat of New Jersey, formed the Congressional Crime Caucus, a bipartisan and bicameral group of seventy-nine legislators dedicated to promoting tough-on-crime legislation. Specter and Hughes were both former prosecutors, as were twenty-eight other founding members of the caucus. This group elicited the support of a wide range of organizations, including associations representing governors, prosecutors, prison officials, and police. Each assumed the caucus would advocate in their interest, but not all groups shared the same goals. The "frustrated" IACP believed the caucus could advance legislation to "provide critical funds to help state and local" police agencies. The National Sheriffs' Association hoped for more "frank exchanges of ideas" between local law enforcement and federal legislators. The progressive and reformist Police Executive Research Forum eagerly anticipated bipartisan cooperation in the future. Ultimately, the crime caucus rejuvenated the dormant effort to produce a federal anticrime bill after Reagan's previous veto.[16]

The National Sheriffs' Association began staging an annual congressional reception on Capitol Hill while Biden was securing his tough-on-crime reputation through negotiations on a new crime bill. The first reception took place in February 1984 at the Longworth Congressional Office Building. Around tables dotted with bouquets of daffodils, tulips, and pussy willows, flickering candles, and chafing dishes piled with hors d'oeuvres, 350 sheriffs and a smattering of other law enforcement leaders met with 250 members of Congress, plus executives of various federal agencies. Sheriffs prioritized the need for federal help on jail overcrowding and drug trafficking, as well as broader financial assistance from Washington, which, they argued, should go directly to counties rather than state capitals. Soon association leaders began receiving consistent invitations to Congress and the White House. And the association's annual conference became an important venue for elected officials of both parties to detail their views on criminal justice. The new version of the National Sheriffs' Association was a matchmaker, connecting its members with legislators in Washington.[17]

Sheriffs found new ways to justify their existence. The DOJ started collecting data on state and local police agencies in the 1980s, using new sampling methods. Researchers found that sheriffs engaged in a wide range of law enforcement duties, but most commonly sheriffs served civil processes, maintained court security, and operated jails. Over 83 percent of sheriffs' offices employed fewer than fifty full-time sworn personnel, and more than 70 percent of them served populations smaller than 50,000. The annual budget for this majority of sheriffs' offices serving small populations rarely broke $1 million, but the twenty-seven sheriffs' offices in jurisdictions counting over 1 million people averaged expenditures above $66 million. Sheriffs used these findings to plead their case. "Take the ball and run," the association president commanded his members, "to the streets, to the courthouse, to the state legislatures and to the U.S. Congress."[18]

LAW AND ORDER IN REAGAN'S WASHINGTON

Immediately after Reagan secured his party's nomination for reelection at the Republican National Convention in Dallas, the National Law Enforcement Council, an unofficial umbrella group of leaders of law enforcement associations, coordinated an Oval Office meeting. The council bestowed a plaque on the president, naming him "a friend of the law enforcement profession." In attendance were, among others, Tom Finn, representing the sheriffs' association; Richard Boyd, national president of the Fraternal Order of Police; Robert Scully, president of the National Association of Police Organizations; and Thomas Iskrzycki, chairman of the National Troopers Coalition. Overcome, Iskrzycki broke into tears upon shaking Reagan's hand. Attorney General Ed Meese lightened the mood by pointing out he was incapable of pronouncing Iskrzycki's name. The council was the brainchild of Ordway P. Burden, gadfly, author, and scion of a wealthy, philanthropically active family. Meese reckoned that Burden, as a private citizen attempting to organize law enforcement associations, embodied the Reagan administration's commitment to private sector "voluntarism." In this gathering, Reagan committed to getting a new crime bill passed, even, he cracked, if it required arresting House Speaker Tip O'Neill.[19]

While campaigning in 1984, both Reagan and his Democratic opponent, Walter Mondale, had committed to expanding federal assistance to local law enforcement, as the National Sheriffs' Association had urged. Mere weeks before the general election, which Reagan won decisively, the president signed the Comprehensive Crime Control Act. Among its suite of harsh policies, the bill increased penalties for drug offenses and eliminated federal parole as well as pretrial release for people accused of drug crimes. Legislators also invented the legal category of "career criminal" by creating a mandatory minimum fifteen-year sentence for gun possession by someone previously convicted of three felony burglaries or robberies. The bill also created the Bureau of Justice Assistance, bringing back some of the financial aid the LEAA had provided, though it reduced the maximum federal contribution to 50 percent, effectively guaranteeing greater expenditures by states and municipalities. The GOP used parliamentary procedure to bypass reluctant Democrats, including O'Neill. Because the bill was attached to must-pass appropriations legislation, many of its provisions slipped through Congress with little debate.[20]

Criticism emerged soon after the bill's passage. Representative Bruce A. Morrison, a Connecticut Democrat, complained that "political grandstanding" had larded the bill with measures that would have few effects on "street crime." The editorial board of the *New York Times* recalled the creation of the LEAA in 1968 as the last time Washington had engaged in a "serious new anti-crime program," lamenting, "Where is there an officeholder willing to sponsor anything more than trivial symbolism?" For his part, Morrison was annoyed that the paper of record appeared unaware that Congress had just approved distributing funds to state and local governments for bolstering "block watches, anti-arson squads, career-criminal strike forces, special training for police." He blamed the Reagan administration for the years of delay after the expiration of LEAA funding. Even now that the 1984 bill had passed, he accused the administration of "dragging its feet" in distributing the newly authorized funds—still another year would pass before states were to submit grant applications. Reagan's alarmist talk about the growing threat of drugs contrasted with his administration's chary approach to the DOJ's new capacities to help police, like the Bureau of Justice Assistance.[21]

Deliberative as the federal government may have been in backstopping local police budgets, the Reagan administration worked relatively swiftly to address the needs of sheriffs. Alongside the passage of the 1984 bill, the administration initiated a separate transfer program designed to allow states, counties, and cities to obtain, at no cost, federal real estate to build new correctional facilities—what amounted to a giveaway to sheriffs contending with overcrowded jails. It was a sign that the National Sheriffs' Association had, in Bittick's view, quickly "moved to the forefront of the law enforcement and criminal justice community."[22]

One provision of the Comprehensive Crime Control Act also changed the game for sheriffs. Title III enhanced the ability of law enforcement agencies to seize property, including in all felony drug cases. The legislation specified that property could be seized and assets frozen prior to indictment. Congress created a new federal fund for depositing the proceeds of seized and then forfeited assets, and it allowed local sheriffs and police to obtain

80 percent of the revenue from forfeitures when they aided federal investigations. Under this "equitable sharing" scheme, the money could be spent on law enforcement exclusively, unlike revenues generated by seizures under state laws. In the words of Attorney General Ed Meese, "forfeited assets can give sheriffs a real boost in their battle with cash-rich drug traffickers."[23]

Where criminal forfeiture depends on a judicial process, the right to an attorney, and a finding of guilt, civil forfeiture is more like a lawsuit that renders the original possessor of the seized money or goods a third party. The seizure occurs before a judgment is rendered, and guilt or innocence is often irrelevant. Rather than proof of a criminal act, suspicion that property has been obtained through illicit means or has been used in a crime is enough. The seized property then can become evidence in a criminal prosecution. Those who face seizures without conviction may need to appeal directly to the police department or prosecutor's office that seized their property or pay for their own legal representation. Seizure requires probable cause, but retrieval requires a preponderance of evidence that the property is not connected to criminality. Police will negotiate over seizing one asset but not another or simply issue an ultimatum: forfeit property or face criminal charges and jail time.[24]

Sheriffs rushed to join multiagency task forces that would enable them to grab assets forfeited in federal investigations. The Reagan administration began orchestrating regional drug task forces in October 1982, building on a Nixon-era model of federal-local collaborations. The first was in south Florida; Reagan put Vice President George H. W. Bush in charge. Two years later, a dozen were operational, with Reagan's budget dedicating just under $106 million to them. Within a decade, 1,000 multijurisdictional task forces existed, both formal and provisional. The federal grant program that was the stepchild of the LEAA would soon be allocating half its funds to such task forces, magnifying the possibility of federal prosecutions of low-level dealers snared in their investigations. Right after the 1984 crime bill's forfeiture provisions incentivized state and local participation, 60 percent of regional task force prosecutions included these agencies' investigators.[25]

Joining the task forces afforded these agencies access to seized and forfeited assets, while the Drug Enforcement Administration covered "operational and equipment costs," including overtime pay for local agencies, and assumed liability in any federal civil suits arising from the investigations (though it disclaimed any responsibility for civil rights violations). Task forces set up in metropolitan areas like San Diego or rural areas like the Cascades would often include representatives from tiny agencies, allowing them to detail a single officer but share equally in the proceeds of seizures. The Drug Enforcement Administration also launched Operation Pipeline in 1984, training over 25,000 police and sheriffs over the next two decades how to spot drug "mules" on highways. One district court judge who analyzed operations of a Colorado drug task force, including officers trained through Operation Pipeline, deemed them to be based on a "racist assumption" that violated "the constitutionally protected rights of blacks and Hispanics to travel and be free from unreasonable seizures." The colloquialism "driving while Black" has its origins in Operation Pipeline's practices: skin color alone could put motorists at risk of a pretextual police stop.[26]

Soon, thanks largely to Representative Hughes, the House Crime Subcommittee chair, and Joe Biden, who became the Senate Judiciary Committee chair in 1987, Congress passed additional bills to extend authority for seizures of "drug-tainted assets" and raise the ceiling for how large cash forfeitures could be without the judicial procedure required for real property. Some of the money would go to victims of the crimes that led to the seizures, but most would not.[27]

Republicans had conjured a kind of alchemy: the administration could cut budgets while law enforcement agencies generated their own new revenue. Attorney General Richard Thornburgh quipped, "It's now possible for a drug dealer to serve time in a forfeiture-financed prison after being arrested by agents driving a forfeiture-provided automobile while working in a forfeiture-funded sting operation."[28]

The National Sheriffs' Association encouraged its members to learn how to take advantage of the potentially rewarding federal funding stream. And it celebrated members who received payouts, like Sheriff Bill Hutson of Cobb County, Georgia, who had instituted a tricounty antidrug unit in 1980. The DOJ's check for $76,639.02 would, he insisted, go to expanding undercover narcotics operations, which might lead to more checks.

One Florida sheriff purchased a new bomb disposal truck with forfeiture funding. The association depicted it in *Sheriff* magazine, along with its accompanying bomb retrieval robot, named Andros. The magazine also lauded former association president Don Omodt of Hennepin County, Minnesota, when his department received the largest single award in fiscal year 1990, $215,474. Over time, the ceremonial DOJ checks grew—physically. For Omodt, the DOJ made it look like he had won the Publishers Clearing House sweepstakes.[29]

By 1990, every state but one had put in place drug-related asset forfeiture policies. Police developed model legislation and lobbied state legislatures to make seizures as easy and lucrative as possible, aligning with liberal federal policies. The National Sheriffs' Association's Law and Legislative Committee, collaborating with several state sheriffs' associations and other law enforcement groups, successfully opposed the first efforts to rein in federal civil asset forfeiture. Recognizing how prevalent asset forfeiture had become, the DOJ convened a working group representing prosecutors and all the major police associations, including the National Sheriffs' Association, which called for a nationwide set of standards, training, and technical assistance.[30]

The problem was that asset forfeiture did not always work smoothly. Long delays in distributing proceeds of federal forfeitures made the goal of fully funding local narcotics policing through seizures almost impossible. And sheriffs too often sought "easy" seizures, rather than more challenging prizes, "from securities to real estate." They found it "too hard to follow the cash trail of other, larger profits." The Police Executive Research Forum warned that the dealers most vulnerable to asset seizures might not be the ones who were most active or dangerous. Because sophisticated traffickers often hid their fortunes in legitimate businesses, the sheriffs' association encouraged sheriffs to look beyond "weapons, cash, cars, planes and boats" and instead focus on "seizing the wealth" criminal enterprises had accumulated. This would send "a chilling message," but it required a "no holds barred" approach. Although tactical seizures "built up motor pools," they contributed to a widespread perception that police were as "money-motivated" as "street-level drug dealers."[31]

The vast majority of individual forfeitures remained small in the 1980s, with medians near what a family might save to make a monthly payment on a Plymouth Voyager, not what a kingpin would spend on a Learjet. Seizures tended to come from drug users, not dealers, who themselves tended to be poor or not to speak English. Equitable sharing did incentivize a pivot to drug enforcement, but at the cost of increased traffic fatalities as police lost interest in highway safety. Speeding tickets reaped puny rewards.[32]

Budget cutbacks pushed many sheriffs to become politically defensive. When a Reagan proposal to cut the federal deficit put federal revenue sharing on the chopping block, the association urged members to call or send telegrams to the White House. When the association defined its legislative priorities in 1986, half pertained to protecting or strengthening federal subsidies, including the top four of eleven.[33]

In the end, asset forfeiture became a kind of dependency for law enforcement. Some sheriffs would cover 40 percent of their costs with forfeitures under state law. The pursuit of big scores had a meaningful effect on day-to-day operations—in states requiring that asset forfeitures fund other agencies like schools, police deemphasized state crimes and focused on federal investigations instead, chasing equitable sharing dollars that they would be able to keep for themselves.[34]

"Strength in numbers!! Unity through participation!!" This was the political rallying cry of one president of the National Sheriffs' Association in the 1980s. As the decade wound down, the sheriffs used this unity to push for continued expansion of the war on drugs. Soon, almost the entirety of the country's political class would find itself chasing the high that came from bipartisanship. Elected officials everywhere could not resist joining the endless fight against drug abuse.[35]

CHAPTER 16

THE BIPARTISAN WAR ON DRUGS

Reagan put his stamp on the war on drugs when he signed the Anti–Drug Abuse Act on the eve of the 1986 midterm elections, but this signature anticrime bill took shape with relatively little involvement by the president or, for that matter, lobbying by police groups. It emerged largely thanks to Congress, particularly the House Select Committee on Narcotics Abuse and Control. Democrat Charles Rangel of Harlem, one of the nation's leading Black legislators, began chairing the committee in 1983, and worked closely with the ranking minority member, Benjamin Gilman, a white Republican from the Westchester suburbs north of New York City.

In contrast to the Reagan administration's inconsistent and lethargic approach to anticrime legislation, Congress acted with alacrity. The signature Anti–Drug Abuse Act further increased penalties for trafficking, and it introduced new grants for states to engage in drug enforcement as well as educational programs. It also contained provisions to expand deportation for drug-related offenses, as well as to expedite issuance of a federal immigration "detainer" of an "alien" arrested for a drug violation by local, state, or federal police. This legislation was also the origin of the 100:1 disparity between crack and powder cocaine for triggering mandatory minimum sentences, all but guaranteeing harsher punishments for Black cocaine users than for white ones.[1]

Together, Rangel and Gilman achieved a few bipartisan objectives. They used the bill to draw together foreign and domestic drug-control efforts. Identifying drugs as borderless, the 1986 bill designated drugs as a national security issue, formally recognizing how the security apparatus already operated. They also took pains to prioritize funding assistance for state and local law enforcement specifically earmarked for narcotics, on top of what was already on offer through the Bureau of Justice Assistance.

Rangel and Gilman used the bill's passage as an opportunity to call out the White House for its failure to live up to its law and order promises in the war on drugs. They poured scorn on the administration's markedly low appropriations for grants to police in its 1987 budget, which Congress overruled. Rangel cracked, "You can shove money down an Administration's throat but when they don't want it they cough it back up." At a hearing where mayors and law enforcement officials expressed alarm about Washington turning off the spigot, Rangel dramatically apologized on behalf of the federal government. It was Washington's fault, he lamented, if mayors issued campaign promises to introduce drug programs in schools or to expand police operations but might not be able to keep those promises. He assured mayors that whatever Reagan desired, "we would not cut and run."[2]

The police organizations played a surprisingly small part in the efforts of Rangel and Gilman. The IACP was experiencing internal turmoil and restructuring, and the echoes of the rank-and-file rebellion meant that mistrust and bad blood existed between management and line officer organizations and among the Fraternal Order of Police and the other organizations that jockeyed to represent patrol officers nationally.

Although urban ills fueled Rangel's eagerness to wage war on drugs, drug smuggling necessarily also touched on rural areas patrolled by sheriffs, particularly in the borderlands. The feds first started reconfiguring Washington's relationship with sheriffs in 1983 by declaring that local law enforcement should cooperate with the Immigration and Naturalization Service. Immigration enforcement had long benefited sheriffs because they operate thousands of jails across the country in places where there are no federal pretrial detention facilities. Sheriffs eventually learned to take advantage of new resources, though they were slow to adapt.[3]

Though they were reliably conservative and anticommunist, sheriffs were at first mostly unwitting participants in Reagan's recrudescent global Cold War, which now targeted migrants who were arriving in the United States after Washington had supported the wars that caused them to flee their home countries. Yet Chicano activists immediately recognized that immigration reform plans the Reagan administration floated in its first year would strengthen the Border Patrol, build new detention facilities, and accelerate deportation of asylum seekers, particularly from El Salvador and Haiti.[4]

Reagan eventually signed the Immigration Reform and Control Act just weeks after signing the Anti–Drug Abuse Act. The two laws ushered in a new enforcement regime, which entailed new scrutiny of legal status, sanctions for employers of undocumented workers, and ramped-up expulsion of undocumented people with criminal charges. These changes shifted how police and sheriffs might interact with those deemed potentially deportable. Some city councils demanded that their police departments refuse to collaborate with the Immigration and Naturalization Service, particularly after immigration officers staged a wave of raids. These agents aimed to gin up anger at undocumented people and bolster support for the immigration bill while Democrats were holding it up in Congress. But for sheriffs, who operated beyond the direct control of local officials, the incentives would become clear, if perverse: collaboration in migration enforcement that led to greater numbers of deportable individuals could mean more money for detaining them.[5]

Two years after Reagan signed the first antidrug bill, not long before he was to leave office, a second Anti–Drug Abuse Act landed on his desk for signature. Bipartisanship and savvy negotiating, led by Joe Biden and cheered by Rangel, had produced the bill, which tightened the knots linking military and police and extraterritorial and domestic law enforcement, and made punishment even harsher.

Although each of the crime bills of Reagan's two terms was, in its own way, an attempt to heed the priorities of numerous legislators and constituencies while finding a solution to apparently inexorable street crime, the bills shared a consistent ambition to spend more money on police. But none of the crime bills of the Reagan-Bush years crossed the red line that the 1968 Omnibus Crime Control and Safe Streets Act had established: direct federal funding to pay the regular salaries of state and local police.

Money for new police programming was far easier to come by. In the words of William Hughes, Arlen Specter's companion in creating the

Congressional Crime Caucus, "more resources were allocated to supply reduction and taken away from demand reduction, which wasn't so sexy," meaning legislators fattened the wallets of cops, not drug counselors, in part by turning cops into antidrug educators, including through programs like Drug Abuse Resistance Education (DARE).[6]

DARE began in 1983 as an educational program in Los Angeles that placed police in school classrooms. But it quickly grew to a national program operating in all fifty states by the end of the 1980s thanks in part to federal grants to establish training programs for police. Cops learned how to provide strong antidrug messages to children while also stressing resistance to peer pressure, personal responsibility, and respect for authority, including cops. In this way, according to one historian, educational funding nevertheless found its way to police headquarters.

The 1986 Anti–Drug Abuse Act allocated less than 20 percent of dedicated funds to antidrug education. The next year, DARE America incorporated as a nonprofit, which allowed the program to draw more easily on corporate philanthropy. Dozens of major companies, from Coca-Cola to Warner Brothers to Lockheed Martin, lined up to bestow donations, enabling DARE America to develop a range of educational materials. This reliance on corporate donations was a response to the Reagan administration's pressure to control drug use through education of potential users while withholding the funding to do so. Though DARE America's nonprofit status allowed it to claim that it was not reliant on federal funding for its nationwide efforts, the cops going into classrooms every day were still paid out of state or local police budgets.[7]

DARE was an educational program, but it also represented a changing national mood. While rap and punk lambasted cops from the margins, DARE helped to seed the field with pro-police cultural messaging. In Columbus, Ohio, four cops and a commercial real estate broker got together as the band Hot Pursuit. Landlocked, they played less yacht rock than cruiser rock, with hooky, upbeat love songs full of references to the job. The girl didn't just drive Officer Randy Moon crazy. "The way she twists my mind is brutalizing me," he sang. Hot Pursuit's album, *Communicate*, was issued as a benefit for youngsters undergoing drug treatment at the destination children's hospital in Columbus. The city's police department funded the band's touring schedule, which reached 200 gigs a year at its peak, including at a White House conference in 1988. Soon the band recorded a tense, moody tune for a DARE music video. The chorus implored listeners to "dare to keep a kid off dope" and "dare to give a kid some hope." Available on VHS, the video featured vignettes of teens "growing up too fast" and escaping a rough home life. Clips of kids getting high were interspersed with live shots of the band performing in uniform, with sidearms. The guitarist wielded a six-string shaped like a semiautomatic rifle.[8]

COPS ON THE CHASE

Reagan's war on drugs reignited faded hopes among police that they might make gains in Washington. The IACP lauded the anticrime legislative push throughout the decade, particularly because of the new funds that were becoming available for innovative police operations. Right after Congress passed the 1984 bill and Reagan approved it, the IACP alerted its membership to the "special importance" of the new Office of Justice Assistance. It made sure to quote the bill's implicit sky's-the-limit funding authorization: "such funds as are necessary."[9]

The chiefs also lent hortatory support to the growing obsession among legislators with drugs. Declaring drug abuse to be "Public Enemy Number One" in an official resolution, the IACP pushed for police to have a central role in demand reduction. That meant "an all-out concentrated campaign," which consisted of education, zealous prosecution, and "the continuance of a high level of enforcement activity." When the president signed the 1986 Anti–Drug Abuse Act, IACP executive director Jerald Vaughn joined the ceremony, "pleased with the additional resources and criminal penalties" the bill afforded.[10]

Yet the new resources and harsher penalties had little positive effect as the 1990s arrived. The war on drugs seemed to be stalemated. In the representative words of a news brief in the police magazine *Law and Order*: "Seizures Up Coke Prices Stay Same." Although counternarcotics spending had doubled in three years and the amounts of cocaine seized had nearly quadrupled, production seemed unaffected. Neither the supply nor the demand diminished. And even if narcotics control did succeed, the indicator would be higher prices.[11]

In this sense, contemporary US narcotics control policy depended on each of its constitutive parts failing. The Drug Enforcement Administration, the Department of Defense, and, eventually, Department of Homeland Security all focused largely on source control, endlessly trying to eradicate the crops that produced the drugs, destroy the manufacturing facilities that processed them, or interdict their transshipment into the United States, while assisting police and militaries in other countries. Because source control did not succeed, domestic law enforcement focused on the demand side, trying to stop drug distribution as close as possible to the consumer or to nail the consumer himself or herself. But consumers did not cease to consume because of the threat of arrest, and low-level distributors did not cease to distribute because of the risk of prosecution. This strategy was a failure, yet each part benefited from the failures of the others, and each failure became a justification for committing further resources, so that it might succeed even though the others failed. If addiction was the driver, it was the addiction of all these different parts to public resources.

The anticrime and antidrug bills of the 1980s were not the result of police lobbying on its own. Police and sheriffs supported aspects of them, but the bills combined so many differing goals and pushed so many of federalism's legislative boundaries that it would be impossible to attribute the spoils they ultimately granted police to a grand plan. Succeeding by failing was not a police-orchestrated conspiracy. Yet the resources hailed police, and the police began to regain coherence as a constituency, as had been the case in the late 1960s with the Omnibus Crime Control and Safe Streets Act when the chiefs were in the lead. The intervening years of rising rank-and-file power, as well as gradual diversification of police forces, had fractured any tenuous settlement within the profession that the chiefs had attempted to impose. And Blue Power stoked its own rivalries. Even the White House had to tread carefully, making sure not to invite International Union of Police Associations president Bob Kliesmet to the same meeting of labor leaders as Fraternal Order of Police president Leo Marchetti. Kliesmet could be "brought over to our side," while Marchetti was considered a reliable "friend." ("For our purposes," an aide suggested, the fraternal order could be considered a labor organization even if it was "not within the traditional mainstream of organized labor.")[12]

But thanks to Mario Biaggi's effort to prevent a rare, or even nonexistent, crime problem—shooting deaths of cops caused by specialized bullets—police would exit the 1980s far more cohesive than they had entered the decade, ready to spring into action when the largest crime bill of all would be on the table.

CHAPTER 17

BULLETPROOF

If the growing police commitment to collective bargaining put cops at odds with the New Right, an even greater gulf would emerge around the Second Amendment. Within the conservative movement, there was disagreement about how weak gun laws should be, but the consensus on the right, aided by millions of dollars from arms industry lobbyists, was that the more restrictive gun laws that accompanied Johnson's War on Crime needed to be reconfigured. Although individual police may have agreed, police union leaders wanted to minimize the risk of injury or death of their members. Loosening gun laws did not seem likely to make cops safer, even if three-quarters of the nearly 50,000 assaults on police recorded from 1967 to 1976, the era when the dangers faced by cops peaked, did not involve weapons.

Violence against police had energized Blue Power. Fear of police getting shot in the line of duty, and anger when it did occur, began to drive police politics at the municipal level in the late 1960s. It was true that in the decade after the Detroit and Newark uprisings, 1,077 police across the country were killed. Police responded to officer shootings with extralegal violence as well as organizing. In Detroit, Baltimore, San Francisco, New York, and many other cities, police had severely cracked down on Black radical organizations like the Panthers after officer ambushes. But suicide killed more officers than homicide, and suicide was a complex problem with no easy solution. Homicides of police seemed easier to fix, but they could also galvanize political change.[1]

The most straightforward response to violence directed at police was to make cops bulletproof. Although body armor is not cheap, police officials always point out that it is well worth the price. One 1978 estimate suggested that it would cost $41.8 million to give every cop in the country a bullet-resistant vest, a small fraction of the LEAA's $647 million budget that fiscal year. But Kevlar, the strong synthetic polymer fiber that would become synonymous with body armor, was developed by DuPont scientist Stephanie Kwolek only in 1965. Before Kevlar became widely available, body armor typically relied on metal or ceramic plates. These were hot, heavy, and restrictive, and officers were reluctant to wear this type of armor.

It was not until 1975 that the much more comfortable Kevlar soft body armor got a trial run in Baltimore. Lightweight, inconspicuous, and easy to put on and take off, the Kevlar vest appealed to Baltimore cops. Commissioner Pomerleau worked to outfit every patrol officer and sergeant with a vest by the end of the year. The Department of Justice then issued new standards for police armor, heavily relying on Kevlar, which helped to convince skeptical cops to adopt body armor more widely.[2]

All that remained was the question of how to pay for all of this new gear. Police had not yet won sufficient power on the national level to pass the kind of legislation that would cover the tab. On the municipal level, activists resented new spending on bulletproof vests to protect cops when Black folks

Lightweight bullet-resistant vest on display, 1975. *U.S. News & World Report* Magazine Collection, Prints & Photographs Division, Library of Congress, LC-U9-31649, f 7A.

remained exposed to police brutality and economic austerity. In 1979, one radical group in New York City decried the underlying argument that "*killer cops* are the *victims*." Despite the "firetrap housing, rampant unemployment, lousy schools, [and] organized crime" afflicting so many in New York, scarce funds were being diverted to officer protection. Body armor for cops would do nothing to ameliorate these "deplorable conditions." The police union's efforts to convince ordinary people that police faced the gravest dangers amounted to a diversionary "attempt to counter the growing struggle of the Black community for human rights."[3]

Nevertheless, many big-city police departments were able to obtain some form of soft body armor for their officers beginning in the mid-1970s. LEAA analysts hypothesized that Kevlar had already contributed to the marked decline in officers killed annually by 1977.

Soon a new worry arose. Certain bullets, designed for police use to penetrate vehicle doors or windshields, were now available on the retail market. These bullets could pose a danger to officers even if they were protected by Kevlar.

What ensued was a striking bifurcation between local and national police politics. As the panic about armor-piercing bullets spread, experts realized that the real danger to cops was self-inflicted: during the summer and winter, the LEAA reported that only 38 and 55 percent of officers, respectively, actually wore the vests. Even when collective bargaining agreements began requiring municipal governments to pay for vests, unions could not force officers to wear them. Locally, the vests became contentious; nationally, the new bullets did.[4]

Some leaders, like Sam DeMilia, the president of the New York City Patrolmen's Benevolent Association, sought to politicize the question of vests, as well as the bullets that could penetrate them. In 1979, he launched a campaign called "I Have a Vested Interest in New York's Finest," encouraging donations to protect his officers. DeMilia's fundraising committee had three co-chairs: a white-shoe lawyer on the benevolent association's retainer, a real estate executive, and DeMilia's buddy Meade Esposito, the cigar-chomping, gravel-voiced Brooklyn Democratic boss. Yoko Ono and John Lennon contributed $1,000 out of "genuine concern" for police officers, a little over a year before Lennon would be felled by an assassin's bullet. Major corporations like Citibank as well as Brooklyn retailers offered sizeable donations, while schoolchildren contributed nickels and dimes. The campaign raised $1.3 million in total. But city investigators soon zeroed in on the Patrolmen's Benevolent Association because it appeared to be purchasing bulletproof vests at inflated prices, without a competitive bidding process. DeMilia welcomed "any and all inquiries" into the purchases. "There has never been anything as clean as this operation," he boasted. This outer-borough braggadocio was a familiar tone to one member of Congress, who was also close to Esposito: Mario Biaggi, formerly a member of the police union DeMilia led.[5]

Around the same time, just as the union was trying to equip all its members with new bulletproof vests, DeMilia claimed that armor-piercing "super bullets" had begun flooding the streets of New York City. But no one knew if there was any truth to the claim. Biaggi made a limited effort at introducing legislation to have the Treasury Department research the bullets. It came to nothing. At the time, one senator's aide called the House "the graveyard of criminal justice legislation." With the outside encouragement of DeMilia, now newly installed as president of the National Association of Police Organizations, the refuge for police unions that refused to affiliate with the AFL-CIO, Biaggi set out to change the tone among his House colleagues.[6]

"UNITY IS ESSENTIAL"

In January 1982, NBC ran a television news segment focusing on the "KTW" bullet: a brass bullet that was coated in Teflon, another DuPont-invented synthetic. It seemed no cop had been confirmed as killed by a KTW bullet at the time that NBC drew attention to it, but no clear data existed either way. After the documentary aired, it became apparent to Mario Biaggi that a patchwork of local bullet bans would not suffice, compelling him to act more aggressively on Capitol Hill. He introduced the Law Enforcement Officers Protection Act in February 1982. Senator Daniel Patrick Moynihan then introduced a companion bill in the Senate. But success still proved challenging.[7]

Biaggi anticipated that the National Rifle Association and police organizations would collaborate to ban the bullets. He was wrong. The rifle association was critical of the documentary, arguing that it revealed information to the general public that only specialists needed to know, and the industry mobilized in opposition to the ban. Meanwhile, many leading police advocates also targeted the documentary itself. One writer suggested the program offered "a blueprint for killing cops," while Associate Attorney General Rudolph Giuliani claimed that simply debating the ban "will encourage assassins and other criminals to search out these particularly dangerous classes of ammunition."[8]

Firearm industry talking points quickly overpowered police defenders. Giuliani argued that even finding a clear definition for "armor-piercing bullets" would pose an insurmountable challenge for any potential bill. Moreover, Giuliani noted that because a bullet's penetrating power would differ when fired from a rifle rather than a handgun, legislation would end up affecting sport shooters. The National Rifle Association's lobbying arm amplified this argument, suggesting the bill would "deprive firearm owners of the use of their weapons." But supporters of the bill started to use a phrase that caught the industry off guard: "cop-killer bullets." Soon, it was on the lips of newscasters everywhere.[9]

Two years later, the Reagan administration finally introduced its own version of the bullet ban. It focused on projectiles marketed as capable of piercing aluminum armor, rather than the Kevlar-based armor available to most officers. In place of Biaggi's commonsense definition of an armor-piercing bullet as a bullet that could pierce armor, the administration followed the National Rifle Association's guidance to substitute a definition based on the metallic composition of the slug, and pointedly left existing bullet stock unregulated. A committee analysis of this version of the bill observed that its effects were likely to be nil.[10]

Mario Biaggi never deviated from his script: he wanted to pass a bill that would protect officers. But he and his aide Craig Floyd knew that the only way they would succeed was if they could demonstrate that a bullet ban had widespread support among police. Biaggi and Floyd took it upon themselves to cultivate that support and train police leaders in how to make their feelings known on the Hill. They would cajole police leaders, and police leaders would then cajole members of Congress. The ban itself was only one goal of the legislative process. The other became the process of organizing the otherwise rivalrous police organizations.[11]

The last time police organizations had put aside their differences was to support the Public Safety Officers' Benefit Act. Propelled by fears of political militants targeting police and signed into law by Gerald Ford in 1976, the bill provided a $50,000 benefit for surviving family of state or local police, firefighters, or prison guards who died on duty, administered by the LEAA. The strongest supporters of the survivor benefit had been Democrats like Biaggi and Peter W. Rodino, plus moderate New York Republican Hamilton Fish Jr. That bill did not have to overcome serious opposition on its way to passage. The bullet ban was different.[12]

Biaggi and Floyd settled on a strategy that would transform short-term failure into success for the most restrictive version of the ban, outlawing importation, manufacture, and sale (including existing stock) of armor-piercing bullets. Because Biaggi's ban had failed to proceed year after year, each time he reintroduced it he had a fresh opportunity to bring police organizations

Biaggi with "cop-killer bullets" display. Mario Biaggi Papers, The Bronx County Archives at The Bronx County Historical Society Research Library.

into his coalition. The strategy, as Floyd put it to his boss, was to "get law enforcement groups to unite behind one bill, which is both strong and politically viable." Biaggi gathered eight police groups one year, then a dozen the next. He told them, as his speaking notes recorded: "We're here to reach agreement on course of action to take—unity is essential—law enforcement community cannot afford to be split on this issue."[13]

Success required that police play an active role, walking the halls of the congressional office buildings while in uniform, in a "coordinated lobbying effort." The plan was to have each group "be responsible for lobbying" specific members of Congress and developing the crucial count of how a vote would play out. Further, Floyd provided action items for the organizations' leaders, including the joint letter they would eventually send to Reagan. He also suggested that cops could author op-eds and letters to the editor and should meet with their local congressional representatives at home, where their organizations were strongest.[14]

In the meantime, Congress had passed the Comprehensive Crime Control Act, which opted for punishment rather than prevention. At Giuliani's suggestion, it contained a mandatory five-year sentence when armor-piercing handgun ammunition was used in a violent crime. But it did nothing to limit the availability of the ammo. Floyd worked with the House subcommittee, led by William Hughes, on a strategy to narrow the differences between Biaggi's bill and the administration's version. They would push forward the ban on sales, which was Biaggi's priority, while dropping other "objectionable" provisions, including a buy-back clause.[15]

Biaggi worked to consolidate police groups behind his bill, rather than the administration's version. But when police groups sent a joint letter to President Reagan, urging his support for Biaggi's bullet ban, in January 1985, not every group signed on. According to Floyd, some organizations had already committed to the administration's version and were reluctant to withdraw support in favor of Biaggi's version, "even though they agreed it was a better bill for police." The Fraternal Order of Police's president supported the bill but, in classic cop circumlocution, "found a lack of interest by interested parties to this legislation for a summit meeting." Biaggi was insistent: the "law enforcement community cannot afford to be split" over details in the legislation, as that would make the passage of any bill unlikely. It was time to unite police into a single lobbying force.[16]

Once it became clear that a ban on sales of existing stock remained the sticking point—not including the ban would be a "serious omission" that "would undermine significantly the effectiveness of the legislation"—the Fraternal Order of Police finally agreed to join its usual antagonist, the IACP, in support of Biaggi's bill. By November 1985, Biaggi had managed to unite a dozen groups that were otherwise typically at odds, including the Fraternal Order of Police, the IACP, the International Union of Police Associations, the National Association of Police Organizations, the National Organization of Black Law Enforcement Executives, and the National Sheriffs' Association. All supported Biaggi's ban on sales, rather than the more limited ban on manufacture and import that the Reagan administration advocated. But there was still one battle with the gun industry left to fight. With Congress debating an even larger firearms bill, the newly unified national police lobby now faced off against the National Rifle Association directly—and with it, policing's contradictory relationship to gun regulation became highly visible.[17]

BULLETS VERSUS GUNS

Over the nearly twenty years since the 1968 Gun Control Act, the firearms industry had built a campaign to unwind restrictions on gun sales. Not long after Reagan took office in 1981, Idaho Republican senator James A. McClure introduced a bill to do exactly that. The Democratic-controlled House dragged its heels, but by July 1985 the latest version of the McClure–Volkmer gun bill had passed the Senate 79–15. The bill, also known as the Firearm Owners' Protection Act, was at once tough on crime and pro-gun, increasing penalties for the use of a gun in drug trafficking offenses while repealing some record-keeping requirements on bullet sales and making it easier to sell firearms across state lines, allowing unlicensed "hobbyists" to sell firearms at gun shows.[18]

The National Rifle Association supported the McClure–Volkmer gun bill while opposing the Biaggi bullet bill, arguing that rank-and-file cops were far more favorably disposed toward gun rights than the leaders who claimed to represent them. There was some truth to this claim—much like the police who criticized documentaries about armor-piercing bullets for teaching the public information that would kill cops, rank-and-file officers complained directly to Biaggi that he was publicizing their vulnerabilities, and that his "big mouth" was responsible for getting officers killed. Nevertheless, the coalition backing Biaggi's bill, including the Fraternal Order of Police, IACP, and National Sheriffs' Association, defied the gun lobbyists, petitioning President Reagan not to sign McClure–Volkmer, and forming the Law Enforcement Steering Committee Against S. 49 to oppose it.[19]

The Law Enforcement Steering Committee succeeded in forcing changes to the gun bill, but the "rift" between the National Rifle Association and police organizations only widened. In the IACP executive director's view, the skirmish over the bill "could best be described as a blood bath, with both sides experiencing a certain degree of damage." The IACP and the National Rifle Association parted ways in 1986, with the chiefs' leadership voting to ban the gun association from exhibiting at the IACP's annual meeting, while also developing new firearms training programs that circumvented the National Rifle Association. Forty years later, the National Rifle Association has not returned to the IACP's annual exhibit hall.[20]

The battle solidified the police lobby into a nearly unified bloc. The IACP's executive director celebrated the "very positive working relationships" among police organizations that had cohered "as they never had before" to oppose this liberalization of gun laws. Yet there was one exception to the otherwise unanimous opposition to McClure–Volkmer: the International Union of Police Associations. Robert Kliesmet had cozied up with the National Rifle Association, leading Biaggi to criticize him personally. Kliesmet, Biaggi complained, had "compromised" the interests of police by becoming "closely involved with a competing special interest group." Isolated, after failing to construct a broad-based national police union affiliated with the AFL-CIO, Kliesmet flaunted his independent streak, in the process marking himself as the champion of rank-and-file officers who favored gun liberalization over bullet bans.[21]

Despite disapproval on the right, Biaggi's bullet ban passed 400–21 in the House in December 1985. Conservative Republican and first-term representative Dick Armey of Texas, who would go on to work with Newt Gingrich as House majority leader, claimed to speak on behalf of police, arguing that the "overwhelming majority" of cops did not support the ban. But with the backing of all the major police organizations, and reluctance among House members to kick the bill to 1986, an election year, the bullet ban had gained a head of steam that the Firearm Owners' Protection Act lacked. Still, a final fight in the Senate loomed, as archconservative Jesse Helms of North Carolina had placed a hold on the bullet ban.[22]

Immediately after the House vote, Biaggi addressed the Law Enforcement Steering Committee. "If not for the substantial and very visible support from the law enforcement community," he confirmed, "there would be no victory to celebrate." The passage of the ban in the House demonstrated "in a very convincing way just how formidable a political force the law enforcement community can be when speaking with one forceful voice." The Fraternal Order of Police's president personally commended Biaggi for getting the bill through the House. "You put your personal and legislative career on the line to back law enforcement throughout this country. We will never forget you!" It was now up to individual police officers to finish the fight, pressuring their senators.[23]

But while awaiting a Senate vote, Biaggi's bill was eclipsed early in 1986 by McClure–Volkmer. It suddenly advanced, causing police to organize more intensely, worried about the switch in momentum. The IACP had previously encouraged its members to call legislators and urge them not to sign a discharge petition, an arcane procedure that allowed a piece of legislation to proceed directly to a floor vote. But, sure enough, Volkmer organized a rare successful discharge petition, pushing the gun bill out of committee. In response, hundreds of cops rallied at the Capitol in uniform on the day of the House vote.

It was a standoff between gun power and Blue Power. The gun lobby maintained the advantage: they had donated $1.4 million to members of Congress running for reelection in 1984, including most who signed the discharge petition. They also had the Reagan administration on their side. Attorney General Meese, branded "the best friend law enforcement ever had" by one police organization official, kept his own skepticism about the liberalization of handgun sales private. IACP executive director Jerald R. Vaughn was shocked: "I'm new to Washington," he lamented, but "I'm baffled by how someone can say publicly they support something and privately they don't." One congressman who refused to speak on the record observed that the gun lobby was simply better at working the Hill: "The average deputy sheriff doesn't know a lot about how the House works." The bill passed the House 248–176.[24]

But the fight was not yet over. Though the president of the Police Foundation had groused that members of Congress were more afraid of the National Rifle Association than of police, conservative congressmen calculated that further opposition to a bullet ban was not worth the political cost. Craig Floyd saw a narrow path to victory through the reconciliation process.[25]

In the end, the final, reconciled version of the bullet ban contained Biaggi's preferences. It preserved the prohibition on sales of existing stocks of armor-piercing bullets that the House version of the bill proposed, absent from the Senate version. Biaggi lauded the "full-forced lobby effort by the law enforcement community" and thanked his House colleague William Hughes, as well as Senators Biden, Moynihan, and Thurmond. To Biaggi's chagrin, Ronald Reagan deprived police organizations of an opportunity to join a signing ceremony at the White House, signing it in California with little fanfare. But the bill had been signed into law just the same. Biaggi had proved that a legislator could herd competing organizations with differing constituencies and goals. His work had "opened lines of communication" among police groups and "laid the groundwork" for further collaboration, according to the IACP's executive director. It was a turning point in the consolidation of police power on the national stage.[26]

McClure–Volkmer was also a turning point for gun policy. It changed the regulatory and record-keeping architecture for gun sales to foster, rather than constrain, their freer circulation. In its wake, the gun control consensus among police organizations frayed. After tepidly supporting the 1993

Brady Bill, which imposed a waiting period for handgun purchases and created a permanent infrastructure for instant background checks, police took the side of the National Rifle Association in support of gun laws that would allow street arrest of violators rather than reduce the availability of guns. The bullet ban had unified police, though what they would do with their newfound power remained an unsettled question.[27]

CHAPTER 18

WEEKEND WARRIORS ON CRIME

After Reagan signed Biaggi's "cop-killer bullet" ban into law in 1986, the term "cop killer" should have receded from politicians' lexicon. But in March 1992, Body Count, a metal band fronted by rapper Ice-T, released a song called "Cop Killer" on its self-titled first album. The compact disc hit stores a month before the verdict in the trial of four police officers charged with assaulting Rodney King, the Black motorist who received a savage beating by police, surreptitiously recorded on a bystander's home video camera. When a mostly white jury found the officers not guilty, Black people rebelled, and Los Angeles burned. It was the largest outbreak of civil disorder since 1968.

"Cop Killer" narrated a surprise attack on police officers as revenge for police abuse. The song's lyrics named Daryl Gates, chief of the Los Angeles Police Department, as well as King. The chorus included the menacing phrase "Tonight we get even." Ice-T called the track a protest and argued that the lyrics embodied the position of someone who was fed up—but who was fictional. He himself had never killed a cop. He pointed out that he was no more a cop killer than David Bowie, who sang about piloting a spaceship, was an astronaut.[1]

In the aftermath of the Rodney King case and the Los Angeles rebellion, police used the Body Count song as a tool to reclaim popular approval and respect, as well as to paint criticism of policing practices as tantamount to threats on officers' lives. The Combined Law Enforcement Associations of Texas, or CLEAT, working with member police unions, pressed Body Count's record label, Warner Brothers, to drop the band and withdraw the album. When the media conglomerate Time Warner resisted, invoking the right of free expression, several other police organizations joined the effort, including the Grand Lodge of the Fraternal Order of Police and the National Association of Police Organizations, as well as the officer unions of New York City and Los Angeles. President George H. W. Bush and Vice President Dan Quayle condemned the track as "sick" and "obscene," respectively. Sixty members of Congress wrote letters to Time Warner in support of police. Police labor expert John Burpo described the controversy as "a textbook example of how police associations can, regardless of their affiliation, work together toward a common goal."

CLEAT decided that the best way to frame the issue was as one of corporate greed, as its leaders worried that demanding censorship would backfire. Whether to demand that consumers boycott Time Warner—"the ultimate act of corporate warfare," in Burpo's view—was a strategic question. The organization wanted to win; what winning would entail was not obvious. But because CLEAT was not a hierarchically organized political party, it could not control the line that members chose. Once the Dallas Police Association asked its own members to boycott the company, CLEAT determined that threatening, rather than launching, a broader consumer boycott would be effective. Meanwhile, Warner Brothers was receiving bomb threats, forcing evacuations as officers scoured the building "looking for bombs which didn't exist." Cops knew the bombs did not exist, according to one executive. As he learned from a buddy on the force, they were the ones calling in the threats.[2]

At a press conference that attracted national media coverage, CLEAT's president, Ron DeLord, made sure to play the song. And he warned Time Warner that he would be organizing outraged police officers to appear at an upcoming shareholders' meeting. Depending on what happened at the meeting, a boycott might ensue. In the meantime, the National Sheriffs' Association passed a resolution calling on Time Warner to stop distributing the song, and the Grand Lodge of the Fraternal Order of Police asked all members across the country to boycott the company. Sales immediately soared. The album went gold—500,000 copies sold by the beginning of August.[3]

In Los Angeles, a small group of police and police family members, organized by CLEAT, showed up at the Time Warner shareholders' meeting. A clutch of supporters of Ice-T showed up to protest too. Although police outnumbered counterprotesters, Burpo also observed that there seemed to be as many reporters as there were police taking part in a picket. Coverage was good, but he noted that this provided a useful lesson for police union organizers: if you do not get a good turnout at a police picket, label the attendees a "representative" group of rank-and-file cops, rather than calling it a "mass" demonstration.

A front group funded by the National Rifle Association, the Law Enforcement Alliance of America, which adopted the obsolete LEAA acronym, claimed to have been the originators of the call to protest Time Warner, indicating that even as Burpo believed the "Cop Killer" controversy fostered cohesion, jockeying for leadership of police, which CLEAT was itself doing, remained inevitable.

At the shareholders' meeting, attendees demanded that Time Warner's chief executive address the controversy. They disrupted the proceedings, preventing him from conducting other business. When he relented, shareholder Charlton Heston offered a dramatic reading of the lyrics of "Cop Killer." DeLord, as well as several other police union leaders, gave "impassioned speeches." Ice-T did not apologize, nor did the company, to the consternation of the police associations that had ginned up the hullabaloo for their own purposes.

A couple of weeks after the meeting, Body Count "voluntarily" removed the album from distribution. On a new pressing of the album, the band replaced "Cop Killer" with a track called "Freedom of Speech," featuring a guest appearance by Jello Biafra, though Body Count continued to play the song live. After the band removed "Cop Killer" from the album, few retailers returned the original pressing in exchange for the new one. Sales of the censored version were unimpressive, while collectors snatched up the original.

CLEAT and other organizations called for a "cease fire" and acknowledged that a consumer boycott of the label would be difficult and fruitless. The president of the New York Patrolmen's Benevolent Association counseled DeLord to declare victory and move on. Nevertheless, some small police organizations like the New York State Sheriffs' Association continued to call for a boycott. After the larger organizations scaled back their vitriol, the astroturf Law Enforcement Alliance of America, which naturally focused most of its work on "protecting law-abiding citizens' Second Amendment rights," claimed credit for "national success by forcing Time Warner to dump the infamous Ice-T," even after executives refused to budge while meeting with the group.[4]

Coming in the middle of an era when politicians had repeatedly courted police with law and order rhetoric stripped of economic follow-through, the "Cop Killer" brouhaha put on display how readily police unified around cultural issues rather than material ones. The Law Enforcement Alliance of America engaged in the fight because it claimed the song had the "potential to impact violent crime by encouraging impressionable youths into acting out." Even as the organization tried to chalk actual violence up to song lyrics, its circuitous phrasing could not help but indicate that causation was complicated. Only political organizing and grandstanding by police could bridge the gap, transforming the song's fantasy into real-world consequences.

But the controversy also highlighted how much disunity persisted within the profession, particularly across the color line. Throughout the spring and summer of 1992, several different African American police organizations, including the National Organization of Black Law Enforcement Executives, refused to condemn Ice-T, arguing that police brutality remained a significant problem and that he was "entitled to voice his anger and frustration with the conditions facing oppressed people." Bruce W. Cameron, the dyspeptic editor of the most conservative police magazine, *Law and Order*, wondered, "Was it simply because the group was black that there were no great denunciations from the liberal side of society—or even the organization representing black police officers?"[5]

One detail lost in the kerfuffle was that Body Count, as a band, appealed mostly to disaffected white teenagers who learned about the song because of the widespread condemnation. My close friend Nick, who attended an elite prep school in Manhattan, turned me on to Body Count in 1993. Though I recalled the controversy that had occurred the prior year, I had never actually heard the band. After the height of their infamy, in December 1992, when Body Count played The Academy, a midtown New York club, Nick joined the mosh-pit fray. To this day, when I think of the song "Cop Killer," I get a mental picture of Ice-T menacingly surveying the crowd from the stage, asking the crowd in his demotic baritone: "What do you wanna be when you grow up?" And teenagers like my pal, a skinny WASP whose dad worked in finance, reaching for the mic to yell "Cop Killer!" At the concert, Nick approached Ice-T, who was sitting in the balcony with his wife, and asked for his autograph while Dirty Rotten Imbeciles began their set. Nick never did obtain "a 12-gauge sawed-off," as mentioned in the lyrics, but he did get the rapper's signature. And Ice-T would go on to become far more famous playing another fictional character on the television series *Law and Order: Special Victims Unit*—a police detective.

COPS ON THE CAMPAIGN TRAIL

Bush had won election as the tough-on-crime candidate, but just like Reagan, he was in no rush to sign major legislation on crime policy. The nugatory measures he did sign, after vociferous and racist fearmongering, opened the door for Democrats to reposition themselves. Both parties aspired to be seen as tough on crime, constantly recalibrating policy gradients in their quest. But neither had any firm idea of how Washington could meaningfully stem crime. "Congressmen and senators are afraid to vote no," New York Democratic representative Chuck Schumer rued, "even if they don't think it will accomplish anything." Police associations had no answer for them—they appealed to Congress and the White House to act to protect and serve police. Allaying the public's fears about crime was not in their interest.[6]

The White House, Congress, and the law enforcement organizations needed cooperation and focus to achieve legislative success. But cooperation was not preordained. When it came to policy, internal disagreements in the profession persisted. Whether a Republican or a Democrat in the White House would be better for police remained uncertain throughout 1992, an election year in which a third-party challenger undermined the Republican incumbent. Like 1968, it was an election year marked by political rebellion about six months before voters entered the booths. But Democrats had learned the lesson of 1968, and Bill Clinton was determined to win by portraying himself as both sensitive to racism and ready to act on crime.

The Law Enforcement Steering Committee had originally formed to oppose McClure–Volkmer's liberalization of gun laws. The group consisted at different points of ten to twelve law enforcement associations, and it had been working since 1988 to craft major new legislation to aid police, in collaboration with Joe Biden and other legislators. The IACP officially quit the group in 1992. It disagreed with the softer position other members advocated on gun policy. But the IACP remained important because of its history in Washington, the prominence of many of its individual members, and its reputation for consistently supporting police professionalism.[7]

By the time of the 1992 election, the International Union of Police Associations was too weak to command much influence, though Bob Kliesmet endorsed Clinton and condemned Bush as a "weekend warrior in his war on crime." Its new political action committee spent just under $10,000 on Democratic candidates that year, a small sum. As novices in the minutiae of federal campaign finance law, its member unions ran afoul of the regulations. For instance, Kliesmet's old union, the Milwaukee Police Association, attempted to donate directly to the international's political action committee. To do so, it had to register with the feds, but the International Union of Police Associations did not want its locals to register independently. Donations had to be returned. Most of the money legally funding the political action committee came in the form of $20 donations from individual cops or their family members across the country. But the committee nevertheless directed donations to candidates representing the districts of their would-be donor member unions, including Milwaukee's longtime Democratic representative, Jerry Kleczka.[8]

Still dominated by rural agencies, the National Sheriffs' Association, for its part, failed to articulate how it could meet the challenge that drove the conversation: street violence in cities. And the US presidential election was sandwiched between elections for the leadership of the Fraternal Order of Police and the National Association of Police Organizations. These leaders would have to work together.

Yet Clinton and the Democrats struggled to prove their anticrime mettle. Biden was perpetually frustrated that the most effective anticrime measures inserted into the bills that Reagan and Bush had signed were the ones originating within his party, under his oversight. "I am going to say something outrageous," Biden railed in the Senate chamber. "I defy anybody in here to show me they have a better relationship with the police organizations of this country." And yet, he complained, "I am characterized as a wide-eyed liberal Johnsonian Democrat."[9]

Biden promised Strom Thurmond that he could get Democrats to pass crime legislation that would also mollify staunch conservatives, ensuring that the GOP still got credit. Biden thus honed a discourse designed to demolish the notion that his party coddled criminals. He embraced conservative repudiations of social explanations of crime, arguing that the new "consensus" was "we must take back the streets." From the floor of the Senate, Biden wailed, "It doesn't matter whether or not they were deprived as a youth. It doesn't matter whether or not they had no background that enabled them to become socialized into the fabric of society. It doesn't matter whether or not they're the victims of society. The end result is they're about to knock my mother on the head with a lead pipe, shoot my sister, beat up my wife, take on my sons." He did not care "what made them do this." Instead, he declared, "they must be taken off the streets."[10]

It was not until 1992, when he was up for reelection, that George H. W. Bush asked Congress to pass a large-scale omnibus crime bill, something Biden had already been working on. Bush's late pivot to focusing on crime earned him some credibility with police, particularly because he framed it as an extension of his tough approach to foreign policy, which emphasized drug trafficking. But when he expressed disgust at the beating of Rodney King, he annoyed many cops. He tried to thread a needle by supporting a federal civil rights investigation into the Los Angeles Police Department while denouncing the rebellion as having nothing to do with civil rights or protest. "It's been the brutality of a mob, pure and simple," he declared, effectively indicating that he saw King's brutalizers in the same light as he did those who rose up against the verdict.[11]

As the election approached, Bush gave what amounted to a campaign speech at the IACP annual meeting in 1992, but the group issued no official endorsement. Bush did propose spending around $1 billion on federal assistance by fiscal year 1993, up from $334 million spent in 1989, and his budget reserved $469 million for direct grants. Wary of this outreach to police, Clinton claimed that regardless of the increases over his time in office, Bush intended to slash $100 million in federal grants to police.

The Fraternal Order of Police endorsed Bush in 1992. Dewey Stokes, the organization's husky national president, had met Bush when the National Law Enforcement Council secured a White House meeting in 1989. At the time, Bush's police agenda remained nebulous. Stokes, by contrast, was vigorous. He defended the need for swift punishment and determinate sentences, "and to hell with all the things" that occurred in defendants' childhoods that might explain their behavior. Stokes came across as street-smart and confident but also knowledgeable about Washington.[12]

The Fraternal Order of Police appreciated that Bush had endorsed a new omnibus crime bill, which he argued was the toughest anticrime legislation ever introduced. But the president's men lobbied the Fraternal Order of Police's board, and Bush reached out directly to Stokes. Bush's chief of staff, James Baker, took advantage of the organization's lack of a codified endorsement process. Twenty-five of forty-seven members of the board supported Bush, enough to clinch the endorsement. But Stokes was reluctant, and he demanded "a little reciprocity" from the president. Stokes wanted action in Washington that would directly benefit police, and he knew that the omnibus bill was primarily the result of collaboration between Biden's office and the Law Enforcement Steering Committee.[13]

Stokes had recently been reelected as national president of the Fraternal Order of Police. He won a second term while pledging police "unity," but the campaign was one of the most contentious in the organization's history. Stokes was a cop from Columbus, Ohio. He had experienced the emergence of collective bargaining rights for police in the state firsthand while leading the city's Fraternal Order of Police lodge. But in 1991 he faced a challenger for the national leadership, Tom Possumato, a detective from Newark, New Jersey.

A supporter with deep pockets backed Possumato. Through its Law Enforcement Alliance of America, the National Rifle Association was trying to get the Fraternal Order of Police to stop pushing for gun control. Ejecting

Stokes from the national presidency seemed the most expedient way to do so. The president of the Law Enforcement Alliance of America claimed that his organization stood for "the line officer, the working stiff," who opposed a waiting period for handgun purchases, unlike Stokes, who was campaigning on the success of the Brady Bill, which had recently passed the House. Possumato denied that he was the National Rifle Association's ringer, but cash that came from the Law Enforcement Alliance of America bought him a high-priced marketing firm, mass mailings, telephone polling, and advertisements. It was not enough, however, to overcome the value of Stokes's reputation in Washington.[14]

Once Clinton won the presidency, Stokes realized that he should work with the new administration, though not all cops were so easily convinced. Bush's actions in the final months of his presidency certainly helped change many minds on this front.

After indicating that he would sign the Brady Bill if it was included in the omnibus crime bill, the president balked—he did not want to sign a gun control bill, but he was wary of rejecting it. A month before the election, Bush's staff made sure the legislation died without a vote, sacrificing Biden's crime bill in the process. Robert Scully, president of the National Association of Police Organizations, complained, "I feel betrayed by the whole process," which had been ongoing since 1988. He placed "blame clearly with the Bush administration." In the aftermath, Stokes and Scully became allies, refocusing their attention on winning passage of the omnibus crime bill. Now when Stokes visited the Clinton White House, he came wearing his police uniform, to show that he meant business.[15]

With Robert Scully as its executive director, the National Association of Police Organizations was now Clinton's most reliable supporter among the dueling police organizations. Although the Detroit-based organization emerged from the wreckage of the International Conference of Police Associations after it affiliated with the AFL-CIO, it remained more closely aligned with the labor movement than with the Fraternal Order of Police. Scully had been a member of the bargaining team of the Detroit Police Officers Association since 1973, after becoming a Detroit cop just months after the 1967 rebellion. And Scully was as convincing as he was persistent, just like Carl Parsell, in whose footsteps he walked. Attorney General Janet Reno referred to her expectation of getting an "incisive comment" from Scully whenever they worked together, while also knowing to expect "trouble" when he approached her, "jaw jutted out." Scully even converted the association's president, Thomas Scotto, a Bush backer from Staten Island, into a Clinton supporter.[16]

Before Clinton's election, the Law Enforcement Steering Committee lacked confidence that Washington was willing to devote significant amounts of money to policing. The group's official blueprint in 1992 was unambitious. Grants for "community policing" were on the table, but the best the group hoped for was a series of studies and research grants, as well as earmarks for programs like DARE, education in prison, and anticrime public service announcements. Clinton's win changed the tone, giving members like Stokes and Scully new self-assurance. All the while, far from the White House, in the nation's cities, cops were ready to take over.[17]

CHAPTER 19

WHO RULES THE CITY?

By the 1980s, New York City had become the epicenter of Blue Power. It was home to the country's largest single municipal police union, the Patrolmen's Benevolent Association, along with four other police unions that represented each rank. The association loomed large in officers' lives even beyond the job, assisting with personal legal matters like divorces or drafting wills, as well as planning for home purchases and retirement. But because of its size, resources, and zero-sum tactics, the Patrolmen's Benevolent Association's power both to control the police department and to shape city and state politics grew redoubtable in the 1980s.[1]

The 1992 presidential election had proven to be a minefield for the national police organizations. Bill Clinton was eager to demonstrate, with the aid of Joe Biden in the Senate, that Democrats could be cops' best friend. It would mean that Democrats had to make sacrifices to those on their right flank, which showed cops that they might still have something to gain from attacking Democratic elected officials. Where the national police organizations found themselves flummoxed, the New York City Patrolmen's Benevolent Association, long familiar with forcing Democrats to bend rightward, plowed through this political minefield, setting a new tone. The benevolent association would again prove that the national blueprint for success of a police union would be drawn on its most familiar home terrain.

In 1989, David Dinkins challenged Ed Koch, a law and order Democrat whose mayoralty had lurched into scandal and political sclerosis by the end of his third term. Dinkins was a progressive former state assemblyman, Manhattan borough president, and most recently the New York City manager of Jesse Jackson's 1988 presidential campaign. After Jackson narrowly beat Michael Dukakis among city voters in the primary election, Dinkins built on Jackson's campaign apparatus to assemble a diverse coalition of unions, cultural workers, and ethnic and racial organizations. Koch won the endorsement of the Patrolmen's Benevolent Association, but it was not enough. City residents sought a new path away from the backroom deals and neoliberal urban redevelopment schemes that Koch endorsed. Dinkins toppled Mayor Koch in the primary, then narrowly defeated Republican challenger Rudy Giuliani by only 3 percent to become the city's first African American mayor.[2]

Crime in New York City is always a national story, and the four serious violent crimes indexed by the FBI—murder, rape, robbery, and aggravated assault—reached their highest level in 1990. Murder incidence remained stubbornly high, at over 2,000 annually, from 1987 to 1994. When it did finally start to decline, ultimately bottoming out at 292 in 2017, the New York Police Department received a great deal of credit. Yet homicide rates declined in similarly precipitous fashion across the United States, as well as in Western Europe, Canada, and Australia, and places where police departments did not replicate New York's tactics. Still, cops felt that they should be lauded for the crime decline and recognized for the difficulty of their jobs. They resented criticism. The mere existence of any civilian oversight, which Dinkins was entertaining while crime was at its peak, implied there was just cause for criticism.

The New York Police Department and its officer unions, in contrast, sought public sympathy with mawkish spectacles. They perfected the practices of honoring injured and slain officers in this period. The Patrolmen's Benevolent Association, assisted by executives of the financial firm Bear Stearns, secured the purchase of a new home on Long Island for Officer Steven McDonald, for instance. He was shot in Central Park in 1986, leaving him quadriplegic. At a ceremony attended by hundreds of cops and well-wishers, the mayor choked up, finding himself too emotional for a speech on the new home's porch. Although the numbers of line-of-duty deaths fluctuated annually, by the late 1980s, with the totals declining, funereal choreography acquired its most potent form. Lengthy processions, with 4,000 or even 8,000 officers lining the streets, became common. The department's Emerald Pipe Band, police brass, and city dignitaries would accompany family members to the services. Irene Herman, widow of Jeff Herman, and Bebe Herman, his mother, were accompanied by 4,000 officers when he was laid to rest. Herman "enjoyed the action," and was killed in the middle of it in 1989 as a member of an anticrime unit. The Patrolmen's Benevolent Association lamented that Herman had been childhood friends with another cop slain the prior year, Bobby Machate. "Cops represent society," an association member wrote. "If you assault a cop, you assault society; threaten him and you threaten everyone."[3]

But in New York City, cops killed and brutalized Black and brown people with alarming regularity. Throughout the 1970s, 1980s, and into the 1990s, names of city residents killed by police accumulated on protest flyers and placards and in eulogies. Clifford Glover. Randy Evans. Arthur Miller. Manuel Martinez. Domingo Morales Jr. Luis Baez. Elizabeth Mangum. Ricky Lewis. Kenny Gamble. Michael Stewart. Eleanor Bumpurs. Edmund

Youth protest after the 1980 police killing of Kenny Gamble and Ricky Lewis in New York City. *Police Magazine*, March 1981, Laurie Peek.

Perry. Federico Pereira. José "Kiko" García. Nicholas Heyward Jr. Pain and animosity accumulated too. Without fail, the Patrolmen's Benevolent Association defended the killer cops. The union's president was widely quoted as urging officers to "shoot first and shoot to kill."[4]

After Officer Stephen Sullivan killed Eleanor Bumpurs, a sixty-seven-year-old Black grandmother, with two shotgun blasts at the door of her apartment during an eviction, the Patrolmen's Benevolent Association spent $15,000 on radio and newspaper ads to defend the officer and "set the record straight." Under the leadership of President Philip P. Caruso, the union also organized a rally of 10,000 police officers outside the district attorney's office after Sullivan was indicted. It was likely the city's largest police demonstration until that point.[5]

Two weeks later, a bomb detonated at the police union's office in Manhattan. The bombing, according to a caller, was in protest of the union's support for "racist murder and killer cops." No one was hurt. But the district attorney subsequently dropped the charges against Sullivan. Nothing that New Yorkers did—not lawsuits, protests, or violence—seemed capable of curbing the city's police department. Instead, the police union was using all of these to get its own way.[6]

As the 1990s arrived, police unions had achieved a modicum of success in most cities, securing decent contracts, including binding arbitration and a host of perks for each individual officer. Two-thirds of all local police agencies now allowed collective bargaining. Control over Washington remained the prize that police organizations coveted, but dominance over state and local politics lent police significant influence over national politics, even if indirectly, with New York City as a leader.[7]

The profession remained overwhelmingly white, and New York City had the lowest percentage of Black officers (though the second-highest percentage of Hispanic officers) among the five largest cities in 1987. Nationally, 85.4 percent of local police, 86.6 percent of sheriffs, and 88.7 percent of state police were white. Entry-level sheriff's deputy positions paid about $1,800 more annually on average than entry-level police positions, though small agencies tended to pay lower salaries at all rank levels. It was possible for a starting officer in New York City with only a high school diploma to earn more than a twenty-five-year veteran chief in a small town. In such big cities, union contracts were the reason.[8]

Winning a contract was never the end of the line for rank-and-file cops and organizers, particularly as budget cuts remained a recurring threat. Chiefs received constant complaints about violent crime from mayors, city councils, journalists, and business and property owners, which meant that they did not relent in pressuring line officers either. In Minnesota, Missouri, and New Jersey in 1989, even before a recession set in the next year, police voiced anger at lagging pay and layoff threats. Familiar tactics like the blue flu joined with public relations efforts, like bumper stickers and posters promoting union objectives, as well as more aggressive approaches.

When the New Jersey state government slashed its emergency funding for "distressed cities," the largely working-class and industrial port city of Elizabeth was in a bind. Rising costs, including for disposing of waste, forced layoffs. The mayor was a deeply conservative and prototypical Reagan Democrat. He determined that up to 221 police, fire, and ambulance workers would be let go. In response, police staged an angry protest that encircled the mayor's house after midnight. No state or county police agency responded to his calls for help. "I was scared for my life," he reported. "I thought they were going to storm the house and burn it down." A couple of days later, an Elizabeth cop held a gun to the head of a trucker who tried to squeeze past a highway blockade that cops were manning as a protest against the layoffs. Despite the promises of labor relations experts, access to collective bargaining had not tempered all rank-and-file fury.[9]

Across the river in New York City, the fury smoldered with police union boss Phil Caruso. Unlike some of his crude and confrontational predecessors, like Ken McFeeley, who organized the "Fear City" campaign, Caruso brought a dignified approach to the position. But he was no less intransigent.

THE ASCENDANT NEW YORK CITY PATROLMEN'S BENEVOLENT ASSOCIATION

The eighth union president in a tempestuous ten-year stretch, Phil Caruso became the most powerful head of the union since John Cassese, because of the results he garnered and his conviction that civil rights protections were overshadowing police officers' rights. Caruso had earned a master's degree while a police officer and strove to develop an analytic method for success at the bargaining table. Caruso also built close ties with the Koch administration when it needed friends. He concurred with Sam DeMilia, who had defeated him in the race for union president in 1977, when he observed that the Patrolmen's Benevolent Association could accomplish the two things that most worried politicians: "help them or hurt them."[10]

Although Caruso dutifully appeared in public—always in tailored suits—he was fiercest behind a desk. His prose, on display in regular columns in the union's magazine, *New York's Finest*, was wordy, pretentious, and vehement. Caruso reserved special spleen for those who also relied on the pen: "Then there are the editorialists, the opinion makers of the media who, with Prussian resolve, proffer oracular wisdom from their oak-paneled bunkers on how to best wage war against crime."[11]

Within the union but well out of earshot, cops labeled Caruso a "dictator." He enforced a code of silence while deploying more than 350 union delegates, almost all white men, as his spies and enforcers. Caruso prized conformity. When nine members objected to an automatic and involuntary payroll deduction of $20, to be deposited with Mario Biaggo's National Law Enforcement Officers' Memorial Fund (his other pet police project, after the bullet ban), Caruso castigated them. He offered to return the money, but he publicly shamed the officers, printing their names in *New York's Finest*. He declared, "You are a disgrace to the entire police service, and you have no valid reason to remain within the ranks of the PBA." He recommended they resign from the union: "We don't want you, and we don't need you."[12]

Together with the legendary negotiator Richard Hartman, Caruso's leadership garnered major gains for police officers, including in retirement benefits, while also keeping pay increases slightly above the inflation rate. In addition, Hartman and Caruso devised a way to extend the time needed for officers to reach salary steps, saving the city money initially, but it meant that as officers stuck around, their pay increased more dramatically than before. In the 1988 contract, incumbents benefited, while young people who hoped to become cops in the future were at a disadvantage, with future starting salaries frozen. The contract also antagonized the heads of other uniformed unions because they had to make unpopular concessions to achieve the wages and benefits Caruso and Hartman negotiated. One called Caruso "The Pope," for acting like he and his members were better than the other unions.[13]

Hartman and Caruso were opposites. Hartman was disheveled and gregarious. Caruso was meticulous and reserved. But they forged a bond lubricated by a gusher of cash. In the election for president of the benevolent association in 1980, Hartman advised both Caruso and his opponent, Charles Peterson, though he secretly funneled more money to Caruso's campaign. He was a bettor and he liked Caruso's odds.

When Hartman became the Patrolmen's Benevolent Association's attorney and chief negotiator, he clocked an annual retainer of $750,000. It would creep past $1 million in short order, then shoot past $2 million. By comparison, his predecessor had been receiving $47,500. When another police union Hartman advised cut him loose, its legal expenses were halved. Tax dollars provided the money that allowed union profligacy, either collected as dues from paychecks or paid into various benefit and legal defense funds and escrow accounts Hartman set up.[14]

Yet Hartman's fees were tolerated in light of his inarguable prowess at the bargaining table. His style could best be described as unorthodox—Hartman once purchased fifty ice cream sundaes to share. He ate three. No one else ate the remaining forty-seven. Hartman also displayed unflagging support for police away from the bargaining table. Cops could dial 212-H-A-R-T-M-A-N at any hour of the day or night to be connected to a lawyer who could aid them in a jam.

Before working for the city police union, Hartman had been responsible for winning "ground-breaking" contracts for police unions on Long Island. Later, hard-line police unions across the tristate area, like Stamford's, also sought his assistance. The better compensation and often easier work for cops on Long Island caused recruitment challenges for the city's police department. But matching the luxurious contracts cops received in Nassau County served as a perpetual goal for the city's unions. Hartman prodded New York City cops to pay attention to what their counterparts in "neighboring jurisdictions" were earning. A 1982 back cover of *New York's Finest* italicized his words: members "deserve to be, as they once were, the highest paid police officers with the best fringe and pension benefits in the country." While lobbying, Caruso's successor would carry two pay stubs with him, illustrating a stark salary difference between two cops: a three-decade veteran in New York City who earned around three-quarters what his son-in-law with nine years on the job in Nassau County took home.[15]

PATROLMEN PLAYING POLITICS

By the time Rudy Giuliani first ran for mayor in 1989, he had already learned that it was better to accommodate Koch's confederates than to vanquish them. As US attorney for the Southern District of New York, Giuliani investigated associates of Koch for corruption, while also seeking dirt on Koch's sexuality. He indicted Mario Biaggi in 1987 in a bribery and kickback scheme involving the defense contractor Wedtech. Biaggi proclaimed his innocence to the end, and he was actually acquitted of separate bribery charges involving his buddy Meade Esposito, the Brooklyn political boss. For extortion and other counts, Biaggi received an eight-year sentence, which the judge would have extended if not for Biaggi's supposedly failing health. He recovered after two and a half years behind bars and unsuccessfully campaigned to return to Congress. The Patrolmen's Benevolent Association was one of nine uniformed unions to endorse him. Caruso declared, "No one has ever championed the cause of police officers more eloquently, more forcefully and more effectively than Mario Biaggi." Giuliani took this plaudit as a challenge.[16]

The Wedtech scandal also ensnared Ed Meese, then Reagan's second attorney general. A key influence-peddling player at the center of the scandal was Meese's "best friend," but prosecutors deemed the evidence against Biaggi to be stronger. Meese eventually resigned in the aftermath of the probe, plus the far more nefarious Iran-Contra affair, though he was never indicted. Meese was so disliked in Washington that local punks in the Dischord Records circle covered the city in hundreds of wheat-pasted posters declaring MEESE IS A PIG. They made shirts too, which became especially popular among bike messengers who delivered packages to the Department of Justice. Biaggi's own defense was that Wedtech would not have needed to bribe a lowly member of Congress. Via Meese's buddy, the company could simply telephone the president's longtime counselor, who was far more powerful. Giuliani's underling rebutted this claim by saying that it did not change what Biaggi had done, while acknowledging in court that, indeed, "Meese was a sleaze," causing some observers to clutch their pearls. It was perhaps the one time that a federal prosecutor found common cause with a punk T-shirt.[17]

But Giuliani's own sleazy behavior ultimately stood out. Giuliani wanted to file his indictment first so that he could determine how his racketeering-fighting acumen would affect his political prospects in an upcoming US Senate race. If he had run against Senator Daniel Patrick Moynihan and won, he would have become New York's junior senator alongside the Republican from Nassau County, Alfonse D'Amato, whom Hartman had "dropped everything" to put into office. Hartman had lined up around 200 police unions to endorse D'Amato. He might have been able to do the same for Giuliani. Regardless, Giuliani wanted to be mayor more.[18]

Caruso was surprised that Dinkins defeated Koch in the primary and Giuliani in the general election of 1989. Dinkins represented the enemy. He was a Black man who believed in rehabilitation for those who committed crimes and disagreed that arresting low-level drug offenders was sound policy. Caruso schemed to make him miserable.

Several months before the election, Dinkins planned to give a speech at Rikers Island, the city's massive jail complex, instead of attending the funerals of two officers who had recently been killed on the job. Giuliani never let Dinkins forget this decision, saying it signaled "his priorities." Soon after winning, a chastened Dinkins skipped a scheduled vacation to attend another two officer funerals. Line-of-duty officer deaths in New York City declined to thirty-two in the decade of the 1990s, from a post–World War II peak of seventy-nine in the 1970s, but each one carried the potential to be political dynamite.[19]

Dinkins was less willing than Koch to give the Patrolmen's Benevolent Association what it expected as its right, including better contract terms than nonuniformed city employees had. When contract talks stalled and the union declared an impasse in 1991, police officers staged a ticketing slowdown. Union delegates spread word of the action, though the union did not officially condone it. Ticket totals plunged by 54 percent; a sergeant quipped, "If these cops slowed down any more, they'd be dead." Arbitration did not go in the union's favor. A lawyer did not help the union's case by suggesting the city save money by spending less on welfare—"a gratuitous shot at the city's first black Mayor," in the words of one labor journalist. Caruso soon initiated a campaign to require arbitration to go before a state board. The city's "puppet Board of Collective Bargaining," according to one police union official, "never decided in a union's favor."[20]

Dinkins also refused to approve a semiautomatic 9mm handgun as the new service weapon for officers. And he created what became known as the Mollen Commission to investigate police corruption. But, despite delaying an incoming police academy class due to budget woes, Dinkins also protected the department from budget cuts and allowed its complement of officers to grow. For one Black communist critic, this only proved that Caruso's union was able to "intimidate elected officials," including Dinkins, who was now "attacking the very base that elected him" by cutting social services, while growing "silent and 'diplomatic'" toward the police department amid "rising police brutality."[21]

In July 1992, a plainclothes officer, Michael O'Keefe, beat and fatally shot an undocumented Dominican immigrant, José "Kiko" García, in Washington Heights. O'Keefe, who played football in high school, started a college degree in English but decided to become a cop when his father got sick. On his first day of patrol in 1986, O'Keefe drew his gun on a stabbing suspect. After six months he requested assignment to the 34th Precinct, in upper Manhattan. A veteran on the force told him it was "the best place for young aggressive cops" because the neighborhood was "a round-the-clock maelstrom of crime." Immediately after the killing, residents of Kiko's block lit fires, tossed bottles, and overturned a car as cops swarmed the neighborhood. One man died after falling from a roof while fleeing police. Protests continued for days, and numerous storefronts were torched. When a muralist painted a tribute to Kiko with the words P.O. O'KEEFE, FUCK YOU! above it, the police department forced the property owner to paint over the first half, leaving the words FUCK YOU on Kiko's memorial. Afterward, in the

Protesters and police in front of the mural commemorating José "Kiko" García in Manhattan's Washington Heights, before and after the police department ordered it modified in 1992. Ricky Flores.

words of one proud participating beat cop, the area was subject to "an absolute saturation of police."[22]

Like all big-city mayors, Dinkins worried about sparking New York's version of the conflagration in Los Angeles after the acquittals in the Rodney King beating. To calm tensions, he hosted García's relatives in city hall, and had the city pay for his funeral. This was the last straw for Caruso. The Patrolmen's Benevolent Association placed full-page newspaper ads denouncing the mayor for commiserating with Kiko's loved ones. (Over a decade later, a jury awarded García's mother $170,600 for false arrest and punitive damages.) The union began plotting its next move soon after the funeral, while still smarting from its lackluster arbitration award. Eyeing his next run for mayor, Giuliani would feed off the energy of the Patrolmen's Benevolent Association. Losing to Dinkins the first time did not deter him—the cops would put him in city hall one way or another.[23]

CHAPTER 20

THE COP COUP

In 1992, the police found their opening in Mayor Dinkins's efforts to temper the racist tough-on-crime politics that perpetually courses through New York City. With Rodney King still in the headlines, Dinkins revived plans for civilian review of police. It would be his undoing.

The New York Police Department had long experience mobilizing constituencies and building political careers out of opposition to civilian review. In the mid-1960s, police protests against civilian review in the city launched John Cassese to national prominence. That mobilization helped touch off the Blue Power movement in the first place. The battle lines of 1992 were inked on a political map that differed little from the one Cassese had helped to draw.

The city's review board, such as it was, had been neutralized by the police department. It was structured to guarantee equal representation of police and the public. Dinkins aimed to remove the police from the board and pull it away from the department. The police unions opposed the board and loathed the notion of granting it independence. Dinkins may have expected pushback from police interests, but what he did not anticipate was how effectively Giuliani would put himself at the center of the fight.

As the city council was set to hear a bill that would satisfy Dinkins's hope to create a review board fully composed of civilians late in the summer of 1992, Caruso convened a protest outside city hall. The demonstration turned out to be just as big numerically as the rally he staged for Officer Sullivan, who killed Eleanor Bumpurs, and the star of the event was Rudy

Giuliani. For him, the demonstration was an opportunity to grab the spotlight and reassert his connection with the white voters who had supported him in 1989. Subsequently called a "mini-riot," a "cop coup," and a "white riot," the rally marked a turning point, a vibe shift, while personally affecting at least three future mayors and two police commissioners. For Giuliani, it outlined the limits he should never again exceed if he wanted to become mayor, as well as just how far he could go before he reached them. The rally proved how much racism the city would tolerate—and reward.[1]

When the morning of Caruso's city hall rally arrived, off-duty police showed up drunk. The union had paid for buses. Some officers brought their kids. Cops carried signs attacking Dinkins in explicit and stereotyped terms, depicting him with an Afro and with oversized lips. One called him a "washroom attendant." Another asked the mayor, HAVE YOU HUGGED A DRUG DEALER TODAY? Another read DUMP THE DINK. Cops chanted, "The mayor's on crack!" and "Dinkins must go!" Some cops, more simply, just bellowed, "Fuck Dinkins!" After a brief bit of marching and copious drinking at nearby pubs, a few officers ascended atop the buses and began chanting "Take the Hall!" It was a threat to overrun the city hall security detail and rush the chambers of the council or the mayor's office. As irate cops swarmed the building's limestone steps, guards braced the door with a metal bar. Other cops jumped up and down on municipal vehicles and the private cars of city officials, including the council speaker, parked outside city hall, denting them. Although the Patrolmen's Benevolent Association planned for 150 marshals to monitor the rally and the department posted 300 uniformed cops at the site, not a single one restrained their fellow officers. Mounted police stood by idly.

Caruso, Giuliani, and his ally Guy Molinari, the conservative Staten Island borough president and former member of Congress, addressed the crowd. Looking beleaguered, Officer Michael O'Keefe, who had killed Kiko García but recently been cleared by a grand jury, also appeared. In O'Keefe's recollection, after a mention by Roy Innis, a Black nationalist affiliated with CORE who had turned to the hard right and befriended Giuliani, "the crowd hoisted me upon their shoulders and crowd-surfed me to the stage." Innis introduced O'Keefe. The officer spoke briefly to thank supporters "who remained in my corner when the mayor was trying to throw me to the wolves." He received the day's strongest applause. He later insisted that he then departed and disapproved of what happened next.[2]

The speakers stood on a platform on the back of a customized bus. It was sponsored by city business leaders as part of the COP-SHOT campaign, which offered a $10,000 "cash bounty on the head of anyone who shoots a police officer." The words TAKE THE CUFFS OFF THE COPS adorned one side of the bus. When Caruso spoke, he called the officers before him "a force for good," in contrast to the civilian review board. It represented "the forces of evil," which were "trying to defeat us."[3]

As Giuliani stepped to the microphone in shirtsleeves, cops chanted, "Rudy! Rudy!" Beside him was "Officer Never Ready," a dummy dressed in a police uniform and chained up, symbolizing the restraint that civilian

"Officer Never Ready" dummy, carted by officers to city hall on September 16, 1992. Willie Anderson/ New York *Daily News* Archive via Getty Images.

review threatened. Giuliani attacked the proposed investigation into corruption, saying it was "to protect David Dinkins' political ass," a discordant point to be made by someone who fought corruption to make his own political name. Feeling the froth in the crowd, Giuliani shouted, "The mayor doesn't know why the morale of the police department is so low." He continued, "He blames it on me. He blames it on you. Bullshit!" The *New York Times* primly disclosed that Giuliani "used an obscenity."

After his speech, Giuliani joined the crowd of cops on Murray Street who were drinking and carousing. One of his supporters mingled in the crowd and tried to register voters among the inebriated cops, dozens of whom were wearing crisp new white T-shirts implying that the next mayor's race began that day. They read DINKINS MUST GO. One officer who did not quite go with the flow chanted, "Daryl Gates for mayor!," referring to the Los Angeles police chief. The primary election, when Dinkins would defend his incumbency, was still 363 days away.

As officers grew angrier and drunker, the n-word flew freely through the mostly white crowd of cops. On the receiving end of the epithet, as well as some punches and kicks, were reporters and cameramen. Jamaica-born city council member Una Clarke also had what she called a "jolting, revolting" confrontation with a beer-swilling cop who blocked her from entering city hall: "This n—— says she is a councilmember; should we let her in?" He wore a blue uniform shirt atop civilian clothes, outwardly blurring his roles that day. The n-word was also reserved for the mayor, but he was not even in the building during the affray because he was attending a funeral uptown. Caruso later denied any bigotry. "Black and Hispanic officers who participated in the rally also heard no racial slurs," he declared. It was the media that displayed "a revolting, unmitigated bias."[4]

Just before noon, as many as 4,000 officers strutted onto the Brooklyn Bridge, just east of City Hall Park. It was a frequent site of protests against police brutality. Now cops mocked their antagonists, chanting, "No justice! No peace!" On-duty officers posted at the foot of the bridge to keep traffic flowing did not interfere. Giuliani later claimed to have had no inkling that the crowd split and thousands had headed toward the bridge while he was to the west on Murray Street glad-handing. But one officer later recalled how it happened: "What I remember was Rudy Giuliani was one of the guys who incited us." The mob of protesting cops blocked traffic and rattled cars, including one carrying the city's first Black council member, Mary Pinkett, and some of her constituents.[5]

After the riot, Dinkins blamed Caruso and Giuliani for the disruption. Caruso apologized to the police commissioner and the "public at large," though not to Dinkins. One increasingly prominent officer, Eric Adams, joined a group of fellow Black cops to demand an inquiry by a special prosecutor into what had happened. Giuliani, however, was defiant. Though willing to admit that he "used unfortunate words," he denied that a riot had occurred. All that had happened was "misconduct." When an incensed Dinkins declared, "If some officers in full view of a camera and public and their superiors or officers would use racial slurs . . . I fear how they would behave when they are out in the streets." Giuliani responded that "the relatively minor occurrence of racial epithets, if they occurred at all, has been made the focus of this rally for political purposes."

Giuliani's political staff worried that his performance—"no portrait of probity"—would hurt him. But his refusal to accept responsibility, and his constant refrain that any criticism of his behavior was mere political point-scoring, lit the path out of the mire. Caruso followed Giuliani's lead, declaring that cops were "pawns in a very complex game of political chess." Their reaction was "human." And the rally "had to take place" to send a message to Dinkins. In turn, Dinkins sent his own message. He did not sign a new contract with the Patrolmen's Benevolent Association before the 1993 election.

No criminal charges were filed against police officers who participated in the riot. Commissioner Ray Kelly ordered forty-two officers reprimanded for their behavior, including one helicopter pilot flying overhead who tooted his aircraft's horn in support. Two cops were suspended. Kelly's office issued a report on the events, which made no mention of Giuliani. The commissioner did tighten the rules on officer use of racial slurs after the riot. Now they were allowed to be uttered only in situations of "extreme emotional distress."[6]

The Mollen Commission soon began its inquiry. It spent eighteen months investigating police corruption and released its scathing full report in July

1994. It concluded that corruption was a "serious problem" in the city. Worse, corruption had adopted a new character, different from the traditional pinch, the accepted bribe, or the blind eye. The "most salient forms" of corruption now included "protecting and assisting drug traffickers for often sizable profits—stealing drugs, guns and money—and often selling the stolen drugs and guns to or through criminal associates; committing burglary and robbery; conducting unlawful searches of apartments, cars and people; committing perjury and falsifying statements; and sometimes using excessive force." Corruption "flourished... not only because of opportunity and greed" but also because of "a police culture that exalts loyalty over integrity." This culture comprised "the silence of honest officers who fear the consequences of 'ratting' on another cop no matter how grave the crime" and oversight by "willfully blind supervisors who fear the consequences of a corruption scandal more than corruption itself." Two of the New York Police Department unions refused to cooperate with the investigation. Caruso skipped a scheduled meeting of all the police union reps with investigators, and the Captains Benevolent Association unsuccessfully sued to dissolve the commission.

Although the Mollen Commission did not argue that corruption was systemic within the department, it did determine that efforts to ignore, downplay, and cover up corruption were pervasive. And the Patrolmen's Benevolent Association, particularly its delegates, who answered to Caruso, played a central role. These factotums urged officers accused of misconduct not to cooperate with internal affairs investigations or with federal agents. They enforced a "code of silence" by "stigmatizing" cooperating witnesses. And delegates also frequently tipped off cops who were secretly being investigated. These actions meant the union "often acts as a shelter for and protector of the corrupt cop."[7]

Caruso's Patrolmen's Benevolent Association supported Giuliani in the 1993 election, funneling money to his campaign through political action committees and vendors. It placed ads across the city, including one in the Jewish part of Crown Heights, which had experienced intense and violent Black-Jewish conflict two years earlier. The ad implied Dinkins was like Hitler. Another ad mocked Dinkins for highlighting his service in the Marine

Corps in World War II because he never went overseas for combat—but no Black Marines were deployed in combat roles. And the union funded a challenge to Dinkins in the primary by Roy Innis. He was unsuccessful, though he did draw away some supporters and garner a quarter of the vote in a low-turnout primary.

The union's actions in 1993 to aid Giuliani and criticize Dinkins treaded on the edge of legality, and they came amid new contract negotiations with the city. Other city unions were also placing expensive ads to pressure the mayor during contract negotiations, but only the Patrolmen's Benevolent Association mocked those other unions as having easy jobs in order to demand higher wages for cops. (City firefighters and sanitation workers die in the line of duty more frequently, however.)[8]

In New York City, no Republican had beaten a Democratic incumbent mayor in the twentieth century. No Republican until Rudolph Giuliani had had such strong support from the Patrolmen's Benevolent Association either. The aid that Giuliani received from the Patrolmen's Benevolent Association was not the only factor boosting his campaign, but it sanctioned the tone he would take.

GIULIANI TIME

In the 1993 mayoral election in New York City, Giuliani squeaked out a victory over Dinkins by about the same margin that had marked his loss four years earlier. As a result, he would become the mayor most closely associated with the city's great crime decline, even though it had started under Dinkins.

Governor Mario Cuomo aided Giuliani by allowing a quixotic referendum to appear on the ballot alongside the Dinkins-Giuliani race. It proposed Staten Island's secession from New York City, an idea underpinned by racist fearmongering about crime. Giuliani campaigned alongside Guy Molinari, shoring up votes in the whitest and most conservative borough, which many law enforcement families called home. Although Giuliani did not explicitly endorse secession, he promised a fair hearing for the idea and a "flexible position," unlike Dinkins, whom he accused of dismissing the idea in an undemocratic way, like a Soviet commissar. Cuomo had no intention of allowing secession anyway. His approval of the effort included a poison pill: mandatory approval by the state legislature. But the referendum helped usher 20,000 more Staten Island voters to the polls than had turned out in 1989. They approved Staten Island's secession.[9]

The city hall riot proved to Giuliani, according to a biographer, that if he avoided any explicit mention of race amid his vicious rhetoric, he could allay the discomfort of white voters who feared embarrassment for supporting otherwise racist policies. He could not have won unless he was running against a Black incumbent, but he insidiously framed his candidacy as opposing the trend of voting with your race. People of color constituted the majority of the city's population, but the majority of registered voters remained white. Enough of them were seeking a colorblind veneer over familiar law and order tones to gravitate to Giuliani's line in the voting booth.[10]

Once in office, Giuliani promptly unleashed the police department. On the streets, young people called the new regime "Giuliani time." Something changed, and kids felt it. "Watch out," they said. "It's Giuliani time." Fervor for secession on Staten Island abated.

The new mayor appointed Boston police commissioner William Bratton as his first new commissioner. Bratton had previously been the head of the New York Transit Police. Through innovations deployed by that smaller police force, Bratton became one of the national figureheads of the crime decline. His relentless focus on metrics, drawing on the crime analysis insights of a transit lieutenant and data maven named Jack Maple, found imitators across the country and even across the globe. Called CompStat, the program drew on old crime-mapping practices, but new technologies allowed nearly real-time location- and trend-based monitoring of crime. One reason for CompStat's popularity was that police commanders felt they finally had discovered the perfect tool for both cutting crime and controlling patrol routines. It was a classic top-down professional imperative, and cops grumbled about the way they were forced to accede to new performance metrics. But the unions also tried to take credit once the numbers turned positive.

Giuliani came to envy the good press and high poll ratings Bratton received. Giuliani wanted Giuliani to get all the credit. Bratton resigned in 1996 after Giuliani "let slip" that he was seeking a private sector position. Giuliani could not fire a man more popular than him, but he could make his position untenable. So he did, and he then basked solo in the spotlight.[11]

For the Patrolmen's Benevolent Association, Giuliani's tight victory turned out to be Pyrrhic. When it came time to negotiate a new contract, Giuliani parted ways with Caruso and repeated the pattern Dinkins had set: the police would not automatically win better terms than other municipal unions whose members were, on the whole, more likely to live in the city. The offer amounted to a wage freeze of eighteen months plus a bonus that did not factor into base salary for calculation of other benefits like pensions. Giuliani promised that something better lay ahead, once city finances improved. Caruso reluctantly swallowed this deal but declined to appear at the city hall announcement of the pact. The union president hung up his designer suits and retired.

Rancor between the Patrolmen's Benevolent Association and the mayor was, in the eyes of one observer, "the singular paradox of the Giuliani era." On a basic level, Giuliani oversaw tough negotiations with all unions representing city employees. But he also was creative. In the name of cost-cutting and efficiency, Giuliani merged the transit and housing police into the New York Police Department, a goal that had eluded prior mayors for decades. The two smaller police departments strenuously opposed the merger. It would have liquidated the two agencies' own unions. The Patrolmen's Benevolent Association thus stood to gain members, and it did not try to block the merger initially. But it soon changed its stance, and in any case the unions were closely linked.[12]

Those links were not all kosher. A top transit police union official and benevolent association lawyers, including Hartman, were later charged with orchestrating bribes to ensure that the lawyers received the transit police union's business. These financial shenanigans were possible only with separate unions representing separate police departments. That could explain why the Patrolmen's Benevolent Association's chief counsel helped write a bill to undo the merger—before he found himself among the figures indicted on racketeering charges.[13]

This turmoil set the Patrolmen's Benevolent Association back just as the national police organizations were finding their footing, figuring out how best to cash in on a promise that emanated from Democratic circles to transform what policing looked like on the streets of the country's cities.

CHAPTER 21

HIRE MORE COPS

Across the country, through the 1980s, a consensus grew that the strong compensation for police recruits that unions had netted was still not enough to replenish the ranks consistently. Worse, new recruits tended to be poorly educated working-class men with little interest in addressing the complex social problems they would face on the beat. And crime continued to rise as if the new hires had no effect at all. Cops complained, and liberal intellectuals raced to save them.

Adam Walinsky, a New York lawyer and onetime aide to Senator Robert F. Kennedy, mapped out a new organization called the Police Corps, in the hope of solving the police manpower problem for good. Inspired in part by the military's Reserve Officers' Training Corps or ROTC, the Police Corps would fund college education for police recruits. In exchange for a commitment to work as a patrol or community liaison officer, the Police Corps would cover tuition. The result, Walinsky hoped, would be a solution to the recruitment and education problems in a single stroke.[1]

There was a precedent for improving the educational attainment of police officers. The Law Enforcement Assistance Administration had funded higher education and other training for police through its Law Enforcement Education Program. The program increased the number of college-educated cops by 15 percent from 1970 to 1974, though it ultimately withered after the LEAA shut down in 1982.[2]

Reformers believed that college education made cops better communicators, as well as less likely to receive complaints or disciplinary infractions, more likely to use discretion "wisely," and more prone to exhibit sensitivity about racial and ethnic differences. Yet Walinsky's new Police Corps idea elicited skepticism. Both union representatives and department administrators wanted more cops, but the idea that young college graduates were the solution irritated many veteran police who fashioned themselves as more blue-collar.[3]

At the heart of the dispute was a long-standing debate over the value of education to policing. Professionalizers argued that lagging police educational attainment hindered departments. Their opponents argued that educational requirements would stymie recruitment. Given that, by the late 1980s, almost 9 percent of Black officers had college degrees, compared to almost 4 percent of white officers, and female officers were approximately ten times more likely than male officers to hold college degrees, if anything it was white male recruitment that would take a hit. New requirements might slit the social and ethnic envelope to which cops were accustomed.[4]

Unions tended to claim that street experience was better training than any college lesson. When, in 1988, the New York Police Department instituted an educational policy mandating two years of college for promotion to sergeant, three years for promotion to lieutenant, and a four-year degree for promotion to captain, the benevolent associations for patrol officers and sergeants sued to cancel it. They argued it created an "unfair" advantage for better-educated officers in promotion. Ultimately, the unions and the department quickly agreed to a limited set of educational requirements for promotion, though college requirements for appointment remained off the table.[5]

The New York Police Department had created its own Police Cadet Corps in 1985. Replicating a model developed by the City University of New York and personally approved by Phil Caruso, the Police Cadet Corps recruited college students and enrolled them in police training part-time during the school year and full-time over the summer. Students were paid hourly for this training and received $4,000 in loans, forgiven after two years as a cop. Upon completion of the two-year apprenticeship, students took the officer exam and received a spot on the preferred promotion list. Attrition rates were about a third, mostly by resignation.

By 1994, 374 Police Cadet Corps recruits had graduated; as a group, they were more diverse than typical recruits, with 22 percent of them African

American men, 24 percent Latino men, and one-third women. A future crime advisor to Bill Clinton, José Cerda, drew inspiration from the program. The department likewise touted the success of the program as a model for what Clinton was trying to achieve as he took up the crime control mantle and even argued that it "has strong support from labor and management alike."[6]

Yet national police leaders were the most consistent opponents of the Police Corps. Robert Scully of the National Association of Police Organizations was impressed by Walinsky's single-minded devotion to the program but nevertheless disapproved. Scully believed that the way to improve policing and expand the number of officers on the street was to allow all cops access to collective bargaining and to improve police compensation. Current cops needed funding, including for better education, but primarily for improving wages and working conditions; what they did not need was an influx of the kind of "idealistic young people" the Police Corps would target.[7]

Conservative legislatures were dubious, both of the $1.7 billion price tag for a national Police Corps and of the underlying goals of the program. One particularly vocal critic was Bruce W. Cameron, a self-described "curmudgeon" who updated *Law and Order*'s editorial line for the 1990s, previously shaped by anticommunist zealot and former FBI special agent W. Cleon Skousen. Besides his conviction that "government spending" was synonymous with "government waste," Cameron would not brook federal interference that might disrupt local police autonomy and discretion. He believed the Police Corps might work if controlled fully at the local level, but that it was not scalable nationally. He proposed an alternative: instead of seeking college-bound teenagers, departments should be incentivized to hire furloughed military members put out of work by cuts to the defense budget.[8]

Other objections were more speculative. Scully wondered if the cerebral Police Corps recruits would panic when "the shooting starts." Or would college-educated recruits spend the minimum required time in uniform and then move on to easier jobs? After graduation, would corps members intentionally get charged with a felony, making them ineligible for police service? They might take the money and run (though it would have already been paid as tuition). James Fyfe, a former New York City cop turned criminology professor, disagreed. He invoked the slogan "Once a Marine, always a Marine" and suggested that something similar would apply, though no one knew for sure how many would quit.[9]

In Washington, congressional Democrats tended to be the program's biggest supporters. Crime-obsessed Arlen Specter, as always, was the Republican exception. With six Democrats and three Republicans as original cosponsors, Specter introduced a Police Corps bill in 1989, which he claimed carried the support of the Fraternal Order of Police, International Brotherhood of Police Officers, and National Association of Police Organizations, among others. The bill stalled in committee. The Senate did approve a pilot program for the District of Columbia, at a planned cost of $25,000 per year for four years for twenty-five students. But it never went anywhere. And the Biden-Thurmond Violent Crime Control Act of 1991, which passed the Senate but ultimately failed, contained $800 million for the Police Corps and $150 million for higher education for current police. For his part, as governor, Bill Clinton supported a small Police Corps program in Arkansas, which came online in June 1992, though Arkansas ranked fiftieth in many categories of government expenditure, including state and local law enforcement. Clinton was one of the charter members of Walinsky's National Committee for the Police Corps. When he first met Walinsky and learned about his program, he joined the committee "on the spot."[10]

There was bipartisan interest in spending money on fighting crime, but the precise admixture of reform and maintenance of the status quo remained up for debate. As a result, powerful voices all settled on a particularly amorphous concept that seemed to appeal to priorities on both sides of the aisle: "community policing." It became a cipher, and few paused to ask what community policing would look like in practice if Washington devoted massive resources to it.

POLICED COMMUNITIES

Community policing became the buzzword of crime policy in the early 1990s, defining the legislation that made its way to the floor during the Clinton administration. Although the 1991 Violent Crime Control Act, introduced by Biden and Thurmond, did include a proposal for the Police

Corps, community policing was not an explicit part of the vision and the term did not appear in the bill. The depth of anger and frustration manifest in the Los Angeles rebellion in April 1992 pushed Democrats to propose a new, apparently more sensitive and sensible approach to policing. When the 1994 bill was finalized, the DOJ created a new office called Community Oriented Policing Services (COPS) to issue the hiring grants.

But what was community policing exactly? The term joins two of the most multifaceted words in the English language. Was a cop still policing while chitchatting with shopkeepers or playing flag football with teenagers, even though this had little obvious connection to crime? And who counted as a community member—urban landlords and small-business owners who lived in the suburbs, or their tenants and clientele? Community policing aspired to afford the community a voice in defining problems, but this voice-centered, participatory approach ran into irresolvable challenges, from delimiting community membership to restricting what outcomes the community could choose. Saying no to police would not be a community-scale option, just as refusal is rarely an option in individual police interactions. Patrol officers, for their part, worried that community policing was labor-intensive. To listen to citizens in the hope of solving community problems, they would have to get out of their cars and hoof it.[11]

The Clinton administration's focus on community policing drew inspiration from the "broken windows" theory that George L. Kelling and James Q. Wilson had explained in a 1982 article in the *Atlantic Monthly*. For Kelling and Wilson, community members defined order, and disorder meant a fissure in community norms. It was not even that a drunk on a corner was disorderly per se, but if a community allowed drunks to be "obstreperous," it might signal that social norms were collapsing, inviting more serious crime. The job of police was to enforce community expectations. Kelling and Wilson acknowledged that those expectations might include racist bigotry in the country's still-segregated cityscapes. "How do we ensure," they asked, "that the police do not become the agents of neighborhood bigotry?" It turned out that "we can offer no wholly satisfactory answer to this important question."

Kelling and Wilson's article, for all its influence, remained ambiguous about the causality of the phenomenon it described. Did low-level crime and visible symbols of disorder lead to more serious crime—as they wrote, "inextricably linked, in a kind of developmental sequence"? Or was it simply that in areas with community policing patrols, residents "seemed to feel more secure than persons in other areas" and "tended to believe that crime had been reduced"?

The article appeared to justify cracking down on low-level or "quality of life" infractions, and it informed the claim some police officials and mayors would make, that graffiti writers, public urinators, litterbugs, and turnstile jumpers were the ones also robbing, shooting, slashing, and raping victims in their cities. Under Bratton, Giuliani's first police commissioner, the New York Police Department explicitly invoked the theory to justify "reclaiming the public spaces" of the city by "systematically and assertively" reducing the "level of disorder," to halt the "downward spiral of urban decay." City council members on the best terms with the police department and able to elicit proactive operations tended to be those in tonier areas, where the fear of decline was palpable. New York's poor, homeless, mentally ill, sex-working, and substance-abusing denizens, mostly Black and Latino, became its targets, often in business and tourist districts, far from where most violent crime was occurring.[12]

Kelling insisted the broken windows theory was not supposed to be a warrant for zero-tolerance policing. In Giuliani's view, zero tolerance meant that any and every time an officer suspected or witnessed a low-level offense, from turnstile hopping to public urination to loitering, it was to result in a stop, summons, or arrest, particularly in business or commercial districts. This police practice of constructing the community through exclusion deviated from the notion of enlisting a preexisting community's support for police operations to maintain its stability. Yet the article facilitated both interpretations, just as some varieties of counterinsurgency theory, its precursor designed to thwart social revolutions, had done in the two preceding decades.[13]

Fundamentally, Kelling claimed that the discretion the theory entailed meant policing should be more like a craft than a bureaucratically administered industry. The subsequent conflation of Bratton's data-driven CompStat with broken windows policing among many commentators misses Kelling's disapproval of managerial controls on patrol activity. Instead, Kelling joined with Bob Kliesmet to argue that police unionism should be tailored in opposition to numbers-driven management imperatives. Kelling and Kliesmet also argued that police unions should negotiate to defend officer discretion in a proactive way, rather than only reacting by defending it after the use of force.

After the police beating of Rodney King in Los Angeles dominated national headlines, the International Union of Police Associations, under Kliesmet's leadership, surveyed its members to determine how the incident had affected them. The organization found that most police unions did not get involved in designing use-of-force policies, though they would necessarily become involved in representing officers who appeared to violate the policies, as in the group of "bystander" officers who faced departmental disciplinary charges in the King attack. Kelling and Kliesmet lamented how unions expressed an interest in shaping these policies when surveyed but failed to do so when the opportunity arose. One survey respondent characterized the distance between the rank and file and management on use-of-force policies: "The managers use pencils; we use force. Since we use the policy, it is only right that we should have a say so in its development." But it remained the case that policies on the use of force or community policing were not yet negotiating issues for most unions. Kelling noted that most unions justified strong officer compensation based on what they claimed was a "heroic" and dangerous fight against "scumbags," but he believed officers should instead be compensated well because of their problem-solving skills, their discretion, their autonomy. And they should try to protect this craft at the bargaining table.[14]

But by the mid-1990s, this discretionary, craft notion of policing was not how police unions, police management, or the political class interpreted the community-oriented imperative. Instead, the Democratic Party bowdlerized the social-scientific underpinnings, took advantage of ambiguities, and stretched the concept, hoping to put thousands more cops on the street to industrialize policing. Following the model of Giuliani's New York, they would aim to arrest every low-level offender in the country over and over again until the offenders relented, evacuating stoops, sidewalks, train stations, parks, and squares.[15]

THE CONTINUED POLITICIZATION OF CRIME

The basic argument for hiring new police was that crime had reached intolerable levels, and the reason was that there were not enough cops on the street to engage in close-contact community policing. By 1994, however, crime had already begun its historic decline, according to FBI statistics. Few noticed. And no one could have known with any certainty that crime would continue to decline, particularly because officials in both parties, as well as police themselves, had long been suggesting it would continue to rise inexorably, perhaps for generations.[16]

But crime's electoral salience seemed to be declining too. In 1992, crime was less of a factor in the election than it had been in 1988, overshadowed by economic concerns. With the midterm elections coming, and Clinton convinced that he would be able to pass major crime legislation before then, Democrats tried to exploit a phantom increasing crime rate. In the spring of 1993, the White House began working in earnest on advancing the crime bill that Biden had been developing for years, based on the notion that crime would never decrease otherwise.

Biden, for his part, was not about to let data get in the way of his two-decade crusade against street crime. He denied the accuracy of the federal government's own crime data to renew his case for congressional action on crime, arguing that no one should "believe that the epidemic of crime in America has been broken." When the Department of Health and Human Services completed a survey that showed a strong decline in cocaine use from 1985 to 1990, Biden released his own study, which argued that the findings underestimated how many "hard-core users" of cocaine and heroin existed in the United States. Not many people did believe the epidemic to be ending—because of this sort of politicization of the data that relocated the problem of crime from the social to the spiritual, where crime was the result of personal demons that could not be measured by scientific methods.[17]

If denying the data did not work, pointing a finger at Washington might. Whether a police official or politician wanted to pillory the federal government or denounce strict gun laws, crime in the District of Columbia was a useful bogeyman. But even the nation's capital, which journalists were calling the "Murder Capital," had seen a decline in homicides from its peak in

1991. The number increased in 1993 from 1992 but declined again in 1994. Nearby Baltimore also saw a dramatic decrease in violent crime (8.1 percent) in the first six months of 1994, which some attributed to awful weather, including a bitterly cold January and snow and ice storms that affected nearly the entire East Coast. Whatever the reason for the decline, the only mention it received in Washington was the claim that it was a blip. That was plausible. But it was nearly impossible to find a member of Congress willing to question whether putting crime at the top of the national agenda was justified.[18]

Elected officials framed their anticrime agenda as responding to ordinary people's fears. Yet it was elected officials, particularly presidents, who drove public concern over crime, with police as eager participants in their appeals. It was less the case that the legislative agenda was driven by popular sentiment than that it shaped popular sentiment. The incidence of crime, whether locally or in nationwide aggregate, was not clearly correlated to public opinion of its importance. Congressional action, therefore, as one study suggested, was appropriately more designed to address public perception than to address the problem of crime.[19]

Even if crime seized Washington's attention during Clinton's first two years in office, Bruce Cameron knew the "real war is taking place in towns and cities across the country." Cameron argued that Clinton chose the wrong tools for this war, including his "emphasis on social programs," which he viewed as "great contributors to the violent crime problems we suffer today." These arguments were standard conservative fare, ringing particularly hollow because Clinton had rejected the social programming conservatives most detested.[20]

Yet whereas Clinton proved willing to adopt block grants to fund welfare, he and his allies in Congress resisted replicating the LEAA by reintroducing block grants to offer funding from Washington to the states for law enforcement. Clinton agreed with Cameron that the real war was in the towns and cities, and he wanted to fund them. Even before passage of the crime bill, he touted DOJ grants for hiring police that afforded $26.3 million to small jurisdictions (large jurisdictions got $14 million). But he refused to relinquish Washington's say over the order of battle by providing totally unrestricted funds. One reason for the restrictions was to foster community policing. But the idea sounded suspicious to conservatives like Cameron. They would never be satisfied that Clinton was not out to replace policing with social programs. In the Senate, Joe Biden set out to prove that the Democrats could satisfy conservatives who wanted more cops on the street.[21]

CHAPTER 22

BLUE POWER CONSOLIDATED

Clinton had never been shy about his support for police as governor of Arkansas, but it was only during his run for the presidency that he transformed it into a mantra: as president, he would hire 100,000 new police officers. The source of the idea was a young advisor on criminal justice, Ronald Klain, who had previously worked in Biden's Senate office. Biden's own discussions with law enforcement leaders had bandied about 50,000 as a possible target, but it was not until two of Clinton's staffers, Bruce Reed and John Kroger, were preparing for a major campaign speech that Klain suggested an even 100,000. After the inauguration, Reed and José Cerda kept up the pressure on this "signature issue," but funding it proved a trickier proposition.[1]

From George H. W. Bush, the Clinton White House inherited an economy still hobbled by recession. Embracing an anticrime agenda made sense to many Democrats who blamed the economic doldrums for the spiking crime rate, but the expense of any solution was daunting. Even Bruce Cameron, who worried that "politically correct federal government programs, where most of the money drains off in layers of bureaucracy, aren't the answer to community problems," eventually conceded that police would need "an infusion of money." Besides, in the early 1990s political landscape, he surmised that Clinton's large-scale crime proposal "has about as much chance of success as a snowball in hell."[2]

The recession had already pitted police agencies against one another on the local level, as the clamor over rising crime and shrinking tax revenues gave way to zero-sum competition between police and sheriffs. After

Clinton's inauguration, this conflict burst into the open when the Pennsylvania state lodge of the Fraternal Order of Police injected itself into a court case that challenged the power of sheriff's deputies to make arrests. The Pennsylvania State Police had been one of the country's original state police departments, modeled on colonial constabularies. It successfully winnowed the role of sheriffs in the state to serving court orders, providing court security, transporting prisoners, and running jails. After a 1990 traffic stop in which a deputy stopped a driver and found him to be inebriated with an expired license, the state lodge delivered an amicus brief arguing that the deputy had exceeded his powers by making any arrest at all.[3]

At base, this dispute about power was also a dispute about money. The fraternal order's worry was that deputies would take away jobs from state police officers or, even more likely, small-town cops. "We don't want to see sheriffs doing police officers' jobs," the lodge president declared. In effect, small towns could obtain free traffic enforcement and other policing by not paying their own officers and instead relying on sheriffs. At the same time, in states where the powers of the sheriff's office were limited, police agencies were increasingly trying to take over jobs usually fulfilled by sheriffs, like court security. Both sides needed a funding fix to head off a spiraling civil war between police agencies and sheriffs' offices.[4]

Yet as of the spring of 1993, it was not at all clear that revenues would be available for police. In response to Republican senators' threats to derail a stimulus bill, Clinton deployed a new tactic to break the GOP's obstruction: going straight to the police. Clinton's staff invited Stokes, Scully, Kliesmet, and police chiefs from Baltimore and the District of Columbia to the White House for a discussion of the economic stimulus.

Many police leaders already supported Clinton's package, hoping that funding for a summer jobs program for young people might dampen crime and disorder—but to clinch police support, the night before the meeting the administration added a direct fiscal infusion for police to their proposal. The president proposed allocating $200 million to rehire officers who had been laid off due to budget cuts in cities and towns across the country, reviving an idea first broached by Mario Biaggi nearly two decades earlier at the height of the urban fiscal crisis, when a short-lived group called the Former Police Officers Association rallied on the Capitol steps, supported by the International Conference of Police Associations. Clinton claimed that if localities matched this appropriation, 10,000 cops might be put back on the street. Adopting language Biden had employed a few years earlier, Clinton called the proposal a "down payment" on his promised 100,000 new cops.

Though the proposed $16 billion stimulus proposal did not succeed in overcoming Republican opposition, Clinton did win the backing of police leadership. Surprised by and enthusiastic about the plan, Scully pleaded with Republicans in the Senate to end their filibuster. Stokes argued that the cost of inaction would be measured in "death, destruction, and mayhem." The proposal dared the GOP to reject support for rehiring police officers. They accepted that dare—but the groundwork had been laid for a much larger bill in the year that followed: the Violent Crime Control and Law Enforcement Act.[5]

The original proposal for what would become the 1994 crime bill was drafted mainly by Joe Biden, coordinating with the chair of the House Judiciary Committee, Jack Brooks, an ornery Texan who, more than anything else, hated being pressured or told what to do. Ceding control to Biden and Brooks, the White House did not even produce its own bill. Partly as a result, an early version of the bill fell short of funding 100,000 new cops. Instead, it called for $3.4 billion to hire 50,000 police while adding 50,000 indirectly through programs like the Police Corps and Empowerment Zones. It was not until the House and Senate conference in July 1994 that the bill was rewritten to hire or rehire 100,000 cops—enshrining what Attorney General Janet Reno called "the centerpiece of the President's anti-crime program."[6]

The details for funding these hires were complex. The DOJ calculated that $8.8 billion would be enough to hire 97,920 cops over six years. Given that, already in 1994, the feds had paid to hire 2,080 cops thanks to $150 million in funds that Congress salvaged from the failed fiscal stimulus, the path to 100,000 was ensured.[7]

Salary numbers were symbolically important. New cops were consistently earning more than firefighters or sanitation workers, though less—"with all due respect," Robert Scully grumbled—than letter carriers.[8]

But police compensation was growing more complex each year. Cops received benefits that nobody carrying a mail sack received. Fringe benefits did vary, but some that unions acquired in negotiations were extravagant. For instance, Toledo, Ohio, offered a payment of $400 annually for occupational stress, "to recognize the unique services performed for the community." Differential night pay and hazard pay for motorcycle, hostage negotiation, bomb squad, or other specialized assignments could be found in many cities. The Clinton administration's primary objective, however, was to support patrol officers on the beat who would become embedded in communities, leaving the details of compensation to individual departments.[9]

These complexities nearly derailed the bill. Because the New York Police Department did not desperately need money for new hires and hoped instead to use funding to support new technology that would allow them to push officers out from behind desks and onto the street, Representative Chuck Schumer became convinced that the bill would need to be altered at the reconciliation stage. To sidestep Schumer's potentially bill-destroying technical modification, Clinton's brainy young aides suggested forcing Schumer's hand by having the president announce some of the provisions with Mayor Giuliani by his side.[10]

Allies with nationwide recognition as crime fighters like Giuliani mattered to the success of the bill, but members of Congress also listened to police in their districts. Before the House was slated to vote on its version of the bill early in 1994, Scully's aide Beth McGee asked the White House if the president would join a "March on Crime," with thousands of cops marching on the Capitol and "calling upon Congress to pass a crime bill immediately to help the police fight the war on crime." The group's hope was that "police clamoring for a crime bill" would be a strong news hook and "generate great media coverage."

Clinton was not interested in leading a huge march of police on the Capitol. Instead, the White House collaborated with the Law Enforcement Steering Committee to organize a show of support for the bill in the form of a police commendation ceremony. It featured the mayors of Newark, Chicago, Los Angeles, and Louisville, who spoke on the South Lawn in front of hundreds of cops organized by the committee's member organizations. Thomas Scotto, president of the New York City Detectives' Endowment Association and the National Association of Police Organizations, brought almost 100 New York City cops to Washington for the event. They set out from a precinct house on his home turf, Staten Island. At the ceremony, Clinton and the mayors urged Congress to pass the crime bill. Then the president awarded certificates to almost 100 cops from all fifty states, marking their "courageous deeds." Hiring 100,000 more cops, he averred, would add many more brave men and women like them to the streets.

That morning, the steering committee privately presented its updated blueprint for combating crime to Clinton in the Roosevelt Room. Clinton applauded the groups' willingness to put aside their differences—chiefs and rank and file, sheriffs and state troopers, local cops and federal agents—"for the good of all." Because committee members had been so closely involved with the bill's creation, the priorities in the blueprint closely matched both the bill the Senate had passed and the one the House was taking up. The blueprint gave pride of place to hiring 100,000 officers for community policing. One hitch was the matching requirement of 25 percent, which police and mayors raised to Clinton, as well as to Reno. The National Organization of Black Law Enforcement Executives supported the bill, but it worried that its core constituent localities, with large Black populations and Black chiefs, might struggle to cover the matching costs. In response, the DOJ floated the idea of a waiver for the most cash-strapped cities. After leaving the White House, police made their way to Congress to hand out a leaflet with the headline "Support Law Enforcement / Vote for the Crime Bill!"[11]

Though still separated from the Law Enforcement Steering Committee, the IACP nevertheless offered its imprimatur to the crime bill. The organization still represented thousands of small-town chiefs across the country, whom the Democrats could not afford to ignore. Increasingly aware of political developments, by the 1990s the IACP had created a legislation committee to monitor new laws that might affect expenditures for law enforcement agencies and to lobby state and federal officials. *The Police Chief* was featuring a monthly "Legislative Alert" section. And a "Congressional Update" sometimes accompanied it, offering a tabular listing of roll-call votes in Congress on legislation of concern to IACP members. The tactics of the rank-and-file insurgency had become commonplace for the largest management organization, which now aimed to make elected officials accountable to police, rather than the other way around.[12]

As the second African American president of the IACP, Sylvester Daughtry Jr. aimed to increase the group's visibility in 1994. He felt he had been successful, with press appearances and "the presence of the association's leadership at numerous meetings and press conferences" with Clinton, Vice President Al Gore, Janet Reno, and the FBI director. Ever skeptical, Bruce Cameron wondered if existing DOJ grant programs were buying the support of the IACP, the National Sheriffs' Association, or even the scrupulously nonpartisan Police Executive Research Forum, which altogether had received almost $1.5 million in the prior fiscal year. But the reality was that IACP officials privately lamented how the hiring program and the ironclad promise of 100,000 new cops steamrolled its members' other priorities, including money for new equipment.[13]

The National Sheriffs' Association concentrated its efforts on Capitol Hill. Representatives of the sheriffs' association did join other members of the Law Enforcement Steering Committee in White House meetings. But Stokes wanted to be at the center of the action and tried to box out competitors. And Clinton's aide José Cerda believed the new president of the sheriffs' association to be "very conservative." The result, after the sheriffs' spat with the Fraternal Order of Police over the Pennsylvania amicus brief, was that the sheriffs had to look for other allies and collaborators. Republican legislators were more receptive, with Senator Bob Dole, for instance, convening a breakfast meeting of his colleagues, which the association's president attended, to discuss Washington's role in fighting crime.[14]

But the police groups remained less powerful on the Hill than the National Rifle Association. Because of the bill's proposed ban on assault weapons, the organization tried to prevent the bill's passage right when success seemed within reach, after both chambers had passed their versions. Thanks to interventions by the National Rifle Association, the House of Representatives voted against allowing the reconciled version of the bill to reach the floor late in the night of August 11, 1994. Before 9 a.m. the next morning, Clinton hastily flew to Minneapolis, where the National

Association of Police Organizations was holding its annual convention. At 1:30 p.m., after thanking his "longtime friend Bob Scully," Clinton spoke to the assembled police officers in front of a banner that read THE EASY WAY OUT IS NOT AN OPTION! It was a reference to the previous night's shocking vote, what Clinton described as "a procedural trick orchestrated by the National Rifle Association and intensely promoted by the Republican congressional leadership." Giuliani and Philadelphia's Democratic mayor, Ed Rendell, joined Clinton on the convention stage to demand speedy passage of the bill. Press coverage of the president's speech was laudatory. But victory was not yet in his grasp.[15]

WASHINGTON REWARDS THE POLICE

After the House vote on the crime bill, GOP critics tried to scuttle the bill entirely. One talking point was that the bill would fund only 22,000 hires, due to insufficient current appropriations and underestimates of the cost. Another was that the assault weapons ban would infringe on the Second Amendment. Some Democrats agreed, while others worried that the ban would unnecessarily harm their prospects at the ballot box.

Although eliminating the assault weapons ban seemed the most obvious way to secure enough votes for the crime bill, Clinton refused to do so. He and Biden also declined any compromise on allocating the money for 100,000 cops. Instead, a revised bill cut crime prevention programs and massaged the ban on manufacture, sales, and possession of military-style semiautomatic weapons and high-capacity magazines. The ban included a sunset clause anyway, meaning it would expire after a decade, and it grandfathered in weapons manufactured before it took effect.

Clinton's police allies defended him to the hilt: Republicans may have questioned the promise that 100,000 officers would be hired, but the Fraternal Order of Police did not. Dewey Stokes, adopting the role of spokesman for all the police organizations, stated that his colleagues had worked for more than six years to get to this point. Stokes also argued that fiscal costs could not be balanced against the costs of human tragedy wrought by violent crime. In the Rose Garden, before an audience of reporters and uniformed cops, Clinton explained how he told police officers he met that "they had never walked away from us" and therefore "Washington should not walk away from them."[16]

With the crime bill's fate on the line, Biden was livid. Thurmond had withdrawn support. So too had others who voted for it at an earlier stage. Biden blamed the National Rifle Association, though complaints now focused on the preventive programs that were supposed to deter social alienation and criminal behavior. Biden had "never been as frustrated in my whole life, to come this close after six years of working with every police organization in this Nation, putting together a bill they have endorsed every time, to be stopped by the NRA and politics." He reminded his colleagues how the bill had come to be, recounting the meetings he had convened with Stokes, Scully, and every other representative on the Law Enforcement Steering Committee. He recounted that he had asked them, "What do you need?" And they replied, "The first thing we need is we need more cops." The bill was not the product of social scientists or social workers. It was not the product of the ACLU, "which I have great respect for," he added snidely. It was the product of police. "I did not call a liberal confab and write it. I did not call Johnsonian liberals, if there are any still alive, and write it." Instead, Biden assured the Senate, "I called the cops."[17]

The turnaround was quick. With the midterm elections looming, and after having sent a message on gun control, the House approved the bill. The Senate followed, passing it at 11 p.m. on August 25, 1994. Several holdouts from the Congressional Black Caucus, including Rangel and former civil rights leader John Lewis, ultimately supported the bill, despite reservations about its expansion of capital punishment. They recognized that the only way to acquire fiscal support for economically struggling majority-Black districts was for it to come packaged as crime prevention, endorsed by police organizations. Success on this legislation came with a heavy cost to the president's domestic agenda, as the Senate failed to vote on his massive healthcare overhaul at the same time. Nevertheless, Clinton was pleased. In gratitude for their support, he sent Giuliani and Rendell one of the bill-signing pens each.[18]

The crime bill contained numerous provisions, but the White House urged Democrats in the House to emphasize the 100,000 new police officers first and foremost, including through op-eds and calls with local officials "trumpeting the potential for new police officers in your district." In addition to recommending photo opportunities with House members walking the beat with community policing officers, the White House suggested that representatives attend the swearing in of newly hired police and invite cops and their children to Washington. The DOJ even set up a toll-free number for members of the public, including police administrators, to call to learn about the hiring program. But the most voluble and visible pitchman for the bill was Clinton himself.[19]

The White House invited 400 police chiefs to a ceremony in October celebrating the bill. The president handed out checks. Although 59 percent of small-town police chiefs, according to one survey, believed most of the funding would go to big cities, Clinton tried to prove them wrong. More than half of the first $200 million tranche of grant funds unlocked early in October went to towns with under 150,000 residents. The chief in Choctaw, Oklahoma, credited the IACP for persisting through the arduous effort to pass the bill over six years and for ensuring that small towns not be left out. His force would nearly double in size thanks to a $368,000 grant issued immediately after the bill's passage. From the White House ceremony, "many small department administrators went home happy."[20]

In October, speaking before a National Association of Police Organizations ceremony honoring the nation's "top cops," Clinton credited the enthusiastic support of police officers for energizing members of Congress to get the bill passed. "If it hadn't been for you, fighting like crazy in the eleventh hour, it wouldn't have happened."[21]

The next week, Clinton addressed the annual meeting of the International Association of Chiefs of Police, celebrating that the bill's funds were already being disbursed. For municipalities with populations under 50,000, grants would be fast-tracked for funding due to a simplified application process that did not require a trained grant writer. To the gathered chiefs, Clinton remarked, "Something else I think that really needs to be pounded home over and over again is that this crime bill was fashioned largely by law enforcement officers." Clinton departed the meeting with an IACP baseball jacket emblazoned with the words AMERICA'S CHIEF on the back.[22]

A garment like that would have been unthinkable for Lyndon Johnson, who painstakingly avoided the appearance of federal control over local police. Small-town chiefs and sheriffs had once been the most reluctant to back federal expenditure, fearing that national funding would erode their local powers. Yet three decades of federal efforts had allayed most fears that police chiefs held about the strings that might be attached. Most police chiefs now wanted money more than anything else, including administrative freedom. Now Washington was able to pay for the direct hiring of police officers, an entailment all the prior crime bills avoided.

The bill's success indicated just how much control local police had won over national politics. Peter Dodenhoff, editor of *Law Enforcement News*, lauded the 1994 crime bill as a "watershed" for the legislative process. It became "a study in interaction between those who make the laws and those who must enforce them." Although many hands created the bill, and the Law Enforcement Steering Committee rightly claimed plaudits, the organizations that deserved the greatest credit—and received it from Clinton—were the IACP, the National Association of Police Organizations, and the Fraternal Order of Police. The bill's success gave police "a tremendous boost within Congress," according to Dodenhoff. They were becoming more than simply props at election time. Now members of Congress would have to heed "what our people want." Even if cops could not all agree on what they wanted, the experience of getting the crime bill passed proved that persistent and patient political activism at multiple scales could reap new and unexpected rewards.[23]

Yet just as had been the case in 1968, Democrats' attempt to capitalize on their crime bill and seize the tough-on-crime mantle fell short. Clinton's party still lost control of Congress in the 1994 midterm elections. And one of the GOP's first orders of business was trying to repeal much of the crime bill that Democrats had just passed.

GOP OVERCORRECTIONS

Republicans swept into Congress with a mandate from the party's new standard-bearer, Newt Gingrich, to deconstruct the state that had been built over the past three decades. Among the party's priorities for a vigorous first

100 days in office in 1995 was to roll back crime prevention policies inherent in the crime bill, and to cut costs.

Where Clinton had doubled annual spending on law enforcement, Republicans proposed to revive some of the most despised aspects of the LEAA by creating a block grant program, while removing even the modest control over state crime control plans that Washington had maintained under the LEAA. Clinton's nearly $2 billion hiring program and matching requirements would be removed and replaced with $500 million in block grants. After the block grant program passed the House on Valentine's Day, Bob Scully of the National Association of Police Organizations remarked, "In one and a half months, the new majority in the House of Representatives has destroyed and gutted what took us six years to put together."

Republicans claimed Clinton's bill was unpopular with police. Because it had passed only a few months before Republicans began the repeal effort, it was still too early for many police administrators to know how the federal spending would affect them. Nevertheless, the White House made sure to line up sheriffs as well as representatives of smaller police agencies, along with national figures like Dewey Stokes, to vouch for the bill.[24]

Leading Democrats in Congress followed suit, aligning themselves with the police groups that had helped them create and then pass the plan in the first place. Minority Whip David E. Bonior stated that "the American people want a crime bill that wears a badge." And the Law Enforcement Steering Committee argued that it knew how police departments operated: an unrestricted infusion of funds was unlikely to be spent on anything other than covering existing costs. The original bill promised advances in street policing in response to purportedly rising crime. Shifting course would mean these came to naught. Only the IACP, representing management, proved agnostic, open either to leaving the bill intact or to switching to block grants.[25]

In the midst of this maneuvering, a tasteless fundraising effort by the National Rifle Association inadvertently shored up police organizations' support for the Clinton administration. The same month that Timothy McVeigh bombed a federal building in Oklahoma City, the National Rifle Association sent an incendiary appeal to its 3.5 million members calling federal agents "jack-booted thugs" and claimed that "in Clinton's administration, if you have a badge, you have the government's go-ahead to harass, intimidate, even murder law-abiding citizens," referring to bungled federal raids in Waco, Texas, and Ruby Ridge, Idaho.

Clinton's staff seized upon the letter, again inviting Stokes, Scully, and other leaders of law enforcement associations to the White House to strategize. Decrying the language in the fundraising letter, the police leaders redoubled their support for the crime bill's hiring program and demanded that Republicans in Congress cease trying to repeal it. National Rifle Association executive vice president Wayne LaPierre unenthusiastically apologized for the letter. However much indignation LaPierre provoked, the debate over assault weapons in Congress had revealed that many backers of the ban held the fantasy that only young Black men in cities desired such weapons. Representing the gun industry, LaPierre needed this fantasy too, for scaring white gun buyers into opening their wallets for protection purposes. Even police who supported the ban recognized that it affected a small slice of the market at that point, and gun control remained a challenge due to wide differences in laws from state to state and city to city. Still, the connection between the hiring grants and gun crime was implicit: putting more police on the beat meant that more Black firearms violators would be arrested, while fewer assault weapons on the street would make cops' jobs safer.[26]

The GOP repeal effort galvanized police leaders, prodding Stokes and others to make their presence again known on Capitol Hill. They also encouraged their members to visit the Hill and speak to their own representatives. Now already looking toward the 1996 presidential election, Stokes remarked, "Anyone in law enforcement has to support those politicians at the local, the state, or the national level that deal with law enforcement up front, on the table, and support the issues that we know, from our membership, [are] important to the police officers working the streets." He concluded, "We're going to hold some of these politicians' feet to the fire."[27]

Clinton promised to veto the repeal measures, but it never came to that. The bombing in Oklahoma City derailed the repeal initiative, while spawning new efforts to pass what became known as the Antiterrorism and Effective Death Penalty Act in 1996, which contained many GOP priorities, such as limits on challenges to wrongful conviction. The Senate declined to take up legislation to match the effective repeal that had passed in the House. The 1994 crime bill remained intact. State legislatures passed bills to cover the necessary 25 percent matching funds for hiring, allowing their states to receive a greater share of the pot. And the DOJ urged municipalities that were still falling short to use asset forfeiture or even other federal grant monies to cover costs. Within about a year, half of all sheriffs were hiring deputies using the new federal funds.[28]

The centerpiece of a complex and multifaceted bill, the aspect that most directly rewarded police support was the promise to hire 100,000 new cops. It took a while to hire officers, train them, and get them on the street. Within four years, one study found, $3.5 billion of the $8.8 billion had been distributed to hire or redeploy 61,000 officers. By decade's end, fourteen of the fifteen largest police departments counted higher numbers of sworn officers.[29]

COPS IN DISARRAY AFTER THE CRIME BILL

Once the crime bill had passed and the repeal efforts had dissipated, police found themselves again at a crossroads. What would the object of their organizing now be? For their part, Stokes and Scully returned to pushing for the national law enforcement officers' bill of rights, which Biden and Brooks had refused to insert into the crime bill for fear of losing the support of the IACP, the National Sheriffs' Association, and many mayors.[30]

Although Stokes and Scully remained supportive of Clinton, including in his 1996 campaign, Stokes ultimately was not reelected as national president of the Fraternal Order of Police. And the organization's relationship with the White House soured, including over opposition to antismoking legislation that Clinton's aides believed would be a net positive for police because it would entail new enforcement. The National Association of Police Organizations and the International Union of Police Associations also opposed the bill. The Fraternal Order of Police, José Cerda regretted, "refuses to meet with us . . . period."[31]

In the main, cops felt antagonized by the Clinton administration. For all that the crime bill had done to support policing, it also created a little-noticed mandate for the DOJ to investigate law enforcement agencies with a "pattern or practice" of constitutional violations. The first case launched in Pittsburgh in January 1997. It led to a consent decree and five years of independent monitoring. This was exactly the kind of oversight and accountability measure that police resented.[32]

That same year, the National Association of Police Organizations organized an open forum to allow officers to challenge Attorney General Reno directly. Several officers complained that the DOJ was too concerned with racism, too mindful of the claims of the NAACP, too eager to prosecute on civil rights grounds after state criminal charges against police had been filed. "You talked about racism," one member explained to the attorney general. "We have to understand that it is a two-way street. And I am not just picking out any group. I think sometimes the Justice Department has to look at the other side."[33]

As Clinton exited the White House, George W. Bush would attempt to win back disaffected rank-and-file officers. He promised the Fraternal Order of Police to make pattern or practice investigations "the exception, rather than the rule," and assured its leaders that even if he did not support a national collective bargaining law for police, as governor of Texas he had made sure state troopers had "a heck of a Christmas party." But the next great opportunity for police would come not from elected politicians but as a consequence of Osama bin Laden's al-Qaeda.[34]

CHAPTER 23

NYPD BLUES

The national calamity of September 11, 2001, put the spotlight back on the largest municipal police force in the country. Twenty-three members of the New York Police Department and thirty-seven members of the Port Authority Police Department were among the 2,977 people killed in the destruction of the World Trade Center. Three hundred forty-three firefighters were killed that day as well. Many more police and firefighters fell ill and died in the years afterward due to the toxicity of the site during the search and recovery phase, which lasted for months. A combination of pension allotments for disability benefits and the victim compensation fund created by Congress has provided resources to police officers and firefighters who could no longer work, as well as the families of the afflicted. The attack on the World Trade Center was devastating to the emergency services of the city, and no member of the fire and police departments was unaffected.

But the 9/11 attack was transformative for the public image of the department, which was at its lowest ebb in years. It empowered police by expanding their mission, while injecting new material resources, and it papered over the differences among police, firefighters, and emergency medical services, to the benefit of police. The attack enthroned the new category of "first responders," which gained popularity in the aftermath by addressing, according to one political theorist, what seemed to be an emergent, diffuse, society-wide threat.[1]

Police benefited from the emergence of this external threat, as "Giuliani time" had been marked by two incidents of gratuitous police violence. In

August 1997, police assaulted and sexually tortured Abner Louima, a Haitian immigrant who worked as a security guard, after a fracas outside a nightclub. The depraved assault of Louima entailed officers raping him with a toilet plunger or broomstick in a bathroom in Brooklyn's 70th Precinct house. Then, in February 1999, a plainclothes "street crime" detail killed Amadou Diallo, a Guinean immigrant and street vendor, by firing forty-one shots at him at the front door of his apartment building. He was unarmed, holding only his wallet.

The Louima attack led the US Commission on Civil Rights to investigate the New York Police Department. It held hearings to assess whether police were systematically violating civil rights, while the city's public advocate requested that the DOJ commence a pattern or practice investigation of the department, using the authority granted by the 1994 crime bill to inquire into unconstitutional policing. Human Rights Watch also conducted its own investigation into policing in the United States, finding that police brutality and abuse nationwide were tantamount to an international human rights violation.[2]

Cops were already under scrutiny, and morale was faltering. After the 1992 city hall police riot, the city council had voted to transform the existing Civilian Complaint Review Board, as Mayor David Dinkins had proposed. It became fully independent of the police department, and it gained subpoena power. Answering a cop's protest sign from that day—ALL CIVILIAN REVIEW? ARE YOU NUTS?—its members would, in fact, all be civilians. Three of thirteen members (fifteen today) would be chosen by the police commissioner, however. More than three-quarters of complaints lodged against the police and processed by the board came from Black and brown New Yorkers, a rate that has stayed steady to the present. After the Louima assault, the city expanded the board's budget and investigative staff. Still, the police department could stymie its investigations, and the commissioner retained final authority on officer penalties.[3]

From 1994 to 1996, New York City paid out $70 million in settlements and jury awards for police misconduct, ranging from false arrest to excessive force to fatal shootings. In 2024 dollars, this amount equaled more than the annual budget of the entire Brooklyn Public Library system. In the year before Louima's arrest and assault, the city issued 503 settlements for police misconduct. The funds did not come from the police budget, meaning there was little pressure or incentive for the department to prevent the officer behavior triggering complaints and lawsuits. The city comptroller, frustrated by these expenditures, recommended putting the department on the hook for half of every payout. That never happened.

Officers themselves rarely paid a cent when sued. Qualified immunity means, in practice, that cops are not personally liable for money damages in lawsuits based on harm inflicted while doing their jobs, including if they violate the Constitution. One study of the forty-four largest police departments found that police officers themselves contributed to settlements or judgments for misconduct only 0.02 percent of the time. In fact, New York City contributed to that tiny percentage. In 34 of 6,887 cases examined in the city, officers did pay some money. This finding was exceptional, and in all but two of the other largest cities, no officer personally contributed to victims' compensation. Laws, policies, and common practices kept officers from having to pay compensatory damages. The original justification for qualified immunity was that officers risked bankrupting judgments without it. But New York City began to indemnify its officers against punitive damages anyway beginning in 1996. Doing otherwise would send a message that city leaders did not support their cops, a message the union would not tolerate. Misconduct may be expensive, but not for its perpetrators.[4]

The Patrolmen's Benevolent Association reliably provided defense attorneys for officers accused of misconduct. It counseled officers not to cooperate with departmental investigators, meaning that disciplinary proceedings would be thwarted, but making lawsuits more likely. Human Rights Watch noted that while Ed Koch was mayor and Phil Caruso led the police union, the city began subsidizing a legal defense fund for officers. The result was that "taxpayers may be charged three times for officers who commit abuses: for their legal defense, for their salaries, and for civil settlements or jury awards."

Caruso's handpicked successor, Lou Matarazzo, entered a new political landscape, with a Republican in both city hall and the governor's mansion by 1995, an alignment that had not occurred in over two decades. Unlike

New York City Patrolmen's Benevolent Association president Lou Matarazzo leads a rally outside the office of the Manhattan district attorney in 1997. Misha Erwitt/New York *Daily News* Archive via Getty Images.

the prolix Caruso, Matarazzo spoke in clipped sentences like he was still a baton-twirling cop on the street. His South Bronx approach mixed rewards with threats, and it played out in Albany and downstate alike as he used the state government to get what he could not obtain from the city. He became adept at playing Albany against the mayor's office, manipulating the contentious relationship between the two fiscally conservative executives. To escape interest arbitration awards adjudicated by the city's Office of Collective Bargaining, Matarazzo worked to shift final decision-making power into the hands of the state's Public Employment Relations Board (PERB). Matarazzo believed that these state-level arbitrators would be less likely to favor the mayor's office.[5]

Matarazzo had learned his union's Albany strategy from Hartman and Caruso. Hartman pioneered it while working for Long Island police unions. One city union official suggested that Hartman got results because he knew that "all you have to do is spread some money around the Legislature." The political landscape was more complicated in the city than on Long Island, but Hartman and Caruso managed to succeed, in part, because they continued to shower donations on state legislators of both parties from the union's considerable war chest. One lobbyist observed that the Patrolmen's

Benevolent Association was a behemoth that "totally intimidated" the "little legislators from outside the city," many of whose members lived in their suburban districts. Even Ed Koch had marveled at the "huge contributions" the benevolent association's lawyers doled out in Albany. The state-level arbitration strategy might allow comparison of city police salaries to the inflated suburban Long Island salaries that Hartman had won, rather than to other city workers' salaries. Matarazzo sought the greatest disparities as the baseline for comparison, which necessitated going statewide.[6]

Building the clout of the Patrolmen's Benevolent Association, Matarazzo spent more time upstate than any of his predecessors. He regularly brought police officers to Albany to sit in on legislative debates and meet with elected officials. Matarazzo also oversaw computerized recording of state legislators' ayes and nays. The benevolent association shared that information readily with members, while also prodding cops to register to vote and turn out in primaries and on election day. Under Matarazzo, the Patrolmen's Benevolent Association's campaign donations soon exceeded nearly every other union's spending in Albany. Major recipients included the Republican majority leader of the senate and speaker of the assembly, a Democrat from Manhattan who did not get along with Giuliani. The Patrolmen's Benevolent Association kept multiple lobbyists in Albany. They were known to "explode into a shouting match" with legislative aides when challenged.[7]

But it was also easy to convince many legislators to support the union's goals. As one Queens assemblywoman remarked, the Patrolmen's Benevolent Association carried "an emotional component that no other union can replicate." Who, she asked, "would want to be against police officers?" The association had an activated membership, money to spend, and a largely positive public image, despite occasional outrages. As one progressive observer noted, most lobbyists had, at best, two of these to offer. The package of all three was rare. For its bipartisan solicitude toward the city's police, the editorial board of the *New York Times* accused the legislature of "spinelessness."[8]

Not all legislators were eager supporters of the city's patrol union, of course. Yet even Republicans who might be wary of siding with a ravenous labor union could ill afford to anger cops, many of whom lived in Long Island strongholds of the state party. Democrats, meanwhile, always worried about appearing soft on crime and knew the union would be merciless with critics. The union's chief counsel and author of the bills he advocated was unabashed in recommending that the union target anyone "against police issues." The goal, he vowed, would be "destruction—political destruction." Beyond letters and phone calls, the union regularly orchestrated visits by cops to legislators' offices, sometimes unannounced, to give their input on how they thought officials should vote. Elected officials from the city delegation also got the message that if they bucked the union, an emergency call to the police might go unanswered, according to an African American state senator. Because cops sent the message, it was not an illegal shakedown.[9]

Matarazzo pounded a winding pathway toward his trophy of a provision to allow the Patrolmen's Benevolent Association to appear before the state's PERB in case of a bargaining impasse. It included lopsided votes in the legislature, governor's vetoes, veto overrides, and a brief ticket-writing strike likely organized by the police union's delegates. In the end, once the provision finally passed, the *Times* grudgingly acknowledged that Matarazzo now seemed to be preeminent in the state.[10]

Yet a lawsuit city hall filed would stop the police union in its tracks, as a court found that the provision for putting police before the PERB was unconstitutional. During the next round of bargaining, Matarazzo faced a weak contract offer from Giuliani, including a two-year wage freeze. Other city employees, not just cops, received the same offer of no increase, but the Patrolmen's Benevolent Association called it "zeros for heroes."

Unwilling to accept equality with other unionized municipal workers, police union delegates voted down "zeros for heroes." Officers engaged in a nine-month ticketing slowdown that reduced misdemeanor, parking, and traffic tickets by 26, 38, and 39 percent, respectively. It was the longest police slowdown in US history. Recalcitrance did not change the offer. The day after the initial rejection of the contract offer, Richie Hartman and his colleague who had written the state arbitration bill were indicted for corruption. A humiliated Matarazzo stepped down as president of the union before the end of his term, putting an end to the dynasty that had passed from DeMilia to Caruso to him. One benevolent association insider griped, "They should never have put all their eggs in that PERB basket; they thought that was the magic bullet."[11]

Hartman, Caruso's star negotiator and an inveterate high-stakes gambler, would be convicted, along with two others. The complex kickback scheme was far from Hartman's first brush with legal troubles due to his gambling. He had previously been investigated but not indicted for withdrawing $817,000 from a benevolent association escrow account and cashing a check for the same amount at the Trump Castle casino in Atlantic City. Caruso testified that he approved the withdrawal, but Hartman ultimately forfeited his law license as a result. New Jersey sued the Trump organization for extending enormous lines of credit to Hartman. The casino's willingness to abet Hartman's gambling habit may not have been solely because the house always wins. Donald J. Trump and Hartman shared a mentor, Senator Joseph McCarthy's acolyte during the second red scare, the lawyer Roy Cohn. Hartman's scandals, along with the wage freeze, created an opening at the top of the Patrolmen's Benevolent Association in 1999. It was the first contested election since 1980, which had landed Caruso in the president's chair.[12]

The police union would select new leadership as outrage over the victimization of Louima and Diallo spurred new political organizing in New York City and beyond. Nationally, the October 22 Coalition's National Day of Protest had launched in 1996. It consisted of demonstrations against police brutality in forty cities. After Louima's gruesome assault, it became an annual event. Often featuring families of victims of police brutality, these demonstrations vocalized collective anguish, constituting a direct antecedent to the Black Lives Matter protests two decades later.[13]

Thousands mobilized to demonstrate outside the 70th Precinct, where Louima was assaulted in the summer of 1997—a massive display of outrage, broken up only by a thunderstorm on a sweltering evening. Then, as news of Diallo's death spread in February 1999, hundreds of New Yorkers quickly rallied outside the Bronx apartment building where police fired the forty-one shots. Protesters soon began staging a vigil in front of One Police Plaza, a block from Giuliani's city hall. After a dozen arrests at this sit-in, civil rights leaders vowed to continue. Ultimately, 1,166 were arrested in a daily routine of civil disobedience. Dinkins, the former mayor, was one of the arrestees. A national rally in Washington, DC, against police brutality drew as many as 25,000 people who chanted, "Amadou! Amadou!" Diallo's father spoke alongside Black leaders, including NAACP president and future Maryland congressman Kweisi Mfume. At a simultaneous rally in Manhattan, Diallo's mother expressed her own grief, but she recognized that "my son belongs to the whole world." When a grand jury delivered indictments of the four officers involved in the shooting, the movement rejoiced. But the officers' union sprang to their defense.[14]

The trial of the officers who killed Diallo was ultimately moved to Albany, ensuring a more police-friendly jury. The prosecution mounted a limp case, and the defense successfully argued that the shooting was reasonable. The four officers were acquitted. The Louima trial began the month after the Diallo shooting. It was complex, marked by duplicity and cover-ups, in part because one of the four accused officers was a delegate of the Patrolmen's Benevolent Association. Louima had sued the union, but its law firm was also representing one of the cops. An appeals court determined there was a conflict of interest. Only one officer was ultimately punished, and who did what remains hazy. Louima received a settlement of $8.75 million. It was the largest ever awarded, with $1.625 million coming from the Patrolmen's Benevolent Association. No police union had ever been responsible for a payout like this.[15]

THE 1999 PATROLMEN'S BENEVOLENT ASSOCIATION ELECTION

Against two longtime union officials, a brash thirty-five-year-old community affairs officer, Patrick J. Lynch, emerged as the upstart candidate in the contest for leadership of the police union. Lynch's father was a subway driver, and the son got a taste of union power joining his old man on the picket line in 1980 during a transit strike. Before long, Lynch was organizing his fellow officers. He began producing a newsletter, *Brooklyn North News*. It lambasted Caruso's reign.[16]

The incumbent union president, James "Doc" Savage, wanted to make a name for himself, as he had been appointed, not elected, to replace Matarazzo. He organized a no-confidence vote in the commissioner about a month before the union election. Lynch supported it but also recognized that it was mostly a ploy to pull votes and capitalize on discontent. Lynch thus campaigned against both the union's leadership and the commissioner, echoing the union's line that command strategies, not officer misconduct, caused high-profile police shootings. But when Savage grew desperate, warning that enforcement tactics threatened "tyranny" and a "police state," Lynch correctly recognized that the rank and file had little appetite for such apparently left-wing or civil libertarian language, rare among police union leaders. He refused to implicate the union's members in command errors.[17]

In a debate, when Lynch accused union official Jimmy Higgins of corruption and nepotism, Higgins reminded Lynch that if he was corrupt, Lynch had benefited from it, as Higgins had secured Lynch his easy job. But the union's members were ready to clean house after "zeros for heroes." In a four-way race, in which Lynch was about two decades younger than his rivals, he garnered 38.5 percent of the 16,000 votes cast. His Voice of the Blue Line slate won all six elections it contested.[18]

In a union where who you knew mattered, Lynch became the first Irish American president after two decades of Italian American leadership. Perhaps more than any other indicator, the election of a guy nicknamed "Paddy," with a proud Italian in the mayor's office, signaled a changing of the guard.

Whom you knew outside the union mattered too. Lynch made the shrewd decision to hire a new chief negotiator—a ringer who had previously worked for Ed Koch and who had been responsible for signing contracts with Caruso larded with benefits for cops. Change was not for its own sake. It was strategic.

In 2001, a new state supreme court ruling found that revised legislation granting New York City police and firefighters access to the PERB was now constitutional. The union exulted, though Matarazzo's promise that state arbitrators would offer gains unavailable otherwise went unproven. The union argued that state-level awards amounted in four years to nearly what city-level awards had totaled in a decade. Hartman, after serving his prison sentence, excoriated union leaders. They used the strategy he and his buddies had devised to obtain gains over four years that he believed should have taken just a year. The union attributed the improvement from "zeros for heroes" primarily to the arbitration venue, but another factor was that the fiscal picture had improved. The 9/11 attack and the election of Mayor Michael Bloomberg had changed both the city's fortunes and policing practices.[19]

Achieving access to the state arbitrators encapsulated the union's approach to politics: overkill. The union was able to get what it wanted because of its resources and relentlessness, but what it wanted turned out not to be as valuable as its leaders assumed. They had political power but lacked political savvy. Union execs like Matarazzo believed that appointed arbitrators could not be trusted to be neutral, nor should cops be subject to the same procedures as every other public sector union. The Patrolmen's Benevolent Association treated an evenhanded approach to its demands as inherent bias against it. Anything less than preferential treatment, which it could receive by turning to the state legislature, was unacceptable. Cops were always the victims, and everyone else but cops benefited from patronage.

On the eve of Lynch's ascent, Anthony Bouza, a former New York cop who became a reformist chief in Minneapolis, pointed out that the Patrolmen's Benevolent Association was "the major obstacle" to a range of command initiatives to change departmental operations, from single-officer patrols to new disciplinary procedures. Obstinacy and unwillingness to change, rather than an active desire to solve challenges facing the police force, let alone those facing the city's residents, characterized the union's culture. Bouza concluded, "Whatever the union supports is most likely to be inconsistent with objective concerns for law and order." In New York City, this maxim united Cassese, Caruso, and Lynch. Crime framed their entreaties, but its decrease was never the purpose.[20]

CHAPTER 24

THE MOST POWERFUL POLICE UNION PRESIDENT

When the Trade Center fell, Giuliani was a lame duck, presiding over a city under the pall of a bursting economic bubble. His emergency services leadership included his lunkheaded former chauffeur, Bernard Kerik, as police commissioner and the former head of the firefighters' union, Thomas von Essen, as fire commissioner. Previously a detective, Kerik did not have a college degree and was therefore ineligible for promotion to captain in the New York Police Department. (He later went to prison.) By contrast, billionaire Michael Bloomberg, the city's richest man, ran as a technocrat, promising expert-led reform while exuding a detached temperament that diverged starkly from Giuliani's acerbic mien. The primary election occurred on September 11, 2001, but voting was halted and rescheduled for two weeks later. Bloomberg defeated his Republican opponent and then triumphed in the general election.[1]

Bloomberg ended up serving three terms as mayor, having convinced the city council to modify the two-term limit. By the end of that third term, Bloomberg's popularity was waning, in part because, after bringing Ray Kelly back to the commissioner's desk, he too oversaw a police department engaged in widespread violations of the constitutional rights of New Yorkers through its industrialization of street pat-downs. The Stop, Question, and Frisk program yielded a peak of 685,000 stops in the year 2011. As Bloomberg's third term was ending, the city's public advocate, Bill de Blasio, campaigned on reining in the New York Police Department. He won and immediately named the jet-setting Bill Bratton, Giuliani's second police commissioner, to lead the department.[2]

A constant throughout these shifts in city hall was Patrolmen's Benevolent Association president Pat Lynch. His resistance to the lures of the type of corruption that had ensnared Caruso's clique and ability to internalize yet supersede the political lessons bequeathed by Blue Power organizers before him like Parsell, Harrington, Crowley, and Kliesmet, plus his own predecessors in New York, made him the "most powerful police union chief in the world," in the proud words of the union's spokesman.[3]

And while former mayor Giuliani translated his long-standing friendship with Donald Trump into a role as counselor to the president after Trump's 2016 election, it was Lynch—despite there being no love lost between him and Giuliani—who best embodied the politics and ideology of Trumpism: impunity, control, and score-settling. You were either his friend or his enemy, and your status could always be reinterpreted. Loyalty, or lack thereof, was paramount. Friends got handshakes and a question or two about the kids and the bathroom renovation. Enemies got threats.

LYNCH TIME

After 9/11, Pat Lynch turned the office of police union president into a national position, far exceeding his institutional base of power and constituency. In the process, he contributed to what political scientists call the nationalization of politics. Scholars fret that our politics are now broken because every school board race is now a referendum on national politics. Irrelevant, hyperpolarized issues define the town square. Lynch was able to nationalize the politics of police unionism as no other figure chronicled in this book managed to do. He also contributed the flipside, treating all national politics as if it were a fight over police compensation, death benefits, pensions, or external oversight. And he treated opponents, whether negotiators from the mayor's office or pastors on the streets chanting "No justice! No peace!," as if they were crazed militants, hell-bent on destruction.

At the outset of his term, Lynch shared the appearance of many young cops. They were often chunky, thanks to sleepless nights, meals eaten from takeout containers on the go, and a few too many beers to unwind and doughnuts to pass the time. Over time, he lost the weight, and his slicked-back hair turned silver-gray. His dark pinstripe suits conveyed his determination. His pleading eyebrows, coming to an inverted V on his forehead, accentuated his words, expressing a mixture of outrage and empathy.

Lynch's approach was populist, and even an eminent liberal journalist referred to him as a demagogue. But more than anything he was like a general fighting a war that was already won. Sure, this or that piece of legislation could sweeten things for officers, and there was always room for more pay and protections. Yet after 9/11, with crime spiraling downward to unthinkably low levels, police in New York had it comparatively easy. In his war posture, therefore, Lynch had little to gain from the mayor. So instead he used his function within the state to go to war first with the mayor and then with the city itself.[4]

The patrol union president's yen for public relations was matched only by that of Bloomberg's police commissioner, Ray Kelly. The commissioner also sought the national spotlight, and counterterrorism duties facilitated grabbing it. Although the department always had a global reputation, and even occasional overseas operations in the past, Kelly committed to refashioning the New York Police Department into a data- and intelligence-driven operation with a global footprint. The badge would have no borders. Counterterrorism operations replicated and even duplicated responsibilities held by federal agencies, including spying on, harassing, and manipulating Muslims and left-wing radicals. Street policing entailed a relentless, block-by-block focus on stopping and frisking young men of color. This combination meant that Kelly's policies created the conditions for the patrol officers Lynch represented to be loathed by large swaths of the city's residents. Lynch took advantage of this symbiosis to plead, in a self-pitying fashion, that his members were underappreciated and undercompensated.[5]

As union president, Lynch remade the union, starting with the association's magazine, *New York's Finest*, in his own image—literally. One emblematic issue a few years into his tenure, dedicated to "The PBA's Progress," included a two-page editorial by Lynch, a two-page interview with Lynch, and a two-page article about the organization that summarized the interview. Like D'Arcy and Crowley of the Bluecoats in San Francisco,

Lynch represented an insurgent faction within the union that gave voice to officer dissatisfaction. Like the Bluecoats, he understood that controlling the union's messaging to its members was essential to the success of his agenda. He needed to cultivate an active constituency.[6]

To do so, Lynch operated at the street level, where his officers were. The aloof Caruso was more comfortable in the city's fanciest restaurants, and Matarazzo was focused on whipping votes in Albany. Lynch made it a point to glad-hand cops and deliver six-foot sub sandwiches to them. As one journalist who profiled him noted, "It takes Patrick Lynch a very long time to get around New York: merely walking to his SUV, parked around the corner from his office at the tip of lower Manhattan, can take 15 minutes. That's because Lynch makes a point of shaking hands with every police officer within about a 20-foot range. A more distant officer will get a wave and a shouted greeting." The cold mien he wore behind a lectern was the opposite of the warmth he delivered to his members daily.[7]

Lynch first proposed renaming his organization the Police Benevolent Association of the City of New York, Inc., discarding the gendered term "patrolmen," in 2002. He succeeded only in 2019, thirty years after Caruso had rejected the same proposal and almost fifty years after the department ceased using the term "patrolman." In 2002, Lynch elevated Mubarak "A.J." Abdul-Jabbar to the third-highest position in the association, making him its first African American vice president. Lynch was devoted to his officers and aware that the department was changing. But above all he was tenacious.[8]

It would be a mistake to attribute Lynch's omnipresence, including in the union's magazine, to vanity. Instead, his concerted effort to meet and hear the average cop (and the cop's family) enabled him to build rapport. It also marginalized the doubters who believed he had failed to live up to his promises, even as he strategically emphasized the shortcomings of each contract he signed. As soon as the ink dried on an agreement, particularly those obtained through PERB arbitration, the union notified city hall of its intent to begin negotiating the next contract. Short contracts kept members engaged, and Lynch commanded their attention through interpersonal solicitude and public bombast.

"More like a politician than a cop" is how one colleague described Lynch. Before he traded his uniform for a suit and tie, he had worked as a community affairs officer in Williamsburg, Brooklyn. Prior to its gentrification, Williamsburg was a gritty industrial zone interlaced with low-rise residential streets, with Puerto Ricans predominating on one side of the neighborhood and Satmar Jews predominating on the other. Lynch gained crucial experience negotiating between the Hispanics and the Hasidics, as local observers labeled them, two striving, family-oriented, pious groups. They ostensibly had little in common but in fact shared a good deal, as Lynch perceived.[9]

Lynch earned his badge in 1984. The era of left-wing political violence in the United States was over by then—with one exception, the aforementioned 1985 bombing of the Patrolmen's Benevolent Association office after its demonstration in support of the officer who killed Eleanor Bumpurs. Yet a key characteristic of Lynch's leadership of the union was never letting this era be forgotten. The union frequently reminded its members of the unsolved 1972 assassination of two officers, Greg Foster and Rocco Laurie, attributed to the Black Liberation Army. And it convened regular catered gatherings of spouses and children of officers who had died in the line of duty.[10]

The Patrolmen's Benevolent Association committed to "keep cop killers behind bars" as long as possible. Lynch reliably referred to their continued incarceration as "one of the most important obligations" New Yorkers had. Association leaders organized press conferences, often accompanied by family members of slain New York officers, anytime parole hearings occurred. Lynch was especially caustic when parole for members of the Black Panther Party or Black Liberation Army became possible. Anticipating future tragedies, the union supported legislation to mandate life sentences without parole for people convicted of killing cops, which the governor signed in 2005.[11]

The union's website has hosted a prepopulated electronic form, "Keep Cop Killers in Jail," that allows anyone to message the New York State Parole Board and urge it not to release any of the currently parole-eligible people convicted of killing police. Users can select by the name of the deceased officer or the name of the "perp," or send a global message about all potential parolees. One click can spawn dozens of messages. Lynch brought what he claimed were printouts of 800,000 such messages to one Albany press conference, though the parole board is not supposed to favor correspondence from people unrelated to victims.[12]

The Black Liberation Army applied the catechism of urban guerrilla warfare to devastating effect, but Lynch's Voice of the Blue Line groupuscule made headlines for a guerrilla raid of its own. In early 1998, they snuck unannounced through a back door into the Broad Street offices of the Patrolmen's Benevolent Association, reporters in tow. Shocked to find a mostly empty office, despite the more than two dozen union staffers on the payroll, they delivered a detailed list of demands to Matarazzo. They pleaded with him to attempt to recover the millions that had been embezzled, gambled, and otherwise frittered away by the Caruso circle, to which Matarazzo had once belonged as a union trustee. Lynch threatened to sue on behalf of the rank and file, while acknowledging that doing so would get him branded as an enemy of the union. He reasoned that these demands were natural for cops: they were looking into a crime. One supporter's eyes twinkled at the prospect that storming the union's office augured a "coup d'état." Within weeks, Matarazzo's handpicked candidates for positions in union leadership across the city were losing elections. He did not need a weatherman to know which way the wind was blowing.[13]

Lynch's obsession with revolutionaries of the past also might have taught him about protest. Although the Patrolmen's Benevolent Association had a long record of staging rallies, including demonstrations that devolved into lawbreaking, Lynch fine-tuned its protest tactics. Two types of protest marked Lynch's innovations. The first was the coordinated mass demonstration with other public sector workers. Lynch walked the tightrope that his predecessors had not been able to. Whereas other leaders of the association contrasted police with sanitation workers or teachers, arguing cops deserved better compensation because their jobs were tougher, Lynch tended to be more circumspect. Although he never shied away from highlighting the dangers police faced, he treated teachers like partners, acknowledging the reality that by the 2000s, cops and teachers did work hand in hand to control juvenile misbehavior. The police union augmented its case for better pay and working conditions by publicly collaborating with, rather than antagonizing, other unions.

The police union's argument was convoluted, however. On the one hand, it recognized that the state arbitration panel had not awarded police contracts that improved greatly on what it might have otherwise received, though police still fared better than any other union in the first state-level arbitration. On the other, it denounced "pattern bargaining" that harmonized offers for all city workers, calling the approach a "one-size-fits-all cop-out." What the benevolent association demanded was a pattern that equalized pay in the city with pay in Nassau and Suffolk Counties, or at the very least rewarded cops for the epochal crime decline that was underway.

Late in the spring of 2004, teachers, firefighters, and police rallied together near city hall. The massive crowd, as many as 70,000 strong, demanded better compensation across the board. This fleeting show of solidarity earned nearly ecstatic press coverage, but Lynch's leadership team soon assured its members that it would reject any offer matching the "horrendous" offer the city's biggest public sector union, District Council 37 (AFSCME), had accepted. Notably, that union was not invited to the major rally. One of its persistent goals was to expand civilianization of the police department, putting its members in clerical and other roles often filled by police officers. The officers' association reviled the prospect of giving up positions.[14]

Civilianization was not the only source of conflict between the benevolent association and other municipal unions. City police were more likely to live in surrounding counties, especially on Long Island, than other city workers. By 2023, only 48 percent of cops lived in the city. Higher salaries for cops would not return to city coffers if property tax revenues went to other municipalities. District Council 37 might have been in an economic conflict with police, but it retained political power in the voting booth, provided its members voted as a bloc. The police union's voting power was diluted by its members' residency outside the city, but it too tried to get its members to vote as a bloc.[15]

The Patrolmen's Benevolent Association was strongest in statewide elections, particularly gubernatorial contests. But it made endorsements both in citywide races and in individual district-based races, such as for city council, so that any police officer living in the city knew how to vote. The union insisted that its endorsement could mean the "likely support" of 50,000 active and retired cops, along with just as many family and friends. But endorsements from the police unions carried great symbolic weight, beyond how they translated into the promise of cop votes. Abdul-Jabbar argued that endorsements could indicate to voters that candidates "are strong on law and order, are friends of police officers on the street, and are in favor of safe streets and justice," meaning in essence that they are "tough on crime." The result was a greater likelihood of receiving campaign donations, particularly from "corporate leaders who recognize that their profits are tied to the safety of the streets."[16]

Because officer votes were not enough to sway a municipal election, the union relied on publicity and protest. The other protest tactic that Lynch implemented was personalized. Serving under a billionaire mayor made it easy for cops to proclaim unfairness. Bloomberg had a private jet; cops wanted exemptions from tolls at bridges and tunnels. But more than the message itself, protest repertoires became highly personalized, echoing what had made the 1992 city hall protest so offensive. Lynch and his team staged loud protests outside Gracie Mansion, the mayor's residence, against "Mayor Money Bags." When internal affairs officers videotaped the union's pickets, Lynch waved a sign berating their "illegal" surveillance. The union also rented mobile billboards telling New Yorkers to call the city's new info number, 311, and demand a raise for cops and firefighters. District Council 37 workers, whose contract Lynch scorned, answered these calls only to hear messages that were meant for the mayor.[17]

Lynch later sent cops out of state to harass Mayor Bill de Blasio while he traveled to an event for progressive Democrats in Iowa. The union members cynically contended that his contract offer was anything but "progressive." When de Blasio dipped his toe into the presidential campaign pool in Florida, Lynch joined retired members of his union and active members of local police associations at a rally. Cops waved orange foam fingers printed with the word "liar." Lynch told a reporter, "He's the worst mayor, he's destroying New York City, we don't want him to destroy the rest of the country." At home, the union engaged in what it called "stalk and talk," haranguing de Blasio outside the Park Slope YMCA where he exercised and a coffee shop he frequented.[18]

These personalized attacks on de Blasio would crescendo in 2014 and again in 2020, but they also showed that old habits die hard. One of the most sordid events of Lynch's tenure came in 2011, when a ticket-fixing probe in the Bronx implicated well over 100 cops, including three Patrolmen's Benevolent Association board members and eight current or former delegates. As one journalist observed, "Some of the most prolific ticket-fixers are union officials simply because they appeared to have been deputized to fix tickets written in other precincts." More than simply looking the other way or exercising discretion, the ticket-fixing entailed destroying or otherwise nullifying summonses after they had been issued. The district attorney indicted sixteen cops, at ranks from patrol officer to lieutenant, for corruption and other crimes. He claimed that ticket-fixing had cost the city between $1 million and $2 million. Officers responded by slackening their issuance of tickets, costing the city that amount in a week or two, then staging a vitriolic protest in late October 2011.[19]

In an event reminiscent of both the city hall riot and the rally outside the very same Bronx courthouse after the indictment of the officer who killed Eleanor Bumpurs, officers interfered with journalists, mobbed the courtroom, and then verbally abused bystanders in front of an adjacent welfare office, chanting "E.B.T.," the term for electronic distribution of food stamps. At issue in this ugly scene was a persistent distributional question in American politics: Who was deserving? Was it cops, deserving not only of largesse but also of impunity, or the poorest denizens of the city, deserving of dignity and a modicum of social support? Cops rendered the answer in zero-sum terms. But some of the benefits recipients volleyed a chant of their own: "Fix *our* tickets!"[20]

This rambunctious cop protest occurred while the Occupy Wall Street protests were unfolding in Manhattan, a borough and a world away. Officers' bigoted invective crushed the thin hopes that some within the Occupy movement held. Cops would harass, divide, corral, pepper spray, and arrest the 99 percent. But they would not join them.

The Occupy movement was a response to the greatest economic crisis since the Great Depression. Because the 2008 crisis revolved around real estate and entailed waves of foreclosures on homes across the country, municipal budgets reliant on property tax revenue were particularly afflicted. New York City managed to weather the crisis without dramatic and long-lasting effects because federal bailouts of Wall Street firms, which inspired the Occupy movement's ire, propped up the city's economy. When Mayor Bloomberg proposed cost-saving layoffs, he heeded Lynch's demands that they not be made "across the board." Some city agencies experienced far deeper cuts than the police department. As Lynch put it, "Not all city services are of equal importance." The crisis eroded Lynch's willingness to put the benevolent association on the same plane as other city unions.[21]

Other cities did not benefit as directly from Washington's bailouts. Police departments across the country had to contend with what seemed like a "new normal." Their budgets were no longer "bulletproof," as an analysis by the Police Executive Research Forum observed. Crime was down. Costs were up. Especially in large cities, where "police departments account for the largest share of municipal spending," the success of police unions was to blame. Worse, as the president of a Fraternal Order of Police lodge in Kentucky warned fellow police leaders, "Often we make the mistake of supporting politicians who don't work for us, because we personally think like they do, even though their political views are bad for labor." Tough-on-crime, conservative elected officials whom police unions supported with votes, endorsements, and donations also tended to favor budget cuts and privatization. During the recession, private security contractors started to replace sworn police in hard-hit municipalities. This switch was abominable to police unions. Cops' strong support for right-wing elected officials started to bite them in the ass.[22]

In New York, cops were growing defensive. The role of the Patrolmen's Benevolent Association in the ticket-fixing scandal was undeniable. Under Lynch's leadership, the union amplified its policy of discretionary "professional courtesy." It meant that cops should never ticket other cops. Their families became exempt too. The argument was that officers brought their stress home, burdening their loved ones. The mark of Lynch's leadership was to make sure that pecuniary benefits, however slight, would be widely distributed.[23]

But members of the union also felt like Lynch had not defended them effectively while the lengthy ticket-fixing investigation was proceeding. Worse, only cops faced any punishment, though officers believed the benefits of quashed tickets went to politically connected individuals, including elected officials. Lynch commented only after indictments dropped, likely out of concern that the union itself might face charges for orchestrating a conspiracy. For his sin of silence, Lynch faced a small revolt of irate Bronx delegates. Like his predecessors and like police union leaders across the country who cultivated an unflinching and angry membership, it was inevitable that Lynch would face objections vocalized in his very terms: cops should be defended no matter what.[24]

PROFESSIONAL COURTESIES

When I first got my driver's license at age seventeen, a relative (not a cop) passed a small card along to me. It carried the logo of a police benevolent association and an assurance that the bearer supported the union. I had no tangible connection to any member of an officers' association, but when I was pulled over for speeding while driving home from high school, I handed the card to the officer, along with my license. He was perturbed when I could not answer his questions about which officer gave me the card. Nevertheless, this cop in suburban New Jersey followed the credo formulated by the first vice president of the New York Patrolmen's Benevolent Association: "The bottom line: do not write over a PBA card." He did not give me a ticket, even though I was an inexperienced driver operating my vehicle recklessly.[25]

All members of Lynch's union received an annual allotment of "PBA cards," wallet-sized documents that bore the union's logo. Officers could give these cards to friends and family. Though they had existed for decades, by the 1990s police unions and even nonunion ethnic organizations for cops across the country were distributing hundreds of thousands of these cards. Though they were not exactly "get out of jail free" cards, they would usually cause officers to issue a discretionary warning rather than a summons. The widespread availability of the cards has perverse social consequences by distributing impunity.

A card is not enough to solve the problems of the police force, including recruitment and retention, though. And impunity may intensify personal dangers for cops. Exemption from traffic citations for officers likely undermined the union's overall goal of protecting its members. Police in New York City, like elsewhere across the country, were more prone to die in vehicular crashes than by homicide. Because of the city's geography and departmental patrol routines, on-duty crashes were not as dangerous as in other places. But fatal off-duty crashes rose from the 1990s into the 2000s. They became even more visible as on-duty fatalities decreased.[26]

Suicide was another major risk officers faced. For many cops, the difficulties of the job did not become a ho-hum routine. Their weight accumulated, particularly after 9/11. In 2019, ten New York City police officers committed suicide, including a one-star chief. (Two died by homicide that year, and zero in each of the prior and subsequent years.) Lynch took the dangers of depression and other mental illnesses seriously as a practical and political challenge. Among cops, suicidal ideation was not always correlated with mental illness. Instead, lending credence to Lynch's critiques of command, researchers have found that "poor management" is a leading cause. Police today exhibit five times the rate of suicide attempts of the general populace, and over 25 percent of cops in one recent study have contemplated, planned, or attempted to kill themselves. Cops call it "Blue Suicide." Lynch addressed these problems in his own uncompromising way. The union issued a public service announcement that began with Lynch saying, "My fellow officers, if you're on the edge and contemplating suicide, don't fucking do it."[27]

For Lynch, personal problems of his members, as well as broader challenges of recruitment and retention, had a common cause: hatred of police, incubated by Black Lives Matter. The movement began to coalesce after the 2013 acquittal of vigilante George Zimmerman for the murder of Trayvon Martin in Florida, and it blossomed nationally in 2014 after the police killings of Mike Brown Jr. in Missouri and Eric Garner in Lynch's own city. Groups in the umbrella coalition of the Movement for Black Lives helped spread and legitimize critiques of policing that de Blasio adopted while campaigning for mayor in 2013, as part of his attack on the city's vertiginous economic and racial inequality, which had only grown after the 2008 economic crisis.[28]

The national climate buoyed de Blasio's confidence in criticizing the New York Police Department, particularly its stop-and-frisk regime. President Barack Obama, the first Black president, appointed the first Black attorney general, Eric Holder. No matter what these leaders promised, police officials were skeptical that the two of them would support law enforcement. In reality, Obama and Holder were partisans of reformism, open to the type of management-led technocratic approaches that had defined the War on Crime under Johnson more than forty years earlier. Ever since, Blue Power had been growing, and reformist police chiefs had to accommodate the power of the rank and file. Even more so than Bill Clinton, Obama held a vision of law enforcement that relied on restoring legitimacy through procedural tinkering. When the country's most sustained protests against policing in decades broke out during his second term, they invigorated this approach but also revealed its limits.

CHAPTER 25

BLUE LIVES MATTER

On July 17, 2014, New York police officers engaged in quality-of-life enforcement in Tompkinsville, Staten Island, attempted to arrest Eric Garner for allegedly selling loosies (individual cigarettes). In the process, Daniel Pantaleo, one of the officers, wrapped his arms around Garner's neck, leading Garner to complain, "I can't breathe." He repeated the phrase eleven times before losing consciousness. Garner would be pronounced dead at the hospital over an hour later. The next day, a grainy video of the arrest recorded by Garner's friend Ramsey Orta rocketed across smartphone screens. The following day, exactly one year after Obama had offered extended, sympathetic remarks about Trayvon Martin, Al Sharpton led a small protest on the site of Garner's arrest.

Immediately after Garner's death, Ed Mullins, the head of the Sergeants Benevolent Association and Lynch's counterpart in the city's next-largest police union and the country's fifth largest, encouraged a work slowdown: "If there's a delay in getting to the next place, so be it." Coming from the leader of the sergeants' union, this prod carried weight for the patrol officers in Pat Lynch's union. This outburst marked a pivot for Mullins, as he began not just to mimic Lynch's rhetoric but even exceed it. He would go on to call Mayor de Blasio a "total nincompoop" and demand that he be "humble" by recognizing that his views, particularly his criticism of excessive stop-and-frisk tactics coordinated by Ray Kelly and Michael Bloomberg, did not represent those of all New Yorkers. The question of whether a registered Republican who lived on Long Island was a tribune for city residents was left unasked and unanswered.[1]

The media landscape was different now, the public sphere transformed. The type of city reporter who had cultivated long-standing ties with powerbrokers, including police union officials, was going extinct. The reach of police-friendly traditional media was shrinking. But cops were now able to broadcast their message directly. Social media also encouraged one-upmanship in pursuit of likes and reposts. Mullins became an adept poster, using the official account of his union as his own mouthpiece, while sworn officers mainly posted anonymously. Memes and hashtags forged discursive communities, though these were always mutating, often by becoming more outrageous.

Hundreds of current and retired New York City officers inhabited a public online message board called Thee Rant. Though material posted on it was often difficult to verify, it did afford a cross-sectional view into the increasing alignment of police officers with right-wing rejections of Obama, Hillary Clinton, and numerous Democratic elected officials in the city.

Police publications, which have provided a great deal of this book's research base, began moving fully online, allowing a wider readership. This accessibility incentivized publications to seek new audiences through clickbait and frothy comment sections. Coverage pivoted from best practices in policing to more openly politicized accounts of the job. A right-wing investor and marketer bought the web magazine *Law Enforcement Today*, turning it into a mouthpiece for extremist political propaganda under the guise of authoritative analysis from police. Even legacy police publications like *Police* and *Law Officer* have shifted toward open partisanship. But newer, born-digital venues have reshaped public discourse about policing, treating the profession, or at least its rank-and-file members, as coeval with the Republican Party. Thebluemagazine.com, Officer.com, Police1.com, and Apbweb.com (American Police Beat) are among the popular sites, while podcasts hosted by police have also proliferated.

This profusion of police perspectives underpins what critics have called "copaganda," which is not simply the widespread availability of police-dominated narratives crafted by the well-funded and sophisticated public information offices of big-city departments. Instead, it is the naturalization of the police viewpoint and police jargon, to the exclusion of alternatives. The summer of 2014 was the moment when this dominance was irrevocably punctured—thanks to Black protest of police violence.[2]

A few weeks after Garner's death, Officer Darren Wilson shot and killed Mike Brown in Ferguson, Missouri. Wilson would claim that Brown punched him through the open window of his vehicle and grabbed his gun. Wilson managed to fire a round that hit the door panel. He described Brown's reaction: "It looks like a demon, that's how angry he looked." Brown ran from Wilson, who shot at him, hitting him six times. Although there was no video footage of the incident, it immediately instigated widespread anger in the deeply segregated environs of St. Louis. Over the coming months, and especially after grand juries failed to produce indictments of either Pantaleo or Wilson, Black Lives Matter became a nationwide and then global rallying cry. Garner's words "I can't breathe," along with the hands-up posture that witnesses claimed Brown assumed, would be replicated by millions across the globe.[3]

In New York, de Blasio responded with consternation when prosecutors decided not to bring charges against Pantaleo. It was just weeks after a police officer shot and killed Akai Gurley in the stairwell of a Brooklyn housing project, inciting new demonstrations. De Blasio reemphasized a point that he had made implicitly while running for mayor with an ad about breaking with Bloomberg's policies: his own son, a tall Black kid, was at risk of police harassment. The city's stop-and-frisk statistics suggested that he was right; young Black men were significantly overrepresented among those stopped. De Blasio and his wife, Chirlane McCray, reported that they counseled their son to take "special care" while interacting with police.

Lynch was outraged. De Blasio had thrown his officers "under the bus," he cried, while they were working long shifts, controlling Black Lives Matter protests and facing protesters' denunciations. The union circulated a petition titled "Don't Insult My Sacrifice." An officer could fill in his or her name and demand that if he or she was killed in the line of duty, the mayor and city council speaker not attend the ensuing funeral. Their "attendance at the funeral of a fallen New York City police officer," it read, "is an insult to that officer's memory and sacrifice."[4]

Protests continued. Graffiti reading NYPD KILLS in massive letters popped up on the Manhattan Bridge on a Friday morning. That Friday night, off-duty police and allies staged a rally outside city hall, promoted on Facebook with the hashtag #ThankYouNYPD. One supporter traveled from Colorado for the event and brought with him shirts that he gave to demonstrators to wear. They mocked Garner's final words, the same three words uttered by at least seventy people killed by police from 2010 to 2020. The shirts read I CAN BREATHE.[5]

On December 20, 2014, the balance of forces changed. A lone gunman ambushed two New York police officers, Wenjian Liu and Rafael Ramos, who were sitting in their patrol car on a Saturday afternoon in Bedford-Stuyvesant. He shot and killed them both. The shooter was from Baltimore. Earlier in the day, he had fired a gun at his ex-girlfriend, wounding her. After attacking Liu and Ramos, he fled into the subway, pursued by police, where he killed himself.

In New York on that morose Saturday evening, the police revolted. At a press conference, Lynch denounced de Blasio, blaming him for the officers' deaths. The blood spilled by Liu and Ramos "starts on the steps of City Hall," he thundered, "in the office of the mayor." Ed Mullins made a similar statement to his member sergeants and on Twitter. These words marked a turning point. Although this book has documented countless incidents of antagonism between police union leaders and elected officials, Lynch, the highest-profile police union leader in the country, took it to an extreme. He opened an irreparable rift with nationwide implications. Even Giuliani thought Lynch went too far.[6]

Lynch believed he was justified in criticizing de Blasio. This ambush shooting was like a prophecy foretold, a replay of the department's darkest moments. Despite false allegations of membership in a Black Liberation Army–like gang, the shooter was no ideologically motivated political militant conducting a clandestine attack. He had posted his plans to kill two cops online, and announced to bystanders what he was about to do. But it did not matter to Lynch. For him, an antipolice ideology had become normalized. While the radicals of the 1970s that obsessed his union drew from esoteric theories of *guerrillismo* imported from distant lands, it seemed to Lynch that now the #BlackLivesMatter hashtag put extremism in the palm of anyone's hand. The mayor, Lynch felt, had spent his campaign and his entire time in office entertaining critics of the police department, if not directly vilifying police.

In reality, de Blasio often praised officers, especially as they were confronting daily protests. His criticisms were measured, focusing on police tactics like stop-and-frisk, as well as violations of civil rights. He emphasized the burden of history, how mistrust lingered but progress was possible. To Lynch, history was not a chain of events leading toward a brighter future but an accumulation of slights and disrespect. History comprised imperfect arbitration awards, unfair internal affairs investigations, expansions of civilian review, lawsuits, retraining, protests, hashtags, and killings of cops.

Police antipathy for de Blasio grew acute. When the mayor and police commissioner strode through Woodhull Hospital, where Liu and Ramos had been rushed and declared dead, officers lining the halls, including Lynch and Mullins, silently turned their backs on them. Then, outside the funeral service honoring Ramos, attended by 25,000 officers from around the country, cops turned their backs on the huge screens outside the church when de Blasio offered brief remarks. Lynch commented that in his thirty-one years on the job, "I've never seen such a show of support as we have today." Bratton denounced the officers' stunt, but Lynch would not. "We have to understand the betrayal that they feel," he insisted.

The mayor, police commanders, and leaders of the police unions convened an unprecedented emergency two-hour meeting, hoping to ease tensions. A spokesman for Lynch's union characterized it as frank but not hostile: "There was no yelling," but "there was no laughing." It did not mend the fissures. Bratton officially asked police officers to engage in "grieving, not grievance" at Liu's funeral a few days later, but many still turned their backs a second time. Lynch argued that the action was not disrespectful because it occurred outside the church, where officers maintained a right to free expression. "This was an organic gesture that started on the streets of New York, and it should be respected."[7]

Blue Power had reared up. I was living in Brooklyn at the time. Although protests against the police did not cease entirely, a chill wind blew. Local television news broadcasts shifted their tone immediately. Promotional clips featuring images of protest marches and placards disappeared. They were replaced by somber depictions of police saluting, families in mourning, flags, and bagpipers.

A new hashtag, #BlueLivesMatter, went viral on social media the night of the shooting, affording supporters of police and opponents of the protest movement their own distinctive, reactionary term. Three men with law enforcement experience immediately decided to form what became a 501(c)3 nonprofit, Blue Lives Matter NYC. In addition to selling branded gear, the organization hosts charitable fundraisers and provides commentary to the media on police-related topics. Other entrepreneurs also began selling pro-police gear. The most popular logo became the thin blue line across a black-and-white US flag. Now the aggressive defense of police, which for decades had been the professional remit of rank-and-file leaders, would be dispersed as a commodified cultural form, available for anyone to purchase and brandish.

Chuck Canterbury, national president of the Fraternal Order of Police, helped to spread the belief that a national wave of ambush attacks on cops was unfolding: a "war on cops." (Despite clusters of violence, social scientists have not found evidence of a sustained increase in such attacks.) Canterbury, the longest-serving president of the organization since Harrington, called on Congress to pass a law that would make violence against police a hate crime, which would entail sentencing enhancements. Hate crime statutes give prosecutors a powerful tool and great latitude because of the vague, subjective character of the concept, which essentially lowers, rather than raises, a bar for assessing intent, conflating different motivations.[8]

Preexisting laws on the books in every state already augmented punishment for violence against police. The Fraternal Order of Police was now calling for occupation to become a protected class akin to sexuality or race, stretching the meaning of an already elusive concept. Soon a bipartisan bill in Congress called the Protect and Serve Act would emerge, supported by the Fraternal Order of Police, National Association of Police Organizations, and National Sheriffs' Association, though not the International Association of Chiefs of Police. The bill proposed new penalties for violence against police, authorizing life sentences for murder of cops. This federal law was not enacted, but a flurry of state and local hate crime laws protecting police ensued. Prosecutors also began charging individuals with hate crimes for abusing cops after the killing of Liu and Ramos. A Black man in Pennsylvania, arrested on suspicion of shoplifting, called officers "Nazis" and "Gestapo." He caught a charge of "felony ethnic intimidation" that was later dropped.[9]

SLOWDOWN

The sharpest reaction to the deaths of Ramos and Liu, however, was in New York City. Officers instantly commenced a multifaceted slowdown. Rather than calling in sick, as in the classic blue flu scenario, officers showed up to work and did nothing. Officially, they were working to rule. Parking tickets, traffic summonses, and even arrests all but ceased in most precincts for up to seven weeks. De Blasio trusted the broken windows theory, believing that its careful application could reduce major crime. Now, though, officers ended proactive enforcement of small-scale offenses. Police aimed to stop de Blasio's mayoralty in its tracks.

Rumors circulated that the Patrolmen's Benevolent Association and the Sergeants Benevolent Association orchestrated the slowdown. Given how the department operated, and the supreme power of union delegates and trustees among the ranks, it would be unimaginable for a job action like this to occur without some coordination by the associations. A journalist received a screenshot of a copy-and-paste message purporting to come from the patrol union on the night of the shooting, though the union denied producing it. Whatever the source, it gained traction among cops. It invoked the Black Power era. It accused the mayor, introducing the idea that his hands were dripping with officers' blood, which Lynch and Mullins would go on to vocalize.

> FROM NYC PBA. Starting IMMEDIATELY—At least two units are to respond to EVERY call, no matter the condition or severity, no matter what type of job is pending, or what the option of the patrol supervisor happens to be. IN ADDITION: Absolutely NO enforcement action in the form of arrests and or summonses is to be taken unless absolutely necessary and an individual MUST be placed under arrest. These are precautions that were

> taken in the 1970's when Police Officers were ambushed and executed on a regular basis. The mayors hands are literally dripping with our blood because of his words actions and policies and we have, for the first time in a number of years, become a "wartime" police department. We will act accordingly. FORWARD MESSAGE IN ITS ENTIRETY TO ANY AND ALL MOS.[10]

If Lynch and Mullins had ordered a slowdown, it would have violated state law. Lynch told reporters that "precautions had to be taken" but there was "NO SLOWDOWN." De Blasio also did not readily confirm it was happening.[11]

The enforcement numbers did not lie, however. Arrests declined by two-thirds, traffic citations by 94 percent. In one week, three turnstile hoppers were cited, as compared to 400 in the same period the prior year. Officers did not issue a single quality-of-life summons on New Year's Eve. Drunk driving citations were minimal.

Fines fell $5 million short of expectations. Bratton spun what was happening by noting that fewer arrests could save the city the cost of overtime pay. This suggestion only revealed how misdemeanor enforcement extracts a double tax from city residents, first as unnecessary fines and time wasted and, second, as pay for police to complete the elaborate paperwork and processing that results.[12]

Critics of the police department pointed out that there was no spike in complaints of crime due to the slowdown. The lack of serious crime when low-level enforcement disappeared was a challenge to the broken windows theory. In real time, a slowdown by the most data-driven department in the country revealed that crime statistics measure enforcement. The camera is actually an engine of discretionary criminalization. The city's most policed groups—Black and Latino young men—suddenly were treated as if they were white. At a rally outside One Police Plaza, Josmar Trujillo, an organizer and fervent opponent of the department, announced, "We're here to say we want a permanency to the slowdown."[13]

It would not be accurate to say that police officers who ceased enforcement were engaged in a backlash against the excesses of the protest movement that swept across the country in 2014. Instead, "frontlash" would be a better characterization, to draw from scholarly analyses of how a lexicon of crime came to be the rejoinder to demands for civil rights. Cops already opposed the movement's demands; now they had the pretext to act on this opposition in new ways. Across the fifty years of history this book documents, rank-and-file police had been rejecting reform and oversight efforts, decrying critics, and calling for better compensation. They have shaped the available discourse in public discussions of crime, politicizing it, to the detriment of the most economically and socially marginalized people in the country—and to their own benefit.[14]

In the 1960s, the political refrain "law and order" came from police experts and leaders before it was adopted by conservative opponents of civil rights like Barry Goldwater, George Wallace, and Richard Nixon. It suggested that the push for Black freedom was tantamount to crime, as it conflated protest with illegality and racial integration with social breakdown. According to this script, cops sat at the vertex, where criminality and political radicalism met. They were the most threatened, but they were also the bulwark against chaos.

In the spring of 2015, another killing by police reignited the Black Lives Matter movement. It also spurred protests that turned into an uprising that resulted in hundreds of arrests, at least $9 million in property damage, and political upheaval. Baltimore police severely injured Freddie Gray while arresting him on a Sunday morning in April. He died a week later. The state's attorney charged six officers in the incident, though none was ultimately convicted. The Department of Justice launched an investigation into the Baltimore Police Department, which followed on the heels of a similar investigation into policing in Ferguson, Missouri. Both used the authority granted by the 1994 crime bill to investigate localities for a pattern or practice of civil rights violations by law enforcement. The charges against the Baltimore officers, and these investigations, which both affirmed widespread violations and resulted in consent decrees requiring reforms, infuriated cops. They saw these actions, overseen by Black officials both in Maryland and in Washington, DC, as conceding to mob action.

In the Black Lives Matter era, a rejoinder conflating crime and protest again emerged. This uncompromising posture elevated the needs of police over all other social and civic goals. It was not a novel response to the killings of Ramos and Liu or to Department of Justice reform imperatives, nor was this law and order idea born after the rebellion in Detroit in 1967 that opened this book. Instead, police have consistently advocated the racist politics associated with the backlash in advance of these crisis moments, seizing upon them to widen the scope of law and order and intensify its appeal.

Yet there was long a pragmatic, tactical dimension to the complaint that protesting for social justice was equivalent to destroying police forces, and even in early 2015 this became clear when Mullins called a temporary truce with the mayor once de Blasio signed a strong contract with the Sergeants Benevolent Association. They even watched a televised Knicks game together. Conviviality between Mullins and de Blasio was brief, however, as the national political landscape began to shift due to Donald Trump's entry into contention for the White House.[15]

De Blasio was also up for reelection in 2016, and the Patrolmen's Benevolent Association campaigned against him. The union purchased ads on the side of trucks that lumbered through the city. I glimpsed one depicting a car on blocks, adorned with language about a return to the "bad old days," even as crime remained low. Lynch and de Blasio never had a rapprochement, and eventually the two stopped talking at all. After de Blasio's reelection, officers ended up working without a contract for several years.

The insurgent union leader who gained power by antagonizing the department, the union leadership, and city hall was losing effectiveness. De Blasio had no incentive to assist Lynch. The signed contract with Mullins, whose base of power was smaller than Lynch's, was a thumb in Lynch's eye. In the spring of 2015, after the slowdown, Lynch faced challengers in his effort to be reelected union president. One of them had been an ally of Matarazzo, and many of his criticisms of Lynch echoed what Lynch had flung at the old guard many years earlier. It was true that the PERB strategy continued to yield unimpressive results. A new pension tier for officers hired after 2009 limited disability coverage, while the practice of "selling out the unborn," or achieving improvements for current officers by sacrificing them for future recruits, continued. Lynch nevertheless won, but he could not reasonably place blame for declining morale or retention and recruitment challenges on the mayor, city council, and governor alone. Within the union, officers may have believed Lynch was self-aggrandizing or otherwise disagreed with him, but they remained powerless, stuck commiserating over coffee, posting anonymously online, or podcasting.[16]

Lynch no longer had his finger on the city's political pulse. He faced the quandary of whether to continue to engage with conservatives in the Democratic Party or pivot toward Republicans in the few areas of the city where they stood a chance. In 2020, much of the union's campaign spending was directed against Democrats. The next year, the one Democratic candidate the union backed failed spectacularly. Lynch supported political gadfly Sal Albanese for a city council seat in a Staten Island district that was home to many cops. The union allocated $376,597 to spend independently on ads, including one that depicted de Blasio and said, "If you hate this guy . . ." then "You'll love this one," pointing to Albanese. But Albanese lost to the Republican incumbent, winning only about 9,600 votes, meaning the union spent over $39 for each one. In Queens, however, the union supported the county Republican Party chair in a council race, painting her Democratic opponent as a "radical, anti-police extremist." The union spent $218,149 on that race. The Republican won.[17]

During the slowdown after Liu and Ramos were killed, Samuel Walker, a preeminent policing scholar, observed that New York City's police unions were "completely unlike those in any city I'm familiar with." Many cities had unions that battled with their police chiefs, but "in New York, the kind of attitude you get from the police unions, it's completely over the top." What was to come in 2020 from Lynch and Mullins would not just be over the top; it would be off the charts.[18]

CHAPTER 26

FUND/DEFUND/FUND

After Donald Trump announced his 2016 run for the White House, the first major police union to endorse him was, tellingly, the National Border Patrol Council. This endorsement in the Republican primary set the stage for the far larger Fraternal Order of Police to endorse him in the general election, after declining to endorse anyone in 2012. Its reach in the Rust Belt swing states and mountain states was more consequential than the Border Patrol union's, and one study showed that it mobilized not only its members but their families to vote for him as well. But members of the National Border Patrol Council would ultimately reap outsized benefits from Trump's rise, in keeping with decades of success courting public opinion and winning the kind of material national support that remained a dream for other police unions.[1]

A small operation for most of its history, the Border Patrol was the beneficiary of a series of favorable Supreme Court decisions in the 1970s. *US v. Brignoni-Ponce* and *US v. Martinez-Fuerte* affirmed its ability to operate mobile patrols and checkpoints within 100 miles of the borders and coastlines, where two-thirds of the American populace resides. Not only were they permitted to stop and question anyone in that zone, but the ordinary standard of reasonable suspicion grew even thinner for the Border Patrol. A hunch based on two factors, including the driver's skin color, the court ruled, was enough to stop a car while patrolling, and a driver passing through a checkpoint could be stopped without cause and the car inspected based on the race of its occupants. These discretionary investigative powers were to be employed only to enforce immigration law, yet the Border Patrol would not be constrained.[2]

Over the course of its history, the National Border Patrol Council emulated the tactics of municipal police unions, but it managed to win nationally where its predecessors were forced to build power on the local level. Allegations of violence by Border Patrol agents against migrants were widespread, and evidence suggested that the Border Patrol's actions were not only violent but ineffective as well—in 1992 the agency employed more than triple the officers it did when Nixon left office, but apprehensions of "illegal aliens" had only doubled to 1.2 million. Still, xenophobia was rising, and the Border Patrol union managed to deflect accusations of abuse and turn them into reasons to ask for more funding.[3]

When in 1992 Border Patrol agents chased a Chevrolet Suburban that crashed in front of Temecula Valley High School, killing six people, the union managed to dodge oversight by blaming management. The incident translated into a funding bonanza, with bipartisan support. By 1994, experts in counterinsurgency and low-intensity conflict from the Department of Defense had helped the Border Patrol formulate a strategic vision of "prevention through deterrence" that made the more urbanized and populated part of the border with Mexico impenetrable, forcing migrants into far more dangerous remote desert crossing zones. One Border Patrol sector chief, Silvestre Reyes, parlayed his oversight of deterrence operations in Texas into an eight-term career in the House of Representatives.[4]

Prevention through deterrence persists in the fencing, razor wire, saw blades, and other menacing and lethal tools, as well as military-grade surveillance technologies, that festoon the border. Over 10,000 people have died due to exposure to extreme temperatures, snakebite, starvation, dehydration, and drowning, all as a consequence of the strategy to use "hostile terrain" as a barrier. Meanwhile, patrolling the border is uneventful. Whether at fixed checkpoints, on mobile patrol, or in the desert scrub, most officers apprehend no more than a couple of unauthorized border crossers each month. Yet to paint the job as risky, Border Patrol has maintained a policy of overcounting violent incidents toward officers and underreporting violence by officers, while considering rocks tossed over the border fence at officers as potentially fatal and worthy of lethal force in response.[5]

Legislation after the 9/11 attack turned the new agency of Customs and Border Protection—which would include the Border Patrol—into the front-line barrier against terrorists. If locating roving migrants across the vast expanse of the desert Southwest was already difficult, finding phantasmic terrorists was impossible. Border Patrol's response, therefore, was to consider any migrant a potential terrorist, manufacturing a fiction that underpins the Homeland Security edifice. This has been a primary goal of the National Border Patrol Council ever since, while agents daily overstep their broad Supreme Court–granted powers to employ skin color as a factor in immigration enforcement by using it for narcotics interdiction and terrorism prevention.

Hiring new agents grew complex after the agency's post-9/11 transformation. Not only did the Border Patrol have to weather Republican efforts at privatization and civil service reform (later watered down by Democrats), but the reorientation of operations had profound ramifications. For decades, the Border Patrol had recruited many of its agents from the border region where Spanish-language skills were widely available. Only after a series of ad campaigns and incentives was the Border Patrol able to recruit new hires from across the country, including people already employed as cops and prison guards. According to one of the Border Patrol union's most candid executives, Art Del Cueto, the result was that too many agents joined without a commitment to enforcing the law. Instead, strong compensation lured new hires, or else anti-immigrant animus pushed them to recruiters.[6]

The paradox of the relationship between the Border Patrol and Donald Trump is that a "Great Wall of the United States" represents an existential threat to the agency. With every new inch of border fence erected, the Border Patrol becomes more superfluous, while prevention through deterrence makes unauthorized border crossers more difficult to track. Plus, interior enforcement by Immigration and Customs Enforcement, the rival sibling within the Department of Homeland Security, has grown in importance. Nevertheless, in 2016 the National Border Patrol Council's president, Brandon Judd, cozied up to Trump. By putting immigration "at the forefront of this presidential campaign," Trump spoke Judd's language. "Mr. Trump will take on special interests," the endorsement read, "and embrace the ideas of rank-and-file Border Patrol agents rather than listening to the management yes-men who say whatever they are programmed to say. This is a refreshing change that we have not seen before—and may never see again."[7]

Border Patrol agents flocked to Trump. Art Del Cueto boasts that he has taken at least seven selfie photos with his "friend" Donald Trump, who was also initially a guest on the National Border Patrol Council's podcast that he hosts, *The Green Line*, while running for president in May 2016. Now retired, Del Cueto still serves as an officer of the National Border Patrol Council, in addition to "broadcasting from the Southern border." *The Green Line* tailored the thin blue line of cop lore to Border Patrol uniforms. In its own promotional materials, the podcast crowed that it turned a talk show into a movement (aided by sponsorship from ultraconservative Breitbart News). It has also served as a mouthpiece for the culture-war diktats of hard-line immigration restrictionists.[8]

As a union representative and a native of the borderlands, the avuncular Del Cueto is savvy about the realities of the job, including the bureaucratic challenges imposed by Washington and operational challenges imposed by the desert Southwest. Like other executives of the National Border Patrol Council, he is an unwavering supporter of Trump, even as Trump's ideas about how to control unauthorized migration and drug smuggling are untethered from the realities Del Cueto and his brethren experience and understand. Trump, however, could be expected to side with Del Cueto in a skirmish over vocabulary: no Border Patrol agent should listen to politically correct Washington bureaucrats and avoid the standard term "illegal alien."[9]

Yet the cultural battles were set pieces in the longer campaign to boost the material baseline for the Department of Homeland Security. The Republican Party's massive spending bill in 2025 awarded more money to the department than it could figure out how to spend. The cash infusion would come first, with planning a secondary concern. But at least 3,000 new Border Patrol hires were authorized, plus $2 billion for retention and hiring bonuses, as well as another $600 million to find recruits who had not yet considered the pleasures of the desert. Immigration and Customs Enforcement fared even better, with money for 10,000 new officers, setting the stage for the national police force that law enforcement advocates have, for the entire history of the United States, claimed would never emerge. Blue

Power's paramount achievements would tend toward suspending all practical and legal impediments to politicized unification of law enforcement.[10]

Despite a shared commitment to Trump, in practice it was inevitable that friction would develop between cops and sheriffs, on the one hand, and immigration authorities, on the other. If Trump's xenophobic pitch has always relied on the false presumption that immigrants bear criminal tendencies, deputizing local police to engage in immigration enforcement makes ordinary crime prevention tough. Cops cannot gain cooperation from noncitizens, including when victimized, if contact might lead to deportation. Crime goes unreported, tips evaporate, and witnesses decline to speak to officers. Police brass know that cooperation is fickle and relationships are fragile. Ideologues spin careless tales that blame everyone but themselves for cultivating mistrust. Demonizing immigrants and pushing them into the shadows creates the conditions for episodes of social disorder that sustain Trump's appeals. But the disorder was only beginning.[11]

DEFUND THE POLICE

"Defund the police" was the plaintive cry that defined the largest wave of protests in US history, sparked by the murder of George Floyd by a police officer in Minneapolis on May 25, 2020. Protests occurred in every state, not only in cities but also in predominantly white towns as well as rural areas. They also spread across the globe. In some locales they persisted nightly for months. In Minneapolis, protesters laid siege to the 3rd Precinct building and burned it to the ground.

"Defund the police" was more than a slogan. It was a demand. And it is also a lens for understanding US politics since the 1960s. "Defund the police" is the spectral flipside of Blue Power. It would not make sense to demand that the police be defunded if they had not become lavishly funded in the first place, a process this book has documented. And, rather than calling for austerity, the demand contained a claim that government expenditures are misallocated, arguing that social and interpersonal harms may be better addressed by affording greater resources to other agencies, from violence interrupters to mental health and addiction counselors. It argues that public safety will come from improving education, housing, employment opportunities, libraries, parks and recreation, and other social services, not continued steep spending on police.

But the demand to defund the police was not only about money. In our society, among government agencies, funding is an index of power. To defund the police would be to disempower them. But Blue Power also explains why police have not yet been defunded.

In late May 2020, after being stuck inside for months due to the COVID-19 lockdown, what brought me outside and into the streets, marching with thousands of strangers, was Floyd's murder. These demonstrations felt different than any I had experienced before. They could be intense and uncompromising, but because they were so massive, they also included hundreds of thousands who had barely ever protested previously. Many who took to the streets were motivated by the timidity of leaders in Washington, whose support for police and promises of reform went nowhere. The demand to defund the police spread like a shock wave across the country.

I had already been studying the police for over a decade by then, but "defund the police" felt fresh and new. Originating with Black-women-led grassroots groups like Chicago's BYP100 and Minneapolis's Reclaim the Block, the call to defund the police was a way of framing the problem that differed from other demands protesters had made during marches and rallies, including disarming, dismantling, and even abolishing the police. Defunding was not maximalist and may have been more palatable than dismantling or abolishing, but as the practical floor beneath those other demands, "defund the police" clicked for millions.[12]

Police unions interpreted the phrase as a dagger pointed at the heart of the project of Blue Power. In New York City, cops acted as if de Blasio had orchestrated the call, lashing out directly at him. On May 30, 2020, the mayor's daughter, Chiara, was arrested during a protest. A cop leaked her booking details. Ed Mullins then amplified the story on social media. Doxxing the mayor's daughter was an unethical and likely illegal act. It illustrated how far astray police union politics had traveled from securing strong wages and benefits, which Mullins had been able to discuss in person with de Blasio just five years earlier—before Donald Trump's successful campaign for the Oval Office. The ability to leak arrest records also indicated how police can wield immense power in our society, quite unlike that of other bureaucrats. Using their operational capabilities to uphold a vendetta against an elected official and target his family member showed how insatiable Blue Power had become. (Mullins would later be indicted on federal charges of defrauding his own union to the tune of over $600,000. He pled guilty in January 2023.)[13]

During the protests, New York City police officers focused on the anonymous protesters demanding that police be defunded, swerving away from typical tactics that focus on lawbreaking. The country's largest and most well-resourced police department rarely responds to demonstrations in anything but swift and uncompromising fashion. It can muster overwhelming numbers of officers. Sometimes there are more cops armed with "hats and bats," or helmets and batons, than protesters. But during those weeks in the spring of 2020, officers seemed to ignore the obviously unlawful activity that was occurring—vandalism, burglary, and looting of commercial strips in ritzy neighborhoods like SoHo—in favor of corralling, intimidating, arresting, and even attacking protesters doing little more than standing in place and chanting. This approach only incited the crowds, leading to mass arrests like the one that ensnared the mayor's daughter.

Crowd-control tactics shifted from their traditional focus on protest form, like blocking car traffic, to focus on protest content, which was avowedly antipolice. The most widely heard chant on the streets, coming from rambunctious teenagers of color of all genders, was "NYPD suck my dick!" Police momentarily seemed to forget that they are supposed to be protectors of capital. They ignored episodes of looting, accompanied by kids singing about the ensuing communal luxury to the tune of the Brooklyn drill track "Dior" by Pop Smoke: "Christian Dior, Dior, I'm up in all the stores / When it rains, it pours." Instead, police stared down protesters enumerating desired municipal budget cuts.[14]

As an uneasy peace returned to New York City's streets over the summer, Pat Lynch decided that he could match this clampdown on local politics with a leap into national politics. Lynch conferred the Police Benevolent Association of New York City's endorsement on Donald Trump's reelection campaign. It was the first time the city patrol union had issued a presidential endorsement, Lynch proudly announced at Trump's golf club in Bedminster, New Jersey. (That was not true; Caruso had supported both Reagan and Bush when other city and state unions endorsed them.) The union was not simply *giving* an endorsement, he brayed. Trump had "earned" it. The president of the Guardians Association, representing Black cops, complained that Lynch did not formally or extensively consult his membership on the endorsement. The one Black member of Lynch's leadership team, Mubarak Abdul-Jabbar, who had retired in 2018, was taken aback. Abdul-Jabbar had donated to Obama; he called the reelection endorsement of "the most polarizing" president "mind-boggling." Demonstrators swiftly organized a rally that took a page from Lynch's own manual. They showed up outside his home in Bayside, Queens. A phalanx of officers and a cordon of metal barricades confronted them. Lynch quipped, "Their campaign of harassment and intimidation might have the politicians running scared, but it will have zero impact on the PBA."[15]

Lynch had already signaled increasing coziness with Trump's Make America Great Again movement by linking with Sheriff David A. Clarke. During the summer of 2015, the police magazine *NY Blue Now* (today *Blue Magazine*), based in New Jersey, put Clarke on its cover and carried an "uncensored" interview with him about policing, protest, and the Black "underclass." Although independent, the magazine was geared toward rank-and-file cops in the tristate area, carrying ads for local realtors, mortgage brokers, doctors, and lawyers offering discounts for union members. Clarke, the elected African American sheriff of Milwaukee County, embodied the Constitutional Sheriffs movement, an extremist splinter faction dedicated to the claim that sheriffs hold greater authority than any federal official. He had even won its 2013 Sheriff of the Year Award. After the *NY Blue Now* interview, Clarke endorsed Trump for president. Lynch subsequently named the Milwaukee sheriff the Patrolmen's Benevolent Association Person of the Year, "an honor normally granted to a prominent New Yorker," as a journalist pointed out. Clarke soon resigned. Numerous misconduct complaints and lawsuits had been lodged against him, including for restraining pregnant women in the Milwaukee County jail and allowing a detainee to die of dehydration. The resignation offered Clarke "the chance to do what I love most—promote President Trump's agenda, including his fierce support for the American law enforcement officer." Clarke became a spokesperson and advisor for the Trump-aligned political action committee America First Action.[16]

Lynch's endorsement of Trump in 2020 indicated alignment with the president's extreme views on policing, which had fissured the profession. Not long after first assuming office, Trump addressed an audience of police officers on Long Island. The reason for the speech was to demand that Congress fund an expansion of the border fence and appoint 10,000 new Immigration and Customs Enforcement agents. Against a wall of blue-uniformed officers, Trump railed against "animals" in gangs like MS-13 who had rendered cities "bloodstained killing fields." Trump also encouraged police officers to be "rough" when making arrests. With trademark knotted phrasing, he told a story, "I said, please don't be too nice." The audience laughed. "Like when you guys put somebody in the car and you're protecting their head, you know, the way you put their hand over? Like, don't hit their head and they've just killed somebody—don't hit their head. I said, you can take the hand away, okay?" Some of the cops in the room clapped and chortled. The Suffolk County Police Department issued a statement that night insisting that it did not condone hurting suspects. And soon chiefs across the country, as well as the IACP and Police Executive Research Forum, denounced Trump's remarks, arguing that they threatened the progress police had made in restoring legitimacy since the killings of Mike Brown and Eric Garner and the resulting Black Lives Matter mobilizations. These police leaders did not perceive, or admit, that this backsliding was the point.[17]

Meanwhile, groups like the Fraternal Order of Police and National Border Patrol Council enjoyed unprecedented levels of access to the White House and used it to their advantage. Because Congress still held the purse strings, 1600 Pennsylvania Avenue was for pursuing culture war battles. When the National Park Service offered a $98,000 grant to researchers at the University of California, Berkeley, to develop educational materials on the Black Panther Party, the Fraternal Order of Police protested directly to Trump, expressing "outrage and shock" that an antipolice organization could be an educational topic. The administration scuttled the funding, an early precedent for the slashing of humanities funding that would occur upon Trump's return to the Oval Office in 2025.[18]

The International Union of Police Associations, still affiliated with the AFL-CIO, endorsed Trump's reelection early, in September 2019. Sam Cabral, the organization's president, contrasted Trump with Obama: "President Trump has done more for Law Enforcement in the past two and a half years than was accomplished in the eight years that preceded his election. He has even undone some of the harmful acts of his predecessor." The schismatic National Association of Police Organizations, now far larger than the International Union of Police Associations, also endorsed Trump, arguing that he was "the Law and Order president," unlike candidate Joe Biden, with whom the national association had maintained close ties in the 1980s and 1990s. These organizations would all endorse Trump again in the 2024 election. Unity among police organizations, fragmented by geography, agency type, and relationship to organized labor, had been elusive for decades. No more. Police organizations now spoke with one voice, in favor of one man.[19]

By the summer of 2020, police seemed unanimous in their support of Trump. Those who did not support him, including police leaders in Democratic cities in Democratic-leaning states, mostly kept quiet. The International Association of Chiefs of Police and Police Executive Research Forum were neutralized politically. Although Obama had supported their preferred technocratic reformism, there was no space for it politically now, as right- and left-wing critics denounced that approach, though for different reasons. The rank and file had never supported reform, while those who demanded that police be defunded rightly saw reformism as a means of restoring legitimacy to a profession that they believed could never be truly transformed.

Biden had once been the greatest friend police ever had in the Senate. But he also could discern that political winds were changing, particularly within his party. To some critics, he was insecure, known for chasing what was popular and endorsing it with the zeal of a convert. To supporters, he was pragmatic. While campaigning, he revisited some of his harshest punitive stances of past decades with regret. Police wanted neither pragmatism nor assent to any criticism. Police chiefs recognized that incidents like the killing of George Floyd destroyed police legitimacy and made their jobs more difficult. Rank-and-file officers would have been affected by defunding, but chiefs were the ones who had to make the case against it when justifying their budgets to mayors and city councils. In a moment when the promise of reform was no longer a palliative, chiefs were adrift. Led by Lynch and other rank-and-file spokesmen, cops found their footing. It became unshakeable.

Trump's unrelenting, loquacious support for police and the pleasure he displayed regarding police misconduct made him the avatar of Blue Power itself. As the publisher of *Blue Magazine* wrote while endorsing Trump: "Eleven years ago," when the magazine launched, "I would never have thought to endorse a presidential candidate." Police opinions differed, and a conscientious editor had to represent them all. "However, in 2020 we now see things we did not see 11 years ago." The magazine also named Trump its Man of the Year.

Lynch followed his endorsement of Trump with a brief speech on the fourth and final night of the 2020 Republican National Convention. The whole adulatory affair was conducted mostly by video due to COVID-19. Addressing a national audience, Lynch toned down his Queens accent, which he tended to amplify while speaking to his "awffisuhs." "We are staring down the barrel of a public-safety disaster," he explained. It was true that since the weather had turned warmer and while the pandemic lockdown persisted, gun crime was up in New York City. He did not accept any police responsibility for this situation. Instead, the reason was simple: "The Democrats have walked away from us." He claimed that "in city after city, they've slashed police budgets." In fact, one study found no evidence of reduced police budgets in 264 major cities in the next fiscal year. Even advocates of defunding could point to only twenty cities that had reallocated funds, to the tune of $870 million out of the $134 billion spent by states and municipalities in fiscal year 2021. Regardless of the accuracy of Lynch's claims, he was condemning local and state officials while defending the incumbent president. He argued that street violence was itself the goal of the Democratic Party, which was beholden to the "radical left." As the only cop to address the convention, Lynch, the longest-serving president of the nation's largest patrol union, finally assumed the role of stentorian national spokesman for rank-and-file police.[20]

Speaking to Republicans, endorsing a Republican, Lynch turned Blue Power MAGA red.

FUND THE POLICE

Donald Trump did not create Blue Power. Yet Blue Power, particularly in its New York outer-borough guise, created the conditions for Trump's rise. And Trump, in turn, enabled Blue Power to realize its boon. He exploded the tendency toward properly calibrated, micromanaged reformist solutions to the problems of policing. Although factions within the Democratic Party tried to restrain the worst police practices, the covenant that sutured different approaches to reform, or its rejection, remained the provision of robust funding. But Trump offered something more.

Even when Trump supporters (including some cops) attacked the Capitol on January 6, 2021, brutalizing officers trying to defend Congress, the police organizations that supported Trump refused to denounce him. And Biden came into office making a simple plea to Congress, in response to the street protests of 2020: "Fund the police."[21]

The clash within the Democratic Party over policing played out in New York City under Lynch's reign: Would lavish funding to guarantee technical law enforcement acumen be enough to stave off critiques from the party's bases, whether highly educated and well-off liberals or the working- and middle-class Black and brown people whose neighborhoods bore the brunt of both crime and policing's worst tendencies? Funding was always the answer. Police pockets were bottomless. Democrats' quest for legitimacy was bottomless in its own way: it aimed to resolve the irresolvable, being tough on crime while respecting the rights and humanity of the criminalized. As Ray Kelly, a combat veteran of the war in Vietnam, once declared, "You can probably shut down just about all crime if you're willing to burn down the village to save it." He was criticizing Bratton's broken windows approach, but he was also uttering a prophecy of his own regime of stop-and-frisk. Each police commissioner was supposedly solving a problem the other had created, and reform remained the perpetual, nebulous plan for the future.[22]

Yet Trump mooted the question by rejecting reformism, however well funded, just as rank-and-file cops had long rejected it, while labeling any critique of policing radical, if not crazy. At the end of Trump's first term, Attorney General William Barr spent his final days in office issuing a report that trolled Lyndon Johnson's President's Commission on Law Enforcement and Administration of Justice by taking the same name. If the 1967 commission represented the apex of professionalizing reformism among police, the 2020 commission represented the apex of rank-and-file reaction, putting "diminished respect" for police as the profession's greatest problem. Trump became the vehicle to carry the resentments felt by police, while offering a capacious and Manichean vocabulary for police supporters. What Trump did from outside policing, Lynch did from inside the profession; he too had already obtained everything he needed, achieved every marker of operational success, but he wanted more.[23]

Trump's transcendent ability was to unify. The history of Blue Power is a history of false starts, detours, compromises, and disunity. One reason is simply that the practical questions of bureaucratic organization were not easily answered, and answers differed across the vast social geography of the country. But Trump's arrival on the US political scene also came at a moment—created the moment—when solving practical questions ceased to be a goal of governance. In the place of governing would be bullying, trolling, and tormenting, hallmarks of Blue Power. Unity came not from disciplined pursuit of goals but in the form of fetishistic loyalty to abstractions. Trump was, by his own description, "your president of law and order." Extravagant, ritualistic incantation substituted for policy. This performance was exorbitant to achieving any concrete social goal, just like Blue Power.

CONCLUSION

This book began with an obscure officer threatening Congress with a national police strike in 1970. There was at the time no clear way to organize such a nationwide action of withdrawing police labor. In the intervening half century, no single national union for police emerged. Instead, many locally based police unions spawned. These local unions are irregularly linked, and though many federated into larger associations, those larger associations, in turn, have competed with one another. Still, although there is no single nationwide organization for police today, rank-and-file officers now constitute the membership of an unofficial political movement.

I have called this gathering storm Blue Power, a term used once by the movement's father, Carl Parsell, president of the Detroit Police Officers Association. Blue Power is both process and goal, medium and outcome. In response to criticism of police violence, police have wielded this power by at long last rolling out the kind of national police strike that would have been impossible in 1970.

The strike launched in Ferguson, then spread to New York, and then to Baltimore in 2014 and 2015, following antipolice protests. And it exploded in 2020. The strike is amorphous, disavowed, and haphazardly organized. It has ebbed and flowed, and it is not geographically even. It manifests in multiple ways. Its effects are varied, and they can be difficult to parse.

Yet according to a range of studies and a variety of statistical evidence, police have "depoliced" as a rejoinder not just to Black Lives Matter but also to smartphone recordings of their activities, vaccine mandates and health risks, bail and sentencing reforms, investigations into civil rights violations and resulting court decrees, "progressive prosecutors," and the demand for defunding police. At the same time, officers are quitting, retiring early, and seeking disability protections. Recruitment has fallen short of targets all over. Officers on duty play smartphone videogames in plain view of taxpayers. Complaints of cratering morale among police are the signal. Cops get frustrated, and enforcement slackens.

During this creeping strike, response times have lengthened, arrests have declined, and traffic enforcement has plummeted. In New Jersey, three unions for state troopers came under investigation for allegedly orchestrating an eight-month slowdown beginning in 2023, reducing citations by 61 percent, after the imposition of antidiscrimination reforms that merely sought to record the racial identity of drivers whom troopers stopped. There and across the country, traffic deaths have increased. Gun homicide increased sharply in many places with the onset of the COVID-19 pandemic and then after the killing of George Floyd. And police "clearance" rates—the number of killings, rapes, and robberies investigators actually solved—remained abysmal.[1]

Amid the uprisings of 2020, on the most frantic nights, officers in big cities stood down when faced with chaos, instead largely focusing on containing peaceful protesters trying to assert their First Amendment rights, calling for changes to the system, for defunding the police. They then used sophisticated crime-fighting tools to monitor and surveil dissenters. In keeping with the broader trend this book has charted, police answered the perceived threat of the diminution of resources through democratic means by asserting their operational power to strangle civic life. Anytime police constrain protest, they are engaged in political activity. But now the political position they were advancing was nothing but Blue Power. The message to elected officials was that of a protection racket: support us, or we will induce mayhem. Even after the uprisings abated, the police withdrawal persisted, manifesting the dystopic right-wing fantasy of a defunded police force.[2]

If we stopped the tape at the end of 2021, we could conclude that crime went up as enforcement declined. And we might posit a relationship: less policing equals more crime. But now there is less crime again, with rates of violent offenses plummeting. In many places where the homicide rate rose dramatically even before 2020, it has fallen more dramatically. Killings by police are not counted in official tallies of crime, but those have increased year by year since 2020. Sheriffs in rural areas are responsible for a growing, disproportionate share, even as some cities have succeeded in reducing police use of firearms.[3]

The rolling police strike has changed enforcement patterns on the street. Police did not desist entirely. But they became reactive, responding mainly to calls or relying on surveillance and technological substitutes for intensive patrol techniques—for example, by chasing suspected gunshots reported through unreliable acoustic sensor technologies. Police turned away from the proactive approaches that experts had inculcated for decades. Multiagency task forces and small units focused on seizing drugs and guns picked up the slack through intelligence-led raids. In Baltimore, Memphis, and Paterson, cities with already aggressive police forces, and particularly corrupt and abusive specialized units, enforcement actually became criminogenic, leaving violence, anger, and mistrust in its wake. Disbanding those units had positive effects, but they eventually tend to spring back up with new names. Then, in Baltimore, Boston, and Chicago—cities that did very little to defund police but did make significant investments in crime prevention through mediation, counseling, and educational, recreational, and social programs for youth—there were steep declines in violence through the summer of 2025, even as cops have frequently harassed rather than cooperated with violence interrupters trying to keep the peace.[4]

The simple linkage of more police and less crime trotted out by advocates of greater investment in policing is spurious. In its simplicity, leaving the rest of our society untouched, it manipulates fears and concerns about safety by proposing an easy answer.

The truth is that the data are complex—and social life even more so. Generalizing explanations of why crime rises or falls inevitably fail. Causality is difficult to pinpoint. But whatever the local story and however much numerical variegation there is in recorded crime, the explanation of what is happening when it comes to the activity of police must include these two words: Blue Power.

It is not the weakness of police that explains the rolling slowdown of recent years, but rather their strength. Typically, a labor strike occurs in response to incommensurable positions held by management and workers, when well-organized workers believe the only way to achieve their goals of better working conditions and compensation is to withhold labor, hitting the boss in the wallet. The analogy is imperfect with police. The wallet is the revenue garnered from taxpayers, and taxpayers are also the ones potentially hurt—though they are not the boss. That is what makes police distinctive. They cannot be voted out, and they constantly rebuke directives from elected officials. Their operational power is impervious to democratic controls—or almost any external levers. Think I am wrong? Try saying no to a cop next time he or she tells you to stop what you are doing. You might be able to do it as a big group, in the form of protest or uprising, but all the people in the group will then be liable to be called criminals. They will again be targets of police operations.

Throughout this book, many times when police have withdrawn, the most policed people have felt momentarily free. Even more than incidents of police violence, petty harassment by police, which is far more common, corrodes civic trust. Intensive policing that doles out summonses and extracts fines and fees to fund governments undermines effective criminal investigation. But police themselves showed that it does not have to be this way.[5]

The paradox of police power is that when police systematically reduce their presence, the possibility of a society no longer shaped by that power momentarily reveals itself. We might recall the phrase of W. E. B. Du Bois, describing when Black people first obtained freedom across the land, and the United States first became something like a multiracial democracy, between emancipation and the end of Reconstruction: they "stood a brief moment in the sun." This vision is one of Blue Power defeated.[6]

Yet the question of how to defeat Blue Power has no easy answer. In fact, the opponents of Blue Power could learn some lessons from the gains of police over the period this book covers. A movement from the left and from below is not equivalent to the movement of police, but there are tactical rhythms that echo. Still, as conservatives have succeeded at weakening the public sector labor movement, including by passing misnamed right-to-work laws, they have often insulated police. In Wisconsin in 2011 and Florida in 2023, new restrictions on collective bargaining in the public sector exempted police, firefighters, and sheriffs. Can the left imagine the inverse, a collective bargaining law that would cover everyone but the so-called public safety professions? Without rank-and-file organizations to marshal political power, of course, the power of police commanders would only increase. The more salient question is, how could the generous compensation that police have obtained, as well as adroit protection by lawyers from abuse by bosses, become available to all types of workers? As more and more avowed democratic socialists are elected to city, state, and national office, the quandary of how to rein in Blue Power will become even more acute.

This book asserts that, in contrast to the vast majority of analyses of policing, even deeply critical ones, police must not be treated as politically inert or neutral crime fighters. Nor is it enough to declare that police uphold a racist status quo or stabilize capitalism's inequities. Police have been engaged in an explicit, specific, self-interested but multifaceted political project for decades. Recognizing this is the first step toward better understanding the country's politics and pathologies. Further, most analyses of police treat crime statistics as objective representations. Yet we would do better to recognize—and refuse—how police instrumentalize crime levels and reporting. Crime becomes a political barometer, setting priorities and shaping the conditions of possibility for action in the political arena.

To focus on the political power of police is not to imply that their regular operations are apolitical. Both in myriad quotidian individual interactions and in large-scale attention-grabbing activities, like subduing protests, it is obvious that, sited at the frontal edge of state power, police are "inherently and inescapably political," in the words of one theorist. Using coercive violence to constrain what activities regular people can engage in, truncating the sphere of politics itself, is, of course, political.[7]

Pivoting from operations, however, *Blue Power* has attempted to open the black box of the police, showing how contention within the profession has meant that political power did not often result from or result in organizational unity. Scholars and policymakers, as well as street protesters, all frequently refer to police in monolithic terms. And there is great value in acknowledging the irreducible character of police power on the street. But the institution is riven with fractures. Whether these fractures create openings for contesting the political power of police, for coalition building by critics of police who may hope to keep rank-and-file officers from battling with elected officials, is a question of political strategy for those who wish to challenge the hold of police on our politics.

After 2020, when police faced the most widespread criticism ever, as well as vocal support in response, they seemed poised to unify. After the killings of Breonna Taylor, George Floyd, and others, multiple bills were proposed in Congress, with differing levels of severity in their efforts to change police practices at the federal level. Federal legislation could have helped police regain some legitimacy while acknowledging the criticisms. All police had to do was assent to the bill with the least severe restrictions—and some tried. The leadership of the IACP and Fraternal Order of Police found themselves on the same side for once and supported a version of a bill whose reforms they could live with. But the intemperate National Sheriffs' Association and National Association of Police Organizations pushed Senator Tim Scott to blow up the negotiations by demanding concessions the bills' backers could not accept. The chiefs and the fraternal order condemned the sheriffs, while the latter split from the National Association of Police Organizations, its ally during the 1990s heyday of willingness among members of Congress to assist police. The result was that there was no reform legislation, and no new funding was forthcoming. Congress moved on. Even if intransigence was not shared equally, the episode embittered police detractors and allies alike.[8]

Critics of police, therefore, should not be quick to assume that divisions in the profession might offer obvious leverage. But it is also clear that police do not benefit from a strategic consensus. Police have often substituted a tactical disposition for a unified strategy. Their leaders have displayed relentless persistence even after losses throughout the period this book covers. Mistakes and miscalculations have ended the leadership careers of numerous figures in this history, but the movement nevertheless continues, fueled by an unwillingness to retreat. And in the face of losses or missteps, police have been flexible about choosing both opponents and venues for contention. A loss at the municipal level is never a defeat. It is instead a prompt to seek gains at the state level. And so on.

Police have forged coalitions attempting to bridge real gaps within the profession. But they still recognize that the localism of their task dictates the necessity of other types of political ties. They are often shaped more by propinquity and pragmatism than by the camaraderie of the badge. Perhaps more than any other political dispensation or tactic, police have benefited simply from bipartisanship. Few commitments among the political class in the United States are held as strongly as bipartisanship in support of the purveyors of state violence. There is no analogue for the left.

Though contemporary police links with organized labor are diminutive, since 2020 activist coalitions have worked to weaken, if not sever, these relationships. The argument was simple: police were far more likely to endanger union members than support them. Union activists campaigned to push the International Union of Police Associations out of the AFL-CIO. One group calling itself Cop-Free AFSCME tried twice to present a resolution to suspend the police group from the labor federation. The first time, in 2020, the resolution never made it out of committee. The second time, its proponents faced a "chorus of boos" before being voted down on the convention floor, around 80 percent to 20 percent. But as rank-and-file activists continue their fight to remake large labor unions along social justice lines, their resolve to disentangle union power from police power is not going away.[9]

This history shows that police took what they needed from organized labor, leaving aside its core value of solidarity. The gains they have made are remarkable. From 1977 to 2021, according to the Urban Institute, state and local expenditures on police increased 175 percent, adjusted for inflation—more than expenditures on health, education, or transportation.[10]

Most police spending today, over 95 percent, goes to salaries and benefits. As a result, per-officer costs are often higher in more expensive states and cities. Large cities like Chicago, Los Angeles, and New York overspend budget projections because officers earn copious overtime pay, sometimes more than doubling individual base salaries and dramatically increasing pension obligations. The residents of New York City annually spent $626 per capita on police in 2020, with officers enjoying benefits unavailable to most other workers: a year of sick leave, retirement after twenty years of service, and a pension, as well as protections from punishment for misconduct (the most common punishment is loss of vacation days). Baltimore spent $840 per capita, the most of any large city. Starting salaries for new recruits there increased in 2021 to $60,000, reaching that target a few years before teachers' starting salaries did. Unlike teachers, cops did not need a college diploma to be hired.[11]

Today, there are more police agencies than ever. They are approved to hire more officers than they can recruit, who stand to earn more money than ever before. And in the aftermath of the 2020 uprisings, legislators in at least ten states advanced efforts to outlaw municipal budget reductions for police. In Texas, the governor signed a bill to penalize jurisdictions that reduce police budgets. It even requires budgets to keep pace with inflation.[12]

By 2024, the Border Patrol was offering recruitment, retention, and relocation incentives. Recruits willing to be stationed in remote areas could garner $30,000 in extra pay. Yet compensation, however strong, was never enough. Border Patrol union members desired something immaterial: a cultural shift away from the pretense that tired, poor, and huddled masses might find refuge in the United States.[13]

Police across the country have followed a parallel path, becoming creative with tools to attract recruits. More generally, police unions have also been so successful in achieving material wins that they have pivoted to the less measurable, sometimes ephemeral, gains that cultural battles can offer. Cultural questions can also allow simpler answers than more material ones, papering over the real differences and disagreements within the profession. In the 1980s, when it was becoming clear that members of the National Sheriffs' Association did not agree on gun control, the organization developed a more outwardly religious and affirmatively Christian stance, including by adding a "Chaplain's Corner" column to its magazine, which addressed members' religiosity by scripting practical advice in spiritual tones.

Yet the shift to battling over cultural dimensions of fealty to police does not mean that the fundamental questions of civil rights, democracy, and whom the state serves are off the table. Instead, these questions, and their material underpinnings, will be addressed, contested, and answered in the domain of political culture. This terrain is not easy for opponents of the political power of police, but they cannot cede it. Surrendering that fight has already granted police the power to veto reforms they oppose, too often with wide assent. Until there is a meaningful check on Blue Power, whenever movements for democracy, racial equality, and freedom take to the streets, the police will always be there to bring them to heel. Cultural transformation must go together with street protest acumen. Although all workers should have access to the types of compensation and benefits available to police with powerful unions, the underlying alteration that must occur is to keep this one peculiar profession from holding primacy in our politics, distorting and dominating the entire sphere.

As easy as it is for many Americans to take for granted policing's role as a bedrock force of order in human society, the rapid rise of Blue Power reveals that police power is neither universal nor apolitical. Its hold on the country's politics was not inevitable. Police have gained extraordinarily powerful backers because of their long-standing willingness to put down protests, strikes, and other mobilizations for racial and economic justice. Police have demonstrated a commitment to maintaining a status quo of splendor for the few and immiseration for the many. But when protesters confronting cops in riot formation find themselves chanting "Who do you serve? Who do you protect?" the answer is not only the power of the titans of capital. It is also Blue Power. And achieving real justice in this country will become possible only once that power is shattered.

ACKNOWLEDGMENTS

I wrote this book because I wanted to read a critical history of the political power of police, and one didn't exist. The book's genesis was over a decade ago, while I was still researching *Badges Without Borders*, which feels like a prior lifetime. I'm grateful for research support I gained along the way from the Charles Warren Center for Studies in American History at Harvard University and the John W. Kluge Center at the Library of Congress. I am also grateful for feedback received while presenting draft chapters to audiences at the Organization of American Historians and Labor and Working-Class History Association conferences, as well as the Johns Hopkins University Modern American History seminar. Conversations with students at Harvard and Johns Hopkins about this work have been helpful and rewarding too. I am also grateful to *Public Culture* and Shamus Khan and Madiha Tahir for convening a workshop and special issue in which I published some of my initial findings.

Thank you to Barae Hirsch, Nicole Rivas, Natalie Wang, Kristian Whitehead, and Caroline West for research assistance. Aaron Bekemeyer, Mike Clarke, Joshua Clark Davis, Angel Gonzalez, Ryan Richardson, and Jane Schrader helped me track down sources. I also relied on the aid of excellent librarians and archivists, including Ellen Belcher, Stefanie Caloia, Joshua Everett, Aiden Faust, Allen Fisher, Heather Furnas, Jason Kaplan, Steven Payne, and Jim Stimpert. Conversations with Steve Fletcher, Craig Floyd, Steve Gettinger, Hervey Juris, Michael S. Serrill, and Mary Washington provided excellent information and context.

I have been in dialogue with a number of journalists and scholars about policing and politics for many years, too many to list here, but I would like to acknowledge the support and camaraderie of, as well as helpful feedback and insights from, Christopher Agee, Aaron Bekemeyer, Jon Ben-Menachem, Dan Berger, Jonathon Booth, PJ Brendese, Shane Butler,

Nathan Connolly, Andrea Conte, Joshua Clark Davis, Max Felker-Kantor, Yance Ford, Julian Go, Victoria Harms, Lawrence Jackson, Jessie Kindig, Julilly Kohler-Hausmann, Mike Koncewicz, Matthew Lassiter, Geo Maher, Brandon McQuade, Tej Nagaraja, Melanie Newport, Sierra Pettengill, Jess Pishko, Imani Naiema Radney, Steph Saxton, Micol Seigel, Stephen Semler, Nikhil Pal Singh, Joe Slater, Brandon Soderberg, Lester Spence, Heather Ann Thompson, Alex Vitale, Tyler Wall, and Baynard Woods. Other friends, including Jill Hubley, James Lynch, and Nick Turner, also provided treasured support. Beverly Gage and Naomi Murakawa both read and provided invaluable feedback on a draft of the manuscript. At Johns Hopkins, Nathan Connolly and Beverly Silver have been crucial supporters and friends; thank you also to Christopher Cannon.

I had one serious emergency eye surgery while writing my first book, and another while writing this book (what will happen if I write another?). I can't thank Mira Sachdeva enough for her excellent care.

The gestation of this book was complicated, but I could not have asked for a more supportive agent than Paul Lucas. I'm indebted to him. I also wish to thank Mel Flashman for connecting us. Brandon Proia was the first editor to take my ideas seriously, well over a decade ago. I'm so thrilled that we were able to work together on this book. His commitment to the project, understanding of my goals, and editorial insights were stellar. Thanks to the rest of the excellent team at Basic Books as well.

This book is dedicated to my mother, who long ago instilled in me the value of reading. Nothing I have done would have been possible without her sacrifices, unconditional love, and endless support. I'm also grateful to my recently departed great-aunt, who always held high standards. We are all in her debt.

My greatest intellectual interlocutor is Christy Thornton. My gratitude for her love, support, and wisdom is infinite. I'm so fortunate to spend this one precious life together with her, my partner and best friend.

NOTES

Introduction

1. "National Police Strike Envisioned," *Afro-American*, July 18, 1970; General Subcommittee on Labor, Committee on Education and Labor, To Amend the Fair Labor Standards Act, House, 91st Cong., 2nd sess., July 9, 1970. Work stoppages—as officers called in sick—grew in popularity over the prior three years.

2. Although at least 80 percent of police unions are independent from organized labor, and therefore tend to prefer the term "association" to "union" (or "lodge," if part of the Fraternal Order of Police), this book will generally use "union" and "association" interchangeably. All relevant local police labor organizations that collect dues act like unions and adopt the tactics of labor. Office of Community Oriented Policing Services, *Police Labor-Management Relations (Vol. I)* (Washington, DC: Department of Justice, 2006). The abolitionist organization Interrupting Criminalization prefers "police fraternal organizations." Interrupting Criminalization, "Fighting the Power of Police Fraternal Organizations: An Organizer's Playbook," n.d., interruptingcriminalization.com/resources-all/fight-the-fop-power.

3. "Police Jam U.S. Capitol in Protest," *Des Moines Register*, October 15, 1970.

4. Scholars have different interpretations of the rise and vicissitudes of law and order politics. See, e.g., five different analyses of law and order: Jordan T. Camp, *Incarcerating the Crisis: Freedom Struggles and the Rise of the Neoliberal State* (Berkeley: University of California Press, 2016); Michael W. Flamm, *Law and Order: Street Crime, Civil Unrest, and the Crisis of Liberalism in the 1960s* (New York: Columbia University Press, 2005); Naomi Murakawa, *The First Civil Right: How Liberals Built Prison America* (Oxford: Oxford University Press, 2014); Jonathan Simon, *Governing Through Crime: How the War on Crime Transformed American Democracy and Created a Culture of Fear* (New York: Oxford University Press, 2009); Vesla Weaver, "Frontlash: Race and the Development of Punitive Crime Policy," *Studies in American Political Development* 21, no. 2 (2007): 230–265. Biden's quote is in Violent Crime Control and Law Enforcement Act of 1994—Conference Report, *Congressional Record*, Senate, 140, No. 122 (August 23, 1994).

5. Keith L. Alexander, Steven Rich, and Hannah Thacker, "The Hidden Billion-Dollar Cost of Repeated Police Misconduct," *Washington Post* (*WP*), March 9, 2022; Sarah L. Swan, "The Plaintiff Police," *Yale Law Journal* 134, no. 4 (2025): 1182–1268.

6. Mark Baker, *Cops: Their Lives in Their Own Words* (New York: Simon and Schuster, 1985), 44; Katie Kausch, "Some Police Contracts Include Perks and Quirks," Newark *Star-Ledger*, January 23, 2022; Katie Kausch, "Cops Make Most Where Crime Is Least," Newark *Star-Ledger*, February 8, 2022.

7. "Cities Map Strategy to Cope with Militant Unions," *U.S. News & World Report*, July 8, 1974, 70–71; "Issues with City and Union Pensions," *Milwaukee Sentinel*, December

20, 1971. On the growth and decline of public sector unions, see Aaron Brenner, Robert Brenner, and Cal Winslow, eds., *Rebel Rank and File: Labor Militancy and Revolt from Below During the Long 1970s* (New York: Verso, 2010); Jane Berger, *A New Working Class: The Legacies of Public-Sector Employment in the Civil Rights Movement* (Philadelphia: University of Pennsylvania Press, 2021); Jon Shelton, *Teacher Strike! Public Education and the Making of a New American Political Order* (Champaign: University of Illinois Press, 2017). An excellent sociological analysis of the political activism of California prison guards from the 1980s to 2000s is Joshua Page, *The Toughest Beat: Politics, Punishment, and the Police Officers Union in California* (New York: Oxford University Press, 2011).

8. GBD 2019 Police Violence US Subnational Collaborators, "Fatal Police Violence by Race and State in the USA, 1980–2019: A Network Meta-Regression," *The Lancet* 398, no. 10307 (2021): 1239–1255.

9. In the past decade, there has been an efflorescence of books on the twentieth-century history of policing in the United States. But the police have yet to be examined as a political actor unto themselves since the professionalization era, and the history of police unionism in this period remains largely untold. But see Aaron Bekemeyer, *The Labor of Law and Order: How Police Unions Transformed Policing and Politics in the United States, 1939–1985* (University of Chicago Press, forthcoming); Imani Naiema Radney, "'No Justice, No Police': Police Activism and Ideologies of Authority in the City of New York, 1965–1999" (PhD diss., New York University, 2026); Geo Maher, *A World Without Police: How Strong Communities Make Police Obsolete* (New York: Verso, 2021); Kristian Williams, *Our Enemies in Blue: Police and Power in America* (Cambridge, MA: South End Press, 2007), as well as, more generally, Christopher L. Agee, *The Streets of San Francisco: Policing and the Creation of a Cosmopolitan Liberal Politics, 1950–1972* (Chicago: University of Chicago Press, 2014); Andrew S. Baer, *Beyond the Usual Beating: The Jon Burge Police Torture Scandal and Social Movements for Police Accountability in Chicago* (Chicago: University of Chicago Press, 2020); Simon Balto, *Occupied Territory: Policing Black Chicago from Red Summer to Black Power* (Chapel Hill: University of North Carolina Press, 2019); Emily Brooks, *Gotham's War Within a War: Policing and the Birth of Law-and-Order Liberalism in World War II–Era New York City* (Chapel Hill: University of North Carolina Press, 2023); Joshua Clark Davis, *Police Against the Movement: The Sabotage of the Civil Rights Struggle and the Activists Who Fought Back* (Princeton, NJ: Princeton University Press, 2025); Max Felker-Kantor, *Policing Los Angeles: Race, Resistance, and the Rise of the LAPD* (Chapel Hill: University of North Carolina Press, 2018); Anne Gray Fischer, *The Streets Belong to Us: Sex, Race, and Police Power from Segregation to Gentrification* (Chapel Hill: University of North Carolina Press, 2022); Beverly Gage, *G-Man: J. Edgar Hoover and the Making of the American Century* (New York: Viking, 2022); Marisol LeBrón, *Policing Life and Death: Race, Violence, and Resistance in Puerto Rico* (Oakland: University of California Press, 2019); Anna Lvovsky, *Vice Patrol: Cops, Courts, and the Struggle over Urban Gay Life Before Stonewall* (Chicago: University of Chicago Press, 2021); Brendan McQuade, *Pacifying the Homeland: Intelligence Fusion and Mass Supervision* (Oakland: University of California Press, 2019); Khalil Gibran Muhammad, *The Condemnation of Blackness: Race, Crime, and the Making of Modern Urban America* (Cambridge, MA: Harvard University Press, 2010); Stuart Schrader, *Badges Without Borders: How Global Counterinsurgency Transformed American Policing* (Oakland: University of California Press, 2019); Micol Seigel, *Violence Work: State Power and the Limits of Police*

(Durham, NC: Duke University Press, 2018); Sarah A. Seo, *Policing the Open Road: How Cars Transformed American Freedom* (Cambridge, MA: Harvard University Press, 2019); Michael S. Sherry, *The Punitive Turn in American Life: How the United States Learned to Fight Crime Like a War* (Chapel Hill: University of North Carolina Press, 2020); Carl Suddler, *Presumed Criminal: Black Youth and the Justice System in Postwar New York* (New York: New York University Press, 2019).

10. Egon Bittner, *The Functions of the Police in Modern Society* (Chevy Chase, MD: National Institute of Mental Health, 1970); Michael K. Brown, *Working the Street: Police Discretion and the Dilemmas of Reform* (New York: Russell Sage Foundation, 1988); Michael Denning, "Everyone a Legislator," *New Left Review* 129 (May–June 2021): 29–44; Ray Gerda, "Police Militancy," *Crime and Social Justice* 7 (1977): 40–48; Mark Neocleous, *A Critical Theory of Police Power: The Fabrication of the Social Order* (New York: Verso, 2021).

11. Jarrod Shanahan and Tyler Wall, "'Fight the Reds, Support the Blue': Blue Lives Matter and the US Counter-Subversive Tradition," *Race & Class* 63, no. 1 (2021): 70–90.

12. The definitive recent book on how, if not exactly why, courts enact deference to police is Joanna Schwartz, *Shielded: How the Police Became Untouchable* (New York: Viking, 2023); see also Anna Lvovksy, "The Judicial Presumption of Police Expertise," *Harvard Law Review* 130, no. 8 (2017): 1997–2081.

13. On these movements, see, e.g., Mariame Kaba, "Illusions of Safety," *The Baffler*, February 13, 2024; Mariame Kaba, "Yes, We Mean Literally Abolish the Police," *New York Times* (*NYT*), June 12, 2020; Andrea J. Ritchie, "The Demand Is Still Defund the Police," *The Abolitionist*, Summer 2021; Dan Berger and David Stein, "What Is and What Could Be," in *Abolition for the People*, ed. Colin Kaepernick (n.p.: Kaepernick Publishing, 2021), 231–237; Ruth Wilson Gilmore, *Abolition Geography: Essays Toward Liberation*, ed. Brenna Bhandar and Alberto Toscano (New York: Verso, 2022); Sandy Hudson, *Defund: Black Lives, Policing and Safety for All* (New York: Pantheon, 2024); Brooke Darah Shuman, Jen Hoyer, and Josh MacPhee, *Defend/Defund: A Visual History of Organizing Against the Police* (New York: Interference Archive, 2022). Numerous organizations have been at the forefront of radical and creative political criticism of police, including 8toAbolition (national), Action Center on Race and the Economy (Chicago), BYP100 (Chicago), Critical Resistance (California), Interrupting Criminalization (national), Movement 4 Black Lives (national), Reclaim the Block (Minneapolis), Police Reform Organizing Project (New York), Stop LAPD Spying (Los Angeles), and W.E.B. Du Bois Movement School for Abolition and Reconstruction (Philadelphia), along with cop-watch, violence interruption, and "safe streets" operations active in cities across the country. Defundpolice.org, maintained by the Community Resource Hub, collects a wide range of resources and information.

Chapter 1: Blue Power's Model City

1. Oral history transcript, Jerome P. Cavanagh, interview I, March 22, 1971, by Joe B. Frantz, Lyndon Baines Johnson Library, Austin, TX (LBJL), 15; B. J. Widick, *Detroit: City of Race and Class Violence*, revised ed. (Detroit: Wayne State University Press, 1989), 155.

2. Art Glickman, "Blue Power: Police in Many Cities Shed Nonpartisan Role for Active Politicking," *Wall Street Journal*, October 30, 1969.

3. Young quoted in Alex B. Elkins, "Battle of the Corner: Urban Policing and Rioting, 1943–1971" (PhD diss., Temple University, 2017), 504.

4. Robert M. Fogelson, *Big-City Police* (Cambridge, MA: Harvard University Press, 1977); Marilynn S. Johnson, *Street Justice: A History of Police Violence in New York City* (Boston: Beacon Press, 2003).

5. Fogelson, *Big-City Police*; Samuel Walker, *A Critical History of Police Reform: The Emergence of Professionalism* (Lexington, MA: Lexington Books, 1977).

6. "Detroit Establishes New Police Merit Board," *Police Chiefs' News Letter*, June 1939, 1.

7. "The NAACP Emergency Conference," *Militant*, June 12, 1943, reprinted in *Fighting Racism in World War II* (New York: Pathfinder, 1980), 336–338; Ray Girardin oral history, by Maurice Kelman, August 6, 1971, reel 9, UP001282, Wayne State University, Walter P. Reuther Library, Oral History Collections, 6–7.

8. James A. Geschwender, *Class, Race, and Worker Insurgency: The League of Revolutionary Black Workers* (New York: Cambridge University Press, 1977), 53; James A. Allen and Doxey A. Wilkerson, eds., *The Economic Crisis and the Cold War* (New York: Jefferson School of Social Science, 1949), 70.

9. "10,000 Demonstrate in Detroit," *Militant*, April 24, 1943, reprinted in *Fighting Racism in World War II* (New York: Pathfinder, 1980), 312–313.

10. Thomas J. Sugrue, *The Origins of the Urban Crisis: Race and Inequality in Postwar Detroit* (Princeton, NJ: Princeton University Press, 1996), 29; George Edwards, *Police on the Urban Frontier: A Guide to Community Understanding* (New York: Institute of Human Relations, 1968); Walter F. White, *What Caused the Detroit Riot: An Analysis* (New York: NAACP, 1943); Dominic J. Capeci Jr. and Martha Wilkerson, *Layered Violence: The Detroit Rioters of 1943* (Jackson: University Press of Mississippi, 1991); Widick, *Detroit*, 103.

11. "Detroit Ordinance Prohibits Uniforms Resembling Police," *Police Chiefs' News Letter*, October 1943, 7.

12. Widick, *Detroit*, 107; Thurgood Marshall, "The Gestapo in Detroit," *Crisis* 50, no. 8 (August 1943).

13. August Meier and Elliott Rudwick, *Black Detroit and the Rise of the UAW* (New York: Oxford University Press, 1979), 195.

14. On the history of the Detroit Police Officers Association, I have benefited enormously from Margaret Levi, *Bureaucratic Insurgency: The Case of Police Unions* (Lexington, MA: Lexington Books, 1977); Justin E. Walsh, *The Fraternal Order of Police 1915–1976: A History* (Indianapolis: Joseph Munson, 1977).

15. "Question of Police Affiliation with Unions Raised in Several Cities," *Police Chiefs' News Letter*, April 1944, 1–2; Levi, *Bureaucratic Insurgency*, 92–93; IACP, *Police Unions and Other Police Organizations* (Washington, DC: IACP, 1944), 18–20.

16. Stuart Schrader, "Cops at War: How World War II Transformed Policing," *Modern American History* 4, no. 2 (2021): 159–170.

17. "The Origins of the LAPD Motto," *The Beat*, December 1963; Regina Varolli, "My Mom Wrote the Motto 'To Protect and to Serve,'" *CulEpi*, June 2, 2020, web.archive.org/web/20200928045337/https://www.culinaryepicenter.com/my-mom-wrote-the-motto-to-protect-and-to-serve/.

18. Hervey A. Juris and Peter Feuille, *Police Unionism: Power and Impact in Public-Sector Bargaining* (Lexington, MA: Lexington Books, 1973), 25.

19. Mark Baker, *Cops: Their Lives in Their Own Words* (New York: Simon and Schuster, 1985), 13, 175.

20. Seymour Martin Lipset, "Why Do Cops Hate Liberals—And Vice Versa," in *The Police Rebellion: A Quest for Blue Power*, ed. William J. Bopp (Springfield, IL: Charles C. Thomas, 1971), 23–39.

21. Vincent J. Roscigno and Kayla Preito-Hodge, "Racist Cops, Vested 'Blue' Interests, or Both? Evidence from Four Decades of the General Social Survey," *Socius*, January 2021, doi.org/10.1177/2378023120980913; Leonard Savitz, "The Dimensions of Police Loyalty," in *Police in Urban Society*, ed. Harlan Hahn (Beverly Hills, CA: Sage, 1971), 213–224; Micol Seigel, *Violence Work: State Power and the Limits of Police* (Durham, NC: Duke University Press, 2018).

22. Levi, *Bureaucratic Insurgency*, 93.

23. Richard T. Cooper, "Civilian Control Still Moot in Detroit," *Los Angeles Times* (*LAT*), June 2, 1969.

24. Patrick V. Murphy and Thomas Plate, *Commissioner: A View from the Top of American Law Enforcement* (New York: Simon and Schuster, 1977), 35; Mark Baker, *Cops: Their Lives in Their Own Words* (New York: Simon and Schuster, 1985), 183.

25. Levi, *Bureaucratic Insurgency*, 93.

26. The African American managing editor of the *Michigan Chronicle* quoted in Sidney Fine, *Violence in the Model City: The Cavanagh Administration, Race Relations, and the Detroit Riot of 1967* (East Lansing: Michigan State University Press, 2007), 13; President's Commission on Law Enforcement and Administration of Justice (PCLEAJ), *Task Force Report: The Police* (Washington, DC: GPO, 1967), 186; Joseph Turrini, "Phooie on Louie: African American Detroit and the Election of Jerry Cavanagh," *Michigan History Magazine*, November–December 1999, 11–17; editorial cited in George Edwards, "The Constitution and the Citizen: The Quest for Balance," in *Police and Community Relations: A Sourcebook*, edited by A. F. Brandstatter and Louis A. Radelet (Beverly Hills, CA: Glencoe Press, 1968), 154.

27. Cited in Widick, *Detroit*, 155.

28. John Ursu to Herman Wilson, Interview with Ray Girardin, n.d., Subject Files of Robert Conot, series 59, Records of the National Advisory Commission on Civil Disorders (NACCD), LBJL, 001346-024-0001, 1; Zachare Ball, "Adventure Always Followed Retired Detroit Policeman," *Detroit Free Press*, February 5, 1987.

29. Herbert T. Jenkins, "Police Challenges and Changes in Atlanta," *The Police Chief* (*TPC*), November 1967, 28–34.

30. Nicholas Alex, *New York Cops Talk Back: A Study of a Beleaguered Minority* (New York: Wiley, 1976), 151–152; Tony Norman, quoted in Ahmad A. Rahman, "Marching Blind: The Rise and Fall of the Black Panther Party in Detroit," in *Liberated Territory: Untold Local Perspectives on the Black Panther Party*, edited by Yohuru Williams and Jama Lazerow (Durham, NC: Duke University Press, 2008), 195.

31. Girardin oral history, reel 9, 31–32; Alex Elkins, "Liberals and 'Get-Tough' Policing in Postwar Detroit," in *Detroit 1967: Origins, Impacts, Legacies*, edited by Joel Stone (Detroit, MI: Wayne State University Press, 2017), 106–116.

32. Frank Donner, *Protectors of Privilege: Red Squads and Police Repression in Urban America* (Berkeley: University of California Press, 1990), 293; "Black Officers and DPD Discrimination," Matthew D. Lassiter and the Policing and Social Justice HistoryLab, *Detroit Under Fire: Police Violence, Crime Politics, and the Struggle for Racial Justice in the Civil Rights Era* (Ann Arbor: University of Michigan Carceral State Project, 2021), policing

.umhistorylabs.lsa.umich.edu/s/detroitunderfire/page/training-and-recruitment; Isaiah (Ike) McKinnon Interview, Part 1, December 3, 2019, Ann Arbor, MI, Policing and Social Justice HistoryLab.

33. John Ursu to Herman Wilson, Interview with Ray Girardin, n.d., Subject Files of Robert Conot, series 59, Records of the NACCD, LBJL, 001346-024-0001, 2; William Serrin, "'God Help Our City,'" *Atlantic Monthly*, March 1969.

34. Girardin oral history, reel 9, 24; Fine, *Violence in the Model City*, 97, 109, 100, 110.

35. Oral history transcript, Jerome P. Cavanagh, interview I, March 22, 1971, 19; "How One City Is Making a Dent in Its Crime Rate," *U.S. News & World Report*, May 21, 1962, 66–67; Fine, *Violence in the Model City*, 114.

36. "C.C.R. 'Early Warning' System," May 1, 1967, projects.lib.wayne.edu/12thstreet detroit/exhibits/show/beforeunrest/panel6; James Mudge, "Mayor's Secret Riot Spy Network Flopped," *Detroit Free Press*, July 27, 1967. I'm grateful to Aaron Bekemeyer for sharing the Mudge article with me.

37. PCLEAJ, *Task Force Report: The Police* (Washington, DC: GPO, 1967), 126.

38. This assessment and even the phrase "army of occupation" were common in Detroit and widespread around the United States. Kieran Walsh Taylor, "Turn to the Working Class: The New Left, Black Liberation, and the U.S. Labor Movement (1967–1981)" (PhD diss., University of North Carolina at Chapel Hill, 2007); Kim D. Hunter and Ed Vaughn, "Detroiters Remember the 1967 Rebellion," *Against the Current*, September–October 1997; Stuart Schrader, *Badges Without Borders: How Global Counterinsurgency Transformed American Policing* (Oakland: University of California Press, 2019); Fine, *Violence in the Model City*; Girardin oral history, reel 9, 26–27.

39. Donald Whitney Berney, "Law and Order Politics: A History and Role Analysis of Police Officer Organizations" (PhD diss., University of Washington, 1971), 219.

40. Fine, *Violence in the Model City*, 115–116.

41. Elkins, "Battle of the Corner"; Juris and Feuille, *Police Unionism*, 143, 156.

Chapter 2: All Power to the Chiefs

1. On Tamm and the IACP generally, see Stuart Schrader, "To Protect and Serve Themselves: Police in US Politics Since the 1960s," *Public Culture* 31, no. 3 (2019): 601–623; Stuart Schrader, *Badges Without Borders: How Global Counterinsurgency Transformed American Policing* (Oakland: University of California Press, 2019), 134–136.

2. "Quinn Tamm, Assistant Director, Retires from FBI," *FBI Law Enforcement Bulletin* 30, no. 3 (March 1961): 10; C. R. Davidson to Mr. Callahan, January 16, 1961, File 1, Section 7, Serial 1, FOIPA 1448029-000, 32. I'm grateful to Joshua Clark Davis for sharing Tamm's FBI file with me.

3. Robert Leary, "Quinn Tamm—Police Trouble Shooter," *Boston Sunday Globe*, January 28, 1962; Drew Pearson and Jack Anderson, "The Last Days of J. Edgar Hoover," *True*, January 1969, 29–33, 98–101. Also, J. Edgar Hoover to Clyde Tolson, John P. Mohr, Cartha De Loach, and J. J. Casper, September 27, 1965; "Quinn Tamm," February 21, 1966; Clyde Tolson to Quinn Tamm, February 13, 1966; all in File 1, Section 7, Serial 1, FOIPA 1448029-000, 87, 109–117, 127.

4. Ford Foundation, *Annual Report: October 1, 1963 to September 30, 1964* (New York: Ford Foundation, 1964); "Efforts to Improve Criminal Justice at the Starting Point," *Detroit*

Tribune, July 11, 1964; Quinn Tamm, "Police Professionalism and Civil Rights," *TPC*, September 1964, 28–32; J. J. Casper to John P. Mohr, August 11, 1964, File 1, Section 7, Serial 1, FOIPA 1448029-000, 71.

5. Patrick V. Murphy and Thomas Plate, *Commissioner: A View from the Top of American Law Enforcement* (New York: Simon and Schuster, 1977), 89, 88; Casper to Mohr, August 11, 1964.

6. George E. Davidson, "Report of the Resolutions Committee: Resolution Number 2," in *The Police Yearbook 1966* (Washington, DC: IACP, 1966), 425; Advisory Committee on Intergovernmental Relations, *Safe Streets Reconsidered: The Block Grant Experience 1968–1975* (Washington, DC: ACIR, 1977), 10.

7. Quinn Tamm, "Strength from Adversity," *TPC*, December 1965, 6; William L. Durer, "Report of the Resolutions Committee [Resolution Number 3]," in *The Police Yearbook 1967* (Washington, DC: IACP, 1967), 286; "Resolutions," *TPC*, December 1967, 40.

8. Daniel L. Skoler to James Flug, August 2, 1966, Org IACP, Office of Law Enforcement Assistance, General Correspondence, 1965–1968, entry 9, box 56, RG 423, National Archives and Records Administration II, College Park, MD (NARA).

9. Alfred E. Lewis, "The Dumb Cop Worries Police Chiefs," *WP*, October 10, 1965.

10. Leonard Downie Jr., "Fight Back at Critics, Police Chiefs Urged," *WP*, October 4, 1966; Carl C. Turner, "Stand and Be Counted," *TPC*, December 1966; Herbert Jenkins, "Police Challenges and Changes in Atlanta," *TPC*, November 1967, 34.

11. Quinn Tamm, "Federal Law Enforcement Assistance," *TPC*, January 1967, 6; Quinn Tamm, "The Safe Streets and Crime Control Act," *TPC*, February 1967, 6; Alfred E. Lewis, "Top Police Aide Assails Civil Rights Disorders," *WP*, October 8, 1965; "Legion Is Warned of 'War' in the Streets," *NYT*, August 28, 1966; Gerald Caplan, "Reflections on the Nationalization of Crime, 1964–1968," *Law and the Social Order* 3 (1973): 583–635; *Controlling Crime Through More Effective Law Enforcement: Hearings Before the Subcommittee on Criminal Laws and Procedures* (Washington: GPO, 1967), Girardin quotes on 307

12. J. J. Casper to John P. Mohr, September 9, 1965, and "Quinn Tamm," February 21, 1966, both in Section 7, Serial 1, FOIPA 1448029-000, 88–91, 109–117.

13. Sidney Rocker to Robert Donlan, June 3, 1971, OLEP 9-4, entry 10, box 47, RG 423, NARA, 2. An IACP grant application to begin gathering intelligence on "militant/extremist groups" in 1971 proved Tamm still had a bit of the Bureau in his blood. But the LEAA rejected it, noting that the IACP appeared "somewhat reluctant to fully accept LEAA direction under existing contracts." Clarence Coster to the Attorney General, January 8, 1971, White House Meeting with Chiefs of Police 6/3/71, Program Correspondence Files of Richard W. Velde, Subject Files, 1969–1972, entry 1, box 8, RG 423, NARA.

14. "Hear One of America's Greatest Criminal Investigators," n.d., File 1, Section 7, Serial 1, FOIPA 1448029-000, 106.

15. "Nation's Police Bid for Power," *Baltimore Sun* (*Sun*), October 27, 1969.

16. Rohit Acharya and Rhett Morris, "Why Did U.S. Homicides Spike in 2020 and Then Decline Rapidly in 2023 and 2024?," Brookings Institution, December 16, 2024; Interview with Richard H. Levine, January 7, 1965, minutes of the Governor's Committee to Review the Baltimore Police Department, box 1, Ralph G. Murdy Collection on Baltimore Criminal Justice, MS-0374 (RGM), Special Collections, Johns Hopkins University, Baltimore (JHU), 14.

17. Ralph G. Murdy to John E. Ingersoll, June 25, 1965, minutes of the Governor's Committee to Review the Baltimore Police Department, box 1, RGM, JHU, 131–133.

18. Alex B. Elkins, "Battle of the Corner: Urban Policing and Rioting, 1943–1971" (PhD diss., Temple University, 2017), 317; Richard H. Levine, "Crime Data Clarified by Footnote," *Sun*, July 29, 1966. I have relied in this chapter on many newspaper clippings collected by both AFSCME and the Baltimore Criminal Justice Commission. Citations to newspapers other than the *Baltimore Sun*, *Washington Post*, or *Afro-American*, all text-searchable by Proquest, will note the file location if found in these clipping files.

19. Ralph G. Murdy to Thomas B. Finan, December 16, 1964, and Ralph G. Murdy to A. Everett Leonard, February 2, 1965, both in minutes of the Governor's Committee to Review the Baltimore Police Department, box 1, RGM, JHU, 15, 69–70.

20. On the city's changing demographics, see Peter B. Levy, *The Great Uprising: Race Riots in Urban America During the 1960s* (New York: Cambridge University Press, 2018), 130–133.

21. "Police Face Rival Groups," *Sun*, February 28, 1966; Elkins, "Battle of the Corner," 318; William F. Schmick 3d, "Police Union Again Sought," *Sun*, December 18, 1966.

22. IACP, *A Survey of the Police Department, Baltimore, Maryland* (Washington, DC: IACP, 1966); Levy, *The Great Uprising*; Frank J. Battaglia, *History of the Baltimore Police Department* (Baltimore: n.p., n.d. [1983?]), 27, Maryland Department, Enoch Pratt Free Library, Baltimore; Lawrence T. Brown, *The Black Butterfly: The Harmful Politics of Race and Space in America* (Baltimore: Johns Hopkins University Press, 2021), 51; Kenneth D. Durr, *Behind the Backlash: White Working-Class Politics in Baltimore, 1940–1960* (Chapel Hill: University of North Carolina Press, 2003); Rhonda Y. Williams, "The Pursuit of Audacious Power: Rebel Reformers and Neighborhood Politics in Baltimore, 1966–1968," in *Neighborhood Rebels: Black Power at the Local Level*, ed. Peniel E. Joseph (New York: Palgrave Macmillan, 2010), 215–241; "Chief of Patrol, Lt. Col. Battaglia Is Riot Control Authority," *Baltimore Police Department Newsletter* (*BPDN*) 3, no. 10 (May 7, 1969): 2 (issues of the *BPDN* are available at baltimorepolicemuseum.com/en/baltimore-police-newsletters).

23. Donald D. Pomerleau biography, n.d., folder 12, Criminal Justice Commission Records, box S1-B2, Baltimore Regional Studies Archives, University of Baltimore (UB); IACP, *Survey*; Richard H. Levine, "A 600-Page Survey Raps City Police," *Sun*, January 10, 1966; "Police Union Is Opposed," *Sun*, September 16, 1966; John Dorsey, "Police Commissioner Pomerleau," *Sun*, April 2, 1967; "The International Seminar," *TPC*, December 1965, 18; Roger Twigg, "Saints Aim Sinful Barbs at Pomerleau," *Sun*, October 28, 1978.

24. Francis B. Burch and Fred Oken to Marvin Mandel, July 23, 1974, folder 20, box 137, AFSCME Office of the President: Jerry Wurf Collection, #682, Walter Reuther Library, Detroit, MI (JWC).

25. Stephen Tabeling and Stephen Janis, *Black October and the Murder of State Delegate Turk Scott* (n.p.: Writers' Branding, 2020), 48; IACP, *Survey*, 210; D. D. Pomerleau, "Departmental Safety Program," *BPDN* 1, no. 13 (August 17, 1967): 1–2; untitled attachment to Ralph G. Murdy to Richard G. Sullivan, May 10, 1967, folder 12, Criminal Justice Commission Records, box S1-B2, UB.

26. Guy Halverson, "The Police Are in Transition," *Christian Science Monitor*, June 29, 1973; "Unlawful Search of the 230," *Afro-American*, January 23, 1965; "Pomerleau, City Council to Meet," *Sun*, March 26, 1968; Frank Donner, *Protectors of Privilege: Red Squads

and Police Repression in Urban America (Berkeley: University of California Press, 1990), 301; "Where Are They Now?," *Your BPD News*, January 2016, 7–8.

27. My understanding of the origins of state control of the city police draws from Stephanie Saxton, "Gold, Coal, and Oysters: Economic Booms, Elite Fracture, and the Origins of Police Departments" (PhD diss., Johns Hopkins University, 2024).

28. Charles Whiteford, "City Police Commended in House, Conduct During Riot Questioned," *Sun*, March 18, 1965; "Source Material on Police," minutes of the Governor's Committee to Review the Baltimore Police Department, box 1, RGM, JHU, 97–104; "Current Police Issues in Baltimore," September 1, 1965, minutes of the Governor's Committee to Review the Baltimore Police Department, box 1, RGM, JHU, 141.

Chapter 3: Blue Power Rising

1. Jerome H. Skolnick, *The Politics of Protest* (New York: Clarion, 1969), 265; Thomas J. Cahill, "Campus Unrest Topic of Address," *Tuebor*, November 1970, 36–37, folder 32, box 19, part 1, Ernest Goodman Papers, Walter P. Reuther Library, Detroit, MI; "Join the P.I.G.S.," *TPC*, July 1970.

2. Alwyn Scott Turner, "Carl Parsell, Cop Turned Union Leader, Is a Living, Breathing Sign of the Times," *Detroit Free Press*, March 23, 1969; Skolnick, *Politics of Protest*, 282. For other early uses of the term "Blue Power," see, e.g., Hans Toch, "Cops and Blacks: Warring Minorities," *The Nation*, April 21, 1969, 491–493; Ed Cray, "The Politics of Blue Power," *The Nation*, April 21, 1969, 493–496; Art Glickman, "Blue Power," *Wall Street Journal*, October 30, 1969, 1, 29; "Blue Power?," *Newsweek* 75, no. 23 (June 8, 1970): 87, 89; William J. Bopp, ed., *The Police Rebellion: A Quest for Blue Power* (Springfield, IL: Charles C. Thomas, 1971).

3. Jarrod Shanahan, "'White Tigers Eat Black Panthers': New York City's Law Enforcement Group," The Gotham Center for New York City History blog, March 21, 2019, gothamcenter.org/blog/white-tigers-eat-black-panthers-new-york-citys-law-enforcement-group.

4. Edward P. Murray, "Should the Police Unionize?," *The Nation*, June 13, 1959, 530–533.

5. Margaret Levi, *Bureaucratic Insurgency: The Case of Police Unions* (Lexington, MA: Lexington Books, 1977), 101; Robert M. Fogelson, *Big-City Police* (Cambridge, MA: Harvard University Press, 1977).

6. Harry Golden Jr., "Poll Shows Most City Employees Support Cavanagh," *Detroit Free Press*, September 29, 1965.

7. Police Dispute Panel, "Findings and Recommendations on Unresolved Economic and Other Issues," February 27, 1968, reprinted in William J. Bopp, "The Detroit Police Revolt," in *The Police Rebellion: The Quest for Blue Power*, ed. William J. Bopp (Springfield, IL: Charles C. Thomas, 1971), 162–172; PCLEAJ, *Task Force Report: The Police* (Washington, DC: GPO, 1967), 134–135; PCLEAJ, *The Challenge of Crime in a Free Society* (New York: Avon, 1967).

8. PCLEAJ, *Task Force Report*, 197.

9. White House Referral to Attorney General, telegram from Carl Parsell, April 27, 1966, Name File, White House Central File, box P641, LBJL; James Vorenberg to Carl Parsell, May 3, 1966, May 1966, Commission Correspondence and Memoranda, Part 1, Records of the PCLEAJ, LBJL, 016514-015-001.

10. Glenn A. Marin, "Lateral Transfer," *TPC*, November 1968, 26, 30; PCLEAJ, *Challenge of Crime*, 283–284; Terry Eisenberg, Deborah Ann Kent, and Charles R. Wall, *Police Personnel Practices in State and Local Governments* (Washington, DC: Police Foundation, 1973), 52.

11. Ray Gerda, "Police Militancy," *Crime and Social Justice* 7 (1977): 43; Hervey A. Juris and Peter Feuille, *Police Unionism: Power and Impact in Public-Sector Bargaining* (Lexington, MA: Lexington Books, 1973), 20, 192n36.

12. National Advisory Commission on Civil Disorders, *Report of the National Advisory Commission on Civil Disorders* (New York: Bantam, 1968), 90; Oral history transcript, Jerome P. Cavanagh, interview I, March 22, 1971, by Joe B. Frantz, LBJL, 31; Levi, *Bureaucratic Insurgency*, 128n47.

13. Levi, *Bureaucratic Insurgency*, 106.

14. "The Kercheval Incident, August 1966," Matthew D. Lassiter and the Policing and Social Justice HistoryLab, *Detroit Under Fire: Police Violence, Crime Politics, and the Struggle for Racial Justice in the Civil Rights Era* (Ann Arbor: University of Michigan Carceral State Project, 2021), policing.umhistorylabs.lsa.umich.edu/s/detroitunderfire /page/kercheval; Howard Kohn, "Pig Riot Manual Exposed!," *Fifth Estate* 84 (July 24–August 6, 1969).

15. Lloyd E. Ohlin, "Effect of Social Change on Crime and Law Enforcement," *Notre Dame Law Review* 43, no. 6 (1968): 834–846; Johannes F. Spreen with Diane Holloway, *American Police Dilemma: Protectors or Enforcers?* (New York: iUniverse, 2003), 86; Sidney Fine, *Violence in the Model City: The Cavanagh Administration, Race Relations, and the Detroit Riot of 1967* (East Lansing: Michigan State University Press, 2007), 119–121; Leonard G. Lawrence, "The President's Message to IACP Members," *TPC*, December 1968, 22–28.

16. Thomas J. Sugrue, *The Origins of the Urban Crisis: Race and Inequality in Postwar Detroit* (Princeton, NJ: Princeton University Press, 1996), ch. 4.

17. Mary M. Stolberg, *Bridging the River of Hate: The Pioneering Efforts of Detroit Police Commissioner George Edwards* (Detroit: Wayne State University Press, 1998); David Carson, *Rockin' Down the Dial: The Detroit Sound of Radio* (Troy, MI: Momentum Books, 2000), 180.

18. Wayne Kramer, "Riots I Have Known and Loved," *Left of the Dial* 4 (2002); Frank H. Joyce, "Cops Riot at Belle Isle: Have Hate-In," *Fifth Estate* 30 (May 15–31, 1967).

19. John H. Burpo, *The Police Labor Movement: Problems and Perspectives* (Springfield, IL: Charles C. Thomas, 1971), 29–30.

20. Fine, *Violence in the Model City*, 118–122.

21. Bopp, "The Detroit Police Revolt," 168; Juris and Feuille, *Police Unionism*, 203n27.

22. Burpo, *The Police Labor Movement*, 32; Jerry M. Flint, "Detroit Police Threatened with Jail," *NYT*, June 18, 1967.

23. Remarks by Mayor Jerome P. Cavanagh at Dinner Meeting of Washington Chapter of Sigma Delta Chi, September 30, 1967, Subject Files of the Office of the Executive Director, series 46, Records of the NACCD, 8, 001346-016-0780.

24. Burpo, *The Police Labor Movement*, 12.

25. Levi, *Bureaucratic Insurgency*, 116; Juris and Feuille, *Police Unionism*, 58, 60; Bopp, "The Detroit Police Revolt."

26. Burpo, *The Police Labor Movement*, 79; Sol Plafkin, "Off Center," *Fifth Estate*, July 1–15, 1967; Ursu to Wilson, n.d., 3.

27. Juris and Feuille, *Police Unionism*, 143.

28. Levi, *Bureaucratic Insurgency*, 118; Plafkin, "Off Center"; Fine, *Violence in the Model City*, 123. The residency requirement became an object of contestation beyond the bargaining process. The Detroit Common Council reintroduced it in 1968. For years afterward, it offered commanders a tool for disciplining officers when they needed to document an infraction. The Detroit Police Officers Association then sued, leading to a state supreme court decision affirming its legality as bargainable in 1971, which the Police Officers Association of Michigan then fought at the state level for three decades until a new state law invalidated residency requirements, resulting in 23 percent of Detroit police living in the city by 2020, including only 3 percent of white officers. Chad Livengood and Annalise Frank, "Reexamining Residency Rules for Detroit Police Officers," *Crain's Detroit Business*, July 26, 2020, crainsdetroit.com/crains-forum/reexamining-residency-rules-detroit-police-officers.

29. Bopp, "The Detroit Police Revolt," 172.

Chapter 4: Collective Bargaining by Riot

1. Today, 12th Street is known as Rosa Parks Boulevard. Oral history transcript, Jerome P. Cavanagh, interview I, March 22, 1971, by Joe B. Frantz, LBJL, 53.

2. W. Eugene Groves and Peter H. Rossi, "Police Perceptions of a Hostile Ghetto: Realism or Projection," in *Police in Urban Society*, ed. Harlan Hahn (Beverly Hills, CA: Sage, 1971), 176; National Advisory Commission on Civil Disorders, *Report of the National Advisory Commission on Civil Disorders* (New York: Bantam, 1968), 84–108; Scott Kurashige, *The Fifty-Year Rebellion: How the U.S. Political Crisis Began in Detroit* (Oakland: University of California Press, 2017); Sidney Fine, *Violence in the Model City: The Cavanagh Administration, Race Relations, and the Detroit Riot of 1967* (East Lansing: Michigan State University Press, 2007), quote on 160.

3. Fine, *Violence in the Model City.*

4. Kim Barker, Michael H. Keller, and Steve Eder, "How Cities Lost Control of Police Discipline," *NYT*, December 22, 2020.

5. William Scott III, quoted in Fine, *Violence in the Model City*, 161.

6. Fine, *Violence in the Model City*, 200.

7. John Hersey, *The Algiers Motel Incident* (Baltimore, MD: Johns Hopkins University Press, 1998 [1968]), 153. Pollard's first name is sometimes spelled Aubrey.

8. Robert A. Mendelsohn, "Police-Community Relations: A Need in Search of Police Support," in *Police in Urban Society*, ed. Harlan Hahn (Beverly Hills, CA: Sage, 1971), 161.

9. Marion E. Walker, *Black Rebellion* (Columbia, SC: National Graphics, 1968), 11.

10. Cavanagh oral history I, 53; Christopher H. Pyle, "Military Surveillance of Civilian Politics, 1967–1970" (PhD diss., Columbia University, 1974), 42.

11. James Mudge, "Permanent One-Man Grand Jury Urged," *Detroit Free Press*, September 21, 1967; Fine, *Violence in the Model City*, 174.

12. Joe R. Feagin and Harlan Hahn, *Ghetto Revolts: The Politics of Violence in American Cities* (New York: Macmillan, 1973), 193–195.

13. Stateside Staff, "This Is What It Was Like to Be a Young, Black Police Officer in Detroit During the 1967 Rebellion," Michigan Radio, July 18, 2017; Wayne Kramer, "Riots

I Have Known," *Left of the Dial* 4 (2002); "Dope-O-Scope," *Detroit Sun*, September 1967, 20; Peter Werbe, "Fifth Estate A-gassed," *Fifth Estate* 36 (August 15–31, 1967).

14. James P. Gillece, John A. Macleod, Gerald J. Rapien, and John P. Rettinger, "Long, Hot Summer: A Legal View," *Notre Dame Law Review* 43, no. 6 (1968): 972; Hersey, *The Algiers Motel Incident*, 54; Interview with John Nichols by Judy Richardson, October 31, 1988, Eyes on the Prize II Interviews, repository.wustl.edu/concern/videos/9c67wr74g.

15. Jerald Francis Robinson, "The Development and Economics of Firefighter and Police Unionism: A Cooperative Study" (PhD diss., University of Illinois at Urbana-Champaign, 1973), 159–161; John H. Burpo, *The Police Labor Movement: Problems and Perspectives* (Springfield, IL: Charles C. Thomas, 1971), 8; "About the ICPA," *The Law Officer* 8, no. 3 (July–August 1975): 27.

16. "Cop Blames Politics," *Chicago Tribune*, July 26, 1967; "Police Group Ponders Resolution on Force," *LAT*, July 22, 1967; Ernest Conine, "Police Violence: Two-Sided Coin," *LAT*, July 26, 1970.

17. "186 Suspended Policemen Reinstated with Back Pay," *Detroit Free Press*, August 3, 1967; J. Anthony Lukas, "Postscript on Detroit: 'Whitey Hasn't Got the Message,'" *NYT*, August 27, 1967.

18. Gavin Mueller, *Breaking Things at Work: The Luddites Were Right About Why You Hate Your Job* (New York: Verso, 2021), 15–16; E. J. Hobsbawm, "The Machine Breakers," *Past and Present* 1 (1952): 58.

19. Burpo, *The Police Labor Movement.*

20. "Fact-Finders Urge Salary of $10,000 for Detroit Police," *NYT*, February 28, 1968.

21. Margaret Levi, *Bureaucratic Insurgency: The Case of Police Unions* (Lexington, MA: Lexington Books, 1977), 121, 130n75; Michael S. Serrill, "Urban Crisis Makes Police Vulnerable—And Angry," *Police Magazine*, Summer 1977, 10.

22. Interview with Nichols by Richardson.

23. "Detroit Riot Loot Is Sold by Police," *NYT*, February 28, 1968.

24. "Police in Detroit Get Pay Raise to $10,300," *NYT*, March 21, 1968; Hervey A. Juris and Peter Feuille, *Police Unionism: Power and Impact in Public-Sector Bargaining* (Lexington, MA: Lexington Books, 1973), 95; Burpo, *The Police Labor Movement*, 11.

25. This discussion of the Detroit pension situation is based on Robert Fogelson, *Pensions: The Hidden Costs of Public Safety* (New York: Columbia University Press, 1984), 119–123; William Serrin, "'God Help Our City,'" *Atlantic Monthly*, March 1969.

26. David Kleinman, "In the Midwest, What's Bad for General Motors Is Bad for Police," *Police Magazine*, May 1981: 23–30.

27. Thomas J. Sugrue, *The Origins of the Urban Crisis: Race and Inequality in Postwar Detroit* (Princeton, NJ: Princeton University Press, 1996).

28. E. W. Kenworthy, "Nixon Vetoes H.E.W. Bill; Cites 'Reckless Spending,'" *NYT*, August 17, 1972.

29. Patrick V. Murphy and Thomas Plate, *Commissioner: A View from the Top of American Law Enforcement* (New York: Simon and Schuster, 1977), 25.

30. "Patterns of Police Brutality/Misconduct," Matthew D. Lassiter and the Policing and Social Justice HistoryLab, *Detroit Under Fire: Police Violence, Crime Politics, and the Struggle for Racial Justice in the Civil Rights Era* (Ann Arbor: University of Michigan Carceral State Project, 2021), policing.umhistorylabs.lsa.umich.edu/s/detroitunderfire

/page/citizens-complaint-bureau-68-70. I am grateful to Matt Lassiter for bringing these incidents to my attention.

31. Dennis A. Deslippe, "'Do Whites Have Rights?': White Detroit Policemen and 'Reverse Discrimination' Protests in the 1970s," *Journal of American History* 91, no. 3 (2004): 932–960; Juris and Feuille, *Police Unionism,* 83; Alex B. Elkins, "Battle of the Corner: Urban Policing and Rioting, 1943–1971" (PhD diss., Temple University, 2017), 487–488.

32. "Parsell's Statement on Assassination," *Tuebor,* November 1970, 1, 4, Ernest Goodman folder 32, box 19, part 1, Ernest Goodman Papers, Walter P. Reuther Library, Detroit, MI.

33. Roger Lane, "Statewide Police Union Formed," *Detroit Free Press,* October 10, 1968; Carl Parsell Scholarship Mission Statement, miape.org/scholarships/103-carl-parsell-mission-statement.

34. Deslippe, "'Do Whites Have Rights?'"

35. James Boggs, "The Myth and Irrationality of Black Capitalism," in *Pages from a Black Radical's Notebook: A James Boggs Reader,* ed. Stephen M. Ward and Grace Lee Boggs (Detroit: Wayne State University Press, 2011), 192.

Chapter 5: Labor Power or Blue Power?

1. Peter B. Levy, *The Great Uprising: Race Riots in Urban America During the 1960s* (New York: Cambridge University Press, 2018), 190–207; Max Johnson, "Agnew Insults Leaders," *Afro-American,* April 13, 1968, 1, 15; Interview with Marvin Mandel, by Nyasha Chikowore and Maria Paoletti, July 12, 2007, Baltimore '68: Riots and Rebirth Oral History Project, UB, 8.

2. Stephen C. Halpern, *Police-Association and Department Leaders: The Politics of Co-optation* (Lexington, MA: Lexington Books, 1974), ch. 2.

3. Ralph G. Murdy, "Is There a Board in Your Future," *TPC,* June 1965, 12.

4. Robert M. Fogelson, *Big-City Police* (Cambridge, MA: Harvard University Press, 1977), 285–286; Justin E. Walsh, *The Fraternal Order of Police 1915–1976: A History* (Indianapolis: Joseph Munson, 1977); Timothy J. Lombardo, *Blue-Collar Conservatism: Frank Rizzo's Philadelphia and Populist Politics* (Philadelphia: University of Pennsylvania Press, 2018). According to Fogelson, after Harrington demonstrated how to win, rank-and-file organizations and their allies defeated proposals to implement civilian review in Baltimore, Cincinnati, Denver, Detroit, Hartford, Los Angeles, Newark, San Diego, San Francisco, and Seattle.

5. Ralph G. Murdy to George Quinn, April 19, 1965, folder 9, Criminal Justice Commission Records, box S1-B29, UB; "Police Face Rival Groups," *Sun,* February 28, 1966; Jerome H. Skolnick, *The Politics of Protest* (New York: Clarion, 1969), 267–268.

6. Stephen C. Halpern, "Power and Policy-Making in Police Labor Relations: The Case of Baltimore," Johns Hopkins Center for Metropolitan Planning and Research, 1974, Maryland Department, Enoch Pratt Free Library, Baltimore, 1. Some estimates of AFSCME police representation are as high as 40,000, but the lower number seems more reliable; Hervey A. Juris and Peter Feuille, *Police Unionism: Power and Impact in Public-Sector Bargaining* (Lexington, MA: Lexington Books, 1973), 28–29; Walsh, *The Fraternal Order of Police,* 278; Fred Barbash and Charles A. Krause, "Baltimore Strike Is Symbolic of Strong Union Growth," *WP,* July 10, 1974; Kenneth D. Durr, *Behind the Backlash: White Working-Class*

Politics in Baltimore, 1940–1960 (Chapel Hill: University of North Carolina Press, 2003), 134–137.

7. Baltimore did not institute civilian review until 1999, and the board's operation today is ineffectual. "Observations on the Baltimore City Police Administration," March 3, 1965, folder 11, Criminal Justice Commission Records, box S1-B2, UB; Earl Kratsch, "How It All Started: The Eulogy for Richard Allen 'Dick' Simmons," August 18, 2013, History of FOP Lodge #3, Baltimore City Police History, baltimorepolicemuseum.com/en/lieutenant-michael-f-black/item/1049-history-of-fop-lodge-3.html.

8. "An Introduction to the F.O.P.," *FOP's Pen*, n.d., Fraternal Order of Police Correspondence, box 2, RGM, JHU, 16; Richard H. Levine, "Visit Is Due by Head of Police Order," *Sun*, February 26, 1966; "Police Form Rival Group," *Sun*, May 28, 1966; Sample Ballot, Personnel Service Board, July 1, 1966–Mar. 31, 1968, box 2, RGM, JHU, 20, 20a, 20b; Richard H. Levine, "Gelston Tells Police to Stop Fraternal Order Formation," *Sun*, July 23, 1966.

9. John J. Harrington, "For Immediate Release," n.d. (February 1966), folder 9, Criminal Justice Commission Records, box S1-B29, UB; "Police Form Rival Group."

10. William F. Schmick 3d, "Pomerleau's Parley Brief," *Sun*, November 3, 1966; Richard H. Levine, "Pomerleau Airs Stand," *Sun*, March 17, 1967.

11. Earl Kratsch, "Maryland State Lodge—The Beginning," Maryland Fraternal Order of Police, mdstatefop.org/history/.

12. "An Introduction to the F.O.P.," 18, 19.

13. "Agnew Joins Police Union," *Sun*, July 30, 1967; Ralph G. Murdy to John E. Ingersoll, June 15, 1965, folder 4, Criminal Justice Commission Records, box S1-B29, UB; William F. Schmick 3d, "Police Union Again Sought," *Sun*, December 18, 1966; "Police Bill Introduced," *Sun*, February 24, 1967; Richard H. Levine, "Raise-Asking Policemen Investigated," *Sun*, January 31, 1967.

14. Juris and Feuille, *Police Unionism*, 69.

15. Donald Pomerleau, "The Eleventh Hour," *TPC*, December 1969; John H. Burpo, *The Police Labor Movement: Problems and Perspectives* (Springfield, IL: Charles C. Thomas, 1971), 67; Fogelson, *Big-City Police*, 218.

16. Alex B. Elkins, "Battle of the Corner: Urban Policing and Rioting, 1943–1971" (PhD diss., Temple University, 2017), 475; Halpern, "Power and Policy-Making."

17. Frank Donner, *Protectors of Privilege: Red Squads and Police Repression in Urban America* (Berkeley: University of California Press, 1990), 298–305; Memorandum of the Meeting of the Committee to Review the Operations of the Baltimore City Police Department, September 7, 1965, minutes of the Governor's Committee to Review the Baltimore Police Department, box 1, RGM, JHU, 175.

18. Senate Investigating Committee Established Pursuant to Senate Resolutions 1 and 151, "Report to the Senate of Maryland," December 1975, 33, 34, 9, 37; James B. Rowland, "Iron Hand Rules Baltimore Cops," *Star-News*, August 5, 1974, clipping in folder 21, box 137, JWC.

19. Judson L. Jeffries, "Revising Panther History in Baltimore," in *Comrades: A Local History of the Black Panther Party*, ed. Judson L. Jeffries (Bloomington: Indiana University Press, 2007), 30; Andrea Conte, "The Framing of Eddie Conway," *Baltimore*, November 2023, 118–127, 202–203; Rowland, "Iron Hand Rules Baltimore Cops"; "50 Students

Protest War Downtown," *Sun*, May 16, 1970; Michael Olesker, "Pomerleau Took Ill-Gotten Secrets to the Grave," *Sun*, January 21, 1992; Edward Walsh, "Baltimore Police Admit Political Surveillance," *WP*, January 8, 1975; George Derek Musgrove, *Rumor, Repression, and Racial Politics: How the Harassment of Black Elected Officials Shaped Post–Civil Rights America* (Athens: University of Georgia Press, 2012), 58.

20. Olesker, "Pomerleau Took Ill-Gotten Secrets to the Grave"; Karen E. Warmkessel and Will Englund, "Mandel Returns to Friends, Offer of a City Job," *Sun*, December 5, 1981.

21. Pomerleau, "The Eleventh Hour."

22. "Tough Commissioner Revitalizes Baltimore's Police," *WP*, May 31, 1969; "Quinn Tamm, Director of IACP, Assesses Department's Reorganization," *BPDN* 3, no. 5 (February 26, 1969), 1–2; D. D. Pomerleau, "In Retrospect," *BPDN* 1, no. 17 (October 11, 1967): 1–3; Burpo, *The Police Labor Movement*, 110; untitled attachment to Ralph G. Murdy to Richard G. Sullivan, May 10, 1967, folder 12, Criminal Justice Commission Records, box S1-B2, UB; Drew Pearson, *Washington Merry-Go-Round: The Drew Pearson Diaries, 1960–1969* (Sterling, VA: Potomac Books, 2015), 563.

23. "Two Testify in Police Paint Probe," *Sun*, November 28, 1967; Mary Curtis and Bill Rhoden, "Police Wives in Fight for Black Captain," *Afro-American*, June 30, 1973.

24. John F. Reintzell, "Elimination of Non-Police Duties a Part of Departmental Improvement," *BPDN* 4, no. 18 (September 9, 1970): 1–2.

25. "Officer Eugene C. Brukiewa Honored," *BPDN* 2, no. 4 (February 14, 1968): 4.

26. "Excerpts Taken from Newscast on Station W.J.Z.-T.V., Channel 13, June 19, 1968," "The IACP and the Baltimore City Police Department," n.d. [June 1968], Ralph G. Murdy to D. D. Pomerleau, June 3, 1968, and Ralph Murdy to Thomas A. Rapanotti, July 3, 1968, all in Union Matters, Dec. 1, 1967–Aug. 31, 1968, box 2, RGM, JHU, 166–168, 133–146, 129, 180–183. See also Michael J. Clark, "Union Queries Police Order," *Sun*, June 20, 1968.

27. Alvin P. Sanoff, "2 Policemen Are Charged," *Sun*, June 29, 1968; Halpern, "Power and Policy-Making."

28. D. D. Pomerleau, Police Commissioner's Memorandum 69-87, July 31, 1969, PSB, April 1, 1968–Dec. 31, 1969, box 2, RGM, JHU, 168.

29. *Brukiewa v. Police Comm'r of Baltimore City*, 257 Md. 36, Md. Court of Appeals (1970); *Flynn v. Giarrusso*, 321 F. Supp. 1295 (E.D. La. 1971); *Muller v. Conlisk*, 429 F.2d 901 (7th Cir. 1970); "Police Labor Law—First Amendment Rights," *TPC*, June 1971, 63; Richard L. Halpert, "The Policeman's Right to Free Speech: *Muller v. Conlisk*," *Indiana Law Journal* 46, no. 4 (1971): 538–543; "Public Safety Labor Relations Center," *TPC*, September 1971, 70–71; William J. Gilkinson to Donald D. Pomerleau, February 24, 1970, reprinted as Appendix B in Burpo, *The Police Labor Movement*.

30. "Narcotics Enforcement Working in Baltimore," *BPDN* 6, no. 1 (January 12, 1972): 1–2; "Narcotics Enforcement: A Progress Report," *BPDN* 7, no. 5 (March 7, 1973): 1, 3; Risa Goluboff, *Vagrant Nation: Police Power, Constitutional Change, and the Making of the 1960s* (New York: Oxford University Press, 2016).

31. Franklin G. Ashburn, "Increased Police Capabilities Facilitated by Federal Grants," *BPDN* 4, no. 19 (September 23, 1970): 1–2.

32. Advisory Committee on Intergovernmental Relations, *Safe Streets Reconsidered: The Block Grant Experience 1968–1975* (Washington, DC: ACIR, 1977), 137; Martin R.

Gardner to Martin Danziger, August 12, 1971, OLEP 9-12, Office of Law Enforcement Programs, General Correspondence, 1968–1972, entry 10, box 48, RG 423, NARA.

33. Coleman A. Young, "Crisis of the Cities—A National Crisis," *Freedomways* 16, no. 3 (1976): 158–159.

34. Virginia Gray and Bruce Williams, *The Organizational Politics of Criminal Justice* (Lexington, MA: Lexington Books, 1980), 55, 66, 33; Vesla Weaver, "The Significance of Policy Failures in Political Development: The Law Enforcement Assistance Administration and the Growth of the Carceral State," in *Living Legislation: Durability, Change, and the Politics of American Lawmaking*, ed. Jeffery A. Jenkins and Eric M. Patashnik (Chicago: University of Chicago Press, 2012), 221–251.

35. Lyndon B. Johnson, Remarks to the Members of the President's Commission on Law Enforcement and Administration of Justice, September 8, 1965, online by Gerhard Peters and John T. Woolley, The American Presidency Project (TAPP); Gerald M. Caplan, "Foreword," in *National Institute of Law Enforcement and Criminal Justice: Annual Report FY 1975* (Washington, DC: Department of Justice, 1975).

36. Halpern, "Power and Policy-Making," 20; Sarah Carey, *Law and Disorder IV* (Washington, DC: Center for National Security Studies, 1976), 39–43.

37. Levy, *The Great Uprising*, 206–222; Brian Purnell, "'Revolution Has Come to Brooklyn': Construction Trades Protests and the Negro Revolt of 1963," in *Black Power at Work: Community Control, Affirmative Action, and the Construction Industry*, ed. David Goldberg and Trevor Griffey (Ithaca, NY: Cornell University Press, 2010), 45; Jeffries, "Revising Panther History in Baltimore"; Akinyele Omowale Umoja, "Set Our Warriors Free: The Legacy of the Black Panther Party and Political Prisoners," in *The Black Panther Party Reconsidered*, ed. Charles E. Jones (Baltimore: Black Classic Press, 1998), 426; Lil' Masai, "Report Concerning Attempted Vamp on Baltimore Chapter," *The Black Panther*, May 19, 1970, 9; Ralph G. Murdy to Deputy Commissioner Poole, March 26, 1970, Union Matters, Mar. 12, 1970–Feb. 19, 1971, box 2, RGM, JHU, 15.

38. Fred Barrash, "Negroes Seek Dismissal of Pomerleau," *Sun*, July 24, 1971; "Governor Mandel Reappoints Police Commissioner," *BPDN* 6, no. 11 (May 31, 1972): 1; "President Richard Simmons Speaks Out Against Anti-Police Parren Mitchell," *FOP's Pen* 4, no. 1 (January 1973): 1, folder 9, Criminal Justice Commission Records, box S1-B29, UB.

39. "Investigation Seen as Plot to Oust Police Commissioner: The Story Behind the Story," *Afro-American*, January 15, 1972; Pam Widgeon, "AFRO Reviews Court Cases of 1974," *Afro-American*, December 28, 1974; Interview with Lee Baylin, by John Schwallenberg, November 20, 2007, Baltimore '68: Riots and Rebirth Oral History Project, UB, 3; Curtis and Rhoden, "Police Wives in Fight for Black Captain."

Chapter 6: Organized Labor's Greatest Advance Among Police

1. Baltimore City Police Union leaflet, n.d., Union Matters, Mar. 12, 1970–Feb. 19, 1971, box 1, RGM, JHU, 34–35; "An Introduction to the F.O.P.," *FOP's Pen*, n.d., Fraternal Order of Police Correspondence, box 2, RGM, JHU, 16; Pay Period Ending 10-14-70, Union Matters, Mar. 12, 1970–Feb. 19, 1971, box 2, RGM, JHU, 68. Also, untitled table of membership, Ralph G. Murdy to D. D. Pomerleau, June 10, 1971, Richard A. Simmons to Donald D. Pomerleau, April 11, 1968, and April 30, 1968, and D. D. Pomerleau to Ralph

G. Murdy, January 28, 1971, all in Fraternal Order of Police Correspondence, box 2, RGM, JHU, 154, 134–135, 33–35, 116–117.

2. Local 1195, Baltimore City Police Union pamphlet, n.d. [May 1970], Union Matters, Mar. 12, 1970–Feb. 19, 1971, box 2, RGM, JHU, 34–35; Stephen C. Halpern, *Police-Association and Department Leaders: The Politics of Co-optation* (Lexington, MA: Lexington Books, 1974).

3. Maryland Police Unions, Member Letter, December 23, 1970, Earl Ralph Kratsch to Bernard F. Norton, January 6, 1971, and William L. Rawlings to D. D. Pomerleau, January 6, 1971, all in Union Matters, Mar. 12, 1970–Feb. 19, 1971, box 2, RGM, JHU, 91–95. See also Gary W. Woodcock, "A Reply to the Union," January 1, 1971, Fraternal Order of Police Correspondence, box 2, RGM, JHU, 143. When I asked him about this document, Kratsch replied that it did not ring a bell: "I am drawing a blank on this." He did verify his signature on the accompanying memo. Email communication from Earl Kratsch, December 16, 2021.

4. "FY 1973 Salary Schedule," *BPDN* 6, no. 14 (July 12, 1972): 2; Kenneth D. Durr, *Behind the Backlash: White Working-Class Politics in Baltimore, 1940–1960* (Chapel Hill: University of North Carolina Press, 2003), 192; "Pay Increase," *BPDN* 6, no. 2 (January 26, 1972), 3.

5. Sarah Carey, *Law and Disorder IV* (Washington, DC: Center for National Security Studies, 1976), 41; "Assaults Increase," *BPDN* 6, no. 13 (June 28, 1972): 3.

6. Roger Twigg, "'72 Police Count Found Drugs Lost," *Sun*, February 20, 1973; Roger Twigg, "Police Source Reports Murder, Heroin Link," *Sun*, January 22, 1973; Donald D. Pomerleau, "You Need to Know," *BPDN* 7, no. 3 (February 7, 1973): 1–2; Roger Twigg, "Pomerleau Said to Learn Jury Secrets," *Sun*, February 21, 1973; Roger Twigg, "Firm Probing Police," *Sun*, February 22, 1973.

7. Stephen C. Halpern, "Power and Policy-Making in Police Labor Relations: The Case of Baltimore," Johns Hopkins Center for Metropolitan Planning and Research, 1974, Maryland Department, Enoch Pratt Free Library, Baltimore; Martin J. Gribbin, "Lodge #3 Continues War on District Court," *FOP's Pen* 3 (October 1972), folder 9, Criminal Justice Commission Records, box S1-B29, UB.

8. Jane Berger, *A New Working Class: The Legacies of Public-Sector Employment in the Civil Rights Movement* (Philadelphia: University of Pennsylvania Press, 2021); "Walkouts Disrupting U.S. Cities," *Chicago Tribune*, July 15, 1974; "Strikes: Pressures from U.S. Labor Mount Since Lifting of Wage, Price Controls," *Christian Science Monitor*, July 16, 1974.

9. Don Wasserman to Jerry Wurf, Baltimore Sanitation Wages—United States Comparison, July 10, 1974, folder 20, box 137, JWC; *The Soul of Baltimore* (WMAR-TV, 1968), archive.org/details/WMAR-DOCS-002.

10. PP.177.124.1, Richard Childress Photograph Collection (PP177), Maryland Center for History and Culture, Baltimore, MD. I am grateful to Victoria Harms for her assistance.

11. Tom Fitzpatrick to Jerry Wurf, Baltimore Sanitation Workers Walkout, July 1, 1974, Maryland Local 1195, folder 20, box 137, JWC.

12. There are two AFSCME-produced timelines of the July strikes in folder 20, box 137, JWC. These timelines and other documents in this collection inform my narrative of the strike.

13. "Baltimore Sanitation Strike Sold Out," *Workers Vanguard* 49 (July 19, 1974): 1, 9.

14. Jim Savarese to Jerry Wurf, Baltimore Strike—City Finances, July 8, 1974, folder 20, box 137, JWC; Douglas Watson, "Baltimore Police Walk Off Job," *WP*, July 12, 1974; Fred Barbash and Charles A. Krause, "Baltimore Strike Is Symbolic of Strong Union Growth," *WP*, July 10, 1974.

15. "News from the Baltimore Police Department," July 25, 1974, folder 21, box 137, JWC.

16. Berger, *A New Working Class*; James D. Dilts, "In $40,000 Tourist Drive: Ad Dubs Baltimore 'Charm City,'" *Sun*, July 11, 1974.

17. Jerry Wurf and Quinn Tamm, "Do Police Have the Right to Strike?," *Sun*, July 20, 1974.

18. Richard Ben Cramer, "Police Union, Rapanotti Fined $35,000 a Day," *Sun*, July 14, 1974; "Fire Sweeps 6 Stirling Street Houses, Dealing a Blow to Homestead Project," *Sun*, July 15, 1974.

19. "City Workers, Police End Baltimore Strike" ("Third Attachment"), folder 20, box 137, JWC; Richard Ben Cramer, "City, Officers Agree on Pay; Cleanup Starts," *Sun*, July 16, 1974.

20. Cramer, "City, Officers Agree on Pay; Cleanup Starts." Pomerleau claimed 565 officers struck; the union claimed the number was closer to 1,300. Over 900 quit the union within a couple of weeks of the strike. "Charm City U.S.A.?," *AFSCME Public Employee* 39, no. 7 (August 1974): 6–7.

21. "Baltimore Police Walk Off Jobs," *Police Labor Review* 4 (October 1974): 3; "Discipline Figures Released in Baltimore," *Police Labor Review* 14 (August 1975): 3; *AFSCME v. Marvin Mandel*, Complaint, 6–7, folder 21, box 137, JWC; AFSCME, "News for Immediate Release," August 6, 1974, folder 21, box 137, JWC; Richard Ben Cramer, "U.S. to Probe Police 'Breach,'" *Sun*, August 7, 1974; "Court Review of Police Discipline," *Sun*, January 10, 1977.

22. Ralph De Toledano, *Let Our Cities Burn* (New Rochelle, NY: Arlington House, 1975).

23. *AFSCME v. Mandel*, 10; AFSCME, "News for Immediate Release," August 6, 1974, folder 21, box 137, JWC; unsigned letter to Marvin Mandel, July 26, 1974, folder 20, box 137, JWC; Welford L. McClellan, "Infiltrators Acted on Own, Former ISD Man Says," *Sun*, March 11, 1975; Pomerleau, "You Need to Know."

24. William Taaffe, "Labor, Politics in Maryland," *Washington Star-News*, August 4, 1974, folder 21, box 137, JWC; Glenn Houlihan, "The Legacy of the Crushed 1981 PATCO Strike," *Jacobin*, August 3, 2021, jacobinmag.com/2021/08/reagan-patco-1981-strike-legacy-air-traffic-controllers-union-public-sector-strikebreaking.

25. "March Against KKK," *People's Tribune* 11 (June 1, 1975); Stephen Tabeling and Stephen Janis, *Black October and the Murder of State Delegate Turk Scott* (n.p.: Writers' Branding, 2020); Gene Oishi, "Swisher's Just an Old-Fashioned Kind of Politician," *Sun*, June 25, 1978; "Another Corruption Case in Maryland: No Tears for Swisher," *Afro-American*, April 14, 1979.

26. Roger Twigg, "City Solicitor Backs Police Dues Checkoff," *Sun*, October 2, 1976; Doug Struck, "City Agrees to Bargaining with a Police Union," *Sun*, March 27, 1982.

27. Harold J. Logan and Douglas Watson, "Garbage Piles Up in Strike," *WP*, July 7, 1974.

28. Woodcock broke with Local 1195 after losing election for its vice presidency in 1969. He soon joined Lodge #3. Gary W. Woodcock, "My Argument with the Union," n.d., Union Matters, Sept. 1, 1968–Mar. 12, 1970, box 2, RGM, JHU, 107; Woodcock, "A Reply to the Union."

Chapter 7: A Colorblind Counterrevolution

1. National Advisory Commission on Civil Disorders, *Report of the National Advisory Commission on Civil Disorders* (New York: Bantam, 1968), 316.

2. W. Marvin Dulaney, *Black Police in America* (Bloomington: Indiana University Press, 1996); N. D. B. Connolly, "Games of Chance: Jim Crow's Entrepreneurs Bet on 'Negro' Law and Order," in *What's Good for Business: Business and American Politics Since World War II*, ed. Kim Phillips-Fein and Julian E. Zelizer (New York: Oxford University Press, 2012), 140–156.

3. James Forman Jr., *Locking Up Our Own: Crime and Punishment in Black America* (New York: Farrar, Straus and Giroux, 2017), ch. 3; C. E. Wilson, "The System of Police Brutality," *Freedomways* 8, no. 1 (1968): 54, 55.

4. Terry Eisenberg, Deborah Ann Kent, and Charles R. Wall, *Police Personnel Practices in State and Local Governments* (Washington, DC: Police Foundation, 1973), 58; Ronald Koziol, "Union Charges Panther Plot to Upset Cops," *Chicago Tribune*, October 1, 1969.

5. John Darnton, "Color Line a Key Police Problem," *NYT*, September 28, 1969; "The Selling of the Black Community by the Guardian Civic League," *The Black Panther* V, no. 19 (November 7, 1970): 4.

6. "EEOC Affirmative Action Guidelines Receive Unfavorable Comment," *Police Labor Review* 45 (March 1978): 14.

7. Tera Agyepong, "In the Belly of the Beast: Black Policemen Combat Police Brutality in Chicago, 1968–1983," *Journal of African American History* 98, no. 2 (2013): 253–276.

8. Candace McCoy, "Affirmative Action in Police Organizations," in *Police Management Today: Issues and Case Studies*, ed. James J. Fyfe (Washington, DC: International City Management Association, 1985), 150; James B. Jacobs and Jay Cohen, "The Impact of Racial Integration on the Police," *Journal of Police Science and Administration* 6, no. 2 (1978): 168–183.

9. Bruce Cory, "In Atlanta, a Furor over Cheating," *Police Magazine*, March 1979, 15–19; Anthony J. Balzer, "Quotas and the San Francisco Police: A Sergeant's Dilemma," *Public Administration Review* 37, no. 3 (1977): 276–285.

10. "Affirmative Racism," *The Black Panther* XVII, no. 14 (September 17, 1977): 2; Dirk J. Beijin, "Group of Racists," *SF Policeman* 10, no. 1 (January 1979): 15; "Supreme Court to Hear Discrimination Appeal by Boston Police, Firefighters," *Police Magazine*, January 1983, 34; Tim Bornstein, "Reverse Discrimination," *Police Magazine*, July 1978, 15; William S. Wells, "Black Policemen Picket Union HQ," *Detroit Free Press*, July 24, 1974; photos in Police—Michigan, 1975, folder 24134, box 609, *The Daily Worker* and *Daily World* Photographs Collection, Tamiment Library/Robert F. Wagner Labor Archives, New York University, New York.

11. "Fraternal Order of Police Must Accept All Officers," *Police Labor News*, July 1974, 12; "Black Officers Resign from Miami FOP," *Police Magazine*, May 1982, 40; Russ Trunzo, "Pigs Unite Against Black People," *The Black Panther* V, no. 7 (August 15, 1970): 23.

12. Ulf Goebel, "Black Policemen Fight Ouster Move by F.O.P.," *Call and Post* (Cleveland), April 18, 1970.

13. See also Trevor Griffey, "'Blacks Should Not Be Administering the Philadelphia Plan': Nixon, the Hard Hats, and 'Voluntary' Affirmative Action," in *Black Power at Work: Community Control, Affirmative Action, and the Construction Industry*, ed. David Goldberg and Trevor Griffey (Ithaca, NY: Cornell University Press, 2010), 134–160.

14. Paul Chignell, interviewed by Olivia Chignell, StoryCorps, November 28, 2016, archive.storycorps.org/interviews/paul-chignell/; Christopher L. Agee, *The Streets of San Francisco: Policing and the Creation of a Cosmopolitan Liberal Politics, 1950–1972* (Chicago: University of Chicago Press, 2014), 237.

15. IACP, *Police Strikes: Causes and Prevention* (Gaithersburg, MD: IACP, 1979), 2; on Feinstein's career, see Rebecca Traister, "The Institutionalist," *New York*, June 6, 2022; Agee, *Streets of San Francisco*, 257.

16. Charles Einstein, "Alioto: His Once and Future Honor," *Los Angeles Times Magazine*, October 24, 1971; Paul Chignell, "Jerry D'Arcy, Leader of the Bluecoats," *POA Notebook* 30, no. 7 (July 1998): 1, 6.

17. Robert A. Jones, "Black Versus White in the Station House," in *The Police Rebellion: A Quest for Blue Power*, ed. William J. Bopp (Springfield, IL: Charles C. Thomas, 1971), 211–217; Daryl Lembke, "Younger S.F. Police Seek Key Offices," *LAT*, February 9, 1970.

18. Paul Chignell, "Jerry D'Arcy—A Man for All Seasons," *SF Policeman*, August 1989, 11; Jerry Crowley, "President's Corner," *SF Policeman*, May 1973, 2; Agee, *Streets of San Francisco*, 243; *Officers for Justice et al. v. Civil Service Commission of San Francisco et al.*, Memorandum and Order, Series 3: National Black Police Association Operating Files, 1966–1984, accession no. 201929-193-0002, African American Police League Records, 1961–1988, Proquest.

19. Nicholas von Hoffman, "Police 'Unity,'" *WP*, May 14, 1969; "Nazi Keeps Police Job," *The Black Panther Intercommunal News Service*, June 8, 1974; Lacy Fosburgh, "Lonely and Full of Hate, She Joined the Nazi Party," *NYT*, June 6, 1974.

20. IACP, *Police Strikes*, 2; Agee, *Streets of San Francisco*, 243; Labor Special Projects Unit, *EEO in Public Safety Agencies* (Rockville, MD: Bureau of National Affairs, 1982), 44–47; Anthony Balzer, "A View of the Quota System in the San Francisco Police Department," *Journal of Police Science and Administration* 4, no. 2 (1976): 124–133; *Officers for Justice et al. v. Civil Service Commission of San Francisco et al.*, Memorandum and Order.

21. "Political Blackmail," *SF Policeman* 4, no. 5 (May 1973): 1; "Persons Behind Federal Legislation," *SF Policeman* 4, no. 6 (June 1973): 1, 4; Jerry Crowley, "President's Corner," *SF Policeman* 4, no. 6 (June 1973): 2.

22. Balzer, "A View of the Quota System," 125, 124; "Police Quotas Set in San Francisco," *NYT*, December 2, 1973; "Federal Court Ruling," *SF Policeman* 4, no. 12 (December 1973): 1, 10.

23. IACP, *Police Strikes*, 2; San Francisco Police Minority Recruitment 1974–1975, Series 2: League to Improve the Community Operating Files, 1963–1984, accession no. 201929-173-0001, African American Police League Records, 1961–1988, Proquest; Labor Special Projects Unit, *EEO in Public Safety*; Balzer, "A View of the Quota System," 133; Bruce Cory, "Minority Police: Tramping Through a Racial Minefield," *Police Magazine*, March 1979, 4–14.

24. *Vanguard Justice Society, Inc. v. Hughes*, 471 F. Supp. 670 (D. Md. 1979); Vanguard Justice Society, Inc., "Our History," vjsinc.org/history.

25. George F. Hoyt and Thomas Rapanotti to Melvin Freeman, November 1, 1973; P. J. Ciampa to Tom Fitzpatrick, May 2, 1974; Tom Fitzpatrick to Jerry Wurf, May 7, 1974; George Hoyt to Jerry Wurf, May 15, 1974; all folder 20, box 137, JWC.

26. Thomas C. Miles, "Could You Afford to Lose Your LEAA Support?," *TPC*, November 1972, 76.

27. "Black Cops Urged to Complain About Bias," *Police Magazine*, March 1978, 49; Cory, "Minority Police"; "Black Cops Sue Federal Crime Agency," *Black Panther Party Intercommunal News Service*, September 15, 1975.

28. Hanes Walton, *When the Marching Stopped: The Politics of Civil Rights Regulatory Agencies* (Albany: SUNY Press, 1988), 163–164; Cory, "Minority Police," 7; Law Enforcement Assistance Administration, October 20, 1980, folder 5, box 2741, part V, NAACP, Library of Congress (LOC), 4.

29. John J. McCarthy, "Harold Breier: Imperious, Old-Fashioned and Chief for Life," *Police Magazine*, November 1981, 21–36; Ronald Howard Snyder, "Chief for Life: Harold Breier and His Era" (PhD diss., University of Wisconsin–Milwaukee, 2002), 5; William I. Tchakirides, "'Accountable to No One': Confronting Police Power in Black Milwaukee" (PhD diss., University of Wisconsin–Milwaukee, 2020); Yohuru Williams, "'Give Them a Cause to Die For': The Black Panther Party in Milwaukee, 1969–77," in *Liberated Territory: Untold Local Perspectives on the Black Panther Party*, ed. Yohuru Williams and Jama Lazerow (Durham, NC: Duke University Press), 245.

30. Harold R. Wilde, "Milwaukee's National Media Riot," in *Cities Under Siege: An Anatomy of the Ghetto Riots, 1964–1968*, ed. David Boesel and Peter H. Rossi (New York: Basic, 1971), 103–110; W. Eugene Groves, "Police in the Ghetto," in *Supplemental Studies for the NACCD* (Washington, DC: GPO, 1968), 103–114.

31. Tchakirides, "'Accountable to No One,'" 361 369.

32. McCarthy, "Harold Breier"; Andrew Witt, "Picking Up the Hammer: The Milwaukee Branch of the Black Panther Party," in *Comrades: A Local History of the Black Panther Party*, ed. Judson L. Jeffries (Bloomington: Indiana University Press, 2007), 193.

33. Promotional Exam Administered, Attachment 6 to James F. Blumenberg to Treadwell O. Phillips, May 27, 1981; George Sanders, untitled timeline, n.d., folder 1; both in box 2741, part V, NAACP, LOC. Also, *League of Martin et al. v. City of Milwaukee et al.*, Plaintiffs' Brief in Support of Preliminary Injunction Motion, folder 3, box 2741, part V, NAACP, LOC; Snyder, "Chief for Life," 59.

34. Letter to Robert Kliesmet, September 25, 1981; Robert Kliesmet to Harold A. Breier, October 29, 1981; both in folder 1, box 2741, part V, NAACP, LOC.

35. McCarthy, "Harold Breier," 27; James Chposky, "Collective Bargaining—Between Rounds," *The Law Officer* 4, no. 6 (March–April 1976): 11; "Justice on Trial," *Newsweek*, March 8, 1971, 17. I am grateful to Heather Furnas for helping me obtain this article.

36. The League of Martin took its name from Martin Luther King Jr. *League of Martin et al. v. City of Milwaukee et al.*, Complaint, folder 1, box 2741, part V, NAACP, LOC; Snyder, "Chief for Life," 61, 63–64; interview of Ron Lindsey by William I. Tchakirides, December 2, 2017, African Americans in the Milwaukee Police Department Oral History Project, 2016–17, University of Wisconsin–Milwaukee Libraries.

37. McCarthy, "Harold Breier," 31, 34, 83.

38. "Milwaukee Union Moves to Curb Power of Police Commission," *Police Magazine*, March 1981, 44–45; Gina Barton, "Daniel Bell Police Death Case Still Resonates 50 Years Later," *Milwaukee Journal Sentinel*, May 27, 2013; Snyder, "Chief for Life," 82–83, 85.

Chapter 8: A Cop in Congress

1. Craig W. Floyd, interview with author, March 30, 2022.

2. Royce L. Givens, "International Conference of Police Associations Newsletter," *San Francisco Police Officers' Association Notebook* (*SFPOAN*) 2, no. 4 (April 1971): 3; Alfred E. Lewis and Paul W. Valentine, "'Bill of Rights' for Policemen Pushed by 126 Congressmen," *WP*, April 27, 1972; "SEIU Creates Division for Police Officers," *AFL-CIO News*, March 4, 1972; Edward J. Kiernan and Nelson De Mille, "H.R. 181 Policeman's Bill of Rights," *The Law Officer* 9, no. 2 (March–April 1977): 10–15.

3. "Congressional Highlights," *TPC*, October 1983, 17; "National Sheriffs' Association Opposing Federal Funding Tied to the Law Enforcement Officers' Bill of Rights," *National Sheriff*, August–September 1989, 46.

4. Craig W. Floyd, interview with author, March 30, 2022.

5. Adam Walinsky, "The Knapp Connection," *Village Voice*, March 1, 1973; "Police Chiefs Confer in Washington," *LEAA Newsletter* 1, no. 12 (September–October 1971): 1, 3–4.

6. PCLEAJ, *Task Force Report: The Police* (Washington, DC: GPO, 1967), 50, 214; Stephen Rushin, "Police Union Contracts," *Duke University Law Journal* 66, no. 6 (2017): 1191–1126.

7. Whitman Knapp et al., *Report on Police Corruption* (New York: City of New York, 1973); Milton Mollen et al., *Commission Report* (New York: City of New York, 1994); Baynard Woods and Brandon Soderberg, *I Got a Monster: The Rise and Fall of America's Most Corrupt Police Squad* (New York: Macmillan, 2020).

8. Kevin Krajick, "Police vs Police," *Police Magazine*, May 1980, 7, 11.

9. Committee on the Judiciary, Subcommittee on Immigration, Citizenship, and International Law, "Public Safety Officers' Benefits Act; and Law Enforcement Officers' Bill of Rights," July 25–26, 1973, House, 93rd Cong., 1st sess., 92.

10. Committee on the Judiciary, "Public Safety Officers' Benefits Act," 87.

11. Homer Bigart, "5,000 Policemen Picket City Hall," *NYT*, June 30, 1965; Christopher Hayes, *The Harlem Uprising: Segregation and Inequality in Postwar New York City* (New York: Columbia University Press, 2021).

12. Jarrod Shanahan, *Captives: How Rikers Island Took New York City Hostage* (New York: Verso, 2022), 120–123; Thomas A. Reppetto, *American Police: A History*, Vol. 2 (New York: Enigma Books, 2012), 117; Paul Chevigny, *Police Power: Police Abuses in New York City* (New York: Pantheon Books, 1969), ch. 6; Hayes, *Harlem Uprising*, 219–240; Ed Cray, "The Politics of Blue Power," *The Nation*, April 21, 1969, 493–496.

13. Hayes, *Harlem Uprising*, 232; Rebecca Hill, "'The Common Enemy Is the Boss and the Inmate': Police and Prison Guard Unions in New York in the 1970s–1980s," *Labor: Studies in Working-Class History of the Americas* 8, no. 3 (2011): 65–96.

14. Kevin Krajick, "New York's Guido: 'Only Simple Fear Will Deter Some People…,'" *Police Magazine*, May 1980, 13–14; Committee on the Judiciary, "Public Safety Officers' Benefits Act," 91, Appendix C, 141–142.

15. Edward Haggerty, "Know Your Bill of Rights," *New York's Finest*, March 1987, 4.

16. Dick Roberts, "The Fraud of Capitalist Politics in New York City," *International Socialist Review* 34, no. 6 (June 1973): 5.

17. FOP Press Release, September 3, 1971, Fraternal Order of Police Correspondence, box 2, RGM, JHU, 155; Stephen C. Halpern, *Police-Association and Department Leaders: The Politics of Co-optation* (Lexington, MA: Lexington Books, 1974), 29.

18. "John J. Gallagher, Ex-Delegate, Dies," *Sun*, May 12, 1989; Richard Ben Cramer, "Friendly Delegates to Continue Togetherness in the Roles of Bridegroom and Best Man," *Sun*, February 5, 1974; "Gallagher Calls District Periled by Drug Pushers," *Sun*, August 18, 1972; "Integration Order Called Aid Peril," *Sun*, August 31, 1974; Dewayne Wickham, "Gallagher Accuses Media of Ignoring Him," *Sun*, August 27, 1975.

19. "Policemen, Wives Demand Rights Bill," *Sun*, March 9, 1973; Committee on the Judiciary, "Public Safety Officers' Benefits Act," 88.

20. "House Panel Passes Police 'Rights,'" *Sun*, March 24, 1973; Justin Fenton, "A Brief Look at How the Maryland Law Enforcement Officer's Bill of Rights Was Passed," *Sun*, February 23, 2016.

21. Charles A. Salerno, *Police at the Bargaining Table* (Springfield, IL: Charles C. Thomas, 1981), 108; Krajick, "Police vs Police"; Samuel Walker, "Police Union Contract 'Waiting Periods' for Misconduct Investigations Not Supported by Scientific Evidence," working paper, July 1, 2015, University of Nebraska at Omaha.

22. Robert D. Gordon, "Legislative Report," *The Law Officer* 8, no. 1 (February 1975): 5.

Chapter 9: From City Hall to the State Capital

1. Paul Chignell, "Jerry D'Arcy, Leader of the Bluecoats," *POA Notebook* 30, no. 7 (July 1998): 1, 6.

2. "S.F.P.O.A. Election," *SFPOAN*, January 1971, 1.

3. Wildcat, "S.F. Workers Battle Mafioso Alioto!," *The Movement*, September 1969, 3, 14; Charles Einstein, "Alioto: His Once and Future Honor," *Los Angeles Times Magazine*, October 24, 1971; Christopher L. Agee, *The Streets of San Francisco: Policing and the Creation of a Cosmopolitan Liberal Politics, 1950–1972* (Chicago: University of Chicago Press, 2014), 238; "Memorandum of Understanding Approved by Commission," *SFPOAN*, November 1971, 1; Jerry D'Arcy, "President's Corner," *SFPOAN*, November 1971, 2.

4. "Biaggi Bill Gains Momentum," *The Law Officer* 5, no. 2 (June 1972): 14.

5. Jerry D'Arcy, "President's Corner," *SFPOAN* 3, no. 5 (May 1972): 2.

6. Chignell, "Jerry D'Arcy"; "Vote for Congressman John Burton," *SF Policeman* 11, no. 10 (October 1980): 6.

7. Carla Marinucci, "Alfred J. Nelder / 1915–2002 / Former S.F. Police Chief a Lifelong Public Servant," *SF Gate*, January 4, 2002; "No Nelder-Never...," *The Gay Crusader* 2, no. 2 (October–November 1973): 3.

8. Alessandro Baccari and Associates, *A Report to the Officers and Members of the San Francisco Police Officers' Association* (San Francisco: Baccari and Associates, 1971), n.p., 2, 9, 10, 11, 42, 12, 53, 22, 31, 39, 94, 99, 155, and passim.

9. Jerry D'Arcy, *SFPOAN* 2, no. 11 (November 1971): 2.

10. Chignell, "Jerry D'Arcy."

11. Paul Chignell, "San Francisco Police Union Leader Jerry Crowley," SFPOA .org, November 1, 2014; Carl Nolte, "Gerald A. Crowley, Who Led Only Police Strike in S.F., Dies," *SFGate*, October 23, 2014; William J. Bopp, Paul Chignell, and Charles Maddox, "The San Francisco Police Strike of 1975: A Case Study," *Journal of Police Science and Administration* 5, no. 1 (1977): 32–42. D'Arcy and Crowley are now deceased. I contacted Chignell, asking for an interview to discuss his ongoing career with the Police Officers' Association. His response: "Thank you for reaching out to me but I do not want to talk to you." Email correspondence with author, May 6, 2022.

12. Mike Hebel, "Commission Approves Political Patronage," *SF Policeman* 6, no. 7 (July 1975): 1, 3; "An Open Letter to SF Policemen, Active and Retired," *SF Policeman* 5, no. 8 (August 1974): 13; Paul Chignell, "Police and Politics," *SF Policeman* 11, no. 1 (January 1980): 10–11.

13. The definitive account of the politics of station closure and reopening is Agee, *Streets of San Francisco*, ch. 7; Chignell, "San Francisco Police Union Leader"; Jimmy the Greek Falzon, "1972 Softball Season Opens," *SF Policeman* 3, no. 3 (March 1972): 8.

14. Jerry Crowley, "President's Corner," *SF Policeman* 5, no. 8 (August 1974): 2; Tony Bell, "Report to Veteran POA," *SF Policeman* 7, no. 4 (April 1976): 9.

15. "Calif. Police Political Action Group Formed," *SF Policeman* 5, no. 2 (February 1974): 1; "Open Letter," *SF Policeman* 5, no. 2 (February 1974): 1.

16. Allen Z. Gammage and Stanley L. Sachs, *Police Unions* (Springfield, IL: Charles C. Thomas, 1972), 58–68.

17. Mike Hebel, "Law Enforcement Legislation," *SF Policeman* 4, no. 6 (June 1973): 3; "Landmark Police Pact Approved," *SF Policeman* 5, no. 5 (May 1974), 1; Bill Hemby, "Calif. Organization of Police and Sheriffs'," *SF Policeman* 5, no. 5 (May 1974): 1; "San Francisco Memorandum Signed," *Police Labor Review*, January 1975, 7.

18. Paul Chignell, "PORAC: A Police Disgrace," *SF Policeman* 7, no. 8 (August 1976): 1, 7; Jerry Crowley, "President's Corner," *SF Policeman* 5, no. 8 (August 1974): 2.

19. Gale W. Wright, "Why Was the SFPOA Involved in Political Endorsements?," *SF Policeman* 5, no. 11 (November 1974): 9; "Learning How to Use Politics," *SF Policeman* 5, no. 2 (February 1974): 5.

20. Edmund G. Brown Jr. to Jerry Crowley and Bill Hemby, *SF Policeman* 6, no. 11 (November 1974), 1; "Election Recommendations/Endorsements: Comparisons and Results," *SF Policeman* 6, no. 11 (November 1974): 8–9.

21. James Chposky, "Cops on Coast Gather to Assert Roles as Political Individuals," *The Law Officer* 4, no. 6 (March–April 1976): 12–15.

22. Chignell, "PORAC: A Police Disgrace"; Paul Grabowicz, "Police Groups Are Wielding More Political Clout," *WP*, October 28, 1979.

23. Paul Chignell, "AB 301 Signed into Law," *SF Policeman* 7, no. 9 (September 1976): 1.

24. Mike Hebel, "Residency Rule Revised," *SF Policeman* 4, no. 2 (February 1973): 1, 12.

25. See, generally, *SF Policeman* 5, no. 11 (November 1974); Anne Chase, "Residency Laws: Should Police Be Free to Live Where They Choose?," *Police Magazine*, January 1979, 62–65; Chignell, "Police and Politics," 11.

Chapter 10: Welcome to Fear City

1. David Greytak, "The Budgetary Effects of Inflation: A Case Study of Expenditures for Police Services," *Journal of Police Science and Administration* 3, no. 4 (1975): 482–485. Ford later claimed never to have said that New York should drop dead.

2. Kevin Baker, "'Welcome to Fear City'—The Inside Story of New York's Civil War, 40 Years On," *The Guardian*, May 18, 2015; Kim Phillips-Fein, *Fear City: New York's Fiscal Crisis and the Rise of Austerity Politics* (New York: Metropolitan Books, 2017); "Assault on Parity," *The Law Officer* 8, no. 1 (February 1975): 9; "Police Layoffs," *The Law Officer* 8, no. 5 (January–February 1976): 20–22; Peter Kihss, "Effort Is Made to Bring Together 26 'Police Oriented' City Unions," *NYT*, June 12, 1978; Peter Kihss, "City Unions Join to Fight Layoffs," *NYT*, July 11, 1975; Edward Hudson, "Ken McFeeley, Union Leader," *NYT*, October 20, 1986.

3. On San Francisco's fiscal situation in the mid-1970s, see Destin Jenkins, *The Bonds of Inequality: Debt and the Making of the American City* (Chicago: University of Chicago Press, 2021), ch. 8.

4. William J. Bopp, Paul Chignell, and Charles Maddox, "The San Francisco Police Strike of 1975: A Case Study," *Journal of Police Science and Administration* 5, no. 1 (1977): 32–42; Al Casciato, "Pay Raises and Benefits," *SF Policeman* 6, no. 7 (July 1975): 12; James Chposky, "Collective Bargaining—Between Rounds," *The Law Officer* 4, no. 6 (March–April 1976): 11.

5. Andrew H. Malcolm, "Emergency Called in San Francisco as Firemen Strike," *NYT*, August 21, 1975; San Francisco Police Strike 1975 (III), Bay Area Television Archive, diva .sfsu.edu/collections/sfbatv/bundles/227915; Kathleen Bianchi, "Policeman's Wife Writes," *SF Policeman* 6, no. 9 (September 1975): 3.

6. IACP, *Police Strikes: Causes and Prevention* (Gaithersburg, MD: IACP, 1979); Joseph L. Alioto, interviewed by Carol Hicke, Bancroft Oral History Office, Berkeley, CA, 1991, 174.

7. Police Commission of the City and County of San Francisco, Regular Meeting Minutes, August 27, 1975, San Francisco Public Library.

8. IACP, *Police Strikes*; Terry Jones, "The Police in America: A Black Viewpoint," *The Black Scholar* 9, no. 2 (1977): 38.

9. Jerry Roberts, *Dianne Feinstein: Never Let Them See You Cry* (New York: HarperCollins, 1994), 131–133; IACP, *Police Strikes*.

10. Chposky, "Collective Bargaining—Between Rounds"; IACP, *Police Strikes*.

11. Bopp, Chignell, and Maddox, "The San Francisco Police Strike," 40; IACP, *Police Strikes*, 24.

12. IACP, *Police Strikes*; Roberts, *Dianne Feinstein*; Bopp, Chignell, and Maddox, "The San Francisco Police Strike."

13. "The San Francisco Police and Firefighters Strike and Its Aftermath," *Police Labor Review*, February 1976, 3; Mike Hebel, "Proposition 'P': Wage Cuts and Early Retirements," *SF Policeman* 6, no. 1 (November 1975): 1.

14. Police Commission of the City and County of San Francisco, Regular Meeting Minutes, September 24, 1975, San Francisco Public Library.

15. Guy Wright, "Admitting the Election Was a Mess," *SF Policeman* 6, no. 12 (December 1975): 5.

16. Jerry Crowley, "Police Assn. Has Positive Goals," *SF Policeman* 6, no. 12 (December 1975): 1; William Safire, "When Cops Become Robbers," *NYT*, August 25, 1975; San Francisco Police Strike 1975 (IV), Bay Area Television Archive, diva.sfsu.edu/collections/sfbatv/bundles/227916; Paul Sweeney, "Hard Times for Police Pensions," *Police Magazine*, November 1982, 27–36.

17. San Francisco voters overall opposed Proposition 13, but white single-family neighborhoods supported it. Jenkins, *The Bonds of Inequality*, 159–169, 202–206. The salary disparity among San Francisco city workers that enraged the striking officers has since switched, with cops earning more on average than any other class of city worker (salary data computed by author from public records).

Chapter 11: A Strike's Aftermath

1. Stephen C. Brooks, "Politics of Crime in the 1970's: A Two City Comparison" (PhD diss., Northwestern University, 1980), 64.

2. Paul Chignell, "Chief Gain and Crime," *SF Policeman* 7, no. 12 (December 1976): 1, 16; Bob Barry, "Assn Crime Bulletins Work," *SF Policeman* 7, no. 12 (December 1976): 16.

3. Randy Shilts, *The Mayor of Castro Street: The Life and Times of Harvey Milk* (New York: St. Martin's Press, 1982), 200–202; Destin Jenkins, *The Bonds of Inequality: Debt and the Making of the American City* (Chicago: University of Chicago Press, 2021), 193–197.

4. Paul Chignell, "Moscone Must Go," *SF Policeman* 8, no. 6 (June 1977): 1; Paul Chignell, "Police and Politics," *SF Policeman* 11, no. 1 (January 1980): 11; Gale W. Wright, "Recap on Election," *SF Policeman* 8, no. 11 (November 1977): 1; William Carlsen, "Ex-Aide Held in Moscone Killing Ran as a Crusader Against Crime," *NYT*, November 29, 1978.

5. "Harvey Milk Talks About Politicians and Lying," *Gay Community News*, February 25, 1978, 6–7, box 18, M&S Collection, LOC.

6. Walter Olesky, "S.F.P.D.'s Gay Recruitment Drive," *Police Product News*, December 1979, 28–32; W. A. Tennant, "Gay Cops," *SF Policeman* 9, no. 10 (October 1978): 9; Stephen H. Leinen, *Gay Cops* (New Brunswick, NJ: Rutgers University Press, 1993), 8.

7. Walter Olesky, "'Straight' Cops Speak Out," *Police Product News*, December 1979, 31; Randy Shilts, "Gay Police—'We're Not All That Different,'" *Police Magazine*, January 1980, 32–33.

8. Quentin Kopp and Dianne Feinstein debate, December 3, 1979, Commonwealth Club of California records, Hoover Institution Library and Archives, Stanford, CA, digitalcollections.hoover.org/objects/1262/quentin-kopp-and-diane-feinstein-debate.

9. Les Ledbetter, "Bill on Homosexual Rights Advances in San Francisco," *NYT*, March 22, 1978.

10. Stephen Warren Solomon and Ralph B. Saltsman, "Proposed Consent Decree," *SF Policeman* 10, no. 1 (January 1979): 1; Shilts, *The Mayor*, 255.

11. "Dianne Feinstein for California Governor (1990)," YouTube, posted by Carrie Chapman Catt Center for Women and Politics, August 17, 2015, youtu.be/1GCZB3UCqRo.

12. Shilts, *The Mayor*, xvi; Mark Powelson and Warren Sharpe, "Straight from the Hip," *The Berkeley Barb*, December 7–20, 1978, 4.

13. My account of White's brief career and the shooting draws primarily from Jerry Roberts, *Dianne Feinstein: Never Let Them See You Cry* (New York: HarperCollins, 1994), 161–172, and Shilts, *The Mayor*; "Transcript of Dan White's Taped Confession (Milk and Moscone Murders)," November 27, 1978, famous-trials.com/danwhite/598-whiteconfession; Paul Chignell, interviewed by Olivia Chignell, StoryCorps, November 28, 2016, archive.storycorps.org/interviews/paul-chignell.

14. An excellent undergraduate essay on the riots and the wave of harassment preceding them is Bruce Martinez, "The San Francisco 'White Night' Riots of 1979," *Historical Perspectives: Santa Clara University Undergraduate Journal of History, Series II* 9 (2004), scholarcommons.scu.edu/historical-perspectives/vol9/iss1/9; Roberts, *Dianne Feinstein*, 186–187; Emily K. Hobson, *Lavender and Red: Liberation and Solidarity in the Gay and Lesbian Left* (Oakland: University of California Press, 2016). The San Francisco Police Officers' Association produced its own investigation into the rioting, serialized in its newsletter in December 1979 and January and February 1980.

15. The Fruit Punch Collective, White Night Riot, GLBT Historical Society, San Francisco, CA, californiarevealed.org/islandora/object/cavpp%3A21040; Wallace Turner, "Coast Police Assail Restraint Order in Riot," *NYT*, May 24, 1979.

16. Ginger Coyote, "Local Newz SF," *Damage*, July 1979, 29; "Revolution Is the Poor People's Crime of Passion," flyer published by the May 21st Defense Fund, San Francisco, 1979, in author's possession.

17. Les Ledbetter, "San Francisco Tense as Violence Follows Murder Trial," *NYT*, May 23, 1979; Roberts, *Dianne Feinstein*, 191; Brad Duncan, ed., *Finally Got the News: The Printed Legacy of the U.S. Radical Left, 1970–1979* (Brooklyn, NY: Common Notions, 2017).

18. "No Confidence Vote for Chief Gain," *San Francisco Policeman* 10, no. 6 (June 1979): 1; "Federal Court Ruling," *SF Policeman* 4, no. 12 (December 1973): 1, 10; "San Francisco Mayor Calls for Police Chief to Quit," *NYT*, July 6, 1979; Chignell, "Police and Politics," 10.

19. Roberts, *Dianne Feinstein*, 184–185; Turner, "Coast Police."

20. *Fresh Fruit for Rotting Eyeballs*, directed by Eric S. Goodfield (Fortified Films, 2005); G. Pascal Zachary, "A Dead Kennedy with a Future," *Boulevards*, October 1979, 21. I'm grateful to Mike Clarke for sharing the *Boulevards* article with me.

21. Tony Rocco, "Biafra 6,591 Votes (3%)!!," *Damage*, January 1980, 18–19.

22. Bob Barry, "President's Report," *SF Policeman* 11, no. 1 (January 1980): 3; Bill Kidd, "Where's Our MOU?," *SF Policeman* 12, no. 9 (September 1981): 9.

23. Stephen Warren Solomon and Ralph B. Saltsman, "Proposed Consent Decree," *SF Policeman* 10, no. 1 (January 1979): 1; Jerry Crowley, "Letter to the United States Attorney General," *SF Policeman* 9, no. 1 (January 1978): 1.

24. "Settlement Reached in San Francisco Discrimination Suit," *Police Magazine*, September 1979, 20; Mike Gannon, "Consent Decree Observations," *SF Policeman* 10, no. 1 (January 1979): 5.

25. "Settlement Reached"; Reporter's Focus on Joseph Hall, folder 4, box 173, part V, NAACP, LOC; "Supreme Court Upholds Disciplining of S.F. Minority Officers," *Police Magazine*, July 1978, 17.

26. *San Francisco Police Officers Association v. NAACP et al.*, Complaint for Damages for Slander, November 14, 1978, 2–4; Memorandum of Points and Authorities in Support of

Motion for Summary Judgment, April 13, 1982, 14, 9; Plaintiffs Answers to Interrogatories Propounded by Defendants NAACP and Joseph Hall, October 23, 1980, 5, all in folders 3–4, box 173, part V, NAACP, LOC.

27. *San Francisco Police Officers Association v. NAACP et al.*, Declaration in Support of Motion for Summary Judgment, March 3, 1982; Memorandum of Points and Authorities in Opposition to Motions for Leave to Amend, October 27, 1980, 9; Robert L. Harris to Richard A. Levine, April 7, 1981; Release attached to Robert L. Harris to Nathaniel Colley, July 7, 1981; Brief of the American Civil Liberties Union of Northern California as Amicus Curiae in Support of Respondents, March 28, 1984, 1; Robert L. Harris to Thomas Atkins, September 28, 1982, all in folders 3–7, box 173, part V, NAACP, LOC.

28. Rodney Williams, "President's Report," *OFJ Journal* III, no. 1 (1983): 3.

29. "September 27, 1983, Board of Directors Meeting," *SF Policeman* 15, no. 11 (November 1983): 10; Williams, "President's Report," 3.

Chapter 12: One Big Police Union

1. "Much More Than an 'Idea'" and "Police and Politics," both in *The Law Officer* 8, no. 3 (July–August 1975): 5, 6–7, 26, 28.

2. Robert D. Gordon, "Remarks Before the IACP 82nd Annual Conference," September 13–18, 1975, Police Labor Relations, Law Enforcement News Collection, John Jay College of Criminal Justice, Lloyd Sealy Library, New York.

3. David Burnham, "Police Planning National Union," *NYT*, May 24, 1970; Allen Z. Gammage and Stanley L. Sachs, *Police Unions* (Springfield, IL: Charles C. Thomas, 1972), 57n89; Edward P. Murray, "Should the Police Unionize?," *The Nation*, June 13, 1959, 530–533; Bruce Cory, "Police Unions Jockey for Position," *Police Magazine*, May 1983, 14; John H. Burpo, *The Police Labor Movement: Problems and Perspectives* (Springfield, IL: Charles C. Thomas, 1971).

4. Gammage and Sachs, *Police Unions*, 54; Hugh O'Neill, "The Growth of Municipal Employee Unions," *Proceedings of the National Academy of Sciences* 30, no. 2 (1970): 1–13.

5. James R. Dorcy, Statement, Illegal Aliens, pt. 5, Hearings Before Subcommittee No. 1, Committee on the Judiciary, House, 92nd Cong., 2nd sess., 1502; official National Border Patrol Council history of affiliation, "About NBPC," n.d., bpunion.org/about-nbpc/.

6. *The Green Line* (podcast), episode 279, October 21, 2019.

7. Frank Del Olmo, "Immigration Service Probe Whitewash, Agent Says," *LAT*, October 6, 1975; Dorcy, Statement, 1503.

8. Del Olmo, "Immigration Service Probe"; C. M. "Buck" Newsome, *Shod with Iron* (Marfa, TX: C. M. Newsome, 1975), 72.

9. "Legislation Urged to Halt Alien Flow," *LAT*, September 22, 1976; "Illegal Aliens Will Be Topic," *LAT*, May 17, 1979; Bob Williams, "Illegal Aliens Win a Beachhead for the Third World," *LAT*, July 9, 1978; Dorcy, Statement, 1502.

10. Gammage and Sachs, *Police Unions*, 55.

11. John Young, "The First Hundred Years: (1969–Present)," *New York's Finest*, November–December 1994, 12–15, 28; Lucy St. John, "New York Labor Begins Showdown," *The Bulletin*, January 25, 1971, 3; "Police Militancy vs. Labor," *Workers' Action*, April–May 1971, 46, 5; Rebecca Hill, "'The Common Enemy Is the Boss and the Inmate':

Police and Prison Guard Unions in New York in the 1970s–1980s," *Labor: Studies in Working-Class History of the Americas* 8, no. 3 (2011): 65–96.

12. Wolfgang Saxon, "Edward J. Kiernan, 77, President Who Strengthened Police Union," *NYT*, January 27, 1999; "ICPA President Arrested," *SF Policeman* 4, no. 8 (August 1973): 1, 8.

13. IACP, *Guidelines and Papers from the National Symposium on Police Labor Relations* (Washington, DC: IACP, 1974); Tim Bornstein, "Police Unions: Dispelling the Ghost of 1919," *Police Magazine*, September 1978, 25.

14. Constitution and By-Laws of the Fraternal Order of Police.

15. Burpo, *Police Labor Movement*, 9–10; Justin E. Walsh, *The Fraternal Order of Police 1915–1976: A History* (Indianapolis: Joseph Munson, 1977), 228, 280; "Capital Police Rally Links A.C.L.U. and Court to Radical Violence," *NYT*, October 15, 1970; John J. Harrington, "Police Reported Angry over Nixon Aid Program," *LAT*, June 26, 1971.

16. "Blackburn Joins in Attacking Police Bill," *Atlanta Daily World*, March 26, 1971; Walsh, *The Fraternal Order of Police*, 291. Gordon's position of executive director became secretary-treasurer in 1975. "Nation's Police Leaders Gather at Seattle for 23rd ICPA Convention," *The Law Officer*, September–October 1975, 24–26.

17. William P. O'Brien, "Unionization, New Dues Structure Are Main Topics at ICPA Conference," in *The Police Rebellion: A Quest for Blue Power*, ed. William J. Bopp (Springfield, IL: Charles C. Thomas, 1971), 79–88.

18. "Activities in Congress," *WP*, September 7, 1972; "Nixon Backed by Units of 155,000 Policemen," *NYT*, July 22, 1972; Michael Zoorob, "Blue Endorsements Matter: How the Fraternal Order of Police Contributed to Donald Trump's Victory," *PS: Political Science and Politics* 52, no. 2 (2019): 243–250; Walsh, *The Fraternal Order of Police*, 286; "Police Want Cop Killing Federalized," *Chicago Defender*, July 17, 1973.

19. Edward P. Murray, "Should the Police Unionize?," *The Nation*, June 13, 1959, 530–533.

20. Allan Dodds Frank, "When All Else Fails, Call the Teamsters," *Police Magazine*, September 1978, 21–34; Bob Fitch, *Solidarity for Sale: How Corruption Destroyed the Labor Movement and Undermined America's Promise* (New York: PublicAffairs, 2006). The Teamsters were readmitted to the AFL-CIO in 1987.

21. Ilene Bergsmann, "Police Unions," *Management Information Service Reports* 8, no. 3 (1976): 1–18; James Chposky, "Why Police Unions Work," *The Law Officer* 8, no. 7 (May–June 1976): 10–13.

22. Walt H. Sirene, "Management: Labor's Most Effective Organizer," *FBI Law Enforcement Bulletin* 50, no. 1 (1981): 4–8.

23. Frank, "When All Else Fails"; James Chposky, "Why Police Unions Work," *The Law Officer* 8, no. 7 (May–June 1976): 10–13.

24. "Much More Than an 'Idea'"; "Police and Politics"; "Why Politics Dominated the Police Convention," *The Law Officer* 8, no. 8 (July–August 1976): 6–9; Edward J. Kiernan, "President's Message," *The Law Officer* 8, no. 8 (July–August 1976): 2.

25. "Police and Politics"; "Why Politics Dominated"; "Candidates Endorsed by Convention in Chicago" and "How Congress Voted," *The Law Officer* 8, no. 8 (July–August 1976): 14–15, 24–31; "ICPA Endorsed Candidates Win Big," *The Law Officer* 9, no. 1 (January–February 1977): 22.

26. Ed Townsend, "Union Wants to Organize Policemen," *Christian Science Monitor*, March 7, 1977; Victor Reisel, "Meany Outflanks Teamsters," *SF Policeman* 10, no. 4 (April 1979): 1; "ICPA Bid to Join AFL-CIO in Trouble," *Police Magazine*, January 1979, 69.

27. "AFL-CIO Official Criticizes Police Unions," *Police Magazine*, March 197), 49; Cory, "Police Unions."

28. "Milwaukee Police Officers Affiliate with AFL-CIO," *Police Labor Review* 58 (April 1979): 13; Joe Patterson, "IUPA, AFL-CIO Meet in San Francisco," *SF Policeman* 10, no. 8 (August 1979): 9.

29. "AFL-CIO Approves New Kiernan, Gordon Group," *Police Magazine*, May 1979, 46–47; Cory, "Police Unions"; "Laboring at the National Level," *Law Enforcement News* 9, no. 12 (June 27, 1983): 4; Ordway P. Burden, "Burden's Beat," *Law Enforcement News* 7, no. 7 (April 13, 1981): 13.

30. "ICPA Wins 4-Year Fight for U.S. Death Benefit," *The Law Officer* 9, no. 1 (January–February 1977): 10; "IUPA Legislative Program—96th Congress," *SF Policeman* 10, no. 8 (August 1979): 9–10; Richard Pearson, "Congressman Tennyson Guyer Dies," *WP*, April 14, 1981.

31. Harold Melnick, "Key Issues in Police Unionism," in IACP, *Guidelines and Papers*, 59.

32. Peter Perl, "Police Vote for Ouster of Union," *WP*, December 16, 1981; David A. Fahrenthold, "D.C. Police Lodge Broke the Law by Selling Hundreds of Whiskey Bottles Online, Investigation Finds," *WP*, December 10, 2021.

33. "Cassese Gets P.B.A. Post for Political Education," *NYT*, August 27, 1975; "Detectives Pull Out of New York PBA," *Police Magazine*, November 1979, 57.

34. "IUPA and IBPO Leaders Talk Merger After IBPO Joins AFL-CIO Service Union," *Police Magazine*, March 1983, 34–35; Robert B. Kliesmet, interview by Peter Dodenhoff, *Law Enforcement News*, January 21, 1985, 9–11; John Burpo, Ron DeLord, and Michael Shannon, eds., *Police Association Power, Politics, and Confrontation: A Guide for the Successful Police Labor Leader* (Springfield, IL: Charles C. Thomas, 1997), 312–313; Frank, "When All Else Fails," 23; Cory, "Police Unions."

35. Kliesmet interview; George L. Kelling and Robert B. Kliesmet, "Police Unions, Police Culture, and Police Abuse of Force," in *Police Violence: Understanding and Controlling Police Use of Force*, ed. William A. Geller and Hans Toch (New Haven, CT: Yale University Press, 1996), 196.

36. Kelling and Kliesmet, "Police Unions, Police Culture," 210; "IUPA's Cabral Is Still the People's Choice," *Law Enforcement News*, July–August 2000.

37. Matthew Cunningham-Cook, "The AFL-CIO's Police Union Problem Is Bigger Than You Think," *The Intercept*, June 18, 2020; Alex N. Press, "On Police Reform, the AFL-CIO Has a Lot of Catching Up to Do," *Jacobin*, June 3, 2021.

Chapter 13: Grievances, Arbitrators, and More Grievances

1. "Police Pilot Must Be Considered for New Position Despite Crash," *Police Labor Review* 50 (August 1978): 4–5; Thomas Morgan, "Juno: Cop on the Night Beat," *WP*, November 23, 1978.

2. Stephen Rushin, "Police Arbitration," *Vanderbilt Law Review* 74, no. 4 (2021): 1023–1078; "Forced Arbitration: Why Cities Worry," in *Police Management Today: Issues*

and Case Studies, ed. James J. Fyfe (Washington, DC: International City Management Association, 1985), 171–180; Michael Z. Green, "Black and Blue Police Arbitration Reforms," *Ohio State Law Journal* 84, no. 2 (2023): 243–301.

3. "Use of Excessive Force Does Not Warrant Discharge," *Police Labor Review* 43 (January 1978): 4; "Suspension for First Offense Too Harsh," *Police Labor Review* 7 (January 1975): 2; "Two-Day Suspension Held Not for Just Cause," *Police Labor Review* 57 (March 1979): 10.

4. "Discharge for Stealing Gasoline Upheld," *Police Labor Review* 8 (February 1975): 6–7.

5. "San Francisco Ordered to Drop Minimum Height Requirement for Police," *Police Labor Review* 22 (April 1976): 11; "Officer's Suspension for Obesity Declared Unfair," *Police Labor Review* 57 (March 1979): 7.

6. "Canine Officer Entitled to Time and One-Half for Taking Police Dog to Vet," *Police Labor Review* 44 (January 1979): 6.

7. Tim Bornstein, "Arbitrator Upholds Order That Police Issue Citations," *Police Magazine*, July 1978, 15; "City Can Unilaterally Institute Campaign for Increased Traffic Enforcement," *Police Labor Review* 46 (April 1978): 4.

8. Peter Feuille, "Compulsory Arbitration and Police Labor Relations," *FBI Law Enforcement Bulletin* 47, no. 6 (1978): 4–10; Stephen A. Plass, "Police Arbitration and the Public Interest," *Harvard BlackLetter Law Journal* 37 (2021): 31–64.

9. John Burpo, *Police Unions in the Civil Service Setting* (Washington, DC: Department of Justice, 1979); Mollie Heath Bowers, "A Study of Legislated Arbitration and Collective Bargaining in the Public Safety Services in Michigan and Pennsylvania" (PhD diss., Cornell University, 1974); Edward J. Kiernan, "President's Message," *The Law Officer* 8, no. 6 (March–April 1976): 2.

10. Philip Shabecoff, "Toledo Walkout Last Week Was an Example of the New Militancy," *NYT*, July 8, 1979; David Kleinman, "In the Midwest, What's Bad for General Motors Is Bad for Police," *Police Magazine*, May 1981, 26; Iver Peterson, "Detroit Mayor Is Warned That Bankruptcy Is Near," *NYT*, April 2, 1981.

11. Bruce Cory, "Police Unions Jockey for Position," *Police Magazine*, May 1983, 12–22; Walter Olesky, "Laugh Lines," *Police Product News*, December 1982, 31–33, 50; Kim Chapin, "Memphis," *Police Magazine*, November 1978, 46.

12. Shabecoff, "Toledo Walkout"; Mary Jo Patterson and Arthur K. Lenehan, "Newark Police Accused of Vandalism After Layoff Announcement," *Police Magazine*, January 1979, 67–68; Patrick V. Murphy, "Guardsmen Must Be Trained as Police for Strikes," *WP*, August 27, 1978; Casey Ichniowski, "Arbitration and Police Bargaining: Prescriptions for the Blue Flu," *Industrial Relations* 21, no. 2 (1982): 149–166.

13. "Des Moines Union Appeals to Public in Newspaper Ads," *Police Magazine*, March 1981, 45; John Burpo, Ron DeLord, and Michael Shannon, eds., *Police Association Power, Politics, and Confrontation: A Guide for the Successful Police Labor Leader* (Springfield, IL: Charles C. Thomas, 1997), 121.

14. "Complaints Against Police," *Stamford Advocate*, January 17, 1978; Kevin Noblet, "Police Sound Off Against Cizanckas," *Stamford Advocate*, November 15, 1979; Jim Mulvaney, "Union's Leader Slams Police Chief," *Stamford Advocate*, April 19, 1979; "Picketing Continues," *Stamford Advocate*, April 12, 1980; Robert E. Tomasson, "It's Rank vs. File in a Rift Dividing Stamford Police," *NYT*, November 5, 1979; Tom Wallace, "The 'Blown'

Police Undercover Caper," *Stamford Advocate*, October 5, 1979; Tom Wallace, "Wide Hunt for Stamford Chief," *NYT*, December 28, 1980; all articles found in Police Department 1977–1980, Stamford Collection, Stamford Public Library, Stamford, CT. See Stuart Schrader, "More Than Cosmetic Changes: The Challenges of Experiments with Police Demilitarization in the 1960s and 1970s," *Journal of Urban History* 46, no. 5 (2020): 1002–1025.

15. "Strikes and Job Actions," *Police Magazine*, November 1979, 55–56; Michael Peter Wigginton, Carl Julius Jensen, and Jessica Michele Vinson, "Hold That Line: The New Orleans Police Strikes," *Criminal Justice Policy Review* 26, no. 3 (2015): 234–251; Sharlene Sinegal-DeCuir, "Mardi Gras Canceled," *64 Parishes*, December 2, 2018, 64parishes.org /mardi-gras-canceled.

16. "Judge Orders Arrest of Striking Officer," *Police Labor Review* 27 (September 1976): 4; "Forced Arbitration."

17. Tim Bornstein, "Poll Shows Police Strikes Unpopular," *Police Magazine*, May 1978, n.p.; Gallup Organization, Gallup Poll #991, 1978; Associated Press/NBC News, Poll #1981-Aug: Reagan/Politics, Cornell University Roper Center for Public Opinion Research, 1981.

18. Wayne W. Schmidt, *Survey of Police Misconduct Litigation, 1967–1971* (Evanston, IL: Americans for Effective Law Enforcement, 1974); Charles E. Friend, *Police Rights: Civil Remedies for Law Enforcement Officers*, 2nd ed. (Wilmette, IL: Callaghan, 1987), 13, 11.

Chapter 14: Blue Power in the Red

1. Kenneth J. Matulia, *A Balance of Forces: Executive Summary* (Washington DC: DOJ, National Institute of Justice, 1982); Lawrence W. Sherman and Robert H. Langworthy, "Measuring Homicide by Police Officers," *Journal of Criminal Law and Criminology* 70, no. 4 (1979): 546–560; "New York City / Police Deaths," CBS Evening News, May 22, 1971, 216945, Vanderbilt Television News Archive.

2. Philip B. Taft Jr., "Policing the New Immigrant Ghettos," *Police Magazine*, July 1982, 10–20, 21–38; Mimi Swartz, "The Killing of José Campos Torres," *Texas Monthly*, February 14, 2023; Charles R. Epp, *Making Rights Real: Activists, Bureaucrats, and the Creation of the Legalistic State* (Chicago: University of Chicago Press, 2009), 75–76.

3. "Police Story," on Black Flag, *Damaged*, SST Records, 1981.

4. Swartz, "The Killing of José Campos Torres"; "Tune Prompts Lawsuit," *Houston Post*, April 4, 1981; "Earl Littman," *Jewish Herald-Voice*, October 5, 2023; "Houston Police Hunt Elusive Punk Rockers," *Police Magazine*, July 1981, 4; Susan Elizabeth Shepard, "A Houston Punk Band's Protest Anthem Still Resonates, Forty Years After Its Release," *Texas Monthly*, March 10, 2021. I'm grateful to Harry Leverette and the other members of AK-47 for sharing materials with me and for permission to reprint lyrics.

5. Advisory Committee on Intergovernmental Relations, *Safe Streets Reconsidered: The Block Grant Experience 1968–1975* (Washington, DC: ACIR, 1977), 26; LEAA, *LEAA Tenth Annual Report: Fiscal Year 1978* (Washington, DC: Department of Justice, 1978), 4; LEAA, *Eighth Annual Report of LEAA: Fiscal Year 1976* (Washington, DC: Department of Justice, 1976), 4; LEAA, *LEAA 1970: Grants and Contracts Fiscal Year 1970* (Washington, DC: Department of Justice, 1970), 13–17.

6. Richard W. Velde to Attorney General, January 13, 1971, Sensitive Memoranda re LEAA Personnel, Transition and DOJ Budget Matters, entry 1, box 4, RG 423, NARA, 2;

Advisory Committee on Intergovernmental Relations, *Safe Streets Reconsidered*, 124; Malcolm M. Feeley and Austin D. Sarat, *The Policy Dilemma: Federal Crime Policy and the Law Enforcement Assistance Administration, 1968–1978* (Minneapolis: University of Minnesota Press, 1980).

7. The time bomb motif appeared frequently. See Robert Fogelson, *Pensions: The Hidden Costs of Public Safety* (New York: Columbia University Press, 1984); John Blackmore, "Pensions: Something Has Got to Give," *Police Magazine*, May 1978, 4–16; Advisory Committee on Intergovernmental Relations, *Improving Urban America: A Challenge to Federalism*, M-107 (Washington, DC: ACIR, 1976).

8. James Chpoksy, "Why Police Unions Work," *The Law Officer* 8, no. 7 (May–June 1976): 10–13.

9. Fogelson, *Pensions*, 2–3; Paul Sweeney, "Hard Times for Police Pensions," *Police Magazine*, November 1982, 27–36.

10. Blackmore, "Pensions," 5.

11. Sweeney, "Hard Times," 33–34.

12. "Pensions: Myth and Reality," *The Law Officer* 8, no. 5 (January–February 1975): 6–10; Blackmore, "Pensions," 6; Fogelson, *Pensions*, 7; Minneapolis Police Department, *Annual Statistical Report, 1976* (Minneapolis, MN: Police Department, 1976).

13. Sweeney, "Hard Times"; Advisory Committee on Intergovernmental Relations, *In Respect to Realities: A Report on Federalism in 1975*, M-103 (Washington, DC: ACIR, 1976).

14. Blackmore, "Pensions"; Nathan Bomey and John Gallagher, "How Detroit Went Broke: The Answers May Surprise You—And Don't Blame Coleman Young," *Detroit Free Press*, September 15, 2013.

15. Patrick V. Murphy, "Guardsmen Must Be Trained as Police for Strikes," *WP*, August 27, 1978.

16. On Carter, the LEAA, and the IACP, see Michael S. Serrill, "Will Congress Defend LEAA from Carter's Attack?," *Police Magazine*, July 1978, 57–59; Elizabeth Hinton, *From the War on Crime to the War on Poverty: The Making of Mass Incarceration in America* (Cambridge, MA: Harvard University Press, 2016), 281–286; Nancy E. Marion, *A History of Federal Crime Control Initiatives, 1960–1993* (Westport, CT: Praeger, 1994); Cynthia Gorney, "Bell Orders Bias Suit Against San Francisco Police," *WP*, December 21, 1977; Warren Weaver Jr., "Kennedy Assails Cuts President Is Proposing for Law Enforcement," *NYT*, January 30, 1979; Law Enforcement Assistance Administration, September 15, 1980, attachment to Yvonne Price to Thomas Atkins, folder 5; part V, box 2741, NAACP Records, Library of Congress, Manuscripts Division, Washington, DC.

17. John Katzenbach, "Overwhelmed in Miami," *Police Magazine*, September 1980, 7–15; "1980: The Year of the Black Revolt," *Socialist Worker*, August 1980, 3; Elizabeth Hinton, *America on Fire: The Untold History of Police Violence and Black Rebellion Since the 1960s* (New York: Liveright, 2021); Aran Shetterly, *Morningside: The 1979 Greensboro Massacre and the Struggle for an American City's Soul* (New York: Amistad, 2024).

18. Richard Allinson, "LEAA: On the Brink of Extinction," *Police Magazine*, July 1980, 58–59; Robert Pear, "Law Enforcement Aid Agency Facing a Phase-Out," *NYT*, March 29, 1980.

19. "Building Unity Against Cutbacks and Repression," *Unite!* 7, no. 9 (May 15, 1981): 3; Brenda Payton, "Police Use of Deadly Force in Oakland," *Black Scholar* 12, no. 1 (1981): 62–64.

20. "Oakland Rejects Tax Increase Despite Rising Crime," *NYT*, April 26, 1981; Patty Hirota, "Party Work in Community Coalition," *Unite!* 7, no. 9 (May 15, 1981): 1–2; *Valentine v. City of Oakland*, October 20, 1983, 148 Cal. App. 3d 139 (Cal. Ct. App. 1983).

21. "Police Spread Thin," *NYT*, June 16, 1981.

22. Payton, "Police Use of Deadly Force"; Robyn C. Spencer, *The Revolution Has Come: Black Power, Gender, and the Black Panther Party in Oakland* (Durham, NC: Duke University Press, 2016).

23. John H. Burpo, *The Police Labor Movement: Problems and Perspectives* (Springfield, IL: Charles C. Thomas, 1971); Ray Gerda, "Police Militancy," *Crime and Social Justice* 7 (1977): 40–48; Hervey A. Juris and Peter Feuille, *Police Unionism: Power and Impact in Public-Sector Bargaining* (Lexington, MA: Lexington Books, 1973); Margaret Levi, *Bureaucratic Insurgency: The Case of Police Unions* (Lexington, MA: Lexington Books, 1977).

24. Gary P. Hayes and Alan Beals, "Preface," in Steven B. Rynecki and Michael T. Morse, *Police Collective Bargaining Agreements: A National Management Survey*, revised ed. (Washington, DC: Police Executive Research Forum, 1981).

Chapter 15: Passing the Torch to the Sheriffs

1. Howell Raines, "Reagan Proposes Revisions of Laws to Combat Crime," *NYT*, September 29, 1981; Lee Lescaze, "Reagan Blames Crime on 'Human Predator,'" *WP*, September 29, 1981; Ronald Reagan, "Remarks at the Annual Meeting of the International Association of Chiefs of Police in New Orleans, Louisiana," September 28, 1981, reaganlibrary.gov/archives/speech/remarks-annual-meeting-international-association-chiefs-police-new-orleans.

2. Neil Henry, "Police Unit Head Blasts Rival Group," *WP*, November 8, 1978; Charles R. Epp, *Making Rights Real: Activists, Bureaucrats, and the Creation of the Legalistic State* (Chicago: University of Chicago Press, 2009), 55.

3. Michael T. Farmer, "Standing Up for Police Professionalism," *NYT*, July 13, 1982; "The International Association of Chiefs of Police . . . ," United Press International, July 8, 1982; John Herbers, "Murphy Assailed by Police Chiefs," *NYT*, July 8, 1982; "The Out-of-Touch Police," *NYT*, July 9, 1982; Epp, *Making Rights Real*, 81.

4. Art Harris, "Lack of Crime-War Funds Deplored," *WP*, November 19, 1982; Margaret Gentry, "The Word from Washington: Tough Talk, but No Money," *Police Magazine*, January 1982, 34–40.

5. Harris, "Lack of Crime-War Funds."

6. "Agency in Justice Dept. to Shut Down April 15," *NYT*, January 1, 1982; Andrew H. Mott, "Block Grants," *NYT*, March 20, 1981.

7. Peter R. Bensinger, "Blank Cartridges," *WP*, October 8, 1981; Nancy E. Marion, *A History of Federal Crime Control Initiatives, 1960–1993* (Westport, CT: Praeger, 1994), 173.

8. Craig W. Floyd, interview with author, March 30, 2022.

9. Jessica Pishko, *The Highest Law in the Land: How the Unchecked Power of Sheriffs Threatens Democracy* (New York: Dutton, 2024); Emily M. Farris and Mirya R. Holman, *The Power of the Badge: Sheriffs and Inequality in the United States* (Chicago: University of

Chicago Press, 2024); Marshall E. Honaker, "A Challenge Toward Professionalism," *Sheriff*, July–August 1991, 7; Johnny Mack Brown, "Sheriff's Department Versus Office of the Sheriff," *Sheriff*, March–April 1993, 9; Larry Amerson and Greg Champagne, "What Is the Legal Meaning of a Sheriff's Oath of Office?," in Martin Alan Greenberg, *Everyone a Sheriff: The Democratization of Crime Prevention in America* (Lanham, MD: Lexington Books, 2021), 307–309.

10. Associated Press, "Nixon Says the G.O.P. Will Need 8 Years to Undo Democrats' Work," *NYT*, May 11, 1981; Edwin Meese III, "Civil and Criminal Justice Expenditures," *TPC*, July 1987, 13; "Reagan Vetoes Multi-$Million Law Enforcement Local Aid Bill," *National Sheriff*, February–March 1983, 26–27; L. Cary Bittick, "Setting an Agenda for NSA Growth," *National Sheriff*, February–March 1983, 41–42.

11. "Cops Miffed at $$$ Stats," *Law Enforcement News* VII, no. 7 (April 13, 1981): 1; Thomas J. Sardino, "President Sardino Takes Office: Speech Highlights," *TPC*, December 1984, 9.

12. Ronald Reagan, "Remarks at the Annual Conference of the National Sheriffs' Association in Hartford, Connecticut," June 20, 1984, reaganlibrary.gov/archives/speech/remarks-annual-conference-national-sheriffs-association-hartford-connecticut. He told the same yarn about having played a sheriff to the IACP meeting three years earlier.

13. L. Cary Bittick, "An Interview with the New NSA Executive Director," *National Sheriff*, April–May 1983, 53–54; Bob A. Ricks, "Model Drug Laws," *National Sheriff*, February–March 1984, 36, 46, 48; "Law and Legislative Committee," *National Sheriff*, February–March 1985, 55; "Law and Legislative Committee," *Sheriff*, November–December 1994, 46.

14. "In 1950 Cale Boggs hoped to make Americans safe from Stalin," campaign ad, Biden for Senate Committee, 1972, in author's possession.

15. Violent Crime Control and Law Enforcement Act of 1994—Conference Report, *Congressional Record*, Senate, 140, No. 122 (August 23, 1994).

16. "Congressional Crime Caucus Formed," *TPC*, August 1984, 73. Also, Norman Darwick to Arlen Specter, April 6, 1984, L. Cary Bittick to Arlen Specter, April 26, 1984, and Gary P. Hayes to Arlen Specter, April 9, 1984, all in Cop Killer Bullets box, Mario Biaggi Papers, Bronx Historical Society, The Bronx, NY (MBP). Also, David Dagan de Picciotto, "Building the Big House: American Institutions and the Rise of Mass Incarceration, 1970–1990" (PhD diss., Johns Hopkins University, 2019).

17. "Congressional Reception," *National Sheriff*, April–May 1984, 18.

18. Bureau of Justice Statistics, "Bulletin: Profile of State and Local Law Enforcement Agencies, 1987" (Washington: DOJ, 1989); "Sheriffs' Statistics: A U.S. Department of Justice Report," *National Sheriff*, June–July 1989, 40–43; Richard L. Germond, "President's Message," *National Sheriff*, August–September 1985, 3–4.

19. Photo ops, President Reagan meeting with the National Law Enforcement Council, Oval Office, August 30, 1984, 06270-4T-W420-I86a, WHTV 1981-89 (Video Collection), Ronald Reagan Library, Simi Valley, CA.

20. Marion, *A History of Federal Crime Control Initiatives*; Elizabeth Hinton, *From the War on Crime to the War on Poverty: The Making of Mass Incarceration in America* (Cambridge, MA: Harvard University Press, 2016); Ted Gest, *Crime and Politics: Big Government's Erratic Campaign for Law and Order* (New York: Oxford University Press, 2001).

21. Bruce A. Morrison, "Letter to the Editor," *NYT*, January 30, 1985; "Gates, Guards, Guns, and Goetz," *NYT*, January 27, 1985; "Justice Assistance Program Underway," *TPC*, May 1985, 82.

22. L. Cary Bittick, "Annual Conference Demonstrated 'Sheriffs Search for Excellence,'" *National Sheriff*, August–September 1984, 52; Public Law 98-473, October 12, 1984; Gest, *Crime and Politics*.

23. "The Federal Surplus Real Property Transfer Program," *National Sheriff*, June–July 1985, 53; Edwin Meese, "Honorable Edwin Meese Addresses 1985 NSA Annual Conference," *National Sheriff*, August–September 1985, 8.

24. The best systematic study of forfeiture is by the Institute for Justice, now in its third edition: Lisa Knepper, Jennifer McDonald, Kathy Sanchez, and Elyse Smith Pohl, *Policing for Profit: The Abuse of Civil Asset Forfeiture*, 3rd ed. (Arlington, VA: Institute for Justice, 2020); Sarah Stillman, "Taken," *New Yorker*, August 12–19, 2013; Katherine Beckett, *Making Crime Pay: Law and Order in Contemporary American Politics* (New York: Oxford University Press, 1997), 93–94; Jackson Smith, "Dirty Money and Financial Inequality in North Philadelphia," *Theoretical Criminology* 28, no. 1 (2024): 50–69; Gary Webb, "A Cop's-Eye View: Settling Accounts up Front, in Cash," *San Jose Mercury News*, August 30, 1993.

25. Marion, *A History of Federal Crime Control Initiatives*, 152; Arnold I. Burns, "Address Before the Southeast Region Drug Task Force Winter Conference," January 1987, Gatlinburg, TN, DOJ; Brad W. Smith, Kenneth J. Novak, James Frank, and Lawrence F. Travis III, "Multijurisdictional Drug Task Forces: An Analysis of Impacts," *Journal of Criminal Justice* 28, no. 6 (2000): 543–556.

26. Richard Bocklet, "DEA-State and Local Task Forces: A Body for Law Enforcement," *Law and Order*, January 1991, 272–279; David Kocieniewski, "New Jersey Argues That the U.S. Wrote the Book on Race Profiling," *NYT*, November 29, 2000; Gary Webb, "Driving While Black," in *"The Killing Game": Selected Writings from the Author of* Dark Alliance, ed. Eric Webb (New York: Seven Stories, 2011), 280.

27. K. Michael Moore, "Asset Seizure and Forfeiture: Marshals Service," *Sheriff*, March–April 1991, 12–15.

28. "Honorable Edwin Meese Addresses"; Burns, "Address"; "Federal Revenue Sharing with Local Law Enforcement," *National Sheriff*, August–September 1987, 33; Stillman, "Taken."

29. "Federal Revenue Sharing"; "Florida Sheriff Seized Drug Money to Buy Bomb Truck," *Sheriff*, March–April 1992, 52; "Hennepin County," *National Sheriff*, June–July 1990, 40.

30. "Asset Forfeiture: Taking the Profit out of Drug Trafficking," *TPC*, September 1987, 13–17; Beckett, *Making Crime Pay*; Gary Webb, "Police Lobbying to Save State Asset Forfeiture Law Drug Wars," *San Jose Mercury News*, September 7, 1993; Kimberly A. Kingston, "Forfeiture of Attorney's Fees," *FBI Law Enforcement Bulletin* 59, no. 4 (April 1990): 27–32; Terrence P. Farley, "Asset Forfeiture Training Initiative," *Sheriff*, May–June 1994, 26.

31. Brooke C. Stoddard, "Asset Forfeitures: A Training and Technical Assistance Project," *National Sheriff*, February–March 1990, 38–40; Darrel W. Stephens to Charles Rangel, March 18, 1987, attached to Select Committee on Narcotics Abuse and Control, House, 100th Cong., 1st sess., Hearing on the State and Local Law Enforcement Assistance

Provision of the Anti–Drug Abuse Act of 1986, March 4, 1987; Gary Webb, "The Money Tree: Sweeping Law Leaves Poor, Vulnerable with Little Recourse," *San Jose Mercury News*, August 30, 1993.

32. Shawn Kantor, Carl T. Kitchen, and Steven Pawlowski, "Civil Asset Forfeiture, Crime, and Police Incentives: Evidence from the Comprehensive Crime Control Act of 1984," *Economic Inquiry* 59, no. 1 (2021): 217–242.

33. "Proposed Revenue Sharing Ax: A Problem for County Law Enforcement," *National Sheriff*, April–May 1985, 58; "Sheriffs Define Legislative Priorities," *National Sheriff*, April–May 1986, 53–54.

34. Stillman, "Taken"; Theresa M. Burick-Seemiller, "Comprehensive Crime Bill of 1990," *National Sheriff*, November–December 1990, 28; Southern Poverty Law Center, "Civil Asset Forfeiture: Unfair, Undemocratic, and Un-American," policy brief, October 2017; Gary Webb, "A Modest Weapon on the War on Drugs Can Be Used as a Bludgeon Against the Innocent: Law Fills Cops' Coffers but Invites Abuses," *San Jose Mercury News*, August 29, 1993.

35. Germond, "President's Message"; "National Sheriffs' Association Support of H.B. 526," *National Sheriff*, August–September 1986, 34.

Chapter 16: The Bipartisan War on Drugs

1. DOJ Criminal Division, *Handbook on the Anti–Drug Abuse Act of 1986* (Washington, DC: DOJ, 1987). The sentencing disparity remained until 2010, when it was reduced to 18:1. In 2022, Attorney General Merrick Garland issued prosecution guidelines to eradicate the disparity, but its legislative elimination, introduced in 2021, stalled. Carl Hulse, "Drug Sentencing Bill Is in Limbo as Midterm Politics Paralyze Congress," *NYT*, April 29, 2022; Glenn Thrush, "Justice Dept. Revises Rules for Drug Cases to Address Racial Disparities," *NYT*, December 16, 2022.

2. Mark Sullivan, "Gilman's Role in Drug Battle," *NYT*, May 3, 1987, "Rep. Charles Rangel, D-N.Y., Sharply Criticized the Reagan Administration," UPI, April 25, 1988; Will Bredderman, "Harlem's Lion in Winter A Requiem for Rangel," *Observer*, February 16, 2016; Clifford D. May, "Washington Talk: Drug Enforcement; Once-Lonely Voice Finds an Audience," *NYT*, June 6, 1988; "Congressional Highlights," *TPC*, June 1985, 72; Select Committee on Narcotics Abuse and Control, House, 100th Cong., 1st sess., Hearing on the State and Local Law Enforcement Assistance Provision of the Anti–Drug Abuse Act of 1986, March 4, 1987, 18, and attached memo, Darrel W. Stephens to Charles Rangel, March 18, 1987, 136.

3. In 1996, Congress formalized the local police role in civil and criminal immigration enforcement, under a section known as 287(g). After 9/11, formal deportations, which might entail lengthy detention in jails or private facilities, increased significantly. The National Sheriffs' Association endorsed 287(g), while the IACP opposed it. Amada Armenta, *Protect, Serve, and Deport: The Rise of Policing as Immigration Enforcement* (Oakland: University of California Press, 2017); Adam Goodman, *The Deportation Machine: America's Long History of Expelling Immigrants* (Princeton, NJ: Princeton University Press, 2020); Jack Norton and Jacob Kang-Brown, "If You Build It: How the Federal Government Fuels Rural Jail Expansion," Vera Institute of Justice, January 10, 2020, vera.org/in-our-backyards-stories/if-you-build-it; Raymond M. Kisor, "Enforcing the Immigration and Naturalization Act,"

National Sheriff, October–November 1984, 33–36; Daniel M. Thompson, "How Partisan Is Local Law Enforcement? Evidence from Sheriff Cooperation with Immigration Authorities," *American Political Science Review* 114, no. 1 (2020): 222–236.

4. Kristina Shull, *Detention Empire: Reagan's War on Immigrants and the Seeds of Resistance* (Chapel Hill: University of North Carolina Press, 2022); J. Gonzales, "Chicanos Blast Reagan's Immigration Plan," *Unity*, August 28–September 10, 1981, 3, 10; "Latino Workers Resist Step Up in Immigration Raids," *Unity*, May 11, 1984, 1.

5. Carly Goodman, *Dreamland: America's Immigration Lottery in an Age of Restriction* (Chapel Hill: University of North Carolina Press, 2023).

6. Nancy E. Marion, *A History of Federal Crime Control Initiatives, 1960–1993* (Westport, CT: Praeger, 1994); Elizabeth Hinton, *From the War on Crime to the War on Poverty: The Making of Mass Incarceration in America* (Cambridge, MA: Harvard University Press, 2016); Charlotte E. Rosen, "The Armed Career Criminal Act and the Puzzle of Federal Crime Control in the Reagan Era: 'It's at the State and Local Levels That Problems Exist,'" *Journal of Policy History* 35, no. 2 (2023): 161–194; Ted Gest, *Crime and Politics: Big Government's Erratic Campaign for Law and Order* (New York: Oxford University Press, 2001), Hughes quote on 115.

7. Max Felker-Kantor, *DARE to Say No: Policing and the War on Drugs in Schools* (Chapel Hill: University of North Carolina Press, 2024).

8. Kevin Joy, "Former Members of Police Band Think Message Still Relevant," *Columbus Dispatch*, November 8, 2013; "Hot Pursuit D.A.R.E." [music video], 1990, Columbus (OH) Metropolitan Library, digital-collections.columbuslibrary.org/digital/collection/ccs/id/19326.

9. "Congressional Highlights," *TPC*, January 1985, 61.

10. "IACP Renews Its Efforts in War Against Drugs," *TPC*, October 1986, 21; "Reagan Signs $1.7 Billion Anti-Drug Bill," *TPC*, December 1986, 14.

11. "Seizures Up Coke Prices Stay Same," *Law and Order*, May 1992, 4.

12. Douglas Riggs to Jim Cicconi, November 7, 1983, Labor Outreach, James W. Cicconi Files, box 10, Ronald Reagan Library, Simi Valley, CA, 40-94-6914308-010-016-2016.

Chapter 17: Bulletproof

1. Henry A. Acosta, "Body Armor: Cost Comparison v. Fatality/Injury Reduction Cost," *TPC*, October 1978, 78–79; subsequent cost analysis is also from this article. Also, James Chposky, "Job Stress," *Law Officer* 8, no. 4 (September–October 1975): 8–11.

2. "Body Armor May Save a Life," *BPDN*, January 8, 1975, 1–2; Rudolph Giuliani, Statement before the Subcommittee on Crime, May 12, 1982, Committee of the Judiciary, House of Representatives, MBP; "NIJ's Bullet-Resistant Vest Standard Reaches Milestone," *NIJ Journal* 249 (July 2003).

3. Moncada Library, "Support the National Black Human Rights Campaign!," n.d. [1978], and "Support the Struggle for Human Rights," *Moncada Library Newsletter* 1, no. 4 (June 1979), 2, The Freedom Archives, Berkeley, CA.

4. Daniel B. Moskowitz, "How to Stop a Bullet and Live to Tell About It," *Police Magazine*, May 1979, 57–61; "Shooting Holes in a Controversy," *Law Enforcement News* 9, no. 6 (March 21, 1983), 8–9, 14; Ronald McBride, "Providing Body Armor," *Law and Order*, January 2002, 85.

5. Transcript of Trial Proceedings, *United States of America v. Mario Biaggi and Meade Esposito*, Eastern District of New York, 1988; *In the Matter of Representative Mario Biaggi: Report of the Committee on Standards of Official Conduct, House of Representatives (To Accompany H. Res. 380)* (Washington, DC: GPO, 1988); "Personalities," *WP*, October 16, 1979; Leonard Ruder, "Bids on Bulletproof Vests in P.B.A. Project Studied," *NYT*, May 16, 1979.

6. Mario Biaggi, "'Cop Killer' Bullets: Six Years Later and Still No Ban," *New York Law Enforcement Journal* 1, no. 1 (March 1986): 2, MBP; John Burpo, Ron DeLord, and Michael Shannon, eds., *Police Association Power, Politics, and Confrontation: A Guide for the Successful Police Labor Leader* (Springfield, IL: Charles C. Thomas, 1997), 314; Stuart Taylor Jr., "Law-and-Order Is Easy to Say, Hard to Legislate," *NYT*, December 13, 1981.

7. Kevin Krajick, "Should This Bullet Be Banned?," *Police Magazine* 6, no. 1 (January 1983): 37–43; David Rowe, "Editorial," *Police Product News*, April 1982, 6; J. V. Vollink, "Choosing Sides," *Law Enforcement News* 10, no. 3 (February 13, 1984): 10; Biaggi, "'Cop Killer' Bullets."

8. Massad Ayoub, "The Killer Bullet: An Officer Survival Perspective," *Police Product News*, April 1982, 22; Giuliani, Statement.

9. Ted Gest, *Crime and Politics: Big Government's Erratic Campaign for Law and Order* (New York: Oxford University Press, 2001), 139; Andrew Kendzie, "Cop Killer Bullet," *National Sheriff*, December 1983–January 1984, 9–10.

10. Committee on the Judiciary, Report on Law Enforcement Officers Protection Act of 1985, November 6, 1985, 99th Cong., 1st sess.

11. "The Cop-Killer Bullet" (ad), *Police Magazine* 6, no. 1 (January 1983): 41.

12. "First-Person Interview: Congressman Joshua Eilberg," *Law Officer* 9, no. 1 (January–February 1977): 12–14; Hamilton Fish Jr., "Letter to the Editor," *Law Officer* 9, no. 1 (January–February 1977): 4; Committee on the Judiciary, Subcommittee on Immigration, Citizenship, and International Law, "Public Safety Officers' Benefits Act; and Law Enforcement Officers' Bill of Rights," July 25–26, 1973, House, 93rd Cong., 1st sess., 54.

13. "Persons Attending December 12, 1984, Meeting on 'Cop Killer' Bullet Bill," "Some Ideas of What Police Can Do," n.d. [November 6, 1985], "Attendees at Nov. 6 Meeting on 'Cop Killer Bullet' Bill," and Craig Floyd to Mario Biaggi, December 11, 1984, all in MBP.

14. "Some Ideas"; Craig Floyd to Mario Biaggi, December 12, 1984, MBP.

15. Craig Floyd to Mario Biaggi, November 30, 1984, MBP.

16. Craig Floyd to Mario Biaggi, December 11, 1984, Robert E. Van Etten et al. to Ronald Reagan, January 10, 1985, and Richard A. Boyd to Mario Biaggi and William J. Hughes, March 7, 1985, all in MBP.

17. Richard A. Boyd and James W. Sterling to Strom Thurmond, July 3, 1985, Richard A. Boyd et al. to Strom Thurmond, July 2, 1985, and "Attendees at Nov. 6 Meeting on 'Cop Killer Bullet' Bill," all in MBP.

18. Jennifer Nislow, "Rallying 'Round the Gun-Control Issue," *Law Enforcement News* 12, no. 4 (February 24, 1986): 1, 7; Kristen Rand, *Gun Shows in America: Tupperware® Parties for Criminals* (Washington, DC: Violence Policy Center, 1996).

19. A. F. Schuster Jr. to Mario Biaggi, April 16, 1986, MBP.

20. John Herbers, "Police Groups Reverse Stand and Back Controls on Pistols," *NYT*, October 27, 1985; Richard Corrigan, "NRA, Using Members, Ads and Money, Hits Police Line in Lobbying Drive," *National Journal*, January 4, 1986, 8–14; "McClure/Volkmer

Falls Short of Original Goals," *TPC*, October 1986, 91; Jerald R. Vaughn, "NRA Challenges Prohibitions on Machine Guns," *TPC*, October 1986, 10.

21. Rand, *Gun Shows in America*; Mario Biaggi, "Rep. Mario Biaggi 'Knocks' *Monitor* Interview," *Monitor* 13, no. 6 (March 31, 1986): 2, MBP.

22. Dick Armey, Dear Colleague Letter, December 16, 1985, MBP; "Congress: Support Your Local Police," *NYT*, October 13, 1985; Craig Floyd to Mario Biaggi, October 16, 1985, MBP.

23. Mario Biaggi to Law Enforcement Steering Committee Against S. 49, December 19, 1985, Richard A. Boyd to Mario Biaggi, December 24, 1985, and Craig Floyd to Mario Biaggi, n.d. [yellow paper], all in MBP.

24. "McClure/Volkmer: This Bill Endangers Police," *TPC*, January 1986, 24–25; Gest, *Crime and Politics*, 137–138; Howard Kurtz, "Meese Upsets Police with Gun Law Stand," *WP*, February 25, 1986; Howard Kurtz, "House Votes to Weaken Gun Controls," *WP*, April 11, 1986.

25. Kurtz, "House Votes"; Craig Floyd to Mario Biaggi, May 7, 1986, MBP.

26. Howard Kurtz, "Ban Voted on Production of Armor-Piercing Bullets," *WP*, March 7, 1986; "Bill to Ban 'Cop Killer' Bullets Goes to Reagan," *WP*, August 15, 1986; News from Congressman Mario Biaggi, August 14, 1986, News from Congressman Mario Biaggi, August 28, 1986, Craig Floyd to Mario Biaggi, August 15, 1986, and FOP to Mario Biaggi, August 14, 1986, all in MBP; Nislow, "Rallying 'Round," 7.

27. L. Cary Bittick, "McClure/Volkmer—A Mixed Victory," *National Sheriff*, June–July 1986, 52; Adam Serwer, "The One Group That Could Make a Difference on Gun Control," *The Atlantic*, June 9, 2022.

Chapter 18: Weekend Warriors on Crime

1. This discussion draws largely on John Burpo, "The Police vs. Time Warner: The Story of David Taking Goliath Out to the Woodshed for a Good Whippin'," in *Police Association Power, Politics, and Confrontation: A Guide for the Successful Police Labor Leader*, ed. John Burpo, Ron DeLord, and Michael Shannon (Springfield, IL: Charles C. Thomas, 1997), 251–258; Matthew McKinnon, "Hang the MC: Blaming Hip Hop for Violence," CBC, February 7, 2006; Ben Apatoff, *Body Count* (New York: Bloomsbury, 2023).

2. Apatoff, *Body Count*, 87–88.

3. Avis Thomas-Lester and Marylou Tousignant, "Reaction to Ice-T Song Heats Up," *WP*, June 25, 1992; Frank Policaro Jr., "A Year in Review," *Sheriff*, May–June 1992, 5.

4. "Rap Song Provokes Boycott," *Law and Order*, August 1992, 4; "A New Voice in Law Enforcement," *Law and Order*, October 1993, 87; "Time Warner Gets Protest on Its 'Cop Killer' Album," *NYT*, July 16, 1992.

5. Jon Pareles, "The Disappearance of Ice-T's 'Cop Killer,'" *NYT*, July 30, 1992; Bruce W. Cameron, "Rap Protest and Cop Protest—Hint of Future Protests," *Law and Order*, August 1992, 1.

6. "Bush Signs Stripped-Down Crime Bill," *CQ Almanac 1990*, 46th ed. (Washington, DC: Congressional Quarterly, 1991), 486–499 (bill details at congress.gov/bill/102nd-congress/senate-bill/618); Gwen Ifill, "Senate's Rule for Its Anti-Crime Bill: The Tougher the Provision, the Better," *NYT*, July 7, 1991.

7. Alexis Herman and Jose Cerda, Meeting with the Law Enforcement Steering Committee, April 13, 1994, Extra Copies of Briefing Papers, April 1994, Executive Office of the President, Clinton Digital Library, 86889.

8. Mitchell Locin, "Clinton: Unite in Crime Fight," *Chicago Tribune*, July 24, 1992; Federal Election Commission filings by International Union of Police Association, docquery .fec.gov/cgi-bin/fecimg/?C00264382.

9. Violent Crime Control and Law Enforcement Act of 1994—Conference Report, *Congressional Record*, Senate, 140, No. 122 (August 23, 1994).

10. David Stein, "The Untold Story: Joe Biden Pushed Ronald Reagan to Ramp up Incarceration—Not the Other Way Around," *The Intercept*, September 17, 2019; Andrew Kaczynski, "Biden in 1993 Speech Pushing Crime Bill Warned of 'Predators on Our Streets' Who Were 'Beyond the Pale,'" CNN, March 7, 2019.

11. George H. W. Bush, "Address to the Nation on the Civil Disturbances in Los Angeles, California," May 1, 1992, *Public Papers of the Presidents of the United States: George H. W. Bush, 1992–1993, Book I* (Washington, DC: GPO, 1993), 685–687.

12. "National Law Enforcement Council," May 3, 1989, C-SPAN, 7499-1.

13. George H. W. Bush, "Remarks to the National Fraternal Order of Police in Cincinnati, Ohio," October 9, 1992, and "Remarks to the International Association of Chiefs of Police in Detroit, Michigan," October 25, 1992, *Public Papers of the Presidents of the United States: George H. W. Bush, 1992–1993, Book II* (Washington, DC: GPO, 1993), 1780–1782, 1974–1978; Ron G. DeLord, "Observations on a State and National Election," in *Police Association Power, Politics, and Confrontation: A Guide for the Successful Police Labor Leader*, ed. John Burpo, Ron DeLord, and Michael Shannon (Springfield, IL: Charles C. Thomas, 1997), 226–230; Ruth Marcus and Ann Devroy, "Police Group Gives Bush Its Blessing," *WP*, October 10, 1992.

14. Gary Lee, "Police Group's Leadership Election Seen as Showdown over Gun Control," *WP*, August 11, 1991; Gary Lee, "Taking the Fight Against Gun Control to the Police," *WP*, August 15, 1991.

15. Mollie Dickinson, "Bush's Assassination of the Brady Bill," *WP*, November 1, 1992; 3.14.93 Crime Briefing, Crime Bill Rally—Event—April 15, 1994 [6], Domestic Policy Council and Jose Cerda, Clinton Digital Library, 86739.

16. 3.14.93 Crime Briefing; "The 70,000 Member National Association of Police Organizations," UPI, September 26, 1984; Address by Attorney General Janet Reno before the National Association of Police Organizations, August 11, 1997, Department of Justice, justice .gov/archive/ag/speeches/1997/811_npo.html.

17. Law Enforcement Steering Committee, "Blueprint for Progress in Policing," 1992, NCJRS, 140096; "National Law Enforcement Council," May 3, 1989, C-SPAN, 7499-1.

Chapter 19: Who Rules the City?

1. Chris Francescani, "Law and Disorder," *New York*, December 7, 1998.

2. "Dinkins Fronts for Wall Street," *Proletarian Revolution* 36 (Winter 1990): 3–5; David Duhalde, "What David Dinkins Taught Us," *Jacobin*, November 25, 2020; Ross Barkan, "New York's Cop Coup," *Jacobin*, November 12, 2021.

3. "A Hero's Welcome," *New York's Finest*, January 1988, 14–15; Rick Moran, "The N.Y.P.D. Buries P.O. Jeff Herman," *New York's Finest*, July–August 1979, 6–7.

4. Stuart Schrader, "Wanted: An End to Police Terror," *Viewpoint*, June 9, 2020; Errol Louis, "Police Brutality: A Backstory," NY1, June 5, 2020; Mariame Kaba, "Resisting Police Violence Against Black Women and Women of Color," remarks at "Invisible No More: Resisting Police Violence Against Black Women and Women of Color in Troubled Times," Barnard College, November 2017, New York, NY; "Koch's Cossacks Kill," *Workers Vanguard*, February 27, 1981; Clarence Taylor, *Fight the Power: African Americans and the Long History of Police Brutality in New York City* (New York: NYU Press, 2019).

5. LaShawn Harris, "Beyond the Shooting: Eleanor Gray Bumpurs, Identity Erasure, and Family Activism Against Police Violence," *Souls* 20, no. 1 (2018): 86–109; Modibo, "A Year Since the Bumpurs' Murder," *Unity* 8, no. 14 (October 25, 1985).

6. "Police Union's Offices in Manhattan Bombed," *NYT*, February 23, 1985.

7. Buck Richter, "Political Action Committee," *New York's Finest*, January–February 1989, 4.

8. Bureau of Justice Statistics, *Bulletin: Profile of State and Local Law Enforcement Agencies, 1987* (Washington, DC: DOJ, 1989); Bruce W. Cameron, "Small Agencies: The Backbone of Law Enforcement," *Law and Order*, June 1994, 1; "A National Review of Wages and Benefits," *Law and Order*, November 1993, 42–54.

9. "Police Officers and Firefighters Protest Pending Layoffs," AP News, April 14, 1989; "The Spring of Their Discontent," *Law Enforcement News* 25, no. 294 (June 15, 1989): 1, 7.

10. Leonard Buder, "DeMilia Wins Voting on P.B.A. Presidency," *NYT*, June 12, 1977.

11. Phil Caruso, "Of Crime and Violence," *New York's Finest*, September–October 1990, 2–3.

12. Russ Baker, "The Rogue Police Union," *Village Voice*, December 7, 1993; Phil Caruso, "PBA President Addresses Objector to Memorial Deduction," *New York's Finest*, January–February 1989, 27.

13. Wayne Barrett, assisted by Adam Fifield, *Rudy! An Investigative Biography of Rudolph Giuliani* (New York: Basic Books, 2000); Richard Steier, "Combative Ex-PBA Head Phil Caruso Is Mourned," *The Chief-Leader*, September 30, 2021; Baker, "The Rogue Police Union."

14. Baker, "The Rogue Police Union"; William K. Flynn and Kevin Rashbaum, "The Fat Cats of PBA, Inc.," New York *Daily News* (*Daily News*), February 2, 1997.

15. Richard Steier, "Top Negotiator, Ruinous Gambler Hartman Dies," *The Chief-Leader*, August 24, 2015; Flynn and Rashbaum, "The Fat Cats"; Matthew Purdy and David Kocieniewski, "P.B.A. and Its Lawyers in a Tangle of Money and Mixed Roles," *NYT*, February 2, 1997; Baker, "The Rogue Police Union"; Richard Hartman, "Your Legal Rights," *New York's Finest*, May 1982, 5, 54; Pam Belluck, "The Street Cop in Pin Stripes," *NYT*, March 6, 1996.

16. Alan Finder, "Police Unions Still Loyal to Biaggi," *NYT*, September 6, 1992.

17. Author correspondence with Jeff Nelson, 2010; Ruth Marcus, "Blaming the Messenger," *WP*, June 23, 1988.

18. George Lardner Jr., "Rep. Biaggi Indicted in Wedtech Case," *WP*, June 4, 1987; Andy Logan, "Around City Hall," *New Yorker*, June 19, 1989, 77–82; Barrett, *Rudy!*, 165–171; Baker, "The Rogue Police Union."

19. Sam Roberts, "Police Funeral: Sorrowful Rite and Potent Symbol," *NYT*, March 20, 1994; D. N. Kyriacou et al., "Police Deaths in New York and London During the Twentieth Century," *Injury Prevention* 12, no. 4 (2006): 219–224.

20. Steier, "Combative"; "Police Contract Talks Stalled, Dinkins Says," *NYT*, March 29, 1991; Ralph Blumenthal, "Officers Write 54% Fewer Tickets to Protest New York Pact Impasse," *NYT*, April 11, 1991; James C. McKinley Jr., "As Police Talks Stall, Motorists Gain," *NYT*, April 4, 1991.

21. Baker, "The Rogue Police Union"; Modibo, "Police Brutality, Fascist Threat on the Rise," *Unity & Struggle* 2, no. 3 (June 1991): 1, 7–8.

22. Larry Celona, "Hero Cop's Story," *New York's Finest*, September–October 1992, 6–7, 23; Donald Dewey, "The 34 Pct.: Improving Its Crime-Fighting Batting Average," *New York's Finest*, Summer 1997, 1, 6–11, 24; Dennis Hevesi, "Upper Manhattan Block Erupts After a Man Is Killed in Struggle with a Policeman," *NYT*, July 5, 1992.

23. "Police Review Board Issue Riles New York City PD Rank-and-File," *Law Enforcement News* 18, no. 366 (October 15, 1992): 3; Dareh Gregorian, "City $lapped for Druggie Death," *NY Post*, September 22, 2004.

Chapter 20: The Cop Coup

1. My account of the police riot draws from Richard Steier, "Top Negotiator, Ruinous Gambler Hartman Dies," *The Chief-Leader*, August 24, 2015; Wayne Barrett, assisted by Adam Fifield, *Rudy! An Investigative Biography of Rudolph Giuliani* (New York: Basic Books, 2000); Ross Barkan, "New York's Cop Coup," *Jacobin*, November 12, 2021; Laura Nahmias, "White Riot," *New York*, October 4, 2021; Peter Noel, "Why Blacks Fear Giuliani," in *Why Blacks Fear "America's Mayor"* (New York: iUniverse, 2007), 3–16; Catherine S. Manegold, "Rally Puts Police Under New Scrutiny," *NYT*, September 27, 1992; Carl J. Pelleck, "A Rally to Remember," *New York's Finest*, September–October 1992, 10–13; and NY1 news segment, September 16, 1992. See also John Ganz, *When the Clock Broke: Con Men, Conspiracists, and How America Cracked Up in the Early 1990s* (New York: Farrar, Straus and Giroux, 2024).

2. Michael O'Keefe to Nicole Rivas, email, July 12, 2023, in author's possession.

3. "New Group Urges 'Cuffs off the Cops,'" *New York's Finest*, September–October 1992, 22.

4. Pelleck, "A Rally"; Phil Caruso, "The Media's Riot," *New York's Finest*, September–October 1992, 2.

5. Richard Steier, "Rudy's Unredeemed Pledge," *The Chief-Leader*, January 19, 2001.

6. "Police Review Board Issue Riles New York City PD Rank-and-File," *Law Enforcement News* 18, no. 366 (October 15, 1992): 3.

7. Milton Mollen et al., *Commission Report* (New York: City of New York, 1994), 1, 10, 66–68.

8. Barrett, *Rudy!*; James Bennet, "Selling Unions Like Soap," *NYT*, April 21, 1993.

9. Catherine S. Manegold, "Giuliani Takes Message to Staten Island Voters," *NYT*, October 26, 1993; Anna Sanders, "Gov. Mario Cuomo and the Staten Island Secession Movement," *Staten Island Advance*, January 2, 2015.

10. Barrett, *Rudy!*, 265–270.

11. David Firestone, "The Bratton Resignation: The Overview," *NYT*, March 27, 1996.

12. David Firestone, "Police-Giuliani Tie: Contract Collapse a Further Blow," *NYT*, January 23, 1997; Steven Lee Myers, "Giuliani Wins Police Merger in M.T.A. Vote," *NYT*, April 1, 1995.

13. John Sullivan, "4 Convicted in Corruption at Union for Transit Police," *NYT*, January 27, 1998.

Chapter 21: Hire More Cops

1. Ted Gest, *Crime and Politics: Big Government's Erratic Campaign for Law and Order* (New York: Oxford University Press, 2001), 161–165.

2. David L. Carter, Allen D. Sapp, and Darrel W. Stephens, *The State of Police Education: Policy Direction for the 21st Century* (Washington, DC: Police Executive Research Forum, 1989), 38, xxii.

3. Carter, Sapp, and Stephens, *The State of Police Education*, xxii; "CJ Leaders Assess the Future of Policing," *Law Enforcement News* 10, no. 3 (February 13, 1984): 1, 10.

4. PCLEAJ, *Task Force Report: The Police* (Washington, DC: GPO, 1967), 126; Carter, Sapp, and Stephens, *The State of Police Education*.

5. Carter, Sapp, and Stephens, *The State of Police Education*, 94–96.

6. New York City Police Cadet Corps, Program Summary, February 1994, and "Raymond W. Kelly Retires," *New York City Police Cadet Corps Newsletter*, Winter 1994, 3–4, 9, both in New York—4, Domestic Policy Council and Jose Cerda, Clinton Digital Library, 96643; Faculty Senate Minutes #183, April 13,1999, John Jay College of Criminal Justice, Lloyd Sealy Library, New York.

7. Robert Scully, "The Police Corps: Agreeing on Aims but Disagreeing on Approaches," *Law Enforcement News* 15, no. 302 (November 15, 1989): 8, 13.

8. Bruce W. Cameron, "Some Things Get Better with Age, Others Don't," *Law and Order*, May 1993, 1; Bruce W. Cameron, "'Bubba' Is Wrong About Police Corps," *Law and Order*, March 1993, 1.

9. Gest, *Crime and Politics*, 172; Timothy M. Dees, "The Police Corps: It May Be a Nice Idea, But . . . ," *Law Enforcement News* 20, no. 399 (April 15, 1994): 15; James J. Fyfe, "We Need More Educated Police Officers," *Law Enforcement News* 15, no. 304 (December 15, 1989): 8.

10. "Sens. Specter and Strasser Introduce Legislation That Would Provide Free College Education in Return for Police Service," Public Relations and Media Files, Group 6, Arlen Specter Senatorial Papers online, University of Pittsburgh, 31735070019595; "Where Ballots and Bullets Converge," *Law Enforcement News* 18, no. 365 (September 30, 1992): 1, 7; Congressional Research Service, "Crime, Drug, and Gun Control: Summary of S. 1241 (102nd Congress) as Passed by the Senate," July 31, 1991, Library of Congress; William J. Clinton, "Remarks Announcing Safe Schools and Police Corps Initiatives in Worcester, Massachusetts," August 27, 1998, TAPP; Gest, *Crime and Politics*, 166.

11. Robert E. Worden and Sarah J. McLean, *Mirage of Police Reform: Procedural Justice and Police Legitimacy* (Oakland: University of California Press, 2017); Tony Cheng, *The Policing Machine: Enforcement, Endorsements, and the Illusion of Public Input* (Chicago: University of Chicago Press, 2024); Marian Bass, "Community Policing Is No Panacea," *The Blue Line* (Buffalo PBA), April 1994, 4.

12. George L. Kelling and James Q. Wilson, "Broken Windows: The Police and Neighborhood Safety," *Atlantic Monthly*, March 1982; Rudolph W. Giuliani and William J. Bratton, Police Strategy No. 5: Reclaiming the Public Spaces of New York, July 6, 1994, New York—1, Domestic Policy Council and Jose Cerda, Clinton Digital Library, 96640.

13. Stuart Schrader, *Badges Without Borders: How Global Counterinsurgency Transformed American Policing* (Oakland: University of California Press, 2019), ch. 8.

14. George L. Kelling and Robert B. Kliesmet, "Police Unions, Police Culture, and Police Abuse of Force," in William A. Geller and Hans Toch, ed., *Police Violence: Understanding and Controlling Police Use of Force* (New Haven, CT: Yale University Press, 1996), 201, 204; John L. Mitchell, "LAPD Discipline Urged for Officer in King Case," *LAT*, December 11, 1992.

15. Michael D. White and Henry F. Fradella, *Stop and Frisk: The Use and Abuse of a Controversial Policing Tactic* (New York: NYU Press, 2016); Paul Schwartzman and John Wagner, "As Baltimore Mayor, Critics Say, O'Malley's Police Tactics Sowed Distrust," *WP*, April 25, 2015.

16. "UCR Down Again for 4th Year in Row," *Law Enforcement News* 22, no. 445 (May 15, 1996): 6.

17. "Where Ballots and Bullets Converge;" "BJS Survey: Overall Crime Dipped in 1990, but Violent Crime Was Up," *Law Enforcement News* 17, no. 333 (March 31, 1991): 3; "Skepticism Greets Latest NIDA Report on Drug-Use Decline," *Law Enforcement News* 16, no. 327 (December 31, 1990): 3.

18. Debbie M. Price, "'Murder Capital' Label Has Long Stalked D.C.," *WP*, April 4, 1989; "Law Enforcement Around the Nation, 1994," *Law Enforcement News* 10, no. 414 (December 31, 1994): 10.

19. Willard M. Oliver, "The Pied Piper of Crime in America: An Analysis of the Presidents' and Public's Agenda on Crime," *Criminal Justice Policy Review* 13, no. 2 (2002): 139–155; Nancy E. Marion and Willard M. Oliver, "Congress, Crime, and Budgetary Responsiveness: A Study in Symbolic Politics," *Criminal Justice Policy Review* 20, no. 2 (2009): 115–135.

20. Bruce W. Cameron, "Fighting Violent Crime," *Law and Order*, July 1993, 1.

21. Dawn M. Friedkin to Bruce Reed and Jose Cerda, February 8, 1994; [Bill Clinton], Community Policing Grants Announcement, February 9, 1994, Domestic Policy Council, Bruce Reed, and Crime Series, Clinton Digital Library, 22599.

Chapter 22: Blue Power Consolidated

1. Ruth Shalit, "The Kids Are Alright," *The New Republic*, July 18, 1994; Ted Gest, *Crime and Politics: Big Government's Erratic Campaign for Law and Order* (New York: Oxford University Press, 2001), 173–174.

2. Bruce W. Cameron, "There's Money Available!," *Law and Order*, September 1993, 1.

3. John Hoffman, "Are Sheriffs Under Fire?," *Law and Order*, July 1993, 90–94; Matthew Guariglia, "On August Vollmer's 1935 *Crime and State Police*," *The Metropole*, May 31, 2022, themetropole.blog/2022/05/31/on-august-vollmers-1935-crime-and-state-police/.

4. Dewey Stokes and Frank Policaro Jr., "Letters," *Sheriff*, July–August 1993, 7.

5. "Law Enforcement Initiatives," April 15, 1993, C-SPAN, 39702-1; James Carroll, "Letter," *The Law Officer* 8, no. 5 (January–February 1976): 5; "Fiscal 1993 Stimulus Bill Killed," in *CQ Almanac 1993*, 49th ed. (Washington, DC: Congressional Quarterly, 1994), 706–709.

6. "Just Call Him 'Anti-Crime Bill,'" *Law Enforcement News* 19, no. 385 (September 15, 1993): 1, 6; The Clinton Crime Plan, October 12, 1993, Domestic Policy Council, Bruce Reed, and Crime Series, Clinton Digital Library, 22506; Janet Reno to Jack Brooks, June

13, 1994, Conference Report, Domestic Policy Council, Bruce Reed, and Crime Series, Clinton Digital Library, 22510.

7. DOJ, Fact Sheet: How the Crime Bill Will Put 100,000 Cops on the Beat, October 6, 1994, Crime Bill—100,000 Cops [I], Domestic Policy Council, Bruce Reed, and Crime Series, Clinton Digital Library, 22544.

8. Thomas Gardner and Drew Wallner, "Police, Fire, and Refuse Collection Personnel and Expenditures—1991," in *The Municipal Year Book 1992* (Washington, DC: International City/County Management Association, 1992), 111–123; Robert Scully, "The Police Corps: Agreeing on Aims but Disagreeing on Approaches," *Law Enforcement News* 15, no. 302 (November 15, 1989): 8, 13; "A National Review of Wages and Benefits," *Law and Order*, November 1993, 42–54.

9. "A National Review of Wages."

10. Rahm Emanuel, Ron Klain, and Bruce Reed to Leon Panetta, July 8, 1994; Debunking the Myths: The 100,000 Cops Program Works, February 10, 1995, Crime Bill—100,000 Cops [I], Domestic Policy Council, Bruce Reed, and Crime Series, Clinton Digital Library, 22544.

11. Beth McGee to Jose Cerda, March 14, 1994; Blueprint for Anti-Crime Legislation, April 14, 1994, Crime Bill Rally—Event—April 15, 1994 [5], Domestic Policy Council and Jose Cerda, Clinton Digital Library, 86738; Law Enforcement Officials' Rally, April 14, 1994, C-SPAN, 56046-1; Angela Mosconi, "100 Island Cops Going on the Road to D.C.," *Staten Island Advance*, April 13, 1994; Bill Clinton, Introductory Remarks, April 14, 1994, Extra Copies of Briefing Papers, April 1994: Meeting with Law Enforcement Steering Committee, Executive Office of the President, Clinton Digital Library, 86889; Law Enforcement Steering Committee, Support Law Enforcement leaflet, April 12, 1994, Crime Bill Rally—Event—April 15, 1994 [6], Domestic Policy Council and Jose Cerda, Clinton Digital Library, 86739; Pierre Thomas and William Claiborne, "Mayors Fear U.S. Funding Plan May Prevent Adding Police," *WP*, April 13, 1994.

12. Stuart Schrader, "To Protect and Serve Themselves: Police in US Politics Since the 1960s," *Public Culture* 31, no. 3 (2019): 601–623.

13. Sylvester Daughtry Jr., "The Year in Review," *TPC*, October 1994, 6; Bruce W. Cameron, "NIJ Friends Get BIG Bucks," *Law and Order*, May 1994; Roy C. Kime to Dan Rosenblatt, April 25, 1997, IACP, Domestic Policy Council and Jose Cerda, Clinton Digital Library, 96963.

14. 3.14.93 Crime Briefing; Herman and Cerda, Meeting; "NSA Meets to Discuss Crime and the Judicial System," *Sheriff*, September–October 1993, 7.

15. Katharine Q. Seelye, "Crime Bill Fails on House Vote, Stunning Clinton," *NYT*, August 12, 1994; William J. Clinton, "Remarks to the Convention of the National Association of Police Organizations in Minneapolis," August 12, 1994, *Weekly Compilation of Presidential Documents* 30, no. 32 (August 15, 1995), 1664–1667; "President Clinton (at Podium)" [photo], *Law Enforcement News* 20, no. 414 (December 31, 1994): 15; Gest, *Crime and Politics*, 238.

16. Crime Legislation, August 15, 1994, C-SPAN, 59525-1.

17. Violent Crime Control and Law Enforcement Act of 1994—Conference Report, *Congressional Record*, Senate, 140, no. 122 (August 23, 1994).

18. Katharine Q. Seelye, "House Approves Crime Bill After Days of Bargaining, Giving Victory to Clinton," *NYT*, August 22, 1994; Yolanda Young, "Analysis: Black Leaders Supported Clinton's Crime Bill," NBC News, April 8, 2016; Steven A. Holmes, "Blacks Relent on Crime Bill, but Not Without Bitterness," *NYT*, August 18, 1994; R. W. Apple Jr., "Clinton's Smiles on the Crime Bill Mask the Pain over Health Care," *NYT*, August 26, 1994; Bill Clinton to Rudolph Giuliani, October 4, 1994, 082323, Subject File, White House Office of Records Management, Clinton Digital Library, 86424; Bill Clinton to Edward Rendell, October 4, 1994, 082323, Subject File, White House Office of Records Management, Clinton Digital Library, 86425.

19. White House Communications, Memorandum for the House Majority Leader, July 22, 1994, Office of Speechwriting and Jonathan Prince, 1994 Crime Bill Strategy Memos, Clinton Digital Library, 34286; Public Law 103-322, "Violent Crime Control and Law Enforcement Act of 1994," 103rd Congress, September 13, 1994; Melinda E. Lund, "COPS Program Proves Itself," *Sheriff*, September–October 1995, 18.

20. Arthur G. Sharp, "Help Is on the Way—Maybe," *Law and Order*, January 1995, 298–301.

21. William J. Clinton, "Remarks to the National Association of Police Organizations," October 14, 1994, *Weekly Compilation of Presidential Documents* 30, no. 41 (October 17, 1994), 2021–2023.

22. Dan Rosenblatt to Jose Cerda, October 6, 1994, Event—IACP Conference, Oct. 17, 1994, Domestic Policy Council and Jose Cerda, Clinton Digital Library, 867731; William J. Clinton, "Remarks to the International Association of Chiefs of Police in Albuquerque, New Mexico," October 17, 1994, *Weekly Compilation of Presidential Documents* 30, no. 42 (October 24, 1994): 2056–2061; Roy Caldwell Kime, "Distribution of COPS Monies Well Underway," *TPC*, December 1994, 8–9.

23. Peter C. Dodenhoff, "LEN Salutes Its 1994 People of the Year, the Makers of the Violent Crime Control Act," *Law Enforcement News* 20, no. 414 (December 31, 1994): 1, 14–15.

24. Debunking the Myths: The 100,000 Cops Program Works, February 10, 1995, Crime Bill—100,000 Cops [I], Domestic Policy Council, Bruce Reed, and Crime Series, Clinton Digital Library, 22544.

25. "Tough Talk, Little Progress on GOP's Crime Agenda," in *CQ Almanac 1995*, 51st ed. (Washington, DC: Congressional Quarterly, 1996), 63–68; Chris Wayne to Political Affairs, October 12, 1995, Crime/Drugs 1996: Clinton Law Enforcement Outreach '96, Domestic Policy Council and Jose Cerda, Clinton Digital Library, 96805.

26. "NRA Executive Issues Apology for Letter Attacking U.S. Agents," *WP*, May 18, 1995.

27. Law Enforcement Stakeout, May 19, 1995, C-SPAN, 65270-1.

28. Liliana Segura, "Gutting Habeas Corpus," *The Intercept*, May 4, 2016; Dick Cox, "Will There Be 100,000 New Cops in 1996?," *Law and Order*, June 1995, 42–44; Lund, "COPS Program."

29. Edward R. Maguire, Jeffrey B. Snipes, Craig D. Uchida, and Margaret Townsend, "Counting Cops: Estimating the Number of Police Departments and Police Officers in the USA," *Policing* 21, no. 1 (1998): 97–130; Gest, *Crime and Politics*, 182–186; Brian A. Reaves

and Matthew J. Hickman, *Special Report: Police Departments in Large Cities, 1990–2000* (Washington, DC: Bureau of Justice Statistics, 2002).

30. Bart Stupak, "The Law Enforcement Officers' Bill of Rights in 1995," February 9, 1995, *Congressional Record* 141, no. 27 (1995): E314; Bruce Reed and Jose Cerda, Memorandum for the President, June 22, 1993, Event—NAPO—6-24-93, Domestic Policy Council and Jose Cerda, Clinton Digital Library, 86775; Robert Hussey and Nicholas Gess, International Association of Chiefs of Police 103rd Annual Conference 1996, October 28, 1996, Domestic Policy Council and Jose Cerda, Clinton Digital Library, 96964, 7; Statement of Senator Joseph R. Biden Jr. Introducing "Law Enforcement Officers' Bill of Rights of 1995," February 1, 1995, Police Officers Bill of Rights, Domestic Policy Council and Jose Cerda, Clinton Digital Library, 97063; "Biden, For Cops: Standards, Support," *Cleveland Plain Dealer*, October 15, 1994.

31. José Cerda, Cops/Tobacco—Update, May 13, 1998, OPD and Automated Records Management System, May 13, 1998 to May 15, 1998, Clinton Digital Library, 25080.

32. Civil Rights Division, *The Civil Rights Division's Pattern and Practice Reform Work: 1994–Present* (Washington, DC: DOJ, 2017).

33. Address by Attorney General Janet Reno before the National Association of Police Organizations, August 11, 1997, Department of Justice, justice.gov/archive/ag/speeches/1997/811_npo.html.

34. Eric Lichtblau, "Bush Sees U.S. as Meddling in Local Police Affairs," *LAT*, June 1, 2000.

Chapter 23: NYPD Blues

1. Diren Valayden, "Normalizing Counterinsurgency in the United States: First Responders as the First Line of Defense," *Small Wars & Insurgencies* 33, nos. 4–5 (2021): 673–692.

2. Marilynn S. Johnson, *Street Justice: A History of Police Violence in New York City* (Boston: Beacon Press, 2003); U.S. Commission on Civil Rights, *Police Practices and Civil Rights in New York City* (Washington, DC: USCCR, 2000); Human Rights Watch, *Shielded from Justice: Police Brutality and Accountability in the United States* (New York: HRW, 1998). The next four paragraphs draw from these sources.

3. For an inside look at New York City's Civilian Complaint Review Board, see Mac Muir and Greg Finch, *Cop Cop: Breaking the Fixed System of American Policing* (New York: Zando, 2025).

4. Joanna Schwartz, *Shielded: How the Police Became Untouchable* (New York: Viking, 2023), ch. 10.

5. Pam Belluck, "The Street Cop in Pin Stripes," *NYT*, March 6, 1996.

6. Richard Steier, "Top Negotiator, Ruinous Gambler Hartman Dies," *The Chief-Leader*, August 24, 2015; Russ Baker, "The Rogue Police Union," *Village Voice*, December 7, 1993; Matthew Purdy and David Kocieniewski, "P.B.A. and Its Lawyers in a Tangle of Money and Mixed Roles," *NYT*, February 2, 1997.

7. Terry O'Neill, "Daring to Amend," *NYT*, February 10, 1996.

8. "Governor Pataki's Brave Veto," *NYT*, February 12, 1996.

9. Clifford J. Levy, "New York City Police Union Pounds Beat in State Capitol," *NYT*, February 6, 1996; James Dao, "For Giuliani, as for Mayors Before Him, P.B.A. Flexes

Albany Muscle," *NYT*, October 15, 1996; "Governor Pataki's Brave Veto," *NYT*, February 12, 1996.

10. "Police Warned on Veto Protest," *NYT*, November 15, 1995; James Dao and Jane Fritsch, "Behind the Scenes, D'Amato Wields Vast Power in Albany," *NYT*, September 30, 1996; Belluck, "The Street Cop."

11. Vivian S. Toy, "Court Voids Law Aiding the Police in Wage Disputes," *NYT*, April 11, 1996; Andrea Cann Chandrasekher, "The Effect of Police Slowdowns on Crime," *American Law and Economics Review* 18, no. 2 (2016): 385–437; David Kocieniewski, "Police Union Head Says He Will Quit Next June," *NYT*, July 16, 1998; Richard Steier, "Matarazzo Got Stuck with the Bill," *The Chief-Leader*, July 23, 1998.

12. "For the Record," *The Chief-Leader*, August 24, 2020; Baker, "The Rogue Police Union."

13. Website of the October 22 Coalition to Stop Police Brutality, Repression, and the Criminalization of a Generation, October22.org.

14. Frank Morales, "Reason, Violence, and the Diallo Verdict," in *Police State America*, ed. Tom Burghardt (Montreal: Arm the Spirit, 2002), 129–139; Michael Cooper, "12 Arrested During Sit-In to Protest Diallo Killing," *NYT*, March 10, 1999; Frankie Edozien, "Diallo Rally Hits D.C.," *New York Post*, April 4, 1999.

15. Leonard Levitt, *NYPD Confidential: Power and Corruption in the Country's Greatest Police Force* (New York: Thomas Dunne, 2009).

16. Mike Claffey, "New PBA Prez' Humble Style and Grand Ideas," *Daily News*, June 13, 1999; Lisa L. Colangelo, "PBA Prez Fights for Reform, Respect," *Daily News*, July 25, 2005.

17. Mike Claffey, "PBA Elects Lynch Its New President," *Daily News*, June 6, 1999; Claffey, "New PBA Prez"; John Marzulli and William K. Rashbaum, "Cop Rebellion Against Safir," *Daily News*, April 14, 1999; Richard Steier, "Savage Steps Out Boldly," *The Chief-Leader*, April 23, 1999.

18. Richard Steier, "Hooks and Doublecrosses," *The Chief-Leader*, January 8, 1999; Richard Steier, "PBA Votes Against the Past," *The Chief-Leader*, June 11, 1999.

19. Police Benevolent Association, "PERB Victory," April 16, 2001, nycpba.org/press-releases/2001/perb-victory/; "PBA Reacts to PERB Award," June 28, 2005, nycpba.org/press-releases/2005/pba-reacts-to-perb-award/; Richard Hartman, "Shilling for Lynch," *The Chief-Leader*, October 14, 2005; John Puglissi, "Anatomy of a PERB Contract," *PBA Magazine*, Summer 2005, 4–5.

20. Anthony Bouza, "NYPD Blues—Good, Lucky, or Both?," *Law Enforcement News* 23, no. 460 (January 31, 1997): 8, 10.

Chapter 24: The Most Powerful Police Union President

1. Thomas A. Reppetto, *American Police: A History, 1945–2012* (New York: Enigma, 2012), 185.

2. Michael D. White and Henry F. Fradella, *Stop and Frisk: The Use and Abuse of a Controversial Policing Tactic* (New York: NYU Press, 2016).

3. Alexander Nazaryan, "Patrick Lynch, New York City's Blue Bulldog," *Newsweek*, October 22, 2014.

4. George Packer, "The Heart of Policing," *New Yorker*, January 6, 2015.

5. Leonard Leavitt, *NYPD Confidential: Power and Corruption in the Country's Greatest Police Force* (New York: Thomas Dunne, 2009); John Tully Gordon and Rebecca Ulam Weiner, "Light Pierces Through: An NYPD Reflection on Loss and Lessons Learned 20 Years After 9/11," *TPC*, September 2021, 34–53; Samir Chopra, "The Deadly Self-Pity of Police," *Refusing to Stick to the Subject* (blog), December 4, 2014, samirchopra.com/2014/12/04/the-deadly-self-pity-of-the-police/.

6. *PBA Magazine*, Spring 2003.

7. Mike Claffey, "New PBA Prez' Humble Style and Grand Ideas," *Daily News*, June 13, 1999; Nazaryan, "Patrick Lynch."

8. Richard Steier, "PBA Comes a Long Way, Finally Takes 'Men' Out of Name," *The Chief-Leader*, January 14, 2019; William K. Rashbaum, "P.B.A. Names Black Officer to No. 3 Post," *NYT*, July 25, 2002; Nazaryan, "Patrick Lynch."

9. Claffey, "New PBA Prez"; Lisa L. Colangelo, "PBA Prez Fights for Reform, Respect," *Daily News*, July 25, 2005.

10. E.g., Joseph Alejandro, "Never-Ending Battle for Justice," and Robert Zink, "The Search for a Killer," both in *PBA Magazine*, Spring 2003.

11. "PBA Fights Parole of Cop Killers," March 23, 2018, nycpba.org/news-items/pba-video/2018/pba-fights-parole-of-cop-killers/; Patrick J. Lynch, "Let Laws Be Their Legacy," *PBA Magazine*, Winter 2005–2006.

12. Jennifer Gonnerman, "Prepping for Parole," *New Yorker*, November 25, 2019; Daniel A. Gross, "The Eleventh Parole Hearing of Jalil Abdul Muntaqim," *New Yorker*, January 25, 2019; Natasha Lennard, "The NYPD Union's War Against Parole Reform," *The Nation*, March 29, 2019.

13. Jim Dwyer, "Cops' Plan vs. PBA Is Revolutionary," *Daily News*, February 10, 1998; Paul Schwartzman, "Failures Fuel PBA Dissent," *Daily News*, March 1, 1998.

14. John Puglissi, "The PERB Arbitration: Round Two" and "City Hall Rally Draws Seventy Thousand," both in *PBA Magazine*, Summer 2004; John Puglissi, "Let the Arbitration Begin," *PBA Magazine*, Winter 2004–2005.

15. Jacob Geanous, "More and More NYPD Officers Opting to Live Outside NYC as Lawmakers Try to Push Residency Requirement," *NY Post*, June 3, 2023.

16. Mubarak Abdul-Jabbar, "The PBA Seal of Approval: A Definite Political Asset," *PBA Magazine*, Winter 2005–2006, 10–11.

17. "Suddenly, Last Summer," *PBA Magazine*, Winter 2004–2005.

18. "PBA in Iowa Protesting the Mayor," YouTube, posted by NYC PBA, December 19, 2017, youtube.com/watch?v=t6Yoa-qAGNo; "NYPD Union Heads to Miami, Protests Mayor De Blasio on His Big Night at Democratic Debate," CBS News, June 26, 2019, cbsnews.com/newyork/news/pba-protest-de-blasio-debate/; Laura Dimon, "Stalk and Talk Led to Raise: PBA Prez," *Daily News*, February 6, 2017.

19. Mark Toor, "Cops Rally in Support of 16 at Ticket-Fixing Bronx Court Hearing," *The Chief-Leader*, November 4, 2011.

20. N. R. Kleinfield and John Eligon, "Officers Jeer at Arraignment of 16 Colleagues in Ticket-Fixing Investigation," *NYT*, October 28, 2011.

21. "Bloomberg Says NYC Must Lay Off Thousands," NBC News, April 8, 2009; "PBA Reacts to Additional Budget Cuts," press release, December 13, 2008, nycpba.org/press-releases/2008/pba-reacts-to-additional-budget-cuts/.

22. Police Executive Research Forum, *Labor-Management Relations in Policing: Looking to the Future and Finding Common Ground* (Washington, DC: PERF, 2011), 1, 21.

23. John Puglissi, "Why Professional Courtesy Is the Right Thing to Do," *PBA Magazine*, Summer 2003.

24. Joseph Goldstein, "Police Union President Faces Revolt in Wake of Ticket-Fixing Scandal," *NYT*, November 11, 2011.

25. Puglissi, "Why Professional Courtesy."

26. Lou Matarazzo, "Some Serious Thoughts for the New Year," *New York's Finest*, Winter 1997.

27. "PERF Members Share Ideas for Preventing Police Suicide," *PERF Subject to Debate*, December 2019, 6; Daniel S. Lawrence, Kathleen E. L. Padilla, and Jessica Dockstader, "Bearing the Badge, Battling Inner Struggles: Understanding Suicidal Ideation in Law Enforcement," *Journal of Police and Criminal Psychology*, 2025, psycnet.apa.org/doi/10.1007/s11896-025-09741-x; George Beck, "Editor's Point of View," *Blue Magazine* 11, no. 1 (2020), 6; "A Message from Pat Lynch on NYPD Suicides," YouTube, posted by NYC PBA, August 5, 2019, youtube.com/watch?v=ZgIUe3xbAd4.

28. Barbara Ransby, *Making All Black Lives Matter: Reimagining Freedom in the Twenty-First Century* (Oakland: University of California Press, 2018). The Movement for Black Lives is a coalition of more than fifty organizations including the original Black Lives Matter group, which has since broken apart.

Chapter 25: Blue Lives Matter

1. James D. Walsh, "New York's Most Virulent Opponent of Police Reform," *New York*, August 19, 2020; Ross Barkan, "Bill de Blasio Grows Cozy with His Old Police Nemesis," *Observer*, February 26, 2015; Ross Barkan, "NYPD Union Boss Wants 'Some Type of Apology' From Bill de Blasio," *Observer*, January 5, 2015.

2. Alec Karakatsanis, *Copaganda: How Police and the Media Manipulate Our News* (New York: New Press, 2025); Pat Blanchfield, "Policing and the English Language," *New Republic*, March 31, 2020; Stuart Schrader, "The Lies Cops Tell and the Lies We Tell About Cops," *New Republic*, May 27, 2021.

3. Krishnadev Calamur, "Ferguson Documents: Officer Darren Wilson's Testimony," NPR, November 25, 2014.

4. "PBA President: Police Officers 'Thrown Under the Bus' by De Blasio in Wake of Eric Garner Grand Jury Decision," CBS News, December 4, 2014; Dante de Blasio, "My Dad Gave Me 'The Talk.' When Someone Called Police, I Felt the Fear," *USA Today*, July 1, 2019; "Don't Insult My Sacrifice," petition, in author's possession.

5. Natasha Velez and Ben Feuerherd, "Vandal Who Wrote 'NYPD KILLS' on NYC Bridge Sought," *NY Post*, December 19, 2014; Maura Grunlund, "Pro NYPD Rally Planned for Dec. 19 at City Hall in Manhattan," *SI Live*, December 12, 2014; Ben Feuerherd, "NYPD Supporters Face Off Against Cop Critics at Rally," *NY Post*, December 19, 2014; Mike Baker, Jennifer Valentino-DeVries, Manny Fernandez, and Michael La Forgia, "Three Words. 70 Cases. The Tragic History of 'I Can't Breathe,'" *NYT*, June 29, 2020; Steven W. Thrasher, "'I Can Breathe,' and the Occasional Fear of Covering Protests," *Contexts*, December 20, 2014.

6. Matt Flegenheimer, "For Mayor de Blasio and New York Police, a Rift Is Ripped Open," *NYT*, December 21, 2014; Alex Altman, "Why New York Cops Turned Their Backs on Mayor de Blasio," *Time*, December 22, 2014.

7. Michael Martinez, Kevin Conlon, and Miguel Marquez, "Tension, Tenderness and a Sea of Blue as Slain NYPD Officer Is Laid to Rest," CNN, December 29, 2014; Matt Flegenheimer and J. David Goodman, "Police Unions' Leaders Air Grievances in 2-Hour Meeting with de Blasio," *NYT*, December 30, 2014; Ashley Fantz, Ben Brumfield, and Holly Yan, "A Second Officer's Funeral, A Second Show of Dissent Toward Mayor," CNN, January 5, 2015.

8. Ryan J. Reilly, "Fraternal Order of Police Wants Attacks on Cops Treated as Hate Crimes," *Huffington Post*, January 5, 2015; Michael D. White, "Ambush Killings of the Police, 1970–2018: A Longitudinal Examination of the 'War on Cops' Debate," *Police Quarterly* 23, no. 4 (2020): 451–471.

9. Emanuella Grinberg, "New Bill Offers Police Officers Protections Similar to Those for Hate Crime Victims," CNN, May 8, 2018; Walter Olson, "Using 'Hate' Label with Crimes Against Cops Goes Too Far," Minneapolis *Star Tribune*, October 18, 2015; Joshua Vaughn, "A Black Man Called the Cops Nazis—and Was Charged with a Hate Crime," *The Appeal*, June 28, 2018.

10. The tweet is available at web.archive.org/web/20141221024905/https://twitter.com/gormojourno/status/546464618315792384. The journalist stated that he received it from "a veteran police officer with a history of providing me genuine PBA memos." Azi Paybarah, "P.B.A. Condemns Mayor, Denies Inflammatory Memo," *Capital NY*, December 20, 2014.

11. Azi Paybarah, "Lynch Cites 'Precautions' but Denies Police Slowdown," *Politico*, January 6, 2015.

12. Patrick McGeehan, "Police Slowdown Cost New York City an Estimated $5 Million in Lost Fines," *NYT*, January 14, 2015; Dara Lind, "The NYPD 'Slowdown' That's Cut Arrests in New York by Half, Explained," *Vox*, January 6, 2015; Larry Celona, Shawn Cohen, and Bruce Golding, "Arrests Plummet 66% with NYPD in Virtual Work Stoppage," *NY Post*, December 29, 2014; Christopher M. Sullivan and Zachary P. O'Keeffe, "Evidence That Curtailing Proactive Policing Can Reduce Major Crime," *Nature Human Behavior* 1 (2017): 730–737.

13. David Kaib, "NYPD Will Not Reform Itself," *Notes on a Theory* (blog), January 15, 2015, notesonatheory.wordpress.com/2015/01/15/nypd-will-not-reform-itself/; Aaron Miguel Cantú, "What the NYPD Slowdown Revealed," *The Indypendent*, January 27, 2015.

14. Vesla Weaver, "Frontlash: Race and the Development of Punitive Crime Policy," *Studies in American Political Development* 21, no. 2 (2007): 230–265; see also Naomi Murakawa, *The First Civil Right: How Liberals Built Prison America* (Oxford: Oxford University Press, 2014).

15. Barkan, "Bill de Blasio Grows Cozy."

16. Mark Toor, "Wilson a New Challenger for Lynch in PBA Race," *The Chief-Leader*, April 13, 2015.

17. Reuven Blau, "PBA Super PAC Tries to Swing Staten Island and Queens Council Races for Police Allies," *The City*, November 1, 2021.

18. David Firestone, "The Rise of New York's Police Unions," *The Guardian*, January 13, 2015.

Chapter 26: Fund/Defund/Fund

1. "National Border Patrol Council Endorses Donald Trump for President," National Border Patrol Council, press release, March 16, 2016, bpunion.org/media-relations/press-releases/national-border-patrol-council-endorses-donald-trump-for-president/; Tom Jackman, "Fraternal Order of Police Union Endorses Trump," *WP*, September 16, 2016; Michael Zoorob, "Blue Endorsements Matter: How the Fraternal Order of Police Contributed to Donald Trump's Victory," *PS: Political Science and Politics* 52, no. 2 (2019): 243–250.

2. Reece Jones, *Nobody Is Protected: How the Border Patrol Became the Most Dangerous Police Force in the United States* (Berkeley, CA: Counterpoint, 2022).

3. United States Border Patrol Fiscal Year Staffing Statistics (FY 1992–FY 2020), August 2021; U.S. Border Patrol Total Apprehensions (FY 1925–FY 2020), U.S. Customs and Border Protection, Stats and Summaries, cbp.gov.

4. John Hunneman, "June 2, 1993," *John Hunneman* (blog), May 31, 2017, johnhunneman.wordpress.com/2017/05; TJ Bonner, statement, August 5, 1992, Operations of the Border Patrol, Subcommittee on International Law, Immigration, and Refugees, Committee on the Judiciary, House, 102nd Cong., 2nd sess., 141–153; US Border Patrol, "Border Patrol Strategic Plan: 1994 and Beyond," July 1994; Daniel Denvir, *All-American Nativism: How the Bipartisan War on Immigrants Explains Politics as We Know It* (New York: Verso, 2020).

5. Jones, *Nobody Is Protected*. Human Rights Watch notes that Customs and Border Protection calculates the number of deaths over 30 years at 10,000; migrant advocates in the borderlands estimate the total to be up to 80,000. Human Rights Watch, "US: Border Deterrence Leads to Deaths, Disappearances," June 26, 2024, hrw.org/news/2024/06/26/us-border-deterrence-leads-deaths-disappearances; Customs and Border Protection, US Fiscal Year Staffing Statistics, 2021; Government Accountability Office, *U.S. Customs and Border Protection: Efforts to Improve Recruitment, Hiring, and Retention of Law Enforcement Personnel* (Washington, DC: GAO, 2024).

6. Douglas A. Brook, Cynthia L. King, David Anderson, and Joshua Bahr, "Legislating Civil Service Reform: The Homeland Security Act of 2002," USMC Naval Postgraduate School, 2006; Norma M. Riccucci and Frank J. Thompson, "The New Public Management, Homeland Security, and the Politics of Civil Service Reform," *Public Administration Review* 68 (2008): 877–890; Art Del Cueto, *The Green Line* (podcast), episode 553, March 13, 2025; Government Accountability Office, *U.S. Customs and Border Protection*.

7. "National Border Patrol Council Endorses."

8. Del Cueto, *The Green Line*, episode 553.

9. Fernanda Santos, "Border Agents: 'We're Not Going to Apologize for What We Believe In,'" *NYT*, March 28, 2017.

10. Justin Doubleday, "DHS Prepares for Unprecedented Spending Surge Under 'Big, Beautiful Bill,'" *Federal News Network*, July 7, 2025.

11. Daniel Del Valle, George Beck, and Joseph R. Uliano, "Securing the Border Saves Lives: Former ICE Director Tom Homan," *The Blue Magazine* 10, no. 6 (2019): 26–30.

12. On the vicissitudes of the movement to defund the police in Minneapolis, both before and after George Floyd's death, see Michelle S. Phelps, *The Minneapolis Reckoning: Race, Violence and the Politics of Policing in America* (Princeton, NJ: Princeton University Press, 2024).

13. Brigid Bergin, "Did a Powerful Police Union Violate the City Charter When It Released Personal Info on Chiara De Blasio?," *Gothamist*, June 8, 2020; Megan Sheets and Shawn Cohen, "Bill de Blasio's Daughter Chiara, 25, Is Arrested," *Daily Mail*, May 31, 2020; Brian Price et al., "NYC Nighttime Curfew, Extra Police Officers Unable to Stop Chaos at Macy's," NBC New York, May 31, 2020; U.S. Attorney's Office for the Southern District of New York, "Edward Mullins, Former President of NYPD Sergeants' Union, Pleads Guilty to Defrauding Union and Its Members," press release, January 19, 2023.

14. Hannah Black, "Go Outside," *Artforum*, December 2020; John Bolger, "Exclusive: NYPD Took Hours to Respond to Mass Looting, Despite Quickly Cracking Down on Protests," *The Intercept*, June 1, 2021; Tobi Haslett, "Magic Actions," *n+1*, May 7, 2021; Jarrod Shanahan and Zhandarka Kurti, "Prelude to a Hot American Summer," *Brooklyn Rail*, July–August 2020. The term "communal luxury" comes from Kristin Ross, *Communal Luxury: The Political Imaginary of the Paris Commune* (New York: Verso, 2015).

15. Kate Stockrahm, "How a Union Boss Thrust the NYPD into MAGA Territory," Columbia News Service, October 16, 2020; "Campaign Notes: 14 New York City Unions Plan to Endorse Reagan," *NYT*, July 21, 1984; Paul Taylor and Edward Walsh, "Rivals Don Kid Gloves at NY Dinner," *WP*, October 20, 1988; Christian Murray, "Protesters Rally Outside the Bayside Home of NYPD Union Boss Pat Lynch," *Forest Hills Post*, August 20, 2020.

16. Emily M. Farris and Mirya R. Holman, *The Power of the Badge: Sheriffs and Inequality in the United States* (Chicago: University of Chicago Press, 2024); Stockrahm, "How a Union Boss"; Nick Gass, "Milwaukee Sheriff at RNC: 'Blue Lives Matter,'" *Politico*, July 18, 2016.

17. "Remarks by President Trump to Law Enforcement Officials on MS-13," July 28, 2017, trumpwhitehouse.archives.gov/briefings-statements/remarks-president-trump-law-enforcement-officials-ms-13/; Cleve R. Wootson Jr. and Mark Berman, "U.S. Police Chiefs Blast Trump for Endorsing 'Police Brutality,'" *WP*, July 30, 2017.

18. Michelle Robertson, "Park Service Cancels Black Panther Legacy Project at Cal amid Conservative Outcry," *SF Gate*, October 27, 2017.

19. "The International Union of Police Associations Formally Endorses the Campaign for the Re-Election of President Donald J. Trump," IUPA press release, September 2019; Donald J. Trump, "Trump Campaign Statement on National Association of Police Organizations' Endorsement for President Trump," July 15, 2020, TAPP.

20. "Patrick Lynch's Full Speech at the Republican National Convention," *PBS NewsHour*, August 27, 2020; Mathis Ebbinghaus, Nathan Bailey, and Jacob Rubel, "The Effect of the 2020 Black Lives Matter Protests on Police Budgets: How 'Defund the Police' Sparked Political Backlash," *Social Problems* 72, no. 3 (2025): 1198–1215; Sam Levin, "These US Cities Defunded Police: 'We're Transferring Money to the Community,'" *The Guardian*, March 11, 2021; Urban Institute, "State and Local Backgrounders: Criminal Justice Expenditures," 2022.

21. "'Fund the Police,' Biden Says at State of the Union," PBS, March 1, 2022.

22. Leonard Levitt, *NYPD Confidential: Power and Corruption in the Country's Greatest Police Force* (New York: Thomas Dunne, 2009), 49.

23. Trump's commission added "the" to its name. President's Commission on Law Enforcement and the Administration of Justice, *Final Report* (Washington, DC: DOJ, 2020), xi.

Conclusion

1. Willard M. Oliver, *Depolicing: When Police Officers Disengage* (Boulder, CO: Lynne Rienner, 2019); Griffin Edwards and Stephen Rushin, "De-Policing: An Updated Empirical Analysis of Crime and Federal Police Reform," *Washington and Lee Law Review* 82, no. 2 (2025): 703–773; Steven G. Koven, "Impact of Pattern-or-Practice Investigations on Crime Rates in Large Cities," *Public Integrity*, January 2025, 1–13; Stephen L. Morgan and Rhiannon N. Miller, "Ferguson, Gray, and Davis with De Sousa, Tuggle, and Harrison Too: An Analysis of Recorded Crime Incidents and Arrests in Baltimore City, March 2010 to March 2020," SocArXiv, May 14, 2020; Andrei Barbos, "De-Policing and Fatal Traffic Crashes," *Economics Letters* 250 (April 2025): 112284; Jacob M. Grumbach, Robert Mickey, and Daniel Ziblatt, "Enough Police, but Not Enough Police Work: An Institutional Explanation of Under-Policing in the U.S.," working paper, July 9, 2025, sites.google.com/view/jakegrumbach/working-papers; Elisa Maria Wirsching, "Political Power of Bureaucratic Agents: Evidence from Policing in New York City," working paper, September 2022, elisawirsching.github.io/research/; Ted Sherman, "State Police Under Investigation After Big Drop in Tickets," Newark *Star-Ledger*, December 12, 2024.

2. Multiple police forces diverted anticrime and other resources toward surveillance of antipolice activists or otherwise attacked or retaliated against actual or perceived protesters after George Floyd's death. See, e.g., Jim Daley, "Surveilling Dissent," *South Side Weekly*, July 7, 2021; Tim Dickinson, "Minneapolis Police Caught on Video 'Hunting' Activists," *Rolling Stone*, October 13, 2021.

3. See the Mapping Police Violence website at mappingpoliceviolence.us. Zusha Elinson, "The Rapid Rise of Killings by Police in Rural America," *Wall Street Journal*, July 10, 2025.

4. Stuart Schrader, "Cop Cities Mock Cities," *Los Angeles Review of Books*, October 12, 2024; Hannah Cheves, "ShotSpotter Is a Failure. What's Next?," MacArthur Justice Center, May 5, 2022; Stuart Schrader, "What *We Own This City* Gets Wrong About Policing," *Boston Review*, June 27, 2022; Katie Mettler, "Baltimore Is Seeing the City's Fewest Homicides in 50 Years. Here's Why," *WP*, July 4, 2025; Richard Fowler, "Inside America's Quiet Safety Revolution: How Local Leaders Are Cutting Crime Without More Cops," *Forbes*, July 17, 2025; Vera Institute, "Crime Is Down in 2025. Trump Doesn't Deserve Credit," June 20, 2025; Baynard Woods and Brandon Soderberg, "Credible Messengers," *The Intercept*, July 26, 2020.

5. Rebecca Goldstein, Michael W. Sances, and Hye Young You, "Exploitative Revenues, Law Enforcement, and the Quality of Government Service," *Urban Affairs Review* 56, no. 1 (2020): 5–31; Monica C. Bell, "Police Reform and the Dismantling of Legal Estrangement," *Yale Law Journal* 126, no. 7 (2017): 2054–2150; Vesla Weaver, Gwen Prowse, and Spencer Piston, "Withdrawing and Drawing In: Political Discourse in Policed Communities," *Journal of Race, Ethnicity, and Politics* 5 (2020): 604–647.

6. W. E. B. Du Bois, *Black Reconstruction in America* (New York: Free Press, 1935), 30.

7. Mark Neocleous, *A Critical Theory of Police Power: The Fabrication of Social Order* (New York: Verso, 2021), 220.

8. Leigh Ann Caldwell, "Police Reform Negotiations in Congress Are Teetering on Collapse," NBC News, June 29, 2021; Catie Edmondson, "Bipartisan Police Overhaul Talks Are Officially Dead on Capitol Hill," *NYT*, September 22, 2021.

9. Kim Kelly, "'Cop-Free AFSCME' Still Fighting to Boot Cops from Their Union," *The Real News Network*, July 20, 2022.

10. Urban Institute, "Criminal Justice Expenditures: Police, Corrections, and Courts," n.d., urban.org/policy-centers/cross-center-initiatives/state-and-local-finance-initiative /state-and-local-backgrounders/criminal-justice-police-corrections-courts-expenditures.

11. Per capita police spending data from Vera Institute of Justice, "What Policing Costs: A Look at Spending in America's Biggest Cities," June 2020, vera.org/publications /what-policing-costs-in-americas-biggest-cities; Jessica Anderson, "Baltimore and Police Union Reach Agreement on Contract That Increases Pay in Effort to Boost Recruitment," *Sun*, October 28, 2021.

12. Megan Munce, "Gov. Greg Abbott Signs Slate of Legislation to Increase Criminal Penalties for Protesters, Punish Cities That Reduce Police Budgets," *Texas Tribune*, June 1, 2021; John Pfaff, "The Greatest Threat to Defunding the Police? State Pre-Emption," *The Appeal*, April 29, 2021.

13. Stephen Barr, "Homeland Security Debate Highlights Split over Union Rights," *WP*, September 4, 2002; Stephen Barr, "Mediating the Fracas over 'Flexibility' at Homeland Security," *WP*, April 7, 2006; Hernan Rozemberg, "Immigration Agents Getting Pay Raises Feds Hopeful They'll Attract Recruits," *Arizona Republic*, January 15, 2003; Karoun Demirjian, "Balancing Border Security," *CQ Weekly*, October 20, 2008, 2810–2816.

INDEX

Christy Thornton

Stuart Schrader is an associate professor of history at Johns Hopkins University, where he is the founding director of the Chloe Center for the Critical Study of Racism, Immigration, and Colonialism. He is also the author of *Badges Without Borders: How Global Counterinsurgency Transformed American Policing*. He lives in Brooklyn.